What Others Are Saying About WAR ON US

"*War on Us* is a remarkably comprehensive, evidence-based examination of the war on drugs and all of its victims. The book is personal and accessible, well-researched, contains excellent source material and, most importantly, provides a blueprint for reform. I highly recommend this book to anyone concerned about the increasing toll of death and destruction resulting from America's longest war."

— *Jeffrey A. Singer, MD, Senior Fellow, Cato Institute*

"This book is a marvelous compendium of the ills of and possible pathways out of our misconceived and deadly War on Drugs. It is highly readable, engaging, fast-paced and covers a breathtaking amount of ground. Thank you for this virtuosic contribution to the growing literature about this national policy debacle."

— *Daniel N. Abrahamson, former director of legal affairs and senior legal advisor at the Drug Policy Alliance, and a law school lecturer on drug law and policy*

"With lively prose and convincing quotes and statistics, Colleen Cowles presents a sometimes-shocking history of the politics behind 'getting tough on drugs' and identifies the many collateral victims of the war, including pain and cancer patients, heartbroken parents, minority communities, intimidated doctors and overburdened taxpayers. She then offers reasoned, logical alternatives to incarceration as a way to solve the massive problems created unintentionally—and sometimes intentionally—by the war on drugs."

—*Jo Ann Skousen, Professor, Chapman University; Founding director, Anthem Libertarian Film Festival; Associate producer, FreedomFest*

"As a retired police detective, I've personally seen the effects of the War on Drugs. Colleen Cowles has captured the day-to-day agony created by this war, for citizens as well as for law enforcement. In one book, she gives the reader valuable insight into the history, the effects, the obstacles to change, and logical alternatives to the war on drugs, and solutions to address the addiction and overdose epidemic that's killing our kids and destroying our neighborhoods."

— *Howard Wooldridge, Citizen's Opposing Prohibition (COPS), retired police detective, co-founder of Law Enforcement Against Prohibition*

"Colleen Cowles shares her knowledge as a researcher, attorney and mother with lived experience. She takes us through the historical facts of 50 years of failed prohibitionist policies on drug use and addiction, demonstrating that the War on Drugs is really a war waged on us all. A must-read for parents, taxpayers, educators, decision makers, criminal justice professionals, and healthcare providers and patients."

— *Gretchen Burns Bergman, Co-Founder / Executive Director of A New PATH and Lead Organizer of Moms United to End the War on Drugs*

"A compelling look behind the scenes on the United States 'War on Drugs' and the ensuing humanitarian crisis facing those living with chronic disease and addiction."

— *Lauren Deluca, President, CIAAG (Chronic Illness Advocacy & Awareness Group)*

WAR ON US

HOW THE **WAR ON DRUGS** AND **MYTHS ABOUT ADDICTION** HAVE CREATED A **WAR ON ALL OF US**

COLLEEN COWLES, J.D.

FIDALGO PRESS
St. Paul, MN

Life stories and examples throughout this book are based on real people and real circumstances, but some names, dates, places, incidents, and details have been changed or omitted for confidentiality, security, safety, privacy, and well-being of those involved, and some examples have been combined for ease in reading and to illustrate points.

Nothing contained in this book is to be considered as the rendering of legal advice for specific cases or situations, and readers are responsible for obtaining such advice from their own legal counsel. This book is intended for educational and informational purposes only.

Use of the pronoun "he" in general discussions is for simplicity only.

Published by Fidalgo Press, St. Paul, MN

Publisher's Cataloging-in-Publication Data
Names: Cowles, Colleen, author.
Title: War on us : how the war on drugs & myths about addiction have created a war on all of us / Colleen Cowles, J.D.
Description: Includes bibliographical references and index. | St. Paul, MN: Hidalgo Press, 2019.
Identifiers: LCCN 2019913701 | ISBN 978-1-7340220-0-1 (pbk.) | 978-1-7340220-1-8 (ebook)
Subjects: LCSH Drugs--Law and legislation--United States. | Drug control--United States. | Drug abuse--Treatment--United States. | Drug abuse--Prevention--United States. | Drug addicts--Rehabilitation--United States. | Substance abuse. | BISAC LAW / Criminal Procedure | LAW / Criminal Law / General | POLITICAL SCIENCE / Law Enforcement | PSYCHOLOGY / Psychopathology / Addiction | SELF-HELP / Substance Abuse & Addictions / Drugs
Classification: LCC HV5825 .C69 2019 | DDC 363.4/5/0973--dc23

To Taylor, whose strength, courage, and determination inspire me every day.

Drug policy & the science
impacting addiction
change constantly.

To receive free, current information on
developments including free updates to this book,
visit www.WarOnUs.com.

Table of Contents

HISTORY REPEATS ITSELF

"You are not responsible for the past, but insofar as you do nothing, you are complicit in the present created by it."

JONATHAN R. MILLER

The War on Drugs is personal for me, beginning with my parents and continuing with my sons. Prohibition that made alcohol illegal from 1920 to 1933 personally impacted my parents' lives. The Drug War nearly cost my son's life.

My father was a proponent of legalizing pot decades before the debate was a common topic of discussion. He saw correlations between the alcohol prohibition of his youth and the drug prohibition of mine. He witnessed the escalation of organized crime in his day, and I witnessed the escalation of drug cartels in mine. He saw deaths due to tainted moonshine. I saw homemade meth affect my children's generation. He saw beer-drinking change to consumption of harder alcohol during prohibition. I witnessed skyrocketing overdose rates due to addition of fentanyl to heroin, cocaine and methamphetamine. Both were a result of prohibition, incentivizing smugglers to concentrate potency to make smuggling cheaper and safer.

During my father's childhood, police shot and killed a courier driving moonshine through the small town where Dad grew up. That death never made sense to my father, who believed the driver was an innocent victim simply trying to earn money to survive the Depression. Now, we have drive-by shootings and innocent victims of turf wars between drug cartels or rival gangs. Those deaths don't make sense to me.

My mother, at the height of the Depression, saved money by living at the county jail where her uncle was sheriff. As a child, I was captivated by her stories of "Uncle John" warning local farmers before federal agents came looking for stills in their barns. Those farmers were in violation of prohibition laws, but the local sheriff knew that notifying them of potential raids could, with little downside, save lives that would be at risk during a raid. The law was so flawed that sheriffs took it upon themselves to minimize the harm. Today, we have law enforcement professionals in multiple jurisdictions refusing to charge individuals for drug possession, locating treatment for them in lieu of arrest. Many of those in the trenches every day understand that drug prohibition is as flawed as alcohol prohibition was. Unfortunately, drug prohibition has gone on for much longer, leaving many more bodies and destroyed lives in its path.

Ultimately, my parents' stories may have saved my sons' lives.

The stories intrigued me as a child, but for years as I focused on my career and starting a family, I paid little attention. Even as a law student and then a practicing attorney, drug policy didn't come to the top of my list of priorities. Then, two sons developed substance use issues, followed by arrests for drug possession, and my world collapsed.

Parents are told "Let them hit bottom. Let them feel the consequences of their choices." Dealing with addiction can be excruciating and confusing, and it was tempting to follow that advice, but my late father's words couldn't be silenced. Was a young courier's death a *natural* consequence of his attempts to make a living? Was prohibition—the 1920s' equivalent of today's drug war—a rational policy? Was it a policy that warranted putting people behind bars? Was prohibition worth killing people and destroying lives in efforts to enforce it?

Those questions also applied to my immediate decisions. Would letting my son's lives be destroyed by a criminal justice system that punishes addiction be a natural consequence of their drug use? Did our current drug policy reduce or increase the chances that our children would develop a substance use issue? If addicted, would the criminal justice system help them to find recovery, or block that path? I wasn't sure, but my parents' stories planted enough doubt to make me look for answers and to resist following conventional wisdom without asking questions.

Ultimately, our sons had very different outcomes, largely due to variations in application of drug policy to their individual situations. One son found success through a compassionate prosecutor and judge who allowed us to get him appropriate treatment and to bypass a long-term record. His experience with the criminal justice system and addiction are far in his past. He enjoys life with his wife and children, and has built a successful career. The issues of his youth have little impact on his current life or opportunities.

Our other son wasn't as fortunate, despite beginning on a very similar path. When he needed help, his probation officer refused to allow us to get him medical treatment and prohibited use of proven medications. Those barriers to treatment led to relapse and additional arrests. He will now forever be identified as a felon. That, in turn, compromises access to treatment for pain due to a misdiagnosed autoimmune disease, as well as restricting career, housing, financial and other opportunities for the rest of his life.

Fueled by my parents' stories and our other son's success, we ultimately gathered the courage to take our son out of state to a qualified addiction specialist, risking his prosecution and ours for defying probation mandates. That decision likely saved his life and led to his recovery. It was worth the risk, but it is inexcusable that our family, or any other family, can be put in the position of having to defy the law to be allowed to seek medical care for a loved one.

Seeing the paths of our two sons was a case study on the enormous effect that criminal justice policy has on success rates and long-term health. Our personal experience showed that punitive policies escalated drug use and established roadblocks to recovery. I wondered, was our experience unique, or was this indicative of the results of large-scale drug policy?

Over more than a decade, in addition to continued personal experiences, I researched, interviewed experts, and, as part of my legal practice and authoring online courses*, worked with other families who'd been impacted. What I discovered was infuriating and disturbing, but my research and discoveries, documented in this book, also gave me hope.

My journey made it clear that our family's experience was not unique, and was actually less severe than what many go through. It also became clear that ignoring drug policy out of a naïve belief that it only impacts those with addiction issues or who use illegal drugs was a grave error.

Victims aren't limited to drug users.

War on Us is the story of how the "War on Drugs" is really a war on all of us, impacting nearly every person, *including those who've never touched an illegal drug*. The effect of drug policy has cascaded far past impacting only those who are self-medicating chronic pain or who fall into the percentage of people whose experimentation with drugs led to addiction. *Your* health, *your* family, *your* assets, *your* safety, and *your* freedom are at risk. From SWAT teams breaking down doors of innocent people to drug cartels killing those caught in the crossfire and over a trillion in wasted taxpayer dollars in the United States alone, the "War on Drugs" is jeopardizing daily life for all of us.

Proven medications are being denied to pain patients regardless of whether addiction is a factor or not. Patients are routinely deprived of medications that had been successfully treating symptoms long term, and are often looked at as suspected drug-seeking "criminals." Out of fear of DEA raids, pharmacists police physicians and other health care

---

* Visit www.WarOnUs.com for information on online courses available, as well as complimentary updates to this book and information on developments on the War on Drugs.

professionals and refuse to fill prescriptions. Health care providers no longer work with their patients to make best health care decisions without risking their licenses, putting themselves at risk of civil or criminal prosecution, or of having their assets seized by the DEA or other law enforcement. Suicide rates are increasing among pain patients forced to reduce or stop their medications. Denial of prescription medications is leading some patients to buy street drugs out of desperation, significantly increasing the risk of tainted drugs and escalating risks of overdose. Patients risk legal consequences created by the same legal system that is denying them access to legal, proven and effective medical treatment.

The attempted solutions have become the problem.

The good news is that we do have answers. Medical and scientific breakthroughs provide many effective treatments without prison and without denying helpful medications to all patients.

The question is no longer how to treat substance use disorder. The question is whether we have the will to implement change to bring our policies from the 1930s to the 21st century. I'm cautiously optimistic. The degree of dysfunction in drug policy opens opportunity. Policy change can bring enormous progress.

Our son once told me, "Mom, they'll never think of me as anything but a criminal." My heart broke for him, but also for all the others impacted by the War on Drugs and myths about addiction. It's time to replace judgment with medical care. It's time to allow opportunity instead of filling prisons. It's time to stop wasting taxpayer dollars and compromising everyone's health care. It's time to stop the stigma and to begin hope and recovery.

This "War" is not a War on Drugs, but a war on people. The people most devastated are the most vulnerable—those with physical and mental health issues and their families. We prosecute them, stigmatize them, and destroy them, emotionally, financially, and legally. Persecuting our most vulnerable cascades to affect all of society.

It's time to end the War on Drugs. It's time to end the War on Us. This book is the roadmap to do just that.

PART 1

THE REAL FACE
OF THE
WAR ON DRUGS

CHAPTER 1

UNINTENDED CONSEQUENCES

"Without reflection, we go blindly on our way,
creating more unintended consequences, and
failing to achieve anything useful."

MARGARET J. WHEATLEY

Ryan, a thin, gaunt-looking young man, squints as he emerges from the huge building, shuffles to a bush 10 steps away, bends over, and vomits. A woman runs to him and hands him pills. Is this a drug deal? An illegal transaction?

This is a mother with her son after his release from jail. He was there for just a few days on a probation hold for a missed appointment, but those few days changed his life. When Ryan reported to lockup, he was assured that the nurse would administer his medications. He never saw them again despite multiple requests, including a formal written demand. Fear of retaliation inhibited further complaints, so he endured life-threatening withdrawal and excruciating pain behind bars. Medical journals said cold-turkey withdrawal from the meds he was on "is dangerous, can cause long term issues with serotonin levels, and can cause anxiety, depression, intense dissatisfaction with life, limb pain, nightmares, suicidal thoughts, fatigue, insomnia, mood swings, paranoia, panic, and drug craving." Ryan has the basis for a lawsuit, but statutes of limitation will expire long before his probation will end, and fear of retaliation is justified. Medications are routinely denied to those behind bars ranging from meds proven successful in treating addiction to those used in treating pain, depression, anxiety and multiple other health issues.

Denial of prescription medications put Ryan at high risk for escalating health issues and intensified addiction. Withdrawal behind bars could have killed him. Stress of incarceration combined with reductions in tolerance levels also significantly increased his risk of overdose upon release.[1] Ryan's short jail stay could have become a death sentence.

———

Maggie has never used illegal drugs, but she needs medications to treat her severe, chronic pain. Her doctor, concerned about being accused of over-prescribing, reduced her pain medications, leaving her in agony and making it hard to get through normal daily activities. The War on Drugs has been expanded to impact legal prescription medications. One pharmacy no longer carries the medications. The new pharmacy requires prescription pickup every seven days. When work requires travel on the medication pickup day, Maggie must choose between being in pain or refusing to travel when scheduled. Her life revolves around which days she needs to have access to the pharmacy, and she lives in fear of being denied medications in the future. An acquaintance has given Maggie information on where to get the medications on the street. Out of desperation, she's considered it, but fears arrest or overdose from impurities and varying concentrations in those street drugs.

———

Jason suffers from paruresis, or bashful bladder, a social anxiety disorder that prevents individuals from urinating in public. The condition affects approximately 11 percent of the population.[2] Jason was arrested for drug possession and is now on probation, which mandates ongoing, monitored urine tests. His inability to produce while an observer stands at his shoulder has been deemed to be a failed test, leading to jail time. Requests for saliva, hair follicle, or blood tests in lieu of urine tests were denied. Jail time led to loss of his job and a criminal record that compromises future career opportunities.

The monkey is off of Melissa's back. She's fought hard to beat her addiction. Medications and hard work in addressing physical and emotional issues led to her successful recovery. The issue is that she's unable to find a place to live. With a felony record for drug possession, applications to rent an apartment have all been denied. Sober houses in her area prohibit use of the medications that are needed for her continued recovery. Living with friends would put them in violation of their lease due to her felony. If roommates have beer in the refrigerator or drugs on premises, Melissa could end up behind bars for a probation violation. She's finally found recovery, yet Melissa is homeless.

Judy posts in a Facebook group: "Does anyone have any suggestions on how to keep my son comfortable? He's on my couch, detoxing from heroin. And, we need an affordable treatment center with an open bed."

The home detox on the couch is due to expense and because the relapse that now requires the detox is a probation violation. If the probation agent hears about it, Judy's son could be locked up for a long time.

As is typical of parents struggling to keep their kids alive, Judy seeks help for her son's serious medical symptoms based on where a bed is available. Other emotional and physical issues often accompany substance use disorder. The best treatment for addiction varies depending on individual needs, yet medical help for diagnosis and assessment of the best treatment protocol for the individual patient is seldom available.

———◆———

Paul was arrested on a drug possession charge and is serving prison time. His parents received an extortion call from gang members. If payment isn't made, the callers threatened, their son's life would end in prison at the hand of gang members who were fellow inmates. The parents' prior contact with the prison gave them little confidence that Paul would be protected, so they paid, and hope another call doesn't demand more. Sleep doesn't come easily as, every night, these parents envision their son locked behind bars with gang members willing to murder—all because he had some pills in his pocket. Paul's parents aren't alone.[3]

———◆———

Justin was arrested with a small quantity of Oxycontin and spent the night in jail, prompting entry into treatment several states away shortly after release. No charges were filed at that time. He completed a 28-day treatment program and a six-month aftercare program. Fifteen months after the arrest, Justin was working at the treatment center, an example for other young men entering the program. Then, he received a call from prior roommates, informing him that a SWAT team looking for him had broken down the door of his previous apartment, terrifying current tenants. Justin had left a forwarding address with the post office. Police or prosecutors could have simply sent a letter.

Justin contacted the court and agreed to report. Upon arrival at a hearing, he was told that nothing he'd done in regard to his recovery since the arrest counted for anything, since paperwork to formally file charges had just been completed, and actions prior to filing of charges were irrelevant. In order to afford travel expenses, fines, costs, and required drug testing and other mandates, he was forced to quit his job at the treatment center and move cross-country to live with his parents.

After dedicating 15 months to his recovery, Justin's risk of relapse just skyrocketed, solely because of prosecutorial delays and policies. His positive work with others at the treatment center ended. If the goal of the criminal justice system is to promote recovery so individuals can succeed, in practice, just the opposite happens in many cases.

THIS is the real face of the War on Drugs.

This modern day prohibition, based on assumptions from the 1930s when we didn't have the benefit of today's science and medicine, is literally killing people, destroying lives, and bankrupting families.

It's normal to believe that if we control the supply of drugs, those we care about will be at lower risk of addiction or overdose. It's also instinctive to believe that if we put drug users behind bars, they'll "hit bottom" and make better choices. When parents see their own children turn into shells of their former selves, focusing on nothing but their next fix, many believe, out of desperation, the advice they hear: "Don't enable. Let them hit bottom. Let them feel the consequences of their choices." It seems like common sense to believe that if prohibitions on drug possession are eased, drug use will increase and lead to higher cost and higher risk for everyone.

But what if these assumptions and these conclusions are the exact *opposite* of what science and medicine tell us? What if we HAVE solutions to this epidemic, but simply haven't had the will to implement them because of old assumptions, fear, stigma, entrenched policies, and pressure from those who profit from prohibition?

It's difficult to research the real application of the War on Drugs. It largely happens behind closed doors including prosecutor and probation offices, jail cells, inside mandated treatment programs with treatment providers forced to share information with criminal justice personnel, or in homes where parents are told that advocating for their children is harmful.

Closed doors, secrets, stigma, and fear are foundations of this "War." Profit, politics of both major political parties, and emotional responses have escalated it and created barriers for change, despite the obvious destruction. Some believe that proponents of drug policy reform simply want easy access to drugs, and ignore or don't care about the issues created by addiction or irresponsible drug use—for individuals or for society. Nothing could be further from the truth. Living our own family's nightmare and working with others who've been affected made me excruciatingly aware of addiction and its casualties. The goal is to minimize the destruction that can be caused by substance use disorder, but emotional reactions are seldom successful and punitive responses are highly destructive. That has been proven by the utter failure of the War on Drugs.

CHAPTER 2

ADDICTION KILLS & DESTROYS LIVES

"The idea that other perspectives exist may not be obvious to those who are in an emotional state of mind."

NABIL N. JAMAL

This book is not a utopian argument that ignores the tears of parents seeing their children's dreams lost, or sobbing over caskets after overdose takes the lives of sons and daughters. This book doesn't ignore the desperation and despair of watching a loved one trying to detox on a couch, or lost on the streets, with family and friends waiting for the dreaded call from jail or from the morgue. We can't ignore the thousands of grandparents whose retirement has shifted to raising grandchildren when their sons and daughters are unable to parent because of addiction or overdose. The assessment in this book doesn't ignore the cost to society and to taxpayers of drug addiction, drug cartels, increased crime, lost productivity, homelessness, medical issues, and spread of disease.

To solve a problem, we must acknowledge it. Addiction, overdose, and some substance use are problems. When politicians or criminal justice professionals attempt to implement solutions, many are legitimately trying to improve on the devastation they deal with on a daily basis. Can we blame a police officer who harshly arrests someone who looks high, when the day before that same officer was rescuing children from a meth house? Can we blame a politician who promotes punitive legislation after being contacted by a grieving mother, asking for harsher sanctions against those who supplied the drugs that took her child's life? Can we blame the judge or prosecutor who has no medical training for mandating drug court for a defendant, not realizing that individuals may be set up for failure because the medical needs of that individual won't be met by a drug court that by design has to be one-size-fits-all and that by law is required to use incarceration as a threat?

While it's important to acknowledge all of the issues created by substance use, it's also important to acknowledge that emotional responses and the gut-wrenching desire to "do something" has backfired, and has contributed to many of the results that continue to escalate the epidemic.

Loss of our children's dreams and sometimes loss of their lives is, in many cases, more because of drug policy than substance use. Incarceration, criminal records, denial of medications, stigma, and loss of opportunities make it difficult to crawl out of a financial and emotional hole.

We now know that isolation and trauma are leading causes of substance use disorder,[4] yet we continue to use isolation and trauma in an attempt to stem the problem.

Overdose rates have escalated partly because the War on Drugs has forced those with issues into the shadows, afraid to ask for help. Funding is allocated to prosecution, incarceration, and supervision instead of treatment, and most of those who do receive treatment fail to receive individualized care based on evidence or medicine.[5]

Individuals lost on the streets may be there because they didn't have access to proper medical care, or basic emotional or physical support. They may have given up hope after their families followed conventional wisdom advising to "let them hit bottom," while an ever more complex system makes it nearly impossible for those in the throes of addiction to advocate for themselves, or to locate or obtain appropriate treatment.

They may also be in the streets in an effort to avoid a legal system whose primary motivation is punitive, and where plea agreements result in harsh punishment with little to no due process.

Grandparents raising grandchildren may be doing so because of addiction or overdose, but may also be put in the parenting position because their son or daughter is behind bars.

Much like what happened during prohibition with the growth of organized crime, drug cartels are a product of our War on Drugs. Collateral damage to innocent citizens increases when arrests create vacant positions within cartels, creating conflict among those competing to fill the shoes of those arrested.[6]

For these results, taxpayers in the United States alone have spent over a trillion dollars on the War on Drugs since 1971. For that money, the United States has the highest drug use in the world, the highest incarceration rates in the world, and the highest overdose rates in the world.[7]

How Big Is the Issue?

Worldwide, according to the United Nations World Drug Report, over 533 people die of drug-related causes every day.[8] This is more than car accidents, more than guns, and more than terrorism. Drug overdose has caused a decline in life expectancy in the United States for the first time in recent history.

Let's put this in perspective. In 2017, in the United States alone, we lost over 72,000 to drug overdose—an increase of 12.5 percent over the prior year. Fentanyl deaths increased by 540 percent in the last three years.[9] In the United States, we lose a person to overdose every seven minutes, and that doesn't include suicides and other deaths related to drug use. That's the equivalent of a terror attack killing over 6,000 people every month—the equivalent of a 911 attack every two weeks.

Baby boomers remember the impact of the Vietnam War. Even those of us growing up in small towns experienced the funerals of those who didn't come home, and saw the agony of those returning with physical and emotional wounds. We're still feeling the effects of Vietnam, including the stigma felt by soldiers returning home, and the cascade effect on their families and their communities. Over a period of 10 years, the U.S. lost over 58,000 soldiers in Vietnam. Overdose fatalities every *10 months* are equal to fatalities in the 10 years of the Vietnam War. In both cases, government policy has been instrumental in creating casualties. The long-term effect of the War on Drugs dwarfs the enormous impact that Vietnam had on all of us.

Incarceration rates in the "land of the free" are astonishing. One of every 18 men in the U.S. is currently behind bars, on probation, or on parole.[10] One in 28 children currently have a parent in jail or prison.[11] Seventy million Americans—one in every three adults—now have a criminal record.[12] The U.S. imprisons blacks at higher percentage rates than South Africa during apartheid.[13] There are more black Americans locked in U.S. prisons or on probation or on parole today than were slaves in 1850—before the U.S. Civil War.[14] The numbers are staggering and shameful.

The system is a wrecking ball of lives. It's nearly impossible for those caught in the system to speak for themselves, or to be believed. When silence based on oppression is the standard, change is slow. The system is so horrendous that, had I not experienced it within our own family, it would be hard to believe the stories of the day-to-day misery, ruined lives, and hopelessness created by the War on Drugs and our overall approach to substance use.

If the purpose of the War on Drugs is to minimize the harm created by drug addiction, then the core questions in determining whether our approach is rational should be:

1. Has the War on Drugs been successful? Has it reduced addiction rates? Has it saved taxpayer dollars? Has it kept citizens free and safe?

2. Is addiction a choice, or is it a health condition? If it's a choice, perhaps punitive policies would reduce addiction. If it's a health condition, then our policies contradict foundational

requirements of criminal law—that people should be punished only for acts for which they had intent, and over which they had control.

The answer to the question of whether the War on Drugs has been successful is clear. It has failed. When government tries to solve a problem, it's typical for costs to soar, regardless of whether the policy is effective or destructive.

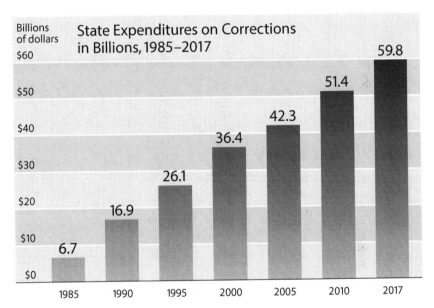

Reproduced/adapted with permission from The Sentencing Project.[15]

As the government doubled-down on failed policies at taxpayer expense, mass incarceration and overdose rates soared.

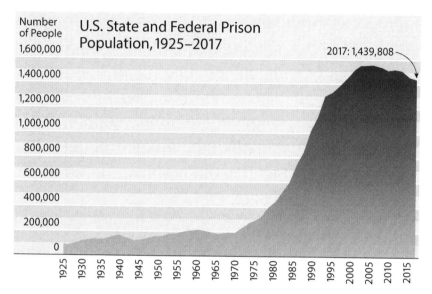

U.S. State and Federal Prison Population, 1925–2017

Number of People

2017: 1,439,808

Reproduced/adapted with permission from The Sentencing Project.[16]

The U.S. has approximately 4.5 percent of the world's population yet incarcerates about 22 percent of the world's prisoners.[17] The War on Drugs has changed the face of the "Land of the Free."

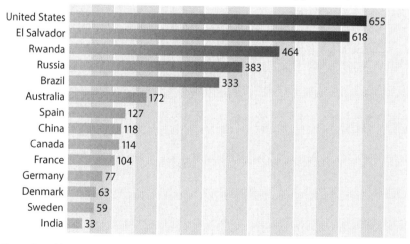

International Rates of Incarceration, per 100,000

Country	Rate
United States	655
El Salvador	618
Rwanda	464
Russia	383
Brazil	333
Australia	172
Spain	127
China	118
Canada	114
France	104
Germany	77
Denmark	63
Sweden	59
India	33

Reproduced/adapted with permission from The Sentencing Project.[18]

As mass incarceration reached unprecedented levels in the United States, the rate of overdose deaths skyrocketed, nearly doubling in a decade.

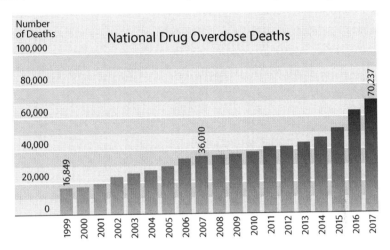

Source: Centers for Disease Control and Prevention[19]

The impact of drug policy does not only affect the young. Overdose rates have escalated in all age groups, with largest increases in ages 25-54. Ages 55-64 also saw significant increases.

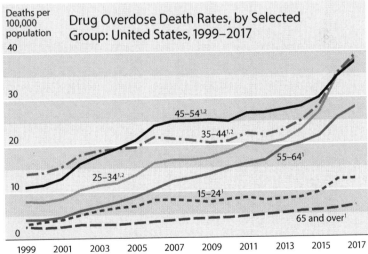

1. Significant increasing trend from 1999 through 2017 with different rates of change over time, p < 0.005.
2. 2017 rates were significantly higher for age groups 25–34, 35–44, and 45–54 than for age groups 15–24, 55–64, and 65 and over, p < 0.05. The rate for age groups 35–44 was significantly higher than the rate for age group 45–54 and

Source: Centers for Disease Control and Prevention [20]

Is there any way to justify spending over a trillion in taxpayer dollars for these results? Why would we continue spending over $51 billion[21] every year to continue these horrific outcomes? There are different approaches that have proven to be successful. We'll discuss alternatives in Part 2, Finding the Fix.

The second question in determining whether our approach to controlling addiction and overdose is rational isn't as straightforward.

CHAPTER 3

IS ADDICTION A HEALTH ISSUE OR A CHOICE?

Definition of Choice: The opportunity or power to choose between two or more possibilities.

MERRIAM-WEBSTER DICTIONARY

Is addiction a health issue or is it a choice? Current policy is enforced by the criminal justice system and punishes drug possession, use, or sale. That policy is clearly based on the assumption that addiction is a choice. As science, medicine, and public sentiment have developed, politicians have voiced various opinions on the choice/disease question, but the application of law continues to be largely punitive. We have hundreds of thousands of people [22] behind bars for drug possession, and millions more under stringent probation requirements or living with opportunity-crushing criminal records. For those on probation or parole or in drug court, a single relapse can create severe sanctions. Current drug policy simply makes no sense if addiction is not a choice.

How can addiction NOT be a choice? These people snort something, pop a pill, or stick a needle in their arm. They're not a sympathetic group. Assuming that addiction is a choice is the most intuitive reaction. After all, there's no one physically *forcing* them to acquire the drug and put it into their bodies in whatever way they're administering it. It's not surprising that the assumption that drug use is a choice is prevalent in policy and in societal beliefs.

The issue is that neither life, nor addiction, is that simple. Addiction is defined as a disease by multiple government agencies including the National Institute on Drug Abuse (NIDA) and the Substance Abuse and Mental Health Services Administration (SAMHSA), as well as the American Medical Association and the American Society of Addiction Medicine.

So, the same government that defines addiction as a disease incarcerates people for drug use—the obvious symptom of that "disease." Hmm. Confusing.

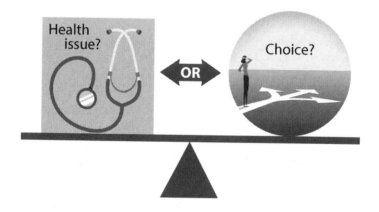

Maybe the issue will be clarified if we look at results. If the choice model and the policies that arose from it are accurate, the War on Drugs should have solved, or at least significantly minimized, drug addiction long ago. Would hundreds of thousands of people choose prison and a high risk of death over ending their drug use? Not likely. Drug War penalties should have changed at least some "choices." Instead, addiction and overdose rates have soared as incarceration rates and other punitive measures have escalated.[23]

Some believe that punishment simply hasn't been harsh enough, and that we should intensify the War on Drugs. [24]

Generally, though, we define insanity as continuing the same action and expecting different results, so we may want to rethink that plan. After more than 50 years of misery and wasted money, might it be worth taking a step back to reassess our original assumption? New research and successful treatment protocols are helpful in answering the question.

One of the most exciting and successful developments in treatment of substance use disorder is use of medications. It may be counterintuitive to use drugs to treat addiction, but the U.S. Substance Abuse and Mental Health Services Administration reports that *medications* cut overdose rates in half! The National Institute on Drug Abuse reports that the medications methadone, buprenorphine, and naltrexone all reduce opioid use, infectious disease transmission, and criminal behavior associated with drug use. They increase the likelihood that a patient will successfully remain in treatment and in long-term recovery.[25] These drugs are on the World Health Organization's list of essential medicines.[26] Medications are now helping many who've struggled long term to return to normal, productive lives.

This raises an important question. If *medications* can lead patients to recovery, then is addiction a moral failing or lack of willpower leading to poor choices? Medications don't remove moral failings, but they do lead to recovery. Is it rational to punish those who don't have access to medications or other care that gives them the medical *ability* to make healthy choices? Medications and other medical care have high success rates, supporting the conclusion that addiction is a medical issue that can be treated medically. If that's the case, punishment is not only inappropriate and ineffective; it's immoral. As a society, few would argue that punishing patients for having a medical condition would be rational or ethical. Yet, that's the approach we apply to patients every day.

The fact that medications save lives and increase rates of recovery is indisputable.[27] Despite this fact, current law and practice largely ignores these medications, and in many cases, restricts or prohibits their use. The majority of jails and prisons, peer support groups, treatment centers, and sober houses *prohibit* use of the medications that have the highest statistical success rate for treating addiction.[28]

Alternate Views and Objections to the Choice and Disease Models

There are alternate views to the more black and white "Choice vs. Disease" model. The disease model minimizes the risk that patients will be blamed and punitive penalties applied. However, some are concerned that the disease model may send the message that the individual has *no* control or personal responsibility in finding recovery. Others worry that the disease model implies a lifelong sentence without possible cure. While the disease model reduces the stigma that often accompanies the belief that addiction is a choice, disease also carries stigma as an impairment or abnormality.

Brain scans showing changes in the brains of those with drug addictions are compelling. If the area of the brain that controls decision-making regarding drug use is compromised, is it appropriate to punish someone for continued drug use? The National Institute on Drug Abuse, states: "Despite popular belief, willpower alone is often insufficient to overcome an addiction. Drug use has compromised the very parts of the brain that make it possible to 'say no.'"[29] However, there are contradictory opinions on this as well, because all experience changes the brain. That is how our brains create memories. Our brains change with other addictions and experiences as well.

Some may argue that, since changes to the brain because of substance use happen only after initial drug use, drug users still bring addiction on themselves.

It's true that if someone never tries a drug, they will avoid addiction. It's also true that, on average, less than 20 percent of all people who try drugs develop addiction. These statistics are very different than what's portrayed in the media, in societal assumptions, and by public policy toward drug use, but numerous studies have come to the same conclusion: Between 80 and 90 percent of drug users do NOT develop substance use disorder. There is one exception to these statistics: Nicotine is the most addictive drug with a 67.5 percent probability rate for transition to dependence.[30]

The National Institute on Drug Abuse estimates that 23 percent of individuals who use heroin develop opioid addiction.[31] In a study assessing 12.3 million methamphetamine users, about 530,000 of them are regular users—which would be indicative of an addiction rate of approximately 23% even if we assume that all regular users are in fact addicted.[32] A study done by New York State Psychiatric Institute at Columbia University estimated a rate of 20.9 percent transition to dependence[33] for cocaine, and 8.9 percent for cannabis.[34]

Averaging statistics for all drugs (excluding tobacco), 10-20 percent will develop substance use disorder. The range depends on whether statistics are averaged for all drugs, or whether the lower addiction rates for cannabis and the larger numbers of cannabis users over other drugs are factored in.

Even using the higher rate of 20 percent addiction, 80 percent of those experimenting with drugs will not become addicted. Statistics are of little comfort to those who tragically end up in the 10-20 percent, but before we judge those in that percentage, we should consider that over 80 percent of individuals who initially make the SAME choices as those who end up addicted are fortunate enough not to have that outcome. For the "lucky" 80 percent, it's easy to advise "Just Say No"—but the very nature of addiction allows that 80 percent to do just that, while the other 10-20 percent are not able to. This creates a paradox. Those who aren't susceptible to addiction believe that their own experience mirrors that of those with substance use disorder. *If I can control my substance use, why shouldn't everyone be able to? If they can't, it MUST be their choice.*

Those with addiction issues have a hard time explaining why or how their responses are different, or why they can't simply stop doing something that is obviously causing them harm. Science now tells us that the addicted brain works differently than that of others. Whether that's due to environmental issues, a history of trauma or isolation, an emotional or physical propensity toward addiction, genetics, or many other factors, what we do know is that addiction is not as simple as "Just Say No."

Unless we want to stigmatize anyone who tries a drug of any type, we should appreciate that similar choices can lead to very different results—not because of a moral failing in those who end up with substance use disorder, but because they were unfortunate enough to fall into the percentage whose physical or psychological makeup or personal history made them susceptible to addiction.

Not everyone who eats candy bars ends up diabetic, but for those who do, we don't incarcerate them for their sugar habit or deny them care. With substance use disorder, in many cases, our criminal justice system adds trauma, stress, and isolation—all life challenges that we now know trigger or exacerbate addiction.

Addiction as a Learned Behavior

Maia Szalavitz, in her book *Unbroken Brain*, argues that because our brain networks motivate us to seek pleasure and avoid pain, addiction is a learning disorder, "a condition where a system designed to motivate us to engage in activities helpful to survival and reproduction develops abnormally and goes awry." Maia goes on to say, "Of course, none of this is to say that addiction isn't a medical disorder or that addicted people shouldn't be treated with compassion."

Maia's discussion is an interesting one. She says that the real issue is the purpose the addictive behavior serves, and how it can be replaced with more healthy pursuits. This analysis—where we focus on best ways of addressing the issue—is rational and productive. She argues that, instead of worrying about how we can "stop the demon drug or activity of the month, . . . what we really need to understand is why and how obsessions and compulsions develop in particular people."

Johan Hari, in his book *Chasing the Scream*[35], says: "It isn't the drug that causes the harmful behavior—it's the environment. An isolated rat will almost always become a junkie. A rat with a good life almost never will, no matter how many drugs you make available to him. As Bruce [Alexander] put it: he was realizing that addiction isn't a disease. Addiction is an adaptation. It's not you—it's the cage you live in." [36] Hari, in his book *Lost Connections*[37], also points out: "The opposite of addiction isn't sobriety. It's connection."

Dr. Carl Hart, chair of the Department of Psychology at Columbia University, agrees that social determinants should be considered. He states in an article in *Nature Magazine*, "Roughly 10 percent of people who try drugs become addicted, and among them you'll find a high prevalence of depression, trauma and other problems like poverty and over-policed neighborhoods . . ." He expresses concern that our focus on the interaction between the drug and the brain leave us focused on either removing the drug from society or studying the brain—rather than looking at potential societal causes and incorporating those into our models for dealing with drugs in our society.

Dr. Gabor Maté, a leading addiction specialist, stated in his book *In the Realm of Hungry Ghosts: Close Encounters with Addiction*, "Not all addictions are rooted in abuse or trauma, but I do believe they can all be traced to painful experience."[38]

The Debate and the Bottom Line

The debate over what is—and is not—a disease has continued throughout time, and can become a hot topic, particularly when definitions impact government funding for treatment and research, insurance coverage, and protocols for care. Definitions can be very important for those purposes. (When considering definitions, it's important to factor in the purpose of those definitions.)

Three primary questions should be essential in assessing drug policy if our purpose is to minimize addiction and the negative impact of irresponsible drug use.

1. How much control does a person with substance use disorder have over drug use?

2. What treatment is most effective and how can we most cost-effectively provide that treatment?

3. How can we change policy to minimize addiction, overdose, and overall harm to society, and what ineffective and destructive policies need to end?

When considering whether to treat addiction as a health issue or as a crime, whether addiction is officially a "disease" or not may be irrelevant. Based on the success of medical treatments, science clearly proves that addiction is a health issue for which individualized medical treatment has statistically been proven more effective than other treatment protocols.

The approach suggested by Dr. Carl Hart, Dr. Gabor Maté, Johan

Hari, and Maia Szalavitz to focus on societal impact on addiction is supported by science and opens opportunities for solutions. History has proven that we'll never successfully remove drugs from society. Drugs haven't even been kept out of prison settings successfully[39] so a drug-free society is clearly impossible. It may also be unwise, since medications have many positive uses. There will always be overlap, with "good" drugs potentially diverted to "bad" uses.

If societal change can make a difference, there is reason for optimism. Each of us can have a part in societal change, not just through advocacy, but on the level of our own families. Reports that trauma and isolation exacerbate addiction should make us seriously reconsider advice that recommends that loved ones "let them hit bottom," thereby contributing to trauma and isolation. As society has used punitive measures, adding stigma, fear, destroyed opportunities, and financial burdens on those with substance use disorder and on their families, the epidemic has grown. That outcome supports current science, which shows that these responses are the exact opposite of what would be effective.

The success of reduced addiction and overdose rates in countries that have replaced punitive policies with those offering treatment by medical professionals confirms the wisdom of those policies. (See Part 2, Finding the Fix.) Addiction is a treatable medical condition. Prosecuting patients is ineffective, costly, wasteful, destructive, and immoral.

Persecuting drug users without addiction issues makes no sense. For the vast majority of drug users who don't develop substance use disorder, what is the legal or moral basis to support prosecution for simply possessing or ingesting a drug? Arrest, prosecution, incarceration, and supervision undoubtedly create stress, trauma, and isolation—all life challenges that multiple studies have now shown trigger or exacerbate addiction. Drug policy itself is potentially increasing the risk that a casual drug user may develop an addiction, or escalating the level of addiction in those who do have a substance use disorder.

If a drug user commits a crime that would victimize another person or their property, we have laws with which to prosecute them for those crimes. Some say drug policy can be justified because drug use could increase the chance that a future activity by the drug user could cause harm. If that's the case, those who drive cars should also be arrested, to prevent potential car accidents. Punishing an act because it could cause harm in the future is wrought with risk of prosecution of innocent victims, planting of evidence[40], and leverage by prosecutors to promote harsh plea agreements based on threats of additional drug charges. It also destroys lives and increases addiction rates, leading to the very risks that the law was supposedly designed to prevent.

The War on Drugs has promoted rampant misinformation, often disseminated by criminal justice employees. Law enforcement and other criminal justice employees are not experts on drugs or addiction, and, based on ongoing negative experiences related to drugs, may understandably be biased.

At a symposium for parents concerned about their children's drug use, a police community liaison officer stated in his presentation, "If someone tries meth, they WILL be addicted, and the ONLY hope for them then is long-term prison—and even then, their chances aren't good." The number of inaccuracies in that one statement was shocking. There is no doubt that methamphetamine addiction is a serious issue, but not everyone who tries meth becomes addicted. Large numbers of people have tried meth without addiction, and treatments for meth addiction are available.[41] Many of those with methamphetamine addictions are self-medicating attention deficit and other disorders. Appropriate treatment, sometimes including medications, can be successful. That officer may have had good intentions and had likely seen the harm caused by addiction, but he was also very misinformed and in his position, that made him destructive.

A combination of factors has led to devastating results. We combine attitudes based on inaccurate, obsolete information, tell loved ones that being involved and advocating is unacceptable, and give those in positions of power the authority to speak as experts and to make decisions behind bars where no one can see what's going on. Regardless of our definitions, regardless of whether addiction is a choice, a disease, or something else, what we're doing has clearly failed. It's time for change.

CHAPTER 4

WHY AN EPIDEMIC NOW? HOW DID WE GET HERE?

"Those who fail to learn from history
are doomed to repeat it."

WINSTON CHURCHILL

Addiction is emotional. It creates fear and panic—for parents, for communities, for taxpayers, and for politicians. It promotes a mentality of "We have to do something." That something, in regard to this topic, has been reactive, with little attention to science, medicine, or analysis of what has worked and what hasn't. That's a prescription for bad results.

The addiction and overdose epidemic can be traced to four historical developments that came together to create a perfect storm. These happened primarily in the United States, which then exported its drug policy worldwide through influence on United Nations treaties and policies.

1. Drug Prohibition

Large-scale prohibition on drug use is, historically speaking, relatively new. It's only in the last century, and primarily in the past 50 years, that we've experimented with the prohibition model. Many substances including cannabis, opium, coca, and psychedelics have been used for thousands of years for spiritual and medicinal purposes.[42] In the 1890s, the Sears and Roebuck catalog offered a syringe and a small amount of cocaine for $1.50.[43]

U.S. Federal Policy

In 1909, the Smoking Opium Act banned the possession, importation, and use of opium for smoking, but still allowed it to be used as a medication. This was the first federal law in the United States to ban the non-medical use of a substance.

In 1914, the Harrison Narcotics Act[44] forced doctors, under threat of felony prosecution, to deny treatment to patients deemed to have addiction issues. In the 1920s approximately 35,000 physicians were indicted for prescribing narcotics to patients, and more than 19 percent of federal prisoners were there for narcotics offenses.[45] Unfortunately, history is now repeating itself. (See # 6, War on Physicians & Pharmacists.)

In 1919, the 18th Amendment to the Constitution began alcohol prohibition. The well-known results, including illegal production and sale of liquor, methanol poisoning, and escalation of organized crime, led to the 21st amendment, which repealed prohibition in 1933. Unfortunately, future policy didn't benefit from lessons learned from the failed prohibition experiment.

When prohibition ended, government agencies previously responsible for enforcing prohibition needed rationale for continued budgets, and bureaucrats wanting to retain their jobs needed a new target. Harry Jacob Anslinger, commissioner of the Federal Bureau of Narcotics from 1930 to 1962, led the punitive approach to addiction, and in doing so, shored up his own power and position. Anslinger was an unabashed racist:

There are 100,000 total marijuana smokers in the US, and most are Negroes, Hispanics, Filipinos and entertainers. Their Satanic music, jazz and swing, result from marijuana usage. This marijuana causes white women to seek sexual relations with Negroes, entertainers and any others." —Harry J. Anslinger

"I wish I could show you what a small marihuana [sic] cigarette can do to one of our degenerate Spanish-speaking residents. That's why our problem is so great; the greatest percentage of our population is composed of Spanish-speaking persons, most of who are low mentally, because of social and racial conditions."
—Harry J. Anslinger

This man, and these attitudes, are the basis for much of today's drug policy. (Johann Hari's book *Chasing the Scream* provides an excellent history of Anslinger's impact on the drug war.)[46]

In 1937, at Anslinger's urging, the Marijuana Tax Act[47] was passed. This law didn't criminalize the possession or use of cannabis, but effectively banned it, including up to a $2,000 fine and five years in prison if taxes weren't paid.

Cannabis was listed as a legal medicine in the U.S. until 1942. According to the *Scientific American*, the American Medical Association opposed prohibiting its use. In 1944, the La Guardia Committee report from the New York Academy of Medicine questioned criminalizing cannabis.[48]

In 1961, under pressure from the United States, the United Nations adopted the Single Convention on Narcotic Drugs. Unfortunately, this international attempt at prohibiting production, sale, and use of illegal drugs made it difficult for countries to experiment with drug policy to determine which policies successfully achieved objectives.

In 1970, the Controlled Substances Act (CSA) was passed in the United States, further escalating drug prohibition, increasing the size of federal agencies dealing with drug policy, and allowing no-knock warrants and mandatory minimum sentencing. A January 29, 1970 *New York Times* article reported passage of the law and the debate (or lack thereof) surrounding it. According to the article, Senator Thomas Dodd, the chief sponsor of the bill, held up a package that he said contained $3,000 worth of marijuana. He then described an Army sergeant in Vietnam who'd called down a mortar strike on his own troops due to "dreadful hallucinations" caused by marijuana. A few minutes later the Senate unanimously passed the bill."[49]

The Controlled Substances Act also created DEA drug schedules. Then Attorney General John Mitchell (of later Watergate fame) included marijuana on the Schedule 1 list of substances, defined as having no medical benefit and a high probability of abuse and addiction. This classification was supposed to be temporary pending further review by a commission appointed by President Nixon.

In June 1971, Richard Nixon officially declared a "War on Drugs." This quote from John Ehrlichman,[50] counsel and assistant to President Nixon, says it all:

"The Nixon campaign in 1968, and the Nixon White House after that, had two enemies: The antiwar left, and black people. You understand what I'm saying? We knew we couldn't make it illegal to be either against the war or black. But by getting the public to associate the hippies with marijuana and blacks with heroin, and then criminalizing both heavily, we could disrupt those communities. We could arrest their leaders, raid their homes, break up their meetings, and vilify them night after night on the evening news. Did we know we were lying about drugs? Of course we did."

In 1972, the commission, led by Republican Pennsylvania Governor Raymond Shafer, unanimously recommended decriminalizing the possession and distribution of marijuana for personal use, but Nixon rejected the commission's recommendations.

The racial component of drug policy illustrated by the Ehrlichman quote wasn't an isolated incident. Legislation making certain drugs legal and others illegal has consistently been based on money, politics, and history rather than on the danger of a drug itself. Drug scheduling, established by the 1970 Controlled Substances Act, is illustrative. Is cannabis, designated as a Schedule 1 drug, *really* more dangerous than morphine, oxycodone, or fentanyl, all designated as Schedule 2 drugs? Physicians and other medical professionals can write prescriptions for morphine, oxycodone, or fentanyl, but have historically been prohibited from prescribing cannabis. Is there any plausible explanation for this other than the political component?

The first anti-opium laws in the 1870s were directed at Chinese immigrants. The first anti-cocaine laws in the early 1900s were directed at black men in the South. The first anti-marijuana laws in the early 1900s were directed at Mexican migrants and Mexican Americans. Even the term "marijuana" was likely used in lieu of the scientific term cannabis because calling it marijuana related it more closely to recreational use by poor Hispanic immigrants. Dr. William C. Woodward, legislative counsel of the American Medical Association appearing at the 1937 hearing on the topic of criminalizing cannabis, accused Anslinger of changing terminology to fool groups that would otherwise have opposed the bill.[51] Today, Latino and black communities are still subject to wildly disproportionate drug enforcement and sentencing practices.[52] (See # 10, War on Minorities.)

Taxpayer cost has escalated tremendously since the inception of the drug war. When President Nixon signed the Comprehensive Drug Abuse Prevention and Control Act in 1971, the annual budget for this "war" was $100 million. Now it's $15.1 billion (with actual costs of enforcement over $51 *billion* annually).[53] The DEA was established by President Nixon in 1973, with an initial budget of less than $75 million.[54] The DEA's budget today is over $2 billion, with nearly 5,000 agents.

In 1984, Nancy Reagan began her "Just Say No" campaign. This campaign promoted the assumption that addiction is a simple choice, and that punishing the wrong choice would effectively minimize addiction rates and protect children from drugs. President Reagan ramped up the War on Drugs, leading to skyrocketing incarceration rates. In the chart below, bars on the left for each category show the number of people behind bars for drug offenses in 1980, with bars on the right showing 2017 rates.

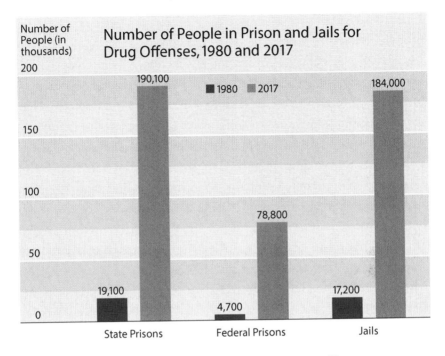

Number of People in Prison and Jails for Drug Offenses, 1980 and 2017

Reproduced/adapted with permission from The Sentencing Project.[55]

Stigma and bias against drug users during the "Just Say No" era are illustrated by comments by then L.A. police chief Daryl Gates, founder of the D.A.R.E. (Drug Abuse Resistance Education) program. He stated in testimony before the Senate Judiciary Committee, "Casual drug users should be taken out and shot."[56] (Gates is also credited with co-creating SWAT teams.)

D.A.R.E. was adopted nationwide in 1983 with no analysis or evidence of whether this would be an effective approach. The programs did not work, with studies showing that D.A.R.E. graduates had no lower drug use, and in some instances, higher drug use than those not exposed to the program.[57]

The lack of foundation for the U.S. drug information campaign mirrored the basis of overall drug policy. Reactive, emotional policies with no evidentiary basis have been the standard for drug policy long term.

In 1988, international efforts at criminalization of personal drug possession were introduced by the United Nations Convention against Illicit Traffic in Narcotic Drugs and Psychoactive Substances[58] which states, in Article 3(2): ". . . each Party shall adopt such measures as may be necessary to establish as a criminal offence under its domestic law, when committed intentionally, the possession, purchase or cultivation of narcotic drugs or psychotropic substances for personal consumption."

In 1988, Joe Biden co-sponsored the Anti-Drug Abuse Act, creating new mandatory minimum sentences for drugs, including sentencing that treated crack cocaine much more harshly than powder cocaine, drugs with the same chemical makeup but used by different racial groups. Black and Latino populations more frequently used crack cocaine, versus more prevalent use of powder cocaine by Caucasians.

Bill Clinton signed the 1994 Crime Law, passing the largest crime bill in the history of the United States. It added 100,000 police officers and provided $9.7 billion in funding for prisons and $6.1 billion in funding for prevention programs (designed with input from law enforcement). This legislation significantly impacted police enforcement of drug laws.[59] The 1988 and 1994 bills combined fueled the drug war.

Drug policy has been a bipartisan failure. During Bill Clinton's 1992 presidential campaign, he advocated for treatment instead of incarceration, but then he escalated the drug war during his presidency. He rejected a U.S. Sentencing Commission recommendation to eliminate the sentencing disparities between crack and powder cocaine. He also ignored recommendations from his drug czar, General Barry McCaffrey, and from Donna Shalala, the secretary of the Department of Health, to end the federal ban on funding syringe access programs.

George W. Bush allocated more money to the War on Drugs than any other administration. His drug czar, John Walters, launched a campaign to promote student drug testing. Rates of illicit drug use remained constant, but overdose fatalities escalated. The Bush years brought increased militarization of domestic law enforcement including 40,000 SWAT raids on Americans annually, largely based on nonviolent drug offenses.

Barack Obama, in his campaign, described the War on Drugs as "an utter failure," criticized the punitive criminal justice system, and called for decriminalization of cannabis. In 2010, he signed the Fair Sentencing Act that reduced the crack cocaine vs. powder cocaine discrepancy from 100:1 to 18:1, but in his first term, did little else to de-escalate the War on Drugs. Medical marijuana raids, prosecutions, and forfeiture actions continued under the Obama administration.[60] His second term improved somewhat. He tolerated state-level legalization of marijuana, removed some of the barriers to medical marijuana research, and shortened more than 1,000 drug offenders' sentences. His crackdown on prescriptions for pain medications began issues for legitimate pain patients and escalated heroin use. At least his drug policies included treatment and harm reduction in addition to the historic punitive measures.

The Trump administration began on rocky ground with the appointment of Jeff Sessions as attorney general. Sessions' quotes, including "Good people don't smoke marijuana" and "I thought those guys [the Ku Klux Klan] were OK until I learned they smoked pot," put fear into the hearts of anyone hoping for drug policy based on science. Despite Sessions' strong stance against cannabis, he was unable to stop the movement toward legalization by states. As of this writing, Attorney General William Barr has pledged to uphold the Cole Memorandum promising not to enforce federal marijuana prohibition in states that have legalized it. Federal legislation to remove marijuana from DEA Schedule 1 classification and to officially delegate cannabis policy to the states is currently being considered. (See #25, The Cannabis Experience.) Cautious optimism is supported by President Trump's signature on the First Step Act[61] and bipartisan criminal justice reform on the federal and state levels.

The First Step legislation expands employment programming for those incarcerated and upon release. It requires the Federal Bureau of Prisons to assist inmates in obtaining social security cards, driver's licenses, and a birth certificate prior to release from federal prison or halfway house. That provision itself will make an enormous difference for those re-entering society, ending the no-man's land that prisoners previously dealt with when released from prison with no evidence of identification.

First Step prohibits restraints on pregnant prisoners and requires corrections officers to complete de-escalation training in an attempt to improve officer responses to inmates. Data collection will be improved under First Step, which requires specific types of information to be collected and provided to the National Prisoner Statistics Program for assessment of who is incarcerated, what programs are offered, who participates in programs, and details on medical care and staffing. The legislation also includes alternatives to prison for low-risk prisoners such as home confinement, expands compassionate and elderly release programs, and requires placement of prisoners as close to family as practicable. First Step mandates evidence-based treatment including use of medications in treatment for substance use disorder. It lowers life sentence mandates for "three strikes" to 25 years, and changes the definition of felonies for three strikes purposes from any felony drug offense to "a serious drug felony or serious violent felony."[62]

Some of the First Step provisions include rights that most citizens would have assumed to be the case without specific mandates, including a requirement that the Bureau of Prisons provide female inmates with tampons or sanitary napkins instead of forcing them to buy them from the commissary. The First Step Act includes several compassionate requirements when a prisoner is diagnosed with a terminal illness. These changes will impact only federal inmates, but will hopefully lead the way to state reforms as well.

Like many before him, President Trump's approach to drug policy has been inconsistent. He has signed beneficial legislation and shown compassion and granted pardons for drug prisoners, overshadowed by what appears to be a continued belief that punishment and "law and order" will solve the epidemic. In March 2018, Trump stated, "If we don't get tough on the drug dealers, we are wasting our time. And that toughness includes the death penalty." President Trump has also praised death penalties for drug dealers in China, as well as Philippine President Duterte's drug policy against drug users as well as dealers, which has led to over 5,000 deaths at the hands of police, and as many as 20,000 more by unidentified gunmen.[63]

The War on Drugs shows enormous hypocrisy and teaches our children disdain for the law. They see themselves and their friends locked up for doing what at least three presidents have publicly admitted to doing.

Barack Obama, in his book *Dreams from My Father*, stated that he "drank heavily," "tried drugs enthusiastically," and tried "a little blow when you could afford it." In a 2008 interview, then Senator Obama, in response to a question about drug use, laughed and stated, "I inhaled frequently . . . that was the whole point."

George W. Bush was arrested for DUI at age 30 when his license was suspended for two years. He also allegedly stated in a taped conversation with a friend, "I wouldn't answer the marijuana question. You know why? I don't want some little kid doing what I tried." Bill Clinton's admission to smoking marijuana was famously followed by his "I didn't inhale" statement. There have been allegations that Presidents Obama, Bush, and Clinton all experimented with cocaine.

Perhaps the good news is that, even if our children have drug histories, they may still become president. The bad news is that continuation of the War on Drugs under the administrations of these and other presidents increases the chance that a child may end up a felon or an ex-con. To date, that has put a damper on career opportunities.

State Prisons and County Jails

When assessing U.S. drug policy, it's easy to focus on federal policy, particularly since approximately half of all federal prisoners are incarcerated for drug crimes. It's important to also understand the impact of state law, since county jails and state prisons house approximately 87 percent of all prisoners held in the United States,[64] including those waiting to be prosecuted and those on their way to prison.

Many assume that jails are less dangerous and better places to be than prison. This is generally not the case. For those who have lengthier stays, many, if given the choice, opt for prison over jail. Since jail is the first stop after arrest, people arriving at a jail may be drunk or high, may arrive with injuries from fights or assaults that led to their arrest, or may be mentally ill with no other place for law enforcement to deliver them. Others, arrested on drug charges, may go into withdrawal after a few days.

Those in jail are less likely to develop attachments than in prison, since inmates come and go frequently. The constant flow of people coming and going can interfere with an inmate's sleep or other scheduling, and can make jails more dangerous than prisons. This is the environment in which we place most drug offenders including first-time "offenders" possessing small quantities. Even a short stay in jail can change identities, making an individual feel like a criminal. It can also act as a "criminal university," with exposure to influences that can change lives in undesirable ways.

Drug Policy Is One of the Direct Causes of the Addiction and Overdose Epidemic

Mass incarceration and criminal records for one of every three American citizens, brought about largely by the War on Drugs, has helped to escalate the addiction and overdose epidemic. When people have to live in the shadows, afraid to seek help out of fear of prosecution, addiction increases. When public funds are spent on law enforcement, prosecution, incarceration, and supervision instead of medical care or individualized treatment, addiction escalates. When career, housing, and personal opportunities are restricted due to criminal records, drug use and risk of addiction increases. When families are destroyed because family members are locked up, children are at higher risk of addiction and incarceration, and the cycle continues.

2. Twelve Steps and Other Treatment—Influences on Criminal Law

Prohibition impacted the availability of alcohol treatment programs, and structure and availability of treatment programs ultimately impacted addiction and overdose rates. Self-help and other programs in existence prior to prohibition had largely ended during prohibition. In 1935, Alcoholics Anonymous filled this void and provided valuable communities of support.

Modern-day treatment protocols weren't available when AA doctrine was developed. Brain scans, medications to treat substance use disorder, and medical research and treatment for the many physical and mental health disorders that often accompany or increase the risk of addiction were not yet available. The foundation of AA did not consider the impact of fentanyl and many other aspects of present-day drug addiction.

Treatment programs that remove individuals from daily routines that include drug use and addictive behavior can be instrumental in making life changes. Twelve-step programs have provided a valuable community and have helped many people (including some of my own family members). The fellowship of others prevents isolation, and is powerful when acceptance counters the stigma felt by those with substance use disorder.

The 12-step doctrine can also add to judgment and stigma when groups are unwilling to accept the success of other treatment methods, or to support those who are partaking in them. Many AA groups are unaccepting of those using medications as part of their treatment, going so far as not allowing those on medications to speak at meetings. That flies in the face of the beliefs of Bill Wilson, one of the founders of AA, who said, "Today, the vast majority of us [AA members] welcome any new light that can be thrown on the alcoholic's mysterious and baffling malady. We don't care too much whether new and valuable knowledge issues from a test tube, a psychiatrist's couch, or from revealing social studies. . . . More and more we regard all who labor in the total field of alcoholism as our companions on a march from darkness to light. We see that we can accomplish together what we could never accomplish in separation and rivalry."[65] Bill W. acknowledged that AA could lead to lack of acceptance of other treatment modalities, stating, "Just because something works for us, that doesn't mean it will work for everyone." Bill Wilson's work included trying to find other types of help for patients.[66]

Bill Wilson's concerns came true. In 1970, Mark and Linda Sobell conducted a study at the Patton State VA Hospital near San Diego to compare success rates of the total abstinence doctrine of AA with a behavior-modification program designed with moderate drinking as a goal. When they published study results indicating that patients in the controlled drinking group had fewer and less severe relapses than those attempting to completely abstain, the fierce attacks on them nearly cost them their careers. Work on the topic was significantly set back.[67]

Controversy about details of the study may be explainable, but the long-term bias against additional studies and rejection of alternatives to AA have resulted in one-size-fits-all peer support approaches, slowing acceptance of advances in science and medicine that can save lives when implemented. These biases even impact solutions for problem drinkers. For example, many with alcohol issues are unaware that taking a naltrexone pill an hour before drinking can effectively curb the craving for alcohol. This technique, the Sinclair Method, has converted some with alcohol use disorder to social drinkers, and has helped others to stop drinking altogether within three to four months. The abstinence-only bias has stymied large-scale publicity or acceptance of this legitimate treatment option. (See Appendix A, Naltrexone.)

Positive developments have occurred, including some treatment centers' acceptance of medications in treatment (including Hazelden/Betty Ford), but the prevalence of 12-step programs, combined with their traditional doctrine that total abstinence for life is required for recovery, contributed to the ongoing criminal justice approach to drug policy.

Twelve-step influence explains prohibitions to use of medications by those in the criminal justice system, despite proof that they are more successful than other treatment protocols. The total abstinence doctrine explains the harsh penalties for relapse, despite relapse happening frequently to patients on the road to recovery.

There are few topics where such black and white rules are mandated, and where anything short of perfection can result in time behind bars. There are no other health issues where patients are forced into peer support groups and punished with denial of care or incarceration if that treatment" is not effective, or if they opt not to participate. Many struggling with addiction have accompanying attention deficit, social anxiety and other health issues. Sitting in peer support groups may not be the best protocol for some of those patients, particularly if participation is not voluntary.

Some studies show that people mandated into AA do worse than those simply left alone.[68] Other studies show that the majority of people recover from addictions without any treatment, regardless of what drug is involved. (This can be a risky path, however, since death by overdose could happen before potential recovery, and because today's stigma and persecution can minimize chances of "aging" into recovery.) Mandating 12 steps or criminalizing drug use and persecuting drug users may actually increase addiction rates and reduce recovery rates.[69]

Twelve-step programs should not replace professional medical treatment or limit availability of other paths to recovery. Replacing medical treatment for cancer with cancer support groups would never be accepted. Unfortunately, 12-step treatment replacing other alternatives is largely what has happened. Twelve steps doctrine provides cover for punitive and perfectionistic criminal justice policies.

In the United States, counties often contract exclusively with one provider to treat drug court participants or other criminal "offenders." More than 44 percent of all referrals to treatment are now made through the criminal justice system[70], which typically mandates 12-step programs. Technically, these mandates violate the establishment clause of the First Amendment to the U.S. Constitution, which prohibits governmental bodies from preferring religion over non-religion or vice-versa. The reality is that few defendants mired in the criminal justice system risk challenging this, or can afford to, so the practice continues on a large scale.

If "offenders" opt not to follow treatment directives, they may be punished with incarceration, even when no medical foundation nor assessment to determine individual patient needs exists and when directives are made by legal professionals without medical training. In turn, legal mandates for attendance have changed the nature of 12-step communities from cooperation to obligation based on threat of harsh penalties for many attendees.

Alternative treatment options are frequently denied to those on probation even if an individual or their family is willing to pay for other services. In some instances, this is because government contracts with providers require minimum quotas. In other cases, it's because of the standard policy of plea agreements to mandate that defendants waive their right to privacy in medical records, authorizing counselors to report back to probation officers. Providers with contracts with specific government agencies are more willing to fully share patient information with probation agents who have the authority to incarcerate the patient based on those reports.

Unwillingness to allow treatment by outside providers may also be because judges and prosecutors are convinced that the treatment by the provider with whom they've contracted is the best for every offender, or because contractual agreements require participants. Either way, these attitudes are arrogant and dangerous, particularly when made without input from medical professionals. This happens every day in the United States.

Seventy-four percent of treatment centers in the United States are 12-step programs, and those seeking treatment are often unaware that other options exist. Seventy-five percent of all treatment centers *prohibit* use of medications despite their success in reducing overdose by 50 percent.[71]

Often, from a practical standpoint, options other than peer support groups don't exist due to lack of funding or lack of trained providers, particularly in regard to physicians and other health care professionals. Traditional health care providers have been largely absent in providing care for substance use disorders, and with the majority of funding allocated to punitive measures, funding for quality treatment is minimal.

The fellowship of AA and those 12-step treatment programs that primarily apply AA principles can be an important component of an overall treatment program, but should not be mandated, or replace, restrict, or conflict with medical treatment. "AA is not really a treatment—it's a fellowship," says William R. Miller, PhD, Emeritus Distinguished Professor, University of New Mexico in the film *The Business of Recovery*.[72] He continues, " If you go to your doctor to be treated for cancer or heart disease you expect your doctor to be doing what the science says is the best treatment available for what you have. That has not been the standard in addiction treatment."

Assessing success rates and considering other alternatives in no way takes away from the historical importance nor the current success of fellowship programs, but substance use disorder should be treated with the same standards as treatment for other physical and emotional health issues. In what other circumstance does treatment bypass medical professionals, blame the patient if a particular treatment protocol is not effective, or criminally prosecute the patient if initial treatment is unsuccessful? In what other circumstance are peer support meetings a prerequisite to receiving medical care?

In many cases, if a patient opts not to attend meetings, medications and other medical treatment is denied or the patient will be terminated from the program. Would we consider denying treatment to a cancer patient or a diabetic if the patient opted not to take part in support meetings? The mentality that meetings are the only way to recover is destructive, and assumes that the same path is appropriate for all patients. This is completely unsupported by evidence, common sense, or medical protocol.

When parents see their children descending into the horrible pit of addiction, getting them into a treatment program—any treatment program—often becomes the primary focus. When an individual in active addiction seeks help, they may not be in a position to assess best options. When stepping forward and asking for help may risk criminal prosecution, social stigma, jeopardizing jobs, housing, or even rejection by loved ones, many don't risk seeking help. If they do seek help, it's often based on desperation rather than research to determine the best individual fit. All of this creates vulnerable consumers.

Funding of treatment may be covered by insurance or government programs, or may be paid for by concerned loved ones. The Affordable Care Act expanded coverage for treatment, but also incentivized abuse of vulnerable patients by those working the system. [73]

Regardless of funding sources, when money and desperation are combined with a lack of standards for sound treatment based on objective science, doors are opened to unscrupulous providers to make huge profits at the expense of patients.[74] Patients who can be subject to arrest and incarceration are unlikely to report abuse. Those who do report are at high risk of being accused of lying. When addiction is involved, some are dishonest, but when an entire group of patients is discounted and have no voice, issues are imminent. When those patients don't succeed, they're often victimized again by criminal justice policies that blame the patient for lack of success, despite never receiving individual care that would significantly increase chances of success.

3. Mental Health Treatment and Deinstitutionalization

History often repeats itself. The history of mental health treatment has directly affected the increase in addiction and overdose. The War on Drugs has provided an avenue to incarcerate patients with mental health issues in lieu of providing the medical services they need. We've come full circle.

In 1841, schoolteacher Dorthea Dix agreed to teach a Sunday School class at a jail outside of Boston and saw the instances of mentally ill patients confined and suffering in horrific conditions. She became America's most famous and successful psychiatric reformer. Her advocacy brought attention to the numbers and conditions of those with mental health issues in jails and prisons, ultimately resulting in large-scale efforts by states to place patients in public psychiatric hospitals rather than in jails or prisons. By 1880, there were 75 public psychiatric hospitals in the United States, with only 0.7 percent of mental health patients in jails and prisons.[75]

These reforms were largely reversed as a result of cries to end institutionalization of mental health patients. These concerns were legitimate, and if community services had been made available, the massive move to "deinstitutionalize" patients may have been a positive one. Instead, the result has been massive closure of state mental hospitals and other institutional facilities that service people with disabilities over the past six decades, with few community-based alternatives made available.[76] Patient numbers dropped from 560,000 housed in institutions in 1955 to approximately 70,000 in 1994 despite significant increases in population and growth of mental health needs.[77]

The failure to provide alternative services for patients who were, or would have been, housed in these hospitals, has been a transition from institutionalization in hospitals to institutionalization in jails and prisons, many times as a result of drug charges.[78] An endless cycle has been created. Mental health services are miniscule and self-medication is common.

Populations needing help are at high risk of incarceration for drug violations. Deinstitutionalization and the lack of services after hospitals were closed has led to jails and prisons filled with those in need of mental health services, to loss of hope, and to increases in addiction and overdose.

Symptoms of serious mental health issues exist in 64 percent of local jail inmates, 56 percent of state prisoners, and 45 percent of federal prisoners.[79] Incarcerating mental health patients and saddling them with criminal records that further compromise opportunities upon release puts these populations at risk of ongoing or escalating addiction, overdose, homelessness, and a continuous cycle of incarceration, release, and return to jail or prison.

In addition to being unethical and cruel, incarcerating those with mental health issues is a waste of taxpayer money. A 2014 report uses Los Angeles County numbers as an example of potential for cutting costs by two-fifths while providing compassionate and more effective services.[80] The annual cost for Los Angeles County to jail an individual with serious mental illness is $48,500. The annual cost to providing community-based services and supportive housing is $20,500. This doesn't consider the benefits of ending the cycle of release and return to jail or the issues with housing mental health patients in a prison setting including impact on other prisoners and increased demands on prison staff. It also doesn't factor in the cost savings of reduced need to build more prisons to house the huge numbers of inmates with mental health needs.

"Deinstitutionalization doesn't work. We just switched places. Instead of being in hospitals the people are in jail. The whole system is topsy-turvy and the last person served is the mentally ill person." —Jail official, Ohio [81]

4. The Opioid Debacle

Villains. It's natural to look for them when we're in pain. When we can identify them, we know who's to blame, and where to direct our anger, frustration, or sorrow.

Throughout the history of drug prohibition, certain drugs have been the designated villains of the time. In the 1980s, it was crack cocaine. In the 1990s, methamphetamine was the target. The new century brought focus to opioids. As addiction and overdose rates escalated and gained more attention, the seemingly clear culprits were the pharmaceutical companies that benefited financially from huge increases in the sale of opioids.

It was an easy assumption to make. In 1995, the FDA approved Purdue Pharmaceutical's drug Oxycontin (trade name for time-released oxycodone) for treatment of chronic pain. Later that year, physicians, hospitals, and accreditation boards adopted the principal that pain is a "fifth vital sign," and new standards for pain assessment and treatment were adopted by the Joint Commission (formerly the Joint Commission on the Accreditation of Healthcare Organizations or JCAHO.) These new standards included patient surveys to rate their health care experiences, incentivizing medical providers to do all possible to receive high ratings from patients. Lawsuits held physicians liable for undertreating pain.[82]

In 1999, the Joint Commission approved new mandatory standards promoting pain assessment and treatment.[83] Insurance companies in the U.S. were also more likely to cover opioid prescriptions than physical therapy or other treatments. All of this opened a perfect door for Purdue Pharmaceutical's marketing campaign to medical professionals.

From 2006 through 2015, the pharmaceutical lobby spent $880 million promoting their interests.[84] While the U.S. government was busy locking up individuals for drug possession and distribution, the Food and Drug Administration was approving distribution of Oxycontin, turning Purdue Pharmaceutical into a billion-dollar company. Purdue Pharmaceutical increased sales of Oxycontin from $48 million in 1996 to nearly $1.1 billion by 2000.[85] In 2012, U.S. physicians wrote 259 million opiate prescriptions—enough for every American adult to have their own prescription, with 19 million to spare.[86] During this same time period, addiction and overdose rates continued to escalate. The villain seemed obvious.

The problem is that the obvious is sometimes incorrect, and may lead to inaccurate assumptions and solutions that can escalate harm and cascade into yet other disasters. Pharmaceutical companies are certainly not blameless. They took advantage of the timing of FDC approval and Joint Commission standards to mass market their product. Some patients developed addictions and some overdosed. The pain for those families cannot be underestimated, and there may be culpability on the part of pharmaceutical companies depending on representations made and other specific facts. However, focusing too heavily on one villain may get in the way of solving the problem and looking at all aspects of the issue.

Could it be possible that increases in opioid prescriptions weren't the sole, or the primary, cause of the overdose epidemic? Could it be possible that reducing those prescriptions won't solve the epidemic, or could actually make it worse?

Pumping huge numbers of pills into the market undoubtedly contributed to today's fentanyl crisis. As opioids became more accessible, more were diverted from patients to recreational users. Ultimately, when Oxycontin accessibility became more restricted, those who had developed addictions moved to heroin. Many used fentanyl, either consciously or due to additives in the unregulated street drugs.

Drug overdose rates from other substances also increased during these years. It's difficult to attribute those overdoses to pharmaceutical companies. The 2018 National Vital Statistics Reports of the U.S. Department of Health and Human Services[87] analyzed substances most frequently involved in drug overdoses in the United States from 2011 to 2016. The report raises questions about whether the fight against prescription opioids is the correct focus.

The Vital Statistics study showed that, in 2011, oxycodone was the number one killer with 5,587 overdose deaths, but that cocaine, heroin, and methamphetamine, all illegal substances, killed a total of over 11,000. By 2016, fentanyl overdoses escalated to 18,335, with heroin, cocaine, and methamphetamine combined killing over 34,000. Oxycodone deaths increased to 6,199.

Most deadly drugs are found in combination with one another.[88] In 68 percent of overdoses involving prescription pain medication, other drugs like cocaine, heroin, fentanyl, alcohol and benzodiazepines were also in the overdose victim's system. In 2017, fewer than 10 percent of all prescription pill overdoses did not involve other drugs.[89]

This brings up the question, "How many overdose deaths were actually attributed to opioids taken by patients for whom they were prescribed?" It appears that the number of overdoses that fit into this category is modest compared with other overdose categories.

There are risks of addiction and overdose with the use of opioids, but based on media reports, it would be easy to assume that if you use prescription opioids, you'll become addicted. According to the U.S. Centers for Disease Control (the same organization that issued 2016 prescribing guidelines that led to tapering and denial of medications), the risk of addiction with long-term use of opioids is from 0.07 percent to 6 percent.[90] The largest study to date, based on over two million patients, showed a 0.022% risk of dying due to medical use of opioids.[91] A 2011 study of chronic pain patients treated in the Veterans Affairs system showed an overdose rate of 0.04 percent.[92] Data is clear that patients using prescribed medications make up less than one percent of opioid overdose deaths.[93] Pain patients are not the primary issue, yet attempted solutions have been directed at them.[94]

The highly publicized "opioid crisis" is actually a crisis of illegal street drugs, with the worst being fentanyl. These drugs were already an issue. Then, access to legal prescriptions was restricted. As pharmaceutical drugs became harder to obtain, use of more dangerous street drugs escalated, as did overdose rates. Medical professionals were threatened into restricting prescriptions for legal medications to patients. Denying medications to pain patients rather than focusing on the fentanyl and other street drug overdose crisis makes no sense, yet is exactly what has happened. Once again, our solution has been based on emotion and has escalated the problem instead of solving it.

The first signal that restrictions on pharmaceutical opioids would lead to increased overdose rates from street drugs was in 2010, when Oxycontin was reformulated in an effort to reduce abuse. The original formulation was extended release that lasted for 12 hours. People who abused it could inject, chew, or snort the pill to get an immediate, full dose of the oxycodone in the pill. Purdue Pharmaceutical's successful reformulation made the pills more difficult to crush and dissolve, reducing misuse by about 40 percent over the next four years. As Oxycontin overdoses declined, heroin overdoses skyrocketed[95] as shown in the following chart. The chart shows recent declines in heroin death rates. Unfortunately, as overdose rates for heroin and for prescription opioids declined, fentanyl overdose rates have skyrocketed, now killing twice as many as heroin.[96]

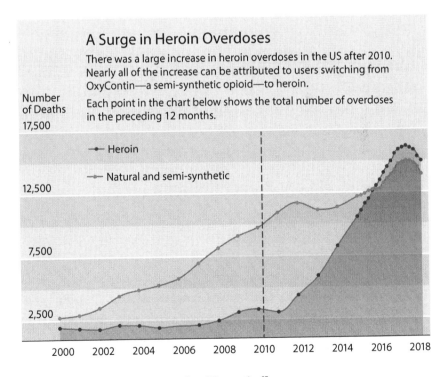

Source: Centers for Disease Control and Prevention[97]

Abby Alpert, coauthor of a paper published in the *American Economic Journal: Economic Policy*, stated: "There was a major shift in the opioid epidemic around 2010 when people shifted from primarily abusing prescription opioids to then abusing heroin and later fentanyl." Research for the paper showed that states that showed the highest increase in heroin overdoses after the reformulation were the same states that had the highest rates of Oxycontin misuse prior to the reformulation.[98]

This balloon effect is typical. Focusing on stopping supply of one substance or source simply makes the issue reappear elsewhere. Unfortunately, policy decisions have not taken this into consideration. The escalation in heroin and fentanyl overdose rates after Oxycontin reformulation forecasted greater issues if Oxycontin prescriptions were further restricted, but these predictors were ignored.

In 2016, the U.S. Centers for Disease Control (CDC) issued new guidelines for prescribing opioids for chronic pain in primary care settings. The prescribing guidelines were supposed to be *guidelines*, and the document specifically stated that the recommendations were for "prescribing opioids for chronic pain outside of active cancer treatment, palliative care, and end-of-life care."[99] Despite that, the guidelines began an era of misery for pain patients caught in the middle of a government in reactive mode as overdose rates continue to climb and physicians and pharmacies try to protect themselves from liability. (See # 5, War on Pain Patients; # 6, War on Physicians & Pharmacists.)

The authors of the 2016 CDC guidelines[100] did not anticipate the large-scale impact of those guidelines on pain patients. They attempted to remedy the issues created by the guidelines, but when momentum begins, it's difficult to rein back in. The CDC guideline authors wrote an essay clarifying that the recommendations were not intended to result in withholding of medications from patients who need them. They specifically renounced "policies that encourage hard limits and abrupt tapering of drug dosages, resulting in sudden opioid discontinuation or dismissal of patients from a physician's practice." [101]

DEA raids, threats of civil and criminal liability, and loss of medical licenses have forced many pain patients off of medications that have worked successfully long term. Health care professionals meeting individually with their patients and assessing their medical needs are no longer the decision-makers. That role has been relegated to bureaucrats who have no relationship with the patient, and in many cases, no medical training. In essence, the War on Drugs has been expanded to include some legal prescription medications.

The U.S. Department of Health & Human Services has recognized that the 2016 Guidelines have created issues. On May 9, 2019, they issued a report entitled "Pain Management Best Practices."[102] The report emphasized the importance of "individualized patient-centered care in the diagnosis and treatment of acute and chronic pain" and "development of an effective pain treatment plan after proper evaluation..."

Some states are also recognizing the issues created. Some state Departments of Health have issued clarifications in an attempt to protect patients, emphasizing that lack of treatment is a departure from physician standards of care. In April 2019, the Washington State Department of Health issued a "Notice of Adoption of an Interpretive Statement," directing ". . . practitioners to not exclude, undertreat, or dismiss a patient from a practice solely because the patient has used or is using opioids in the course of normal medical care. While in most circumstances a practitioner is not legally required to treat a particular patient, the refusal to see or continue to treat a patient merely because the patient has taken or is currently using opioids is contrary to the clear intent of the Commission's rules governing opioid prescribing. Ending opioid therapy or initiating a forced tapering of opioids to a particular MED level for reasons outside of clinical efficacy or improvement in quality of life and/or function or abuse would violate the intent of the rules."[103]

The issue has become so serious that at the AMA's 2018 interim meeting, several resolutions were passed to formally push back against what the AMA refers to as "misapplication of the CDC's guidelines" by regulatory bodies, insurers, legislators, pharmacists, and pharmacy benefit managers. The AMA resolutions state that doses higher than those recommended by the CDC may be necessary and appropriate for some patients, and take issue with regulatory bodies that subject physicians to oversight and potential sanctions solely based on opioid dosages prescribed. The AMA resolutions recognize the importance of individual treatment of patients by physicians, based on physician expertise and patient needs.

These steps will hopefully ease medical provider and pharmacist concerns and reinstate patient levels of care, but as DEA raids, bad public relations, and the risk of lawsuits continue, it will take a long time for physicians and pharmacists to resume normal practice without concern. Traditional malpractice remedies should remain in place, but increased scrutiny on pain and addiction practices has had a chilling effect. In the meantime, stigma for those needing pain medications runs high, patients suffer in untreated pain, and some die. Many practitioners will leave, or not enter, these areas of practice where medical professionals are so badly needed.

There's no doubt that Purdue and other pharmaceutical companies pursued profits to the detriment of the patients they claimed to be serving. Estimates are that the Sackler family who owns Purdue were once worth over $13 billion,[104] earned primarily from aggressive marketing and sale of Oxycontin. They are currently facing multiple lawsuits.

Pharmaceutical companies may not be a sympathetic group, but legal claims against them may be tenuous. They were manufacturing and selling products approved by the FDA and prescribed by licensed medical providers acting under Joint Commission mandatory standards for pain assessment and treatment.[105] Many cases have settled, with pharmaceutical companies attempting to minimize potential liability.

In August 2019, an Oklahoma lower court held Johnson & Johnson[106] liable under a claim of public nuisance, a legal argument typically used to silence noisy neighbors. A North Dakota court[107] dismissed a suit against Purdue Pharmaceutical that used this argument (among others), expressing concern that using a nuisance statute in this context could open huge numbers of claims simply because an action annoyed the public. "Nuisance thus would become a monster that would devour in one gulp the entire law of tort . . ." The defense in that case also pointed out that the pharmaceutical company was marketing substances approved by the FDA.

Government entities' use of funds from settlements or lawsuits to cover costs of treatment and other services for those addicted could be beneficial. As pharmaceutical companies assess potential for liability, however, future access to medications needed by patients could be impacted. Will pharmaceutical companies invest funds into research, approval, and distribution of pain medications or medications to treat addiction, or will fear of liability minimize that research or access to medications or increase prices for patients? Could our reaction to this crisis be laying the foundation for the next one, where shortages of medications may leave patients in pain, drive yet more people to fatal street drugs or turn patients needing substances into criminals?

Restricting access to pain medications for those who need them won't solve today's overdose epidemic. Lawsuits may satisfy the need to find and to punish a villain, but it's also important that those lawsuits don't take the focus off of our current challenges or create new ones.

Let's take a closer look at the impact of these policies on day-to-day life for affected patients.

CHAPTER 5

THE WAR ON PAIN PATIENTS

"The biggest risk for chronic pain patients isn't addiction; it's suicide."

UNKNOWN

If you or someone you love may be in need of pain medications, you have reason to worry. If issues have not yet impacted you, you could be one car accident or one surgery from disaster because of current regulations on pain medications.

We are in the midst of a medical emergency directly caused by attempts at controlling the addiction and overdose epidemic. This emergency impacts millions of pain sufferers who need medications for medical treatment. Many who are being deprived of medications have used them successfully long term, and are now being tapered, or in some cases cut off cold-turkey. This change in treatment has nothing to do with their personal medical needs or a change in their health, but on the hysteria that has led to illogical and harmful responses.

As discussed in the previous chapter, government policies are putting a barrier between practitioners and their patients, leaving some patients with the decision of living with excruciating pain or seeking substances on the street, increasing risk of overdose. Lack of access to medications is converting some from being patients to becoming criminals at risk of prosecution and incarceration simply for seeking substances they can no longer access legally. Others are turning to suicide.[108] At a recent meeting of the American Medical Association, the organization's president shared a story of a patient whose pharmacist called the patient a "drug seeker" and refused to fill the prescription the doctor had written to treat the pain from prostate cancer, which had spread to the patient's bones. Three days later, the patient attempted suicide.

Long-term use of opioids to treat pain is no more addictive than using insulin long term to treat diabetes. According to the American Society of Addiction Medicine, "Addiction is characterized by inability to consistently abstain, impairment in behavioral control, craving, diminished recognition of significant problems with one's behaviors and interpersonal relationships, and a dysfunctional emotional response."[109] Simply needing a medication for a medical purpose is not addiction. Receiving prescription medications for medical issues is not a negative to society, and is certainly not something that patients should be punished or stigmatized for whether that medication is to treat addiction, pain, or any other health condition. That should be obvious, yet every day, pain and other patients are deprived of medications and treated like criminals.

The sad result is that all of this suffering has done nothing to stem addiction or overdose rates, and likely increased them. As of 2018, opioid prescriptions were at an 18-year low[110] and the rate of prescribing had dropped every year since 2011[111], yet opioid overdose deaths have skyrocketed since then.[112]

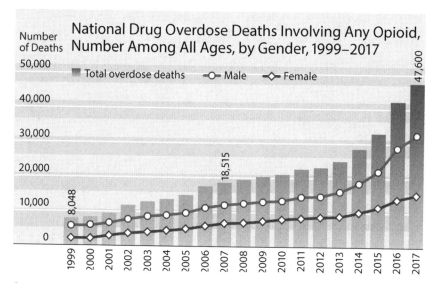

National Drug Overdose Deaths Involving Any Opioid, Number Among All Ages, by Gender, 1999–2017

Source: Centers for Disease Control and Prevention [113]

The CDC guidelines (discussed in #4 under The Opioid Debacle) were never meant to apply to patients currently taking opioids. They provide no basis for forcibly tapering patients off of opioids who are doing well. There's no evidence to support this practice,[114] but patients' lives continue to be destroyed.

In a recent nationwide survey of 3,000 pain patients, 56 percent reported disruptions in care, outright denial of pain medications, or abandonment by their physicians. Of those whose care was disrupted, 55 percent reported experiencing adverse health consequences, and 62 percent reported hopelessness or thoughts of suicide.[115] These are real people in debilitating pain whose lives have been turned upside down. Pain patients report greater incidence of disability caused by pain relapses created by interruptions in medications, negatively affecting lives and increasing cost to taxpayers.

Surgical patients have been made to suffer without pain medications, and Stage 4 cancer patients have been denied pain medications. Even if they were susceptible to addiction, keeping them in excruciating pain cannot be justified.

It's likely that issues will escalate further. Despite FDA notices of shortages of critical care and palliative medicines,[116] on September 11, 2019, the DEA issued a press release announcing their proposed reduction in opioids that can be manufactured in the U.S. in 2020 compared to 2019.[117] The press release states "DEA proposes to reduce the amount of fentanyl produced by 31 percent, hydrocodone by 19 percent, hydromorphone by 25 percent, oxycodone by nine percent and oxymorphone by 55 percent. Combined with morphine, the proposed quota would be a 53 percent decrease in the amount of allowable production of these opioids since 2016."

The drug cartel kingpins must be celebrating. Once again, the solution has escalated issues and created new ones. In this case, attempted solutions to the addiction and overdose crisis have set medicine back decades and created an abusive, perverted process that penalizes patients needing care and the medical professionals who want to provide that care. The impact of regulations or misinterpretations of those regulations are difficult to roll back. The clarifications and resolutions to undo the harm may be helping in some cases, but widespread reports of tapering and denial of medications continue. Proposals and new regulation also continue to fuel the agony of pain patients. Continued reactive efforts at controlling overdose are created without evidence that they will be effective. This generates new issues as quickly as the existing ones are remedied, and sometimes existing issues are exacerbated.

In addition to CDC prescribing guidelines, 48 U.S. states, the District of Columbia, and Puerto Rico have enacted Prescription Drug Monitoring Programs (PDMPs) in an attempt to control doctor shopping.[118] While these regulations may benefit some, they also make it more difficult for patients to seek new medical professionals if they're unhappy with current care, may deter a patient from initially seeking medical treatment, and may make a practitioner reluctant to prescribe pain medications, even if the medical provider believes those prescriptions are the best avenue of medical treatment.

PDMPs were ostensibly set up to protect patients, but have resulted in access to patient medical records by law enforcement with no warrant or probable cause. In an era where medical records are closely guarded from families under HIPAA regulations, those same records are accessible to the DEA.

In May 2019, the State of New Hampshire refused to allow DEA access to its state PDMP records without a warrant signed by a judge. The state lost on the circuit court level but has appealed. The state is disputing the DEA's argument that people have no reasonable expectation of privacy in their prescription records because of the "third-party doctrine." That legal theory asserts that a person loses fourth amendment protections in information voluntarily shared with a third party. New Hampshire's argument should be compelling. Patients do not voluntarily share their information in the PDMP database. The DEA argument that patients give up privacy rights when sharing medical information with their doctor or pharmacist is ludicrous. This would require patients to choose between accessing health care and giving up confidentiality rights to their health information. This is most certainly not a viable, voluntary choice.

The DEA has prevailed in previous cases, but attitudes have changed, and arguments relying on the "third-party doctrine" in regard to cell phone records have been lost.[119] An amicus brief filed in this case includes convincing arguments for denial of PDMP requests for records from the DEA unless a warrant is obtained.[120]

It's amazing that our tax dollars are spent on attorneys representing the DEA in an effort to breach confidentiality between medical providers and patients, and on states having to defend patients' rights. The DEA hides behind the goal of addressing the addiction and overdose epidemic. Their actions escalate the very issues they claim to solve. Patients are afraid to come forward and seek medical attention. Physicians are afraid to address those medical needs in the best way possible as determined by the physician's medical expertise and individual contact with the patient. Civil liberties go by the wayside as drug warriors continue to apply and fight for punitive policies that have failed horribly for over 50 years.

The federal government incentivizes denial of prescriptions to patients in other ways, using the number of prescriptions as the sole factor regardless of individual patient needs. Funding is given to medical providers who reduce the number of prescriptions written.[121] Congress is considering additional regulations including limitations on initial opioid prescriptions to small doses, restriction of prescription package sizes, and tamper-proof packaging that may be difficult for pain patients to open.[122] These types of restrictions are already in place in many U.S. states.

In 2016, Massachusetts became the first state to limit first-time opioid prescriptions to seven days.[123] Inspired by the CDC Guidelines, over half of U.S. states have now passed legislation restricting quantities of opioids that may be prescribed and restricting the length of prescriptions, sometimes as short as a three-day supply.[124] The need to refill a prescription every three to seven days is an extreme measure, particularly when inability to refill can compromise health or lead to withdrawal. The constant need to refill medications increases the chance of an issue with paperwork or medication availability that can create delays. Life happens. Being obligated to appear at a pharmacy every three to seven days is oppressive and dangerous.

In Florida, for example, prescriptions for all Schedule II drugs cannot exceed a 3-day supply[125] This includes pain medications, ADHD prescriptions, antidepressants, methadone, a medication used to treat substance use disorder and others. These restrictions can be problematic, particularly in a state where authorities recommend retention of a 14-day supply of medications as a precaution when potential for hurricanes is present. If a hurricane or other emergency occurs on a refill day, not only are patients dealing with those emergencies; they are also deprived of medications that could put them into acute pain, withdrawal or overdose on street drugs.

Going on and off of medications is unhealthy, compromising health. A one percent potential overdose rate does not balance these atrocious restrictions, which could escalate medical issues or overdose due to the need to seek street drugs when prescriptions aren't available. Most would assume that, before passing such onerous restrictions, sound evidence would support the benefits. The truth is just the opposite. "To date, there is no data on whether and to what extent these laws mediate opioid-related morbidity and mortality, as well as whether they are associated with negative unintended outcomes."[126] The severity of the injury or surgery is irrelevant. Laws supposedly exempt chronic or cancer pain patients, but in practice, those patients are often affected.

Imagine being in severe pain, having trouble getting out of bed, yet needing to go to the pharmacy every three days just to stay out of acute pain, with ever-present concern that you'll be accused of being a "drug-seeker." Major pharmacy chains like Walmart, Express Scripts, and CVS have imposed supply limits, delaying or denying refills for long-term pain patients despite the fact that the CDC guidelines were intended to apply only to patients who had not previously taken opioids. Pain patients report feeling stigma, having to justify their need for prescription medications used to treat a medical issue.

Pharmacies and medical providers balance risk vs. benefit. As a result, some practitioners are simply deciding not to practice in areas related to pain management, and some pharmacies no longer carry certain medications. If your pharmacy tells you they no longer carry your medication, you're a casualty of these policies.

In addition to pharmacy or government restrictions, insurance mandates can also impact access to medications. Even when monthly prescription pickup is allowed, application of rules can border on absurd. Michelle had looked forward to her trip across the country for a cousin's wedding for a long time. She'd saved for it. She'd planned around it, and obtained approval from her doctor to fill her prescriptions a day early. When she arrived at the pharmacy, she was told that they could not fill the scripts until the next day after 8 a.m. because that would be the "correct" amount of time since the last refill. She asked if this 24-hour pharmacy would allow her to pick up at 6 a.m. so she could still make her flight at 9 a.m. The pharmacy refused.

Michelle's options were to leave for her trip without medications, to cancel her trip, or to pay out of pocket for the medications. Going on the trip without medications would put her in excruciating pain and potential withdrawal. Since the medications are classified as controlled substances, filling the script out of state was not allowed. If she cancelled the trip, along with the frustration of missing the wedding, she'd forfeit money already spent on the flight and other deposits. Her other option was to pay for the scripts out of pocket, which she did with family help.

A highly anticipated vacation turned into tears and stress at the pharmacy. No reimbursement from the insurance company was possible. Denial obviously had nothing to do with safety since privately paying quickly solved this issue. Government, insurance, and pharmacy rules are putting patients into untenable positions, and making them prisoners of visits to pharmacies. This restricts travel, freedom, and basic human rights.

Inaccurate claims of high rates of opioid patient overdose have caused enormous harm to patients who need these medications. Many have had medications cut off cold-turkey, not because their physician thought that was the best medical practice, but because their physician or pharmacist was in fear of prosecution, loss of license to practice, or DEA raids. While consideration of risk of addiction and overdose from prescription medications is important, it's also essential to balance the downside of reducing availability to medications. Results of these policies include increases in suicide, use of black market drugs, horrendous pain and decrease in quality of life for patients, many who've successfully been using these medications for years.

As with the War on Drugs, the U.S. has exported its War on Patients. In a May, 2019 report,[127] U.S. politicians accused the World Health Organization of being corrupted by pharmaceutical companies. Experts report that this allegation has decreased access to morphine for millions of people dying in acute pain in poor countries.[128]

Pain patients deprived of badly needed medications sometimes blame addiction patients for creating the pain caused by denial of prescriptions. The tragedy is that the rights of patients of all types are violated every day as a direct result of government drug policy. Pain patients, as well as patients struggling with substance use disorder (many with accompanying health issues including chronic pain), are denied medications that would be of help in treating their health issues. If all patients unite to advocate for their rights, advocacy will be more powerful.

Many patients are impacted on multiple levels. Real lives and real agony is involved. Human rights are being trampled, yet few talk about it. The political and societal reaction has not only failed to solve the problems, but has fueled them. Scientific foundation is absent, inconsistency is rampant, and judgment and emotion are guiding principles. Drug policy impacts everyone's access to health care. When it fails, our health, freedom, and financial stability are all compromised. When looked at as a whole, the inconsistency and lack of evidence to support policies that so often lead to death and misery is astounding.

We've failed to help those with substance use disorder, while denying medical care to patients and treating them as criminals. The opioid debacle is a prime example of a government pendulum swinging far to one side and then far to the other, wreaking destruction and death as it swings.

CHAPTER 6

THE WAR ON MEDICAL PROVIDERS & PHARMACISTS

"I think the biggest challenge is that doctors are no longer in charge. But at the same time it is our licenses and our liability [at risk]."

KRIS EMILY MCCRORY, M.D., FAMILY MEDICINE PHYSICIAN BASED IN SCHENECTADY, NEW YORK

Physicians are being targeted along with their patients, and it's affecting everyone's health care. With the aging of the population and the escalation of the addiction and overdose crisis, we are in desperate need of pain management and addiction physicians. These are tough areas of practice, often dealing with underinsured populations whose health issues compromise full-time employment. Medical professionals in these specialties deal with the frustration of patients with chronic conditions, and don't get the satisfaction felt by other specialties of delivering babies or of surgically curing patients. Instead of incentivizing the more difficult addiction and pain management specialties, physicians in these areas are now at risk of DEA raids, criminal or civil prosecution, or loss of licenses to practice.

It's true that some physicians and pharmacists have used opioids to create wealth for themselves, essentially acting like drug dealers, with all of the accompanying victims and all of the legitimate outrage. We also have police who take advantage of their positions, teachers who sleep with their students, and politicians who take payoffs for votes and special favors.

In those cases, we don't threaten all police, teachers, or politicians, or blame citizens, students, or voters. We don't suspect all professionals of being guilty simply because they are part of a profession with some bad actors. In the case of physicians and pharmacists, if they dispense opioids for their patients—even those patients whose lives depend on those medications—they're treated as suspects and live with concerns that their licenses may be lost, or worse yet, that they could be criminally prosecuted for distribution of drugs or for murder if a patient dies.

Physicians now have to defend treatment of their patients to non-medical bureaucrats. The DEA has broken down clinic doors and confiscated physicians' homes and other assets with no criminal charges filed, using civil forfeiture statutes. (See # 18, You'd Like to Keep Your House?) Doctors may also be criminally prosecuted as drug dealers for writing prescriptions for their patients. Pharmacists are in fear of their licenses as well, leading them to "police" doctors or put themselves at risk of raids and prosecution.

Reporters' comments may destroy medical professionals' reputations, including those simply trying to effectively treat patients who live in excruciating pain. Geraldo Rivera and Martha McCallum, both respected American reporters, got caught up in the emotion of overdose tragedies when discussing the arrest of 60 physicians accused of overprescribing opioids on the Fox News program "The Story With Martha MacCallum" on April 17, 2019. They painted a dark picture of physicians and pharmacists. Martha began with "It just sounds like murder to me. When you know that someone is an addict, and you are a professional doctor or pharmacist and you are giving them these pills anyway, could it be seen as some form of manslaughter?" Geraldo clarifies that it depends on the facts, but then compares physicians, dentists, and pharmacists to street level drug dealers.

The interview cuts to a pharmacist who'd been "visited" by the DEA that morning, and answered "no comment" to Geraldo's questions: You MUST have known that particular doctors were prescribing too many opioids? "No comment." How do you feel about the DEA visiting your store this morning? "No comment." Cut back to the interview, with shaking heads and rolling eyes, obviously convicting the pharmacist based on his "no comment" answers. McCallum: "I think all of these people should be, you know, talk about a good reason for a perp walk. I mean, you put all of these doctors and pharmacists out there and [Geraldo:"Yes, shame them."] you make everybody else look at them and think twice when they're filling these prescriptions." [129]

The physicians and pharmacists discussed in this segment had just been arrested. It's possible that they were all guilty and should be prosecuted, but evidence was not yet available to the reporters. The addiction and overdose epidemic creates panic, even in reporters without facts and without considering the cascade effect of their proposed solutions. If a patient has an addiction issue, should they be denied medications for the rest of their lives? Do we really want pharmacists policing, and adjusting, prescriptions written by doctors who know the individual patients' background and medical needs? Do we want bureaucrats in Washington dictating medical care for pain patients? That's exactly what's happened.

Could it be possible that physicians afraid of the DEA, liability or negative publicity are no longer prescribing medications that people are desperate for, driving them to seek street drugs laced with fentanyl and other impurities, and where dosages are impossible to determine? Might the judgment, stigma, and potential risk to physicians and pharmacists propagated by those journalists and others (who may have good intentions but are jumping to emotional conclusions) be fueling the overdose crisis they're accusing others of escalating?

This isn't the first time in history that physicians, and by extension their patients, have been the scapegoats of the War on Drugs. We're revisiting the Harrison Act of 1914, which indicted and jailed physicians for treating their patients. After utter failure, those policies ended when prohibition was repealed. History is repeating itself. Lessons from the failures of the Harrison Act have been forgotten. Must we continue to repeat the fiasco yet again?

"I am hearing more physicians become completely demoralized by what [the Electronic Health Records system] has done to their ability to really provide the kind of personalized and quality patient care [they] wish to give to their patients."–Catherine Hambley, Ph.D.

CHAPTER 7

THE WAR ON SUBSTANCE USE PATIENTS

"If you can, help others; if you cannot do that, at least do not harm them."

DALAI LAMA XIV

Imagine a life-threatening health issue that's impacted you—or someone you love. Now imagine there's a medication that would cut the fatality rate in half, and would treat symptoms to give a good chance at a normal life. Exciting?

But what if most doctors weren't allowed to prescribe that drug, most patients weren't told about it, and standard treatment protocols ignored the medication—or worse yet, refused to consider it. What if even friends and family had a bias against the treatment that you knew would give the best chance for recovery? What if you were ON this medication and it was working for you, but the government made you discontinue it, with a judge mandating a protocol that he or she believed would be better despite having no medical expertise? Or, based on a symptom of your condition, what if you were put in jail and medications were taken away, causing you to go through withdrawal behind bars?

This is EXACTLY what's happening with treatment of substance use disorder every day in America.

Science has made amazing advances in the treatment of substance use disorder, and, as discussed earlier, use of medications is the most immediate and cost-effective evidence-based treatment technique available today.[130] Addiction is an emotional topic, and changing long-standing assumptions isn't easy. There's a lot of pain, for individuals, their families, and for society, including professionals working in the system. Accepting that drug addiction can be treated with . . . well . . . DRUGS *is* counterintuitive. Accepting that drugs just might be a solution to addiction made my head spin, but desperation is a fast track to being open to any potential solution.

The benefits of using medications in treatment are scientifically indisputable. This is now accepted science. Dr. Mary Jeanne Kreek, head of Rockefeller University's addictive diseases laboratory who helped develop methadone as a treatment for addiction points out that medications correct endorphin deficiencies that develop during opioid use.[131] Proof is compelling that replacement therapy medications stabilize brain receptors, medically allowing the brain and the body to establish a new normal.[132]

Economically and socially, medications make sense. They're less expensive and, according to multiple studies, for many, are more effective than other forms of treatment.[133] Reallocating funds from prosecution and incarceration to treatment would support scientific approaches, respect patient rights, and save lives.

Multiple types of medications are available for use in treatment for substance use disorder. There are pros and cons to each. Coordination of potential medications and other services to the individual needs of each patient is essential, as it is with any health issue. (See Appendix A for details on various medications available.)

Despite proven success, barriers to use of this treatment are astronomical. Our relationship to these medications is nothing short of bizarre.

Medications to treat substance use disorder are completely unavailable in 75 percent of countries worldwide.[134] Where they are available, many criminal justice settings, peer-support groups, treatment centers, and sober houses prohibit their use.

In the United States, physician authorization to prescribe buprenorphine, one of the most popular medications to treat substance use disorder, is restricted.[135] In 2018, according to the Substance Abuse and Mental Health Services Administration, more than 900,000 U.S. physicians were authorized to prescribe oxycodone. Only 38,633 were authorized to prescribe buprenorphine, the medication to treat addiction to oxycodone. A practitioner waiver and certification are required before a medical provider can write buprenorphine prescriptions. Then, the number of patients who may be served by each physician is restricted, increasing cost and accessibility for patients.[136] None of these restrictions apply to oxycodone prescriptions.

We sometimes wonder why patients struggling with substance use disorder reject the idea of treatment. Many patients believe that their only "treatment" alternative is peer support meetings and total abstinence for life. Other alternatives or protocols are frequently not offered or available.

As discussed earlier, medications in treatment have the highest success rate and are the most cost-effective treatment available today. It's mind-boggling to consider that the punishment for displaying symptoms of substance use disorder often includes denial of the very medications that are the best treatment for that disorder.

For those who are aware of medications, who aren't under court supervision prohibiting their use, and who can locate and afford a physician and medications, substantial barriers *still* exist. (You may recognize some of the issues as similar to those discussed earlier as applied to pain patients.) Let's look at the whole picture, to consider what the substance use patient is up against.

○ Parents and other loved ones are told that helping a person struggling with addiction can be harmful "enabling", making many unwilling to help to find the best treatment alternatives. Many families are uninformed and unsupportive of treatment using medications.

○ Stigma is high, with patients frequently accused of not being in "real recovery", including at many meetings attended for purposes of peer support. Patients attending meetings that are supposed to promote open discussion and trust often don't disclose that medications are helping them in their recovery out of fear of stigma or rejection.

○ Depending on the provider, patients risk denial of medications if they miss a required counseling appointment or fail to comply with all provider mandates. Provider requirements are becoming more stringent as medical professionals try to protect themselves from DEA, license, or liability issues that could arise if a patient missed an appointment and still received a medication. Perfection is a high standard, but for those on medications, one missed appointment can lead to denial or delay of prescription refills, despite much higher risk of relapse and other medical issues for the patient if medications are withheld.

○ As physicians encounter more issues and risk with prescribing medications, patients worry about losing access to their medications if a physician decides to discontinue those prescriptions for any reason, or if the physician retires or changes areas of practice. Locating a new physician authorized to prescribe medications for substance use patients is difficult, and protocols vary from physician to physician, so changing providers can be risky.

○ If a patient finds a physician who will prescribe, the pharmacy may opt not to fill prescriptions.

○ Tight timelines on prescriptions make patients hostage to refill dates. Travel and other calendaring is subject to being at the pharmacy on specific dates. Concern that medications may be denied at any point by prescribers or pharmacists can create ongoing anxiety.

○ Housing issues are common, with sober housing either prohibiting medications or with pressure from house managers advising "Get off those medications".

○ Drivers licenses in some jurisdictions may be put in jeopardy if a blood test shows the presence of medications used to treat substance use disorder, even when no impairment exists.

○ Cold-turkey withdrawal may be forced if a patient ends up in jail or on probation (even on a traffic violation or for nonpayment of a fine).

○ With other medical treatment, it is common to make adjustments in medications to determine what is most effective for the individual patient. With medications treating addiction, modifying medications could risk a relapse, which in turn could end in a prison sentence instead of simply adjusting the treatment to a more effective medication for the patient. These fears make patients resistant to medication assessment and adjustment that, for any other health issue, would be standard protocol.

○ With the implementation of Prescription Drug Monitoring Programs (PDMP) and DEA access to those records, patients fear criminal prosecution based on medical records that should be confidential between physician and patient, but no longer are.

○ Substance use treatment records of all types are at risk of losing confidentiality protections that have existed long term under federal regulations.[137] Changes are now under consideration that could include these records in standard medical records and in the PDMP program, so all health care professionals would have access to them. The proposal would make it easier for other agencies to access records, and courts would be allowed to seize all records (with definitions loosely written, potentially making it possible to allow access based on a drug charge. Proposals have also been made that would allow courts access to records, even if the patient is not the one accused of committing the alleged crime.).

These proposed rule changes open huge areas of concern that law enforcement could access records, or that broader disclosure could impact child custody, jobs and housing.[138] Threats of changes like these present more obstacles to those seeking treatment, who are concerned that if they seek help, records will not remain confidential, leading to more stigma or persecution.[139] As a society, we want to incentivize those who need help to come forward to receive it. Proposals like these do just the opposite.

○ Career opportunities can be compromised. Some employers believe that treatment medications are the equivalent of illegal drug use, leading to job termination or refusal to hire those on these prescription medications. Even within the treatment industry itself, this is a risk. Peter, who'd been employed by a treatment center as a successful drug and alcohol counselor for over five years, was fired when his boss learned that he was on methadone. A counselor with personal experience with one of the most successful treatment protocols available today was not only prohibited from sharing his knowledge, but lost his job because of the medical care that had led to his 14 years of successful recovery.

Amazingly, in many cases, the medical profession itself prohibits use of medications in treatment for medical professionals who develop substance use disorder. Medical providers who develop addictions are typically referred to state physician health programs (PHP). If the provider follows the treatment and monitoring plan established by the PHP, the PHP recommends that the state licensing board reinstate the license to practice. The amazing fact is that many state PHPs prohibit use of medications, the treatment protocol proven to have the best success rate.[140]

○ Prior authorizations are particularly problematic with medications for treatment of substance use disorder, creating deadly delays before prescriptions can be filled. In January 2019, Barbara L. McAneny, president of the American Medical Association (AMA), wrote an essay advocating for removal of prior authorization requirements for medications used in treatment of substance use disorder. "When it comes to treating patients with OUD [Opioid Use Disorder], we know what works. MAT [Medication-Assisted Treatment] for opioid use disorder saves lives. MAT helps people maintain recovery, saves money, reduces crime, and helps people regain their health and their lives." She continues, "When patients seek help, it is unconscionable to make them wait days or weeks for the right treatment. There is no valid reason to delay or deny medically proven care that can help end the nation's opioid epidemic and improve patients' health and lives."

This analysis should apply to all patients needing prescriptions, but with the risk of overdose for addiction patients, advocating for an end to delay in receiving those medications is a good beginning. Some states have entered into agreements with insurers to waive prior authorizations for addiction medications.[141]

Considering all of these obstacles, if YOU had a substance use disorder, would you put yourself in front of these blockades to attempt to get evidence-based treatment, or might you simply give up hope and continue to use street drugs?

All of the challenges with use of medications in treatment are the result of policies that are supposedly in place to help those with addiction issues. Instead, patients risk excruciating withdrawal each time barriers prohibit access to medications. Body chemistry is compromised, further increasing the risk of relapse or escalating addiction. Risk of incarceration because of a relapse is increased. The abstinence-only mentality runs deep. Lives are lost because old assumptions continue and scientific proof that medical treatments work is ignored.

The fact that medications save lives and increase rates of recovery is indisputable.[142] The barriers to use of this treatment are astounding and heartbreaking, and are a window into how policy and stigma have directly escalated addiction and overdose rates. If we ignored science and medicine and placed these barriers on treatment of *any* health issue, we'd have an epidemic.

Imagine you have symptoms of diabetes. What would typically happen? You'd see a doctor trained in that medical specialty. Tests would be completed, assessing your individual medical condition. An individualized medical plan would be completed, which may include insulin or other medications, ongoing medical care, and lifestyle changes. You may incorporate lifestyle changes, but may periodically slip on birthday cake or other favorites.

Now, let's imagine a different "treatment" scenario. Let's imagine that someone saw you eating that cake, and police arrived. You're arrested, with the risk of jail time and a criminal record. What if individualized treatment and medications were denied, and peer support meetings were ordered as treatment. Then *you* were accused of not wanting to recover if that "treatment" wasn't effective. If insulin was given, you're told it's only temporary, and you should "Get off that drug" as soon as possible.

By the way, ATTORNEYS, not doctors, are directing your treatment. If you refuse their treatment, you may be put behind bars. And, as a kicker, family members and other loved ones are told that they should withdraw support, and that advocating for good care would be harmful because, after all, you're a diabetic. Do you think you'd succeed? If we're successful in treating other medical conditions with medical treatment, why wouldn't we do that for substance use disorder?

Are medications a magic answer? No. They are not a one-size-fits-all solution any more than any other treatment protocol, for any medical issue. Medications ARE an indisputable weapon in the fight against substance use disorder. They are much more effective when medications are available immediately when needed, and when they can be used without adding further stigma and fear.

In a perfect world, everyone with a health issue could take a year or more, enter an alternate world with less stress, and take time to change their life. When this is available, treatment without medications can be successful. There are some who can white-knuckle withdrawal and change their lives, but when relapse can lead to deadly overdose or to years in prison, this is a risky approach. Dr. Nora Volkow, director of the National Institute on Drug Abuse, is leading a study using brain scanners at the National Institutes of Health's research hospital. The study will assess whether use of medications may also help to heal the brain more quickly than total abstinence.[143]

Medications are statistically the most successful method of treating substance use disorder at the lowest cost.[144] Successfully treating addiction would benefit *everyone* who needs health care, freeing up medical personnel and resources. It would minimize crime, remove much of the income of drug cartels, and stop filling our prisons with people convicted of drug possession. We'd all benefit.

In many cases, denial of medications harms addiction patients on two levels since many patients need medications to treat substance use disorder and are also in need of medications to treat pain and other underlying issues.

Treatment utilizing medications is now a fully accepted technique. The director of the National Institute on Drug Abuse says these medications are "an essential component of an ongoing treatment plan" that allow people to "regain control of their health and lives." The American Society of Addiction Medicine has called for expansion of treatment with medications. Members of Congress have introduced bills to expand use of medications in treatment. Michael Botticelli, former director of the Office of National Drug Control Policy, stated, "Medication Assisted Treatment saves lives while increasing the chances a person will remain in treatment and learn the skills and build the networks necessary for long-term recovery."

Far too many families are losing their sons and daughters when availability of treatment including medications may have saved them and allowed them to live fulfilling lives. Medications are available. What's missing are open minds and policies that don't punish patients for using a proven medical solution.

CHAPTER 8

THE WAR ON ALL PATIENTS

"In my opinion, our health care system has failed when a doctor fails to treat an illness that is treatable."

KEVIN ALAN LEE

Failure to effectively treat substance use disorder overwhelms the medical system and compromises health care for everyone. A Columbia University study[145] concluded that risky substance use and addiction account for one-third of hospital inpatient costs. The study also determined that failure to treat addiction through appropriate medical care contributes to more than 70 other health conditions requiring medical treatment including HIV, hepatitis B & C, tuberculosis and other infectious diseases, various cancers, heart disease and stroke, pulmonary disease, cirrhosis, pancreatitis, pregnancy complications, and accidents and trauma. It also co-occurs with and exacerbates attention deficit, depression, anxiety, bipolar disorder, schizophrenia, post-traumatic stress disorder, eating disorders, and gastrointestinal issues.[146]

Substance use disorder overwhelms medical resources and compromises availability of medical care for all of us. Ignoring modern science to properly treat addiction is putting everyone's health at risk, and ultimately costs taxpayers much more than it would cost to properly treat addiction in the first place.

Some may react to these statistics with anger. It may be counter-intuitive to suggest improving care for substance users, even as a method of improving everyone's health care. Why not punish "them" and treat us? That's exactly what the War on Drugs has attempted over the past 50 years. Those are the policies that have brought us to the current crisis—not only for those with addiction issues, but for all of us. Punishment escalates issues that can successfully be treated medically. If medical treatment is provided, we end the cycle of punishment and crisis and begin implementing long-term, successful solutions.

While we try to incarcerate our way out of the addiction and overdose epidemic, nearly 90 percent of patients needing treatment for substance use disorder are unable to get it[147], resulting in visits to emergency rooms and physicians, exhausting medical resources for all. Emergency room visits are a very inefficient method of treating ongoing medical issues. Fear of criminal sanctions and lack of funding for long-term treatment creates a disincentive for those struggling with addiction to seek help until an emergency arises. This, in turn, escalates medical costs and minimizes access to medical services for the entire population.

In many cases, the challenges of different types of patients converge in one human being. Many who end up with substance use disorders also have chronic pain or mental health issues. Addiction often arises from self-medicating undiagnosed or untreated medical conditions. Then, the criminal justice system adds punishment, shame, cost, and lack of opportunity. Medications are prohibited to treat the substance use disorder, and it becomes nearly impossible for many to receive treatment with medications for the underlying medical issue.

What physician wants to risk the wrath of reporters or investigators for prescribing a pain medication to someone with a history of addiction? The individual's lack of initial diagnosis and treatment spirals into a lifelong prohibition on treatment, combined with lifelong stigma and punishment. Many of these people populate our prisons. Had funds been used to provide appropriate medical care instead of prosecution, incarceration, and supervision, many would have normal lives, be productive taxpaying citizens, and contribute to their families and to society. Those opportunities are lost, yet few are aware because these victims sit silently behind bars or in shame on the streets, reporting to probation officers and suffering in silence. Those who do speak are often disregarded and shamed. In the meantime, the general public is largely unaware that the effects of the War on Drugs include decline of health care services for all patients.

"The state of our nation is only as good as the state of our health."
–Delos M. Cosgrove, M.D.

CHAPTER 9
THE WAR ON SAFETY

"The rights of every man are diminished when the rights of one man are threatened."

JOHN F. KENNEDY

In America, time for police to solve real crime is compromised because of focus on drug arrests. In 2017 alone, 1,632,921 drug arrests were made, with 85.5 percent of those solely for possession. While law enforcement focuses efforts and funding on nonviolent drug possession arrests, over 38 percent of murders, 62 percent of rapes, and 87 percent of burglaries go unsolved.[148] Focusing officer time on drug arrests instead of violent crime jeopardizes the safety of citizens.

Why would police pursue drug possession cases instead of cases involving violent crime? Two incentives explain these strange priorities. First, police departments compete for federal anti-drug grants, with number of arrests and drug seizures strengthening their application for those grants. The grants also incentivize departments to pay for SWAT team armor and weapons, further militarizing our police forces.

Secondly, the ability of police departments to pad their own budgets using civil forfeiture statutes makes drug arrests more lucrative than pursuing other types of arrests. (See # 18, You'd Like to Keep Your House? The War on Your Assets.)

The War Extends to a War on Police

Ron Serpas, a former New Orleans police superintendent and co-founder of an initiative called Law Enforcement Leaders to Reduce Crime and Incarceration, stated "The way our country is currently approaching criminal justice is not ensuring public safety but is making our jobs more difficult. Arresting low level offenders prevents us from arresting high level offenders."

The War on Drugs has attempted to control supply of drugs for over 50 years through law enforcement and harsh criminal penalties. The goal of reducing crime by removing drug dealers and users from neighborhoods has clearly failed. Many officers who risk their lives every day, who have dedicated themselves to keeping all of us safe and to being there when help is needed, are instead spending their time searching for drugs, arresting low-level drug users, and seeing the revolving door of arrest, release, and re-offense with little progress made. They see the public losing their trust, making it more difficult for them to solve serious crime, and they see their reputations and their own lives at risk because to many, they are considered to be the enemy. In many neighborhoods, the police are perceived as the persecutors rather than the protectors. That makes careers in law enforcement much less rewarding than when police were more universally perceived as public protectors who were there to help.

This, in turn, could escalate issues of police violence and lack of empathy. A recent study scanning public Facebook accounts of approximately 2,900 officers from eight departments, and 600 retired officers from those same departments[149], found that one in five current officers and two in five retired officers studied made public posts or comments that applauded violence against Muslims, women, and criminal defendants. Those were just the public comments. This puts motivations and judgment calls made by these officers into serious question.

Dr. Gabor Maté states in his book *In the Realm of Hungry Ghosts*, "Cops are not necessarily predisposed to harshness, but a loss of humane interaction inevitably results whenever an entire group of people is delegitimized while another group is granted virtually unrestrained physical authority over them." [150]

Policies promoted by the government may be attracting law enforcement candidates with a greater propensity toward physical force. Law and order politicians who've supplied law enforcement with military equipment like armored vehicles and SWAT gear create fear and an "us vs. them" mentality between police and citizens. When an arrest can destroy your life through incarceration, supervision by probation, and criminal records, and when, in the United States, approximately 77 million, or *one in three adults now have a criminal record*,[151] fear by the public is justified. When police hear of officers shot while simply sitting in their cars, their fear is justified as well.

For police and for citizens, fear is dangerous. The War on Drugs has put a strain on relationships between police and the public in many neighborhoods, resulting in increased danger for law enforcement, as well as suspect shootings by police. Many dedicated police officers are becoming scapegoats for the frustration and the fear created by the War on Drugs.

This "War" has diminished quality of life for officers. For the past three years, police suicides outnumbered line-of-duty deaths.[152] Law enforcement professionals have access to drugs and have high-stress careers. These factors can increase the risk of addiction. Dr. Michael Genovese, a clinical psychiatrist and chief medical officer at Acadia Healthcare, told *The Fix*, "Not only are law enforcement officers not immune to addiction, but they are also more susceptible to addiction because the stress of their jobs renders them so."[153]

Police officers who develop substance use issues are in a particularly precarious position since their job is arresting those who have the same issue, and appearing weak to peers is risky for an officer. This makes coming forward or asking for help very difficult, increasing the risk that law enforcement professionals may be operating under the influence.

SWAT raids and other situations where they wield a weapon put them in positions where their judgment can be the difference between life and death. Barriers to asking for help also put officers at risk of overdose.

The degree of drug use by police officers is unavailable. In most cases, law enforcement officers are only drug tested when initially applying to the force or after an accident, shooting, or other incident.[154] One retired officer told this author off the record, "Testing would reduce the force too much, especially in management where cocaine use was prevalent."

Ending the War on Drugs would solve issues for law enforcement and for the public. Some law enforcement agencies have taken it upon themselves to locate treatment in lieu of arrest of suspects with substance use disorders. In other jurisdictions, law enforcement has decided to end the cycle, no longer arresting those using or possessing drugs, and instead referring citizens to treatment. (See # 24, De Facto Decriminalization.) Results have been positive.

In those jurisdictions, trust has been rebuilt, communities have once again become assets rather than liabilities in solving other crime, and officers are once again achieving their goal of keeping the public safe, of being trusted public servants, and of knowing they're making a difference. These outcomes could be available to all citizens if we embrace science and medicine—and reallocate the funds now wasted on the War on Drugs to medical treatment. Most people see the value of helping those with substance use issues to find appropriate treatment in lieu of prosecution and incarceration. Although it may seem different, the result is the same as ending the war on all drugs, allowing for compassion, treatment, and access to pure, regulated drugs, increasing safety for all of us.

Attitudes of law enforcement are changing, and multiple groups of current and former law enforcement professionals are working to end drug prohibition and to treat substance use disorder as a medical issue instead of a criminal matter. These professionals have been on the front lines of this war, have seen the destruction, and understand the importance of ending it.[155]

Law enforcement opinions about criminal justice and the War on Drugs are changing worldwide. Suzanne Sharkey, former constable and undercover officer at Northumbria Constabulary in the U.K., states: "When I look back at my time in the police I feel ashamed, I feel a sense of failure. I feel ashamed that I wasn't arresting career criminals; I was arresting people from poor socially deprived areas with little or no hope whose crime was nonviolent drug possession, a complete failure of the War on Drugs. I believe that one of the biggest barriers for people with problematic substance misuse to seeking help and treatment is the current drug policy. It does nothing; it achieves nothing except creating more harm for individuals, families and society as a whole. All of us know the problems and what we need to do but rather than be united by the problems let's be united by the solutions. Solutions based in health, education and compassion rather than criminalisation."[156]

Street Gangs and Cartels

The War on Drugs also increases crime due to conflicts between competing street gangs and drug cartels. Mexican drug cartels' wholesale earnings from illicit drug sales range from $19 to $29 billion annually.[157] The drugs themselves don't create these massive profits and the violence that accompanies them. Traffickers earn exorbitant profits and continue to be incentivized to traffic drugs and to do whatever it takes to protect their markets only because of drug prohibition. If drugs were legal and regulated like alcohol and tobacco, the cartels' monopoly on drug supply would end, as well as much of the danger to the public in terms of violence and in tainted street drugs. [158] When billions of dollars are involved, crime and corruption to protect those profits is a predictable result, leaving little regard for public safety.

Jeffrey Singer, a surgeon in Phoenix and a senior fellow at the Cato Institute, stated, "At the end of the day, the drug overdose problem is the result of sociocultural dynamics intersecting with drug prohibition— and all the dangers that a black market in drugs present. Prohibition also presents powerful incentives to corrupt doctors, pharmacists, and pharmaceutical representatives who seek the profits offered by the underground trade."[159]

Even when arrest of major drug kingpins is successful, the result is an increase in crime and violence as competing interests fight to fill the gap left by the arrest.[160] Suppliers will always fill the gap. Despite the arrest and conviction of Joaquin "El Chapo" Guzman, the DEA estimates that Mexican heroin production increased 37 percent in 2017.[161]

Attempting to control supply of drugs is a fool's errand. Additionally, the illegal drug trade leaves a vacuum for dispute resolution, leaving innocent victims to get caught in the crossfire. Disputes can't be resolved in court, so they're resolved in the streets.

Homelessness and Health

Over 75,000 people are homeless in New York, with over 90 percent of those in New York City. Some 55,000 are homeless in Los Angeles alone, an increase of 75 percent in the six years from 2012 to 2018. Increased housing regulation resulted in higher real estate costs, and replacement of older buildings with new development created shortages of affordable housing. The War on Drugs and the addiction epidemic also escalated homelessness. Substance use can lead to homelessness, but homelessness can also lead to substance use as a way to cope with the stress of lack of housing.

Criminal records have made huge numbers of potential tenants ineligible for housing. Landlords often won't rent to those with records, and felony convictions disqualify many from public housing.[162] For those who would be eligible to rent, compromised career opportunities because of criminal records make rent unaffordable. (See # 12, The War on Housing.)

Homeless individuals are much more vulnerable to interactions with the police and are more likely to be arrested, so the issue of criminal records and its impact on housing can become a downward spiral.[163]

Homelessness creates health and safety issues for all citizens. Homeless populations in Los Angeles have likely led to rats infesting L.A. City Hall. Public outcry has increased as human waste, leftover food, and used needles have accumulated on the streets. LA had a recent outbreak of typhus, a disease spread by fleas on rats and other animals.

Various cities with homeless populations are experiencing increased incidents of Hepatitis A and tuberculosis.[164] The resurgence of these diseases risks not only homeless populations, but others living in the proximity, and ultimately anyone coming into contact with someone infected while in these locations.

According to studies, a quarter to a third of all homeless individuals are hospitalized during a given year, and also use emergency room services more frequently than the general population.[165] This is an inefficient method of health care, monopolizes the system, and spends taxpayer money.

Homelessness is a complex subject, but when individuals are denied housing options because of criminal records for drug possession, the issues are escalated and the health, safety and survival of those "criminals" as well as lives of community members are put in jeopardy.

Have You Been "SWATTED"?

SWAT (special weapon and tactics) raids are a safety hazard for police as well as for citizens. SWAT raids have increased by 15,000 percent from the late 1970s to today, resulting in 50,000 to 80,000 SWAT raids annually in the U.S. alone.[166] The idea that if you're doing nothing wrong you have nothing to worry about is naive. SWAT used to be primarily for hostage or active shooter situations. Now, approximately 80 percent of all SWAT raids are to search for drugs, and many are "no-knock" raids where police are authorized to enter premises without first knocking and announcing their presence or purpose.[167] An anonymous tip can result in your door being broken down, with you, your children, and your pets at risk of being shot or traumatized.

Children are present in 14 to 25 percent of SWAT raids. In many cases, police knew that children would be present.[168] Raids routinely include use of battering rams and heavily armed men. Concussion grenades are also used on some occasions. At a time when science has clearly indicated that childhood trauma increases the risk of addiction in the future, traumatizing children under the guise of controlling drug use is absurd. Additionally, many raids could be avoided by simply checking an address or other information readily available online to minimize the risk of "SWATTING" innocent people.

SWAT is no longer used solely in emergency situations, and there is evidence that little effort is put into avoiding use of SWAT. The fallout of SWAT raids can cascade. As mentioned in Chapter 1, SWAT raided the residence of an innocent family 15 months after Justin, the previous resident, had entered treatment for a substance use disorder. Was Justin a threat, making a SWAT raid imperative to locate him? He'd been arrested shortly before his move, but was never charged until his file came to the top of a prosecutor's pile 15 months later. At the time of the SWAT raid, he'd completed a seven-month extensive treatment program and was working at the treatment center showing new residents that success was possible. He'd left a forwarding address with the post office. Had law enforcement simply checked the forwarding address, he could have easily been found. Sending a letter notifying him that charges had been filed and that he should make contact would have prevented trauma to an innocent family, minimized risk inherent with storming into a home with guns, and saved significant amounts of taxpayer money.

SWAT raids put your pets at risk. A program specialist with the U.S. Department of Justice estimates that 25 to 30 pet dogs are killed by police every day and calls this trend an epidemic.[169] Others estimate that as many as 10,000 family dogs may be killed annually. Totals could be higher, since most police agencies don't track officer-involved shootings involving animals, and some families are afraid to report or to complain. Police have immunity from prosecution unless their actions are "plainly incompetent" or they violated the law. These are high burdens of proof so many citizens see little benefit in reporting these shootings.

The increase in pet deaths has been a direct result of the increased militarization of police and the escalation in SWAT raids on homes, often based on an unsubstantiated complaint from an anonymous source. When terminology like "you've been SWATTED" is added to our vocabulary, we have an issue.

Anyone who's loved a family pet should consider the trauma of having police break down a door and shoot your dog, sometimes in front of children. Consider what this does to overall community trust of police, and the impact of that distrust on success in solving other crime. If this happened to you, would you call police to protect you if you were in trouble in the future? Would you freely offer information on a police investigation on another matter? SWAT and the fear created by these raids leave a large segment of the population afraid to make use of police protection, considering a call to police more dangerous than lack of protection. That's a tragedy for police and for the public.

You may have never touched a drug, but your family pet and your family could be in jeopardy. Is there enough of an upside to balance this risk? Even if drugs were possessed in a home for which a tip is given, is it worth breaking down doors with guns ready for use in order to keep someone from taking a drug? Without current policy, drugs wouldn't be clandestine. The chances would be much greater that they'd be stored in pharmacies or with other regulated distributors.

Exporting the War on Drugs and the Casualties

U.S. drug policy has promoted drug wars in other countries, causing over 250,000 deaths and over 40,000 disappearances in Mexico. According to the Mexican government over 164,000 people were killed in Mexico's Drug War between 2007 and 2014 due to violence related to the War on Drugs, with many innocent victims caught in the crossfire of competing drug cartels. Fatalities have continued to increase. In 2018, fatalities increased by 15 percent over 2017 deaths with over 30,000 more lives lost.[170]

Comparing Drug War deaths in Mexico alone to those killed in conflicts in Afghanistan and Iraq during the same time period puts the devastation into perspective.

Killings in Mexico v. Civilian Deaths in Afghanistan and Iraq Since 2007

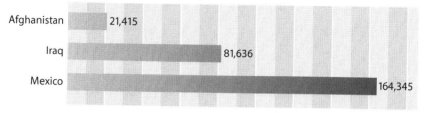

Source: Instituto Nacional de Estadistica, Geografia, e Informatica (Mexico), Iraq Body Count; United Nations[171]

Since 2014, the end of the chart above, the mayhem has escalated even further.

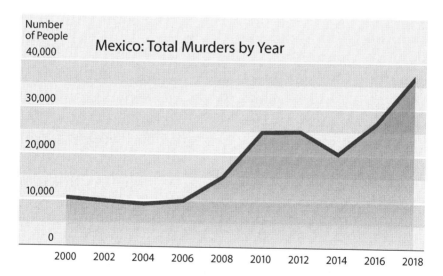

Source: Instituto Nacional y Estadistica, Geografia (INEG)[172]

Terrorism is funded with dollars created by black market drugs. Some terrorist groups fund their activities by trafficking drugs themselves. In other cases, terrorists control regions where illicit drugs are grown and place a tariff on drug traffickers. Either way, the War on Drugs creates the high value on illegal drugs, which are then used to finance terrorism.[173]

Annie Machon, former Mi5 officer tasked with investigating terrorist logistics, states, "On the one hand we have prohibition that pushes the War on Drugs underground and creates huge conflicts globally. On the other hand we are fighting the war on terror which is largely funded by this War on Drugs. So it strikes me as illogical unless it's a very clever circular business model that has been only too successful."[174]

A particularly insidious part of history is the U.S. government's protection and indirect financing of the Afghanistan drug industry, while also spending your tax dollars to persecute drug users. Alfred McCoy, Harrington Professor of History at University of Wisconsin-Madison, in his article "America's Drug War is Ruining the World," reports: "While mobilizing Islamic fundamentalists to fight the Soviet occupation of [Afghanistan] in the 1980's, the CIA tolerated opium trafficking by its Afghan mujahedeen allies while arming them for a guerrilla war that would ravage the countryside, destroying conventional agriculture and herding." This activity on the part of the United States laid the foundation for increases in opium production from 250 tons in 1979 to 4,600 tons by 1999.[175] These results didn't stop U.S. foreign policy from flying in the face of strong War on Drugs policies at home.

McCoy further reports: " . . . to capture the Taliban-controlled capital, Kabul, the CIA mobilized Northern Alliance leaders who had long dominated the drug trade in northeastern Afghanistan, as well as Pashtun warlords active as drug smugglers in the southeastern part of the country. In the process, they created a postwar politics ideal for the expansion of opium cultivation. Even though output surged in the first three years of the US occupation, Washington remained uninterested, resisting anything that might weaken military operations against Taliban guerrillas. Testifying to this policy's failure, the UN's Afghanistan Opium Survey 2007 reported that the harvest that year reached a record 8,200 tons, generating 53 percent of the country's gross domestic product and accounting for 93 percent of the world's illicit narcotics supply."[176]

All taxpayers should be horrified that, while putting our children in cages for minor drug possession in the United States, the same government was responsible for drastically escalating opium production and knowingly financing those suppliers.

The foundation for the War on Drugs is the government's supposed belief that drug supply can be controlled. While they claim this and destroy lives for low-level drug possession, they not only fail to control supply, but use our tax dollars to escalate it, destroying lives on both sides of the ocean. The number of lives affected has reached historic and catastrophic levels.

Immigration issues are also increased due to drug cartel violence. High profitability of the illegal drug trade has made cartels powerful in Central America and Mexico and led to corruption of police with bribes and threats. In Mexico, an estimated 92 percent of crimes go unreported.[177] Criminal gangs have spread through Central America and Mexico, making daily life dangerous and hopeless for those not connected to the cartels. The *New York Times* quoted a Honduran pastor "You never call the cops. The cops themselves will retaliate and kill you."[178] A young Guatemalan told a reporter, "Unless you are connected to one of the families that run this country, there is no future here. Either you work for the narcos or go north."

There are obviously many factors in the ongoing immigration debate, but ending the War on Drugs would significantly reduce the power and presence of the drug cartels that are making life a living hell for many.

Lack of opportunity leads to increased crime. When nonviolent drug offenders have criminal records, career opportunities and housing alternatives are limited or nonexistent. If ongoing fees to cover probation supervision costs aren't paid, penalties include incarceration. The War on Drugs has been an unintended recruiting agent for drug cartels, converting low-level drug offenders into street dealers, sometimes to earn money with which to pay fines, fees, and costs of "supervision" to avoid jail for nonpayment.

SWAT raids, drug violence due to the War on Drugs, misallocated resources resulting in unsolved crime, lost opportunities leading to criminal activity, and much of the population unwilling to work with police on real crime impacts the safety of all citizens. If the goal of the War on Drugs is public safety, it's failed badly.

CHAPTER 10
THE WAR ON MINORITIES

"The War on Drugs will go down in history as
the most racist crusade since slavery."

THOR BENSON

We've discussed the racist foundations of the War on Drugs. There's no doubt that this "War" has destroyed lives of every color, but racial inequities of drug policy are particularly tragic.

This short segment on the topic in no way minimizes the importance of the issue. Much has been written on the racial disparities of the War on Drugs.[179] Statistics illustrate the point. Based on the most recent census statistics, this is the breakdown of the number of incarcerated people per 100,000 in various ethnic groups:

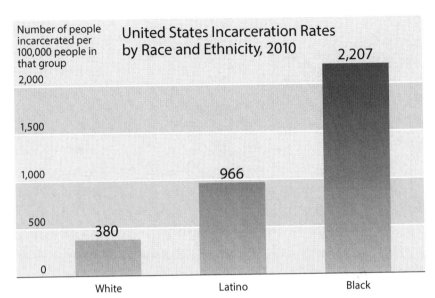

Number of people incarcerated per 100,000 people in that group

United States Incarceration Rates by Race and Ethnicity, 2010

Source: Calculated by the Prison Policy Initiative from Bureau of Justice Statistic, Correctional Population in the U.S., 2010 and U.S. Census 2010 Summary File 1.

Reproduced/adapted with permission from Prison Policy Initiative[180]

In the United States, one in every 20 black men over the age of 18 is in state or federal prison, compared to one in 180 white men. In five states, between one in 13 and one in 14 black men are in prison.[181] A black child born today is less likely to be raised by both parents than a black child born during slavery.[182] In major cities across the country, 80 percent of young African Americans now have criminal records.[183] Almost 80 percent of prisoners serving time for a federal drug offense and 60 percent of those in state prisons are Latino or black.[184] Black Americans account for 12.5 percent of all substance users, but 30 percent of all drug-related arrests are of black "offenders."[185]

The higher numbers of minorities behind bars is partly due to higher rates of incarceration after arrest and imposition of longer sentences for minorities. Black Americans are nearly six times more likely to be incarcerated for drug-related offenses than white Americans.[186]

Whether admitted openly or not, some believe that minorities are arrested more frequently and serve longer sentences because they simply offend more frequently, use or deal in higher quantities of drugs, or are a greater danger to society. An extensive 2018 study analyzing over 700,000 cases disproves all of these assumptions.[187]

Black and Latino men in the United States are under siege, and are at greater risk of arrest, conviction, and long periods of incarceration than the rest of the population. As discussed in chapter 4, the foundations of the War on Drugs were blatantly racist. Unfortunately, those foundational attitudes have continued in the application of this "War".

Ending the War on Drugs would end these inequities and would prevent them from attaching to other races or groups of people. The racial history and continued unfairness and inconsistency in the application of drug policy are more reasons to end it.

CHAPTER 11

THE WAR ON PARENTS

"We all want to protect our families from the potential harm of drugs. But if our children do develop a drug problem, surely we will want them cared for as patients in need of treatment and not branded as criminals."

KOFI ANNAN, FORMER SECRETARY GENERAL, UNITED NATIONS

Parenting a son or daughter with substance use issues is like being in a boxing ring with at least three pro fighters. Your child takes a swing that hits you in the gut, the criminal justice system nails you in the forehead, and societal myths and judgment from others take the legs out from under you.

Imagine lying in bed at night, phone always close at hand, on alert for a dreaded phone call. It could be "This is a call from the County Jail." Your heart sinks, knowing that the life-saving medications your child takes daily will likely be withheld, creating excruciating pain, withdrawal behind bars, and significantly higher chances of overdose upon release. Past experience may tell you that nursing staff is overworked, overwhelmed, and largely untrained to deal with detox. You may also be aware that physicians may only visit weekly and that it's likely that a physician won't see your son or daughter, even if in medical trouble. If you're a parent who's seen the system operate, you're aware that prisoners are forbidden from seeing their own physicians, even if they could pay for it out of their own pockets.

Imagine knowing that your child's arrest may lead to years in prison or a felony conviction that will compromise opportunities for a lifetime, that to avoid that outcome takes money that's badly needed for treatment, and that even then, defense may not be successful. And imagine that your child is there because of a few pills in a pocket, a missed appointment, or simply because he or she looked suspicious to someone. He or she might be there because of a desperate need for medical care that has been unaffordable or unavailable. Perhaps your child is no longer open to help because prior treatment consisted of lectures, guilt, and a message that total abstinence for life was the only alternative. Maybe enduring ongoing threats of incarceration and wearing the "criminal" label destroyed self-esteem and hope.

The dreaded call could also be from the morgue, telling you that all hope for your child is gone—that you'll never hear that laugh or see that smile again. You'll never feel her hug or wipe his tears. You'll never watch your child enjoy his children, build her career, or hold your hand as you grow old. You'll never witness the gifts you know your child could have shared with the world. You know that despite the scorn, the stigma, and the persecution, your child's life had meaning, and the loss of that life is a tragedy. And you know that it's a tragedy that could have been avoided if the War on Drugs hadn't built barriers to getting appropriate help, and created a wall of stigma that was simply too high to climb.

Those who personally experience a child's addiction don't often talk about the details. We're programmed not to. After all, much of the world believes a child's addiction is the parent's fault, and even those who don't buy into that are told that a parent's "job," when a child has substance use issues, is to "let them hit bottom." Essentially, parents are told to let their children die; that to advocate for our children is somehow enabling that will harm them. Put yourself in the place of that parent, in constant worry about your child, while being judged and stigmatized. Imagine knowing that solutions that could save your child are blocked based on nothing more than ignorance, bias, and history that have culminated in today's War on Drugs.

A simple nasal spray can save the life of someone who overdoses if only someone close has it available. Many parents know that people, including perhaps their own family and friends, sometimes believe this nasal spray shouldn't be made available, because they don't believe that a parent's son or daughter is worth saving. That stigma is based largely on a criminal justice system that defines addiction as a crime, classifying patients needing help as criminals.

Imagine knowing that, if your child needed medical help to save his or her life, others witnessing the overdose may opt not to help out of fear of their own arrest.

Imagine knowing that your son or daughter is at high risk of death, and knowing that this impending death could be avoided if we looked at science, provided medical help for a medical issue, and stopped persecuting those who are least able to shield themselves from being decimated by the persecution.

Imagine knowing that your child, like every other human being, wants to succeed, but either can't because substances control his or her life or because opportunities have been blocked—in multiple ways—every day.

Consider a typical week in the life of a son or daughter—perhaps *your* son or daughter. Physical and/or mental health issues are likely a big factor in life. Addiction often comes from self-medicating physical or emotional pain that isn't properly treated. Escalation of addiction is often a result of the War on Drugs, which allocates resources to punishment instead of treatment, leaves patients in the shadows out of fear of prosecution if help is sought, and traumatizes patients through arrest, prosecution, long and onerous supervision requirements, and criminal records that can compromise opportunities for life.

Some parents believe the traditional approach. "Just pray," they say. Prayer, faith, and many other things may help, but if we promoted ignoring treatment for cancer or a broken leg and suggested "just pray" to resolve the issue, as parents we'd be subject to prosecution for child endangerment. Yet, mandated 12-step programs, a faith-based program using a higher power, is the government's mandated go-to treatment protocol. Medications and other treatment protocols are frequently denied, even if the patient, the family, or other financial sources are available to cover the cost or when insurance or other programs would cover treatment.

Life revolves around stopping the pain of potential withdrawal. This may be because of active addiction. It may be after a patient is in recovery, constantly concerned about not being able to get the prescription medications that prevent relapse or treat chronic pain and other medical issues. Denial of access to medications and other medical care converts focus on succeeding in life to focus on having continued access to medications.

If drugs are involved, criminal justice is likely already at the door or on its way to enter your life. Imagine the difference if parents and their children could come out of the shadows, ask for individualized medical care, and receive it without concern about police, arrest, prosecution, or potential time behind bars. How many lives would be saved if the right medical protocol could be determined without the risk of incarceration if testing a protocol created a relapse on the way to finding what works for this patient? How many parents' retirement funds would remain intact, or if used, would be applied to medical care instead of legal fees, fines, and subsidies to children who have been shut out of housing and career options? How many parents wouldn't be grieving the loss of their children?

Parents who are involved find themselves in a battle with a system that should share the parents' goals: an individual's recovery and return to being a productive citizen. Instead, families watch in horror as prosecutors mandate steps that often "undo" progress made.

One mother states: "I'm so angry! The last time I checked with the inpatient treatment that the court would approve, the waiting list was 4 months, so we sold some assets to be able to afford to pay the bond so we could bring our son home and try the medication the drug court wouldn't let him take. He's been doing great, started school, and is working two jobs. A bed opened up today at the rehab and the DA wants him to go into treatment, but the treatment center won't allow the medications that are working for him, and going into treatment will end his jobs and his school. What he's doing is working, but if we don't do what the prosecutor is demanding, they'll send our son to prison for two years. This is crazy! What do we do??"

Unfortunately, these challenges are typical in the lives of parents, and of individuals under court supervision.

Parents struggle along with their children, whether in active addiction or in recovery but still impacted by criminal records. What should a parent do if a son or daughter has done what's needed to get their life back on track, yet is railroaded by a court prosecuting earlier charges, or is unable to find housing because of a criminal record? When children are born, most parents plan for the future and protect themselves against unexpected occurrences with health insurance, life insurance, and college savings plans. Insurance to cover the costs of the War on Drugs isn't available, yet can bankrupt individuals and their families.

The onslaught is ongoing and unpredictable. A felony can impact housing and job opportunities for life, as well as increasing the risk of additional arrests and progressively harsher punishment. Families live in constant fear that a minor infraction will lead to life-changing sanctions when prior records increase penalties, and when even short-term incarceration jeopardizes medical care. Anxiety, depression, and PTSD are not uncommon in parents dealing with these always-present worries.

When the topic of drug legalization comes up, we're sometimes told that legalization sounds crazy. If we want to truly see crazy, look no further than current policies, resulting in wasted money, wasted time, wasted lives, and agony for all involved.

CHAPTER 12
THE WAR ON HOUSING

"Housing is absolutely essential to human flourishing. Without stable shelter, it all falls apart."

MATTHEW DESMOND

When parents watch their children grow into adults, they hope their children will be happy. They hope they will lead fulfilling lives. And they envision them having a secure roof over their heads.

When a criminal record destroys the opportunity for housing, it also destroys hope, health, and opportunity. Without housing, it's nearly impossible to find employment. It's impossible to maintain a healthy lifestyle, to have access to clean food and water, or to simply get a good night's sleep. Maintaining basic dignity and self-esteem can be an insurmountable goal. This is the punishment put on patients with substance use disorder every day because of criminal records.

Landlords are hesitant to take risks on someone with a criminal record. Assumptions are made that the record indicates dishonesty or disrespect for property. If an individual is in active addiction, these assumptions may be accurate, but criminal records create issues long after potential renters have turned their lives around.

Even landlords who understand that criminal records don't always create bad renters are concerned about liability. If an issue arises, the landlord could be accused of ignoring warning signs due to the criminal record, opening the landlord up to greater risk of being sued. With plenty of renters available, why take the risk?

Probation requirements restrict the geographic area in which those with a criminal record can seek housing. Probation requires residence in the county where supervision is assigned unless probation is officially transferred to another county. Transfer is a risky proposition, since new probation agents and new rules can be far different from jurisdiction to jurisdiction. Geographic restrictions further limit the chance of finding a landlord who will accept a renter with a criminal record.

Many townhome and condo associations forbid owners from renting to those with criminal records, and some local governments have passed ordinances *requiring* landlords to conduct criminal record searches prior to renting to an applicant.[188]

For married couples, if the spouse without the record rents a property, he or she may be in violation of the lease if an individual with a criminal record is allowed to reside there.

Friends will sometimes allow someone with a criminal record to live with them, hiding the roommate from the landlord. Whether this is out of friendship or to have another person with whom to share rental costs, the unreported renter is at risk. If a disagreement arises or if the friend changes their mind on a whim, the result can be homelessness. None of the standard protections for a renter apply, leaving those with criminal records vulnerable. They can be set up as easy targets for demands for anything from higher rent payments to sexual favors.

The unreported roommate has no legal authority to control what goes on in a house where they reside as an unreported occupant. The presence of drugs or alcohol could create a probation violation, resulting in jail time for the person simply trying to find a place to live. In today's society, it's difficult to find housing where there's no risk that a roommate might have beer in the refrigerator or a joint somewhere in the home.

Regardless of whether those substances are legal in the jurisdiction, they are prohibited by most probation mandates.

Renters who aren't on the lease can also run into issues with probation simply for reporting an address that isn't officially theirs, while being deprived of having an address because of the very criminal record for which they're on probation.

Can families be of help? The War on Drugs has minimized those opportunities as well. If drug use on the property is suspected (even if never proven), the family home may be at risk of seizure under civil forfeiture law. (See # 18, You'd Like to Keep Your House? The War on Your Assets.) Additionally, parents who allow adult children to live with them while on probation risk home searches or unannounced visits from the probation officers. The risk of SWAT raids and other police activity increases when an occupant has a criminal record.

Is public housing an option? Federal low-income housing programs (Section 8 or housing choice voucher programs) provide housing subsidies for low-income renters. Department of Housing and Urban Development (HUD) regulations require all public housing agencies to conduct a criminal background check as part of the application screening process for all applicants, and to prepare a written plan that includes their policies regarding criminal background checks and their policies on eligibility for those with criminal backgrounds.

In regard to drug crimes, if methamphetamine was sold anywhere near public housing facilities (regardless of how long ago that incident happened), denial is mandatory. In all other cases, decisions can be made on a case-by-case basis, but in many cases, a felony conviction, and especially a felony less than five years old, will likely result in denial of eligibility. *Additionally, not only are those with criminal histories typically denied eligibility, but eligibility can be denied to family members of those with criminal convictions.* This prevents families from providing housing to those getting back on their feet. Even a visit from someone with a drug felony can result in eviction of the whole family, putting an obstacle to family relationships, further isolating the person with a criminal record. This increases the shame, stigma, and lost opportunities for felons, and increases the chance of reoffending or turning to other crime out of frustration or desperation.

In addition to resulting in denial of an initial application, these rules can cause the eviction of individuals or their family members from public housing due to a conviction, so at the same time that a family member is facing criminal charges, the whole family is at risk of becoming homeless.

Some states make felons ineligible for residency in veterans' homes or skilled nursing facilities.

By process of elimination, sober housing often becomes the only alternative available to those with a criminal record, and particularly those with a felony. Sober housing can be a good alternative for some. They have a degree of structure (which varies from house to house). Other residents have also struggled with substance use disorder. A sense of community and camaraderie can be built. Early in recovery can be a lonely time, so a sober house can fill an important gap and help someone new to recovery to build a social foundation.

Sober housing is generally expensive. A shared room can be equivalent to the cost of renting an apartment. Sober housing can minimize issues inherent with living alone, but these houses are often crowded, with many occupants recently out of in-patient treatment, bringing the drama and the noise that can accompany that group.

Individuals sometimes find themselves in sober housing as the only alternative to sleeping on the street because of limitations due to a criminal record. For someone in long-term recovery or someone who ended up with a record for drug possession who does not have a substance use issue, these houses are typically not a good fit. Sober houses may also be problematic for someone whose recovery is not based on 12 steps, since most sober houses mandate regular attendance at 12-step meetings and acceptance of those principles.

Use of medications may be prohibited or, at a minimum, frowned upon in sober housing. Sober houses often come with lists of rules administered by house managers who've gone through treatment themselves. This can be helpful, or can create huge issues. A glimpse into an interview with a house manager can provide insight into attitudes and challenges that can result from those attitudes:

"The first thing you need to do is get off those meds." We're sitting in a sober house interview conducted by the house manager. He's talking about Suboxone, a medication prescribed by the psychiatrist treating the proposed resident of this sober house. This medication has helped this individual toward successful recovery after four failed attempts in 12-step programs. We'd called in advance to be certain this sober house allowed use of medications in treatment, and had been assured that they did. "We understand and support evidence-based treatment" the owner of this group of sober homes told us before we'd scheduled the appointment.

The sober house manager—turned medical advisor—was specifically directing a potential resident to ignore advice of his addiction psychiatrist and his therapist who holds a master's degree in behavioral health counseling. Prior to giving this blanket advice, the house manager asked no questions about the individual's diagnosis, situation, or history, yet knew the "answer" to his issues.

It was clear that life in this sober house could be unpleasant for any resident using prescription medications as part of a recovery plan. An unhappy house manager who perceives that the resident isn't following his rules could mandate removal of the resident from the house, jeopardizing recovery and, if the resident is under court supervision, potentially create a probation violation and time behind bars simply for not being a good fit for this sober house.

This meeting, and the "advice" given, would be laughable if it wasn't so sad, so dangerous, and so widespread. Families striving to help a loved one find recovery are vulnerable and often listen to anyone in a position of authority, whether that person is actually qualified to give advice or not. If cancer patients who'd successfully beat their cancer began "advising" cancer patients that the type of chemo that had worked for them was the only way for anyone to beat cancer, they'd have a credibility issue, and perhaps a legal one as well. The advice is clearly well-meaning, but that makes it no less dangerous—and it's freely given to those backed into a corner with few options other than the street.

When it comes to addiction, advice based on personal experience and anecdote is traditionally accepted, with the credentials of many counselors limited to their own success in a particular program. In recent years, more and more programs and sober houses state that they are "evidence-based," but that term is tossed around like baseballs at a little league game. Many so-called evidence-based programs would have a difficult time providing the scientific or medical evidence upon which their programs are actually based.

In 2016, U.S. Department of Housing and Urban Development (HUD) issued guidelines for interpreting fair housing standards in regard to applicants with criminal records.[189] The guidelines acknowledge that drug policy is clearly racist, so if a landlord has a blanket policy of not renting to those with a criminal record, that policy is much more likely to punish a minority than a non-minority. For that reason, the guidelines indicate that denial of housing to a minority applicant because of a criminal record may be considered to be a discriminatory practice.[190]

Consider this more carefully. The same government that continues the War on Drugs openly admits that those policies are so racist that minority individuals with criminal records should not be denied housing because of criminal records created by those racist policies. Those denied housing who don't fall under minority status are, for the most part, out of luck.

The reality is that most applicants don't have the time or money to sue and proving reasons for denial of housing can be difficult. Most felons and many with other criminal records are denied housing with little recourse unless they can afford to purchase a property.

Housing issues for those with criminal records are fundamentally monetary. Criminal history is generally not considered when applying for an FHA or USDA mortgage, and most home sellers simply want to sell their home and don't care if a buyer has a criminal record. Those with criminal records who can afford to buy real estate, or who have families who can afford to buy, don't suffer the indignity of homelessness.

Buying a home is financially impossible for many after paying legal fees, fines and health costs, and whose wages have been reduced due to career-killing criminal records and time lost behind bars.

In cases where it is feasible for parents to purchase a property to prevent their child from being homeless, a huge dilemma is created. Do parents tie up family finances that may be essential for treatment or other medical needs for themselves or their children, or do they refuse and see their child live on the streets? Should a property be purchased now, when the son or daughter hasn't yet decided if this is where they want to live long term? Do parents use retirement funds to provide housing for their children? Parents weigh their own financial security against seeing their child on the streets, knowing that homelessness leads to an increased risk of relapse, arrest, or death. These are decisions now made by parents in the United States every day.

Homeless populations lead to depreciated property values, spread of disease, and increased crime. Residents of neighborhoods with people living on the streets often don't realize that their tax dollars created criminal records and loss of opportunity that directly led to the homeless encampment.

CHAPTER 13

DRIVER'S LICENSES—THE WAR ON INDEPENDENCE

"Let the punishment fit the crime."

W. S. GILBERT

"It's only a misdemeanor. I don't understand why you think this is a big deal." The prosecutor was responding to questions about a charge for driving under the influence. The charge was based on an arrest in a parking lot.

Emma had been released from the hospital five days earlier after undergoing major surgery. She'd been parked, waiting to meet a friend for coffee, decided to put her head back and rest, and had fallen asleep in the car. When police pulled in behind her, approached, and asked her to step out of the car, she wasn't worried. She had prescriptions for all medications she was taking. It was 7 a.m. There was no evidence of alcohol use, then or anytime in the past few years. She wasn't a drinker. It didn't matter. She was arrested.

She ended up in a hospital for a blood test, and was then locked in a jail cell with a mattress soaked in urine from a previous occupant.

Why was she there? Emma had failed to pass the sobriety test, unable to stand still on one leg for 30 seconds with hands held at her side without moving. The incisions in her side from the recently removed chest tubes were still painful. Pneumonia was still lingering, but the surgeon thought release from the hospital would be preferable to the bacteria present there, and movement would help to re-inflate the lung. Standing on one foot for 30 seconds with arms held directly at her side was simply not achievable. That, combined with prescription medications in her purse landed her behind bars.

Corrections officers at the jail mandated that she pull the urine-soaked mattress to the floor to put it under the bedspring, refused to replace it, and required her to climb to the upper bunk to sleep. Prison staff had been notified of her health issues, by her and by her concerned family. They simply didn't care. When a parent called the jail nurse to provide medical information, he was told, "Your daughter is an adult. You shouldn't be calling. I have a lot of people to take care of. I have no idea who your daughter is. I can't give individual attention." It took 36 hours to get Emma released, with no charges filed.

The experience had been traumatic, but she thought it was behind her. She later learned that criminal charges could be filed at any time within the next 18 months to three years (depending on what was charged), and that, if charges were filed, a warrant could be issued for her arrest with no prior notice.

A week later, Emma received a notice that her license had been revoked, and that to get her license back after the period of revocation, a $700 fine would have to be paid. The revocation was effective prior to the right to any hearing or right to defend against charges. If a hearing was desired, an application would have to be filed and a $300 fee paid, after which a hearing would be scheduled within 60 days.

Emma found herself subject to two different potential charges and two different proceedings. The jail stay and the risk of future criminal charges fell under criminal statutes. The loss of her driver's license was a civil proceeding under implied consent statutes, which are effective in all 50 U.S. states.

Implied consent laws apply if a driver either refuses to submit to a sobriety test requested by an officer, or if a driver tests over the limit of alcohol or other substances. Emma had prescriptions for the medications found in her blood. This provided her with an affirmative defense to the driving under the influence (DUI) charge, but her license was revoked before she had an opportunity to assert this defense. Her choices were to go without a license or to pay the fine and either obtain an occupational license or install an interlock ignition system in her vehicle. The occupational license would work, except that Emma's work hours were erratic, so it was nearly impossible to establish set hours and days when she would need to drive. The interlock ignition system would require paperwork, further cost, and installation of a unit in her car into which she'd breathe each time she needed to drive. Installing an interlock system in her car when she wasn't a drinker seemed crazy, but she found that this might be the least restrictive alternative in her case. Either way, additional expense was significant, but if she didn't come up with the money, she'd lose her job.

Use of medications for various circumstances can risk an experience similar to Emma's. Individuals who take medications to treat substance use disorder are at risk of arrest for DUI. In some states, a prescription provides an affirmative defense. The affirmative defense does not prevent the experience that Emma encountered, though, of time in jail and loss of license until hearings are held (and fees and costs paid up front). During that jail time, it is typical for medications to be withheld, putting patients into withdrawal and significantly increasing the risk of relapse and overdose upon release.

In some states, there is no affirmative defense, so despite having prescriptions and regardless of whether medications impacted the ability to drive, a patient can be charged and convicted of DUI simply for having certain substances in their blood.

The loss of driver's licenses, or the risk of being arrested for DUI because of methadone in the blood, is a huge issue for those who need to travel to a methadone clinic daily. Some patients travel significant distances to get to the nearest methadone clinic, making public transportation or getting rides from others impractical. Loss of licenses or risk of DUI charges deny patients the ability to access the medical treatment that minimizes the risk of relapse and the actual risk of driving under the influence.

Having driver's licenses at risk is one of many disincentives for patients to utilize the treatment that has been proven to be most effective. These laws directly increase addiction and overdose rates, and increase the risk that those in untreated, active addiction will be behind the wheel, putting others on the road at risk.

In Emma's situation, at least the suspicion was related to driving. However, within our criminal justice system, driver's licenses are used like weapons even when the offense has nothing to do with driving. In 1991, as part of the escalation of the War on Drugs, Congress threatened states with reduced highway funding if they didn't automatically suspend the driver's license of anyone convicted of a drug offense.[191] Many states added loss of driver's licenses on top of other criminal penalties. The result is huge numbers of license suspensions and state agencies overwhelmed with the cost and time spent in processing these revocations. Individuals find themselves choosing between risking arrest for driving without a license or losing jobs, missing doctor appointments, or simply being unable to get to the grocery store. Communities with few alternatives for transportation and poor or minority communities are disproportionately affected.

Alexandra Natapoff, in her book *Punishment Without Crime*, citing a New Jersey study, reports, ". . . following license suspension, 42 percent of people lost their jobs. Of those who lost their jobs, 45 percent could not find another one, and for those who did find another one, 88 percent earned less than they did when they had their license."[192]

As states have begun taking a closer look at the effect of these and other unsuccessful drug policies, many have begun to repeal these laws, using a provision of federal law that allows them to opt out of the automatic license suspensions while retaining their highway funding.[193]

In conjunction with driver's license revocations, classes, probation meetings, and court appearances are mandated, leaving some defendants with mandates but no transportation to be able to comply. Finding transportation to ongoing court appearances, probation appointments, and other requirements can become an enormous issue for those on long-term probation. Cost can be prohibitive, and added time required in using public transportation can jeopardize employment. Jeopardizing income can, in turn, lead to incarceration for nonpayment of fees and fines. Penalties for missed appointments or unpaid fees include incarceration and extension of periods of supervision, creating yet more fees and mandates and an ongoing downward spiral.

In many cases, licenses are suspended with no notice provided, or with notice long after the revocation began. In these instances, if an accident occurs, insurance may be compromised and charges for operating without a license may be filed even if the driver had no notice that the license had been suspended. If another offense occurred, even if the driver was unaware of the revocation, driving without a license can trigger more severe penalties.

If a driver is driving under the influence, jeopardizing the safety of others on the road, penalties are warranted. When driver's licenses are revoked for charges that have nothing to do with driving or under circumstances where the ability to drive is not impaired, these penalties, even if charged as misdemeanors, are a "big deal."

The prosecutor's bewilderment that a misdemeanor would cause concern is not unusual. For them, it's just paper pushing to get another case off the desk. For defendants, the threat of a charge, whether a misdemeanor or a felony, can be life altering. Imagine knowing that, at any time, you could be arrested and jailed with no advance warning because a file came to the top of a prosecutor's pile and a decision was made to file charges. Thousands of people live with these threats hanging over their heads on an ongoing basis. Their fear is warranted. It's not unusual for charges to be brought long after the time of an arrest. Cases can be brought any time before statutes of limitations expire, which can be years depending on the type of charge and the jurisdiction. Lives can be uprooted far past the time of an arrest, and uncertainty can be difficult to live with.

Citizens may believe they're immune to these issues if they don't drive after drinking or using drugs, but you could become a casualty simply by being in a vehicle. In December 2016, Dasha Fincher was a passenger in a car that was pulled over by police in Georgia allegedly for window tinting that was too dark, but that was determined not to be a violation. Officers found plastic bags in the back seat that they tested and identified as methamphetamine. Dasha told officers that the substance was cotton candy that had sat in the sun, but was arrested for possession and trafficking of methamphetamine. Dasha's bail was set at $1 million, too high for her to afford the bond, so she sat in jail for three months waiting for test results from the Georgia Bureau of Investigation.

In March 2017, test results were returned saying there were no controlled substances confirmed. It took another two weeks, until April 4, for Dasha to be released from jail. From December to April while Dasha was incarcerated because of cotton candy in her car, she missed the birth of twin grandsons and her daughter's miscarriage. Dasha also states that she was refused medical attention during her incarceration. She is suing[194], so this case has received publicity, but arrests, accusations, costs, delays, and false positives and multi-month delays on drug tests happen every day. This is not an isolated incident. These issues impact real people and real lives.

CHAPTER 14

LIQUID GOLD—THE WAR ON DIGNITY

"In our time, the symbol of state intrusion into the private life is the mandatory urine test."

CHRISTOPHER HITCHENS, LOVE, POVERTY, AND WAR: JOURNEYS AND ESSAYS

The drug testing industry has become so lucrative that urine samples are referred to as liquid gold. With the concern about addiction and overdose, urine tests have become big business and come at huge cost to patients and taxpayers. Companies have taken advantage of the concerns driven by the addiction and overdose epidemic to make enormous profits, while leaving those subjected to the tests humiliated, with pants at their ankles with someone looking over their shoulder. Even if a drug test isn't observed, standing in line to get your "cup" destroys self-esteem. Patients are considered guilty until proven otherwise.

Drug testing has become pervasive. It's not only used in the criminal justice system upon arrest and ongoing as part of probation, but by schools, parents, physicians, and employers. The expense is staggering. The federal government's annual expenditure for drug testing is more than the entire EPA annual budget. Spending on urine screens and related tests quadrupled from 2011 to 2014 to an estimated $8.5 billion annually, yet there are no national standards for who gets tested, how often, or for which drugs.[195] In 2014 and 2015, Medicare alone paid $1 million or more to health care professionals at more than 50 U.S. pain management practices[196], including tests to determine whether Grandma is doing PCP, ecstasy, or cocaine. Not surprisingly, positive test results were minimal. An assistant U.S. attorney in Florida assessing potential issues stated, "We're focused on the fact that many physicians are making more money on testing than treating patients."[197]

Despite stories of wasted money, miscarriages of justice, and ongoing humiliation of those tested with no evidence of guilt, in an era of drug addiction and overdoses, at first glance, drug testing still seems compelling. Any parent who has ever experienced the anguish of seeing their child decline, wondering to what extent drugs are involved, and which drugs may be involved, understands the urge to drug test. It seems logical for schools to test students in an effort to curb the destructive nature of drug addiction in the school setting. Employers have an interest in preventing employees from performing work under the influence of drugs. Law enforcement's use of drug testing allows them to identify illegal drug use, and to have evidence for prosecution. Pain clinics and physicians want to know that medications aren't abused and want to protect themselves from liability to the extent possible.

What could possibly go wrong? Plenty.

Inaccuracy

Drug tests are slow and often inaccurate. Approximately 5-10 percent of tests result in false positives, and 10-15 percent in false negatives. More than 300 over-the-counter drugs and foods can affect urine tests. While the vast majority of tests are accurate, when incarceration, loss of jobs, loss of family support, or other life-altering consequences are caused by test results, inaccurate results impact enormous numbers of people. Over 150 million drug tests are conducted annually.[198] *Even a five percent false positive rate would impact 7.5 MILLION individuals.*

If a drug test is failed, it's important to re-test and to use more accurate testing before accusations are made, but many are impacted by multi-month delays. During that time, they may be incarcerated or put under major stress and suspicion while waiting for outcomes of the retest. The period of uncertainty and the lack of trust created by accusations can do immense damage to individuals and to relationships.

Criminal Justice

Those on probation, sometimes for years, are required to call in to determine whether a drug test is required. Drug tests impact work schedules, and sometimes cost jobs. Ongoing stress can trigger medical issues, including relapse for those with substance use disorder. What could be more stressful than an ongoing requirement to urinate in a cup that could result in being put behind bars? This ongoing humiliation becomes life for those arrested with drug quantities smaller than a penny. Even if a substance use issue does exist, wouldn't it make more sense to fund medical treatment instead of spending millions of dollars to humiliate individuals and threaten them with incarceration?

Medical Disability

Paruresis, or bashful bladder (a form of social anxiety), makes it difficult or impossible for an individual to urinate in public. According to the International Paruresis Association, approximately 7 percent of the public, or 220 million people worldwide (21 million Americans), may suffer from paruresis. It is recognized as a disability under the Americans with Disabilities Act, and is classified as a social phobia in the Diagnostic and Statistical Manual of Mental Disorders (DSM-IV 300.23). Those suffering from this medically accepted disability simply cannot provide a urine sample under the conditions typically required by probation. This can lead to severe sanctions due to a medical disability. The option for hair follicle, blood, or saliva testing is often not given, even if the individual is willing to pay for it personally.

It's easy to shake our heads in disbelief when an individual says they aren't able to provide a urine sample. The immediate assumption by many is that this is simply another way to attempt to beat a drug test when the person being tested knows they won't pass. While this is certainly a possibility, it's also true that the person may actually be *unable* to give a urine sample.

Paruresis makes it difficult or impossible for the individual to urinate in the presence of others, when under time pressure, or when others are close by or might hear them. The factors triggering symptoms are the *essence* of the drug tests typically given by police, probation, and parole officers. If an individual has a tendency toward paruresis, adding the threat of incarceration, potential hostility of those observing the urine test, and the fear of accusations from probation or parole officers can exacerbate the symptoms. Paruresis sufferers can end up incarcerated due to probation or parole violations for not providing urine samples, or being deemed to "flunk" a urine test solely because they can't produce. Many sufferers have lost jobs, not because of actual drug use, but because of an inability to produce samples. The Paruresis Association provides advice to those who face criminal or career issues due to paruresis.[199]

For employers, schools, and government, the cost of testing large numbers of people to "catch" each drug user can translate into extremely high costs per user caught. In school settings, many times positive results do little to help the individual, and in some cases, increase isolation by restricting someone who tested positive from beneficial school activities and groups.

Some states drug test welfare recipients in an effort to save money, or to dissuade individuals from using illegal drugs. Some states have considered drug testing for food stamps and unemployment benefits. The argument can sound compelling. After all, some people have to submit to drug tests given by their employers. Why shouldn't those receiving taxpayer dollars submit to the same requirements? First, requiring employees to submit to drug tests for anything other than in situations where safety would be compromised is unwise.[200] Duplicating the issue for those receiving public benefits isn't the way to solve the problem.

Bottom line is that the cost of testing compared to money saved by denying benefits to those who test positive has been a money loser in every state in which testing has been applied.[201] Legal issues and the cost of legal defense add to costs.

Requiring public benefits recipients to submit to testing also increases stigma around substance use disorder and causes fear of losing benefits, minimizing chances that an individual needing help will seek it. The fear of testing and the requirements of conducting the test may scare those needing benefits from applying for them even if they're not drug users, which is particularly problematic in families with minor children. Fear may be justified due to the risk of false positives with drug tests.

The U.S. government classifies substance use disorder as a medical issue and defines it as a disability under the Americans with Disabilities Act.[202] Denying benefits because of a medical issue is illegal. Multiple lawsuits have delayed testing of applicants or recipients of the Temporary Assistance for Needy Families (TANF) for a variety of reasons, so legal issues and cost to defend these cases should be factored into any cost-benefit analysis. On February 26, 2013, a panel of the U.S. Court of Appeals for the 11th Circuit found in *Lebron v. Florida Department of Children and Families* that drug testing of welfare recipients without a foundation for suspicion is unconstitutional under the Fourth Amendment, and that requiring consent to testing as a condition to receipt of benefits violates the doctrine of unconstitutional conditions.[203]

Before the Florida law testing benefit recipients was struck down, they spent $118,140 on testing, which was $45,780 more than the state saved by denying benefits to the 2.6 percent of applicants who tested positive. Florida then spent hundreds of thousands of dollars defending lawsuits that they lost.[204] These laws humiliate people, increase addiction rates, put children at risk, and cost taxpayers more money than not testing. Unless the sole reason for testing is a conscious desire to humiliate and shame those seeking public benefits, there is no legitimate foundation upon which to base these policies. For the few who fail tests and are denied benefits, families and individuals are at risk of homelessness, increasing risk of crime and health risks to neighborhoods.

Is drug testing of students effective and worthwhile? In June 2002, the U.S. Supreme Court, in a 5-4 decision in *Pottawatomie County v. Earls*, held that random drug tests for all middle and high school students participating in competitive extracurricular activities are permissible. This covers only students in extracurricular activities, giving a disincentive for students to participate.

A National Institute on Drug Abuse (NIDA) study showed moderately lower cannabis use when school testing was done, but an increase in other drugs.[205] This makes sense, since cannabis detection is easier since it stays in the system for up to a month. Students may switch to more illicit drugs like opioids, methamphetamine, and barbiturates that stay in the system for shorter periods of time so are less likely to be detected. This is a very negative unintended consequence of drug testing.

Schools opting to drug test under the provisions of the *Pottawatomie* case are limited to middle and high school students participating in competitive extracurricular activities. More and more studies show that addiction is caused and escalated by lack of connection and other social issues. Removing students who test positive from extracurricular activities or creating barriers to taking part in those activities may be incredibly harmful to those students, pushing them toward, rather than away, from increased drug use.

Additionally, failing a drug test does not mean the student is addicted to drugs, but being classified as a drug user may push that student to identify more closely with others in that category. This result is not beneficial for a student who may have simply been caught at a time of experimentation. Research shows mixed results on student testing. A 2013 study concluded that testing is a relatively ineffective drug-prevention policy. A study funded by the National Institute on Drug Abuse found that student athletes who participated in randomized drug testing had overall rates of drug use similar to students who did not take part in the program, and in fact some indicators of future drug use increased among those participating in the drug testing program.[206]

The American Academy of Pediatrics states "there is little evidence of the effectiveness of school-based drug testing in the scientific literature."[207]

Parents often wonder if they should drug test if they suspect their child of drug use. When a home test comes back positive (assuming it's not a false positive), if it helps parents to take steps to get an assessment and to potentially get help if substance use is an issue, then it may be worth considering. However, there are negatives to parental testing that should be considered.

A negative result can be falsely reassuring and dangerous. The false result could be because the child tested is not a drug user, but may also be because the test was inaccurate, or because it happened to be conducted during a time when drug use wasn't recent enough to be picked up. The negative result may also be because the child found a way to beat the test. Either way, it can give false reassurance to parents and, despite suspicious or unacceptable behavior, may delay getting needed help.

A positive result may create overreaction, or if inaccurate, can destroy relationships and increase the risk that the child will "live up to expectations." Experts have expressed significant concern about the impact on relationships and the atmosphere in the home when parents conduct drug tests. The American Academy of Pediatrics states, "Drug testing poses substantial risks—in particular, the risk of harming the parent-child and school-child relationships by creating an environment of resentment, distrust, and suspicion."

As we look at the challenges and costs of drug testing, it's important to decide what we'll do with the results. What's our purpose? Is it to minimize drug use? Studies have proven that drug tests aren't successful in doing that, and may actually increase use, particularly of harder drugs that show up in tests for a shorter period of time. Is it to determine who needs help? If that's the case, programs should be in place to assure that help is available. In most cases, test results are not used for this purpose and funds with which to provide help are unavailable. If testing won't improve long-term results, then there is little benefit to offset the significant disadvantages of testing.

CHAPTER 15

THE ULTIMATE NANNY STATE— THE WAR ON FREEDOM

"When a man is denied the right to live the life he believes in, he has no choice but to become an outlaw."

NELSON MANDELA

Probation. It sounds like a non-invasive way to keep tabs on those who could be risks to the community without putting them behind bars. How difficult could checking in with a probation officer once in a while be?

In reality, life on probation in the United States varies tremendously depending on the state, the county, and even the particular agent assigned to the case. There are some probation officers who genuinely want to help, and supervise those assigned to them in an effort to transition them out of the criminal justice system to success in life. Unfortunately, many other probation agents use threats and what, in any other circumstance, would be categorized as verbal abuse to keep their "offenders" in line.

3.8 million people in the United States are still on probation, which includes 56 percent of adults in the criminal justice system.[208] When those on parole are added to the probation rolls, 4.5 million—the approximate population of Los Angeles—are under supervision.[209] Over

75 percent of those under supervision were convicted of nonviolent offenses.[210] Adding those behind bars, a total of 6.7 million people in the U.S. are under correctional control.

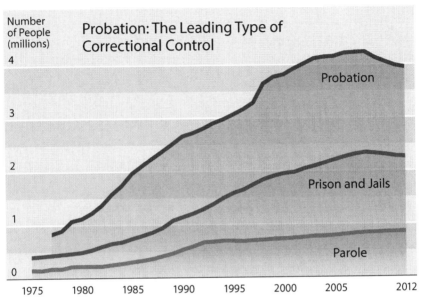

Number of People (millions)

Probation: The Leading Type of Correctional Control

Probation

Prison and Jails

Parole

1975   1980   1985   1990   1995   2000   2005   2012

Compiled from Bureau of Justice Statistics' *Annual Probation Survey and Annual Parole Survey* data series and Prison Policy Initiative Tracking State Prison Growth in 50 States.

Reproduced/adapted with permission from Prison Policy Initiative [211]

Periods of probation are in addition to periods of time for processing plea agreements, which can take months. Multiyear probation sentences are handed out like candy at a parade. Offenses resulting in probation don't have to be serious crimes. Depending on jurisdiction, possession of a few joints could result in long-term probation.

Lengthy periods of probation make it difficult for those in the system to assert rights, even in extreme circumstances of abuse of power by corrections officials or others. Few behind bars or "in the system" want to poke the bear that controls their life, and deadlines for lawsuits to be filed expire long before terms of supervision end. When periods of incarceration are followed by years of probation, few take the chance to complain about mistreatment, propagating a system where abuse of power can occur at the hands of criminal justice employees who buy into old assumptions about addiction and harshly apply those biases behind closed doors. Statutes of limitations for suits against jail personnel are as short as 90 days and often come with stringent requirements of notice to the same authorities that have control over their supervision. These constraints, in addition to various other "qualified immunity" statutes restricting lawsuits against public officials, leave those under supervision of the state very vulnerable.

"Offenders" (the term utilized in probation agreements in many jurisdictions) agree to the terms of probation to avoid incarceration, but probation often leads to incarceration anyway. Even individuals sentenced to probation for minor offenses can end up incarcerated if they can't afford to pay the fees charged for their supervision, can't make it to every appointment, or fall out of compliance in one of many ways. Technical violations are the primary reason that probation results in time behind bars. The following chart shows the numbers of violations leading to incarceration, with people going from probation to incarceration being far larger than those incarcerated for new offenses.

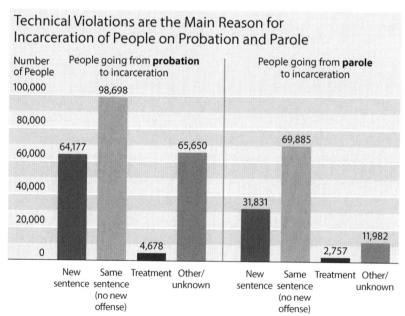

Technical Violations are the Main Reason for Incarceration of People on Probation and Parole

Source: Bureau of Justice Statistics, *Probation and Parole in the U.S. 2016* App. tables 3 and 7 (showing 2016 data)

Reproduced/adapted with permission from Prison Policy Initiative [212]

The stress of probation can lead to relapse or to simply giving up. The standard is perfection, and anything short of that over a multiyear period can lead to time behind bars.

Many agents use common sense and don't want to send people to jail, but the reality is that personality conflicts, personal situations of the agent (we all have bad days), and many other factors can impact an individual's judgment. The way the law is written and applied puts an offender's freedom into the hands of one person with subjective decisions binding. Consider living under provisions like those described below, knowing that if the probation agent decides that you didn't comply based on their judgment, the result would be going to jail.

While it's true that decisions of an agent can be appealed, appeal can be risky. Appeals may be denied since appeal is based on the perceptions of the agent vs. that of the "offender." Then, the rest of the term of probation may be served under an irritated agent—an undesirable scenario for anyone on probation.

If a probation violation can end in incarceration, why would an individual on probation violate? The answer: Because it's nearly impossible to fully comply. Financial inability to pay probation fees can lead to incarceration. Those on probation, often for years, are perpetual second-class citizens, walking on eggs, and begging for the right to simply live their lives. Many probation provisions are so subjective that an offender is unable to effectively argue if an agent says the requirement wasn't complied with.

Here are some typical probation mandates from actual written agreements offenders have been required to sign for the privilege of being on probation in lieu of immediate lockup. These agreements waive basic civil rights. It's obvious, when reviewing these mandates, that they were written with a violent criminal in mind, rather than a person possessing a small amount of a substance, which is the basis for most arrests.

Permission to Live

The defendant's freedom and lifestyle are in the hands of the agent for the extent of the probation, with few rights of privacy.

"You shall inform your agent of your whereabouts and activities as he/she directs."

"You shall provide true and correct information verbally and in writing, in response to inquiries by the agent."

"You shall follow any specific rules that may be issued by an agent to achieve the goals and objectives of your supervision. The rules may be modified at any time, as appropriate."

"You shall submit a written report monthly and any other such relevant information as   directed by your agent." (Not only subjective, but if the offender has poor organizational or writing skills, it could result in jail.)

Searches and Drug Testing

If the defendant resides with others, the home is subject to search without notice at any time, discouraging friends or family from sharing housing. This can result in financial issues and isolation, all triggers for misery and for relapse. If alcohol or firearms are in a shared home, it is a probation violation. A gathering in the home where alcohol is served could create a probation violation for the offender, even if alcohol had nothing to do with the offense, and even though the offender is not consuming alcohol. Some probation officers may not enforce all of these rules, but rules of probation give them the legal right to do so.

Drug testing could arguably provide positive accountability, but as previously discussed, the cost, time requirements, and procedures can become problematic. Drug testing and other requirements are scheduled at the convenience of criminal justice professionals, with the offender complying or risking sanctions for a probation violation. Work schedules typically aren't considered. Time off to take tests can compromise jobs. For those working night shifts and then having to wake up to check requirements and comply, insomnia issues may be created.

Restrictions on entering establishments where alcohol is sold can lead to isolation. In areas where pool leagues and weddings are held in places where alcohol is served, prohibiting an individual from participating for a period of years puts individuals in positions of embarrassment or stigma, or deciding whether to take the risk of being arrested for attending a function.

Typical probation rules include:

> "You shall make yourself available for searches or tests ordered by your agent including but not limited to urinalysis, breathalyzer, DNA collection and blood samples or search of residence or any property under your control."

> "You shall not enter into or be on the premises of any bars, taverns, liquor stores, beer tents or establishments where the primary source of income comes from the sale of alcoholic beverages."

> "You shall not associate with or be around any persons that are actively using or possessing alcohol or illegal drugs."

Changing Jobs or Vehicles; Banks and Credit Cards

Should the penalty for possession of a joint or a pain pill remove a person's right to change jobs, to move, to change vehicles, or to apply for credit without permission for an extended period of time? Restrictions in typical probation agreements are stringent:

> "You shall not change residence or employment unless you get approval in advance from your agent, or in the case of emergency, notify your agent of the change within 72 hours."

> "You shall not purchase, trade, sell or operate a motor vehicle unless you get approval in advance from your agent."

> "You shall not borrow money or purchase on credit unless you get approval in advance from your agent."

Additionally, with terms of probation lingering for years, job opportunities in other jurisdictions are lost since those on probation must live in the county of supervision, and are unable to move to other jurisdictions without onerous paperwork and the risk that the probation agent in the next jurisdiction might be worse. Positions requiring travel are extremely difficult, and those living near state borders where work may require travel into the next state can find themselves begging probation officers for ongoing travel passes. Some agents require notice of a week or more to obtain a travel pass. Others process them immediately upon request. Variations are often dictated more by the personality of the agent than by formal rules. This is just one of many ways that a controlling or vindictive agent can compromise opportunities for those on probation.

Ongoing Fees

Fees for probation fall on the offender, along with court costs and fines. If fees aren't paid, it can result in jail time and/or extensions of probation, creating a true downward perpetual spiral of more costs and requirements. Too frequently, parents whose finances have already been decimated by treatment, counseling, testing, and other costs are faced with also helping their children to cover these costs in order to extract them from the system and give them a chance at a fresh start.

> "You shall pay monthly supervision fees as directed by your agent. You shall pay court obligations as directed by the agent."

Employment and School Mandates

While it's a noble goal for "offenders" to be fully employed or to go to school, requiring this as a condition of probation can be problematic. At the same time that a public record and ongoing requirements of meetings with the probation officer make full-time employment more difficult to obtain, failure to comply can result in jail. Meetings are mandatory and may compromise employment either because of scheduling difficulties or because the offender is forced to notify the employer that s/he is on probation to explain the need to take time off. This is not a way to endear oneself to an employer.

School is also a great goal, but student loans may not be available if there's a felony conviction, and for others with a history of substance use disorder, admission to school, qualifying for loans, or covering costs may simply not be feasible. The "shall" in the rule again threatens the offender with jail for something he or she may not be able to comply with.

> "You shall obtain and maintain full-time employment, school or a combination of both."

Public Shame

Conviction records, including the terms of plea agreements, are published in the newspaper in some jurisdictions. If negotiations on the plea are delayed, this publication can occur long after the offense, creating obstacles and humiliation for individuals who've worked to proceed down a positive path since the offense occurred. Plea agreements sometimes make offenses sound more serious than they are. (See # 17, Bargain or Bars?) When the choice is jail or a plea—even if the plea is severe and not representative of the offense—most offenders choose the plea, which often includes years of probation.

Recovery vs. Criminal Law

If the goal of drug policy is to assist in recovery from substance use disorder, then it would seem logical that the positive aspects of good treatment, counseling, or life-skill programs be incorporated into criminal penalties. The truth is that the two systems are total opposites.

Good science-based treatment promotes honesty. In our criminal justice system, speaking without representation, sharing past issues, or saying the wrong thing can have grave results. The system cultivates distrust and fear. Taxpayer funds are used to subsidize the cost of court-mandated counseling, yet offenders fear opening up to these counselors because probation agreements mandate waiver of confidentiality, authorizing counselors to report to probation officers who have the right to incarcerate the individual for anything said to the counselor. Taxpayer money is wasted to pay for these counseling sessions where opening up to the counselor could put the patient behind bars. These practices also taint offenders against legitimate, confidential counseling in the future that could be very helpful in working through issues, including those created by the criminal justice system.

Good treatment teaches the importance of taking personal responsibility for your past, present, and future actions. Our criminal system takes responsibility from individuals, whether through incarceration or through being required to get permission for daily living as part of probation mandates. Parents are accused on harmful "enabling" when they advocate for their children. Probation is enabling on steroids at the hands of the state.

Good treatment recognizes the importance of having hope and building self-esteem. The criminal justice system destroys hope and self-esteem, consistently sending the message "you aren't important," "you are flawed," "you are unworthy." The requirement of obtaining a probation agent's permission for many life activities for an extended period of time, the constant threat of jail hanging over your head, being subjected to mandatory court appearances (and accompanying attorney's fees) month after month at the whim of the prosecutor, or mandatory meetings with probation officers, all leave offenders in a state of fear, shame, and low self-esteem. Living with a permanent public record requires constant explanation, apology, and ongoing challenges in many aspects of life. This can be exhausting, and is the antithesis of building hope and self-esteem.

Good treatment focuses on building strong, healthy relationships with family. The criminal system wears families out, destroys finances, and adds incredible stress. Many probation agents and corrections officers are defensive about family questions or intervention of any kind. Families learn quickly that contact with criminal justice will likely be adversarial, and that advocating for a family member risks retribution from probation or corrections officers. Families are already worn out from the emotional and financial aspects of addiction and dealing with the criminal justice system. They've been told that it's best to let their loved one "hit bottom." Offenders stuck in a system that decimates their self-esteem daily often end up with little family support and little hope.

Good treatment promotes financial responsibility and working toward achievable and fulfilling goals. The criminal system puts unreasonable financial demands on offenders, with threats of jail if fees, fines, and costs aren't paid on time. Getting ahead financially under these rules is challenging, and sometimes impossible. Many simply give up.

Good treatment provides a foundation of appreciation and gratitude. The criminal justice system creates fear, fatigue, and resentment.

Envision being arrested with a small amount of a substance in your pocket, and then living with these restrictions for a period of one to three years. It's easy for those not directly involved to judge individuals who end up in the system long term, but once in the system, even for a minor infraction, getting out is difficult. Probation violations can lead to new charges and extended terms of probation. The risk of future arrest is much greater for someone who has a prior record. Law enforcement officers use their discretion in making arrests. When a prior record exists, it's much easier for them to presume guilt and make the arrest. Sanctions become more severe with each incident.

Probation for drug possession "offenders" is incredibly expensive for taxpayers with little to show for it but agony, stress, and loss of hope for individuals. Worry about being put in a cage is constant for individuals, simply because they possessed a substance. These harsh penalties aren't because of dishonesty or violence or even because a victim was harmed. They're inhumane, arbitrary, destructive, and a waste of taxpayer dollars.

If probation effectively helped people to find recovery or even reduced addiction and overdose rates, perhaps the denial of civil liberties and the enormous cost to taxpayers could be justified. There is absolutely no evidence that this is the case. Studies have shown that providing behavioral health and other medical services to those with substance use issues and applying resources to supervise people who actually present a high public safety risk achieves the best results for individuals and communities.[213]

CHAPTER 16

THE SCARLET "F"—THE WAR ON OPPORTUNITY

"In court, judges tell people that their conviction carries
a sentence of years, or probation. The truth is far more
terrible. People convicted of crimes often become social
outcasts for life, finding it difficult or impossible to rent
an apartment, get a job, adopt children, access public
benefits, serve on juries, or vote."

JAMES FORMAN, JR.

Convicted felon. Dangerous felon. There are no positive adjectives that
go with the "felon" label. A search for synonyms of *felon* brings up *convict*,
delinquent, loser, outlaw, con, evil, and *cruel*.

Many people are afraid of felons, assuming they must be dangerous,
dishonest, or outcasts of society. Few employers want to employ them.
Few landlords want to rent to them. Simply watching a *Law & Order*
television show makes it clear that the felon should be the first to be
suspected of the next crime. What parent wants their son or daughter
bringing a felon home to dinner? Stigma is huge and opportunities are
slim.

What's not highly publicized is that the felon may be a scared kid caught with a small amount of a substance in his pocket or in her blood. Most felony drug arrests are for minimal drug quantities. A study published by the *UC Davis Law Review* reports that 40 percent of drug arrests are for a quarter of a gram or less of a substance. That's .0088 of an ounce—less than the size of a penny in your hand. Twenty percent of arrests are based on between one-quarter of a gram and one gram, which is still only .035 of an ounce, moving up to the size of a U.S. quarter. Less than one percent of arrests are for a kilogram or more.[214] More than 80 percent of arrests for drug law violations are for drug possession alone.[215]

The person with the felony may be someone who was self-medicating chronic pain or mental health issues and either couldn't get a prescription or didn't take the time or have the money to go to a doctor. If a prior drug charge appears on a record, it becomes even more difficult for an individual to get basic medical care to treat pain or other issues. Punishment instead of treatment perpetuates the issue.

Felonies can be "earned" in other ways. A probation violation for a non-felony drug charge can result in a felony bail jumping charge. Bail jumping may bring visions of a defendant on a fast track out of the country, but is defined simply as the "intentional failure to comply with conditions of bail." This can apply to any probation violation, including missing an appointment, failure to notify a probation agent of a change in employment or other information, a relapse, or failure to meet any of the requirements discussed in the previous chapter. Probation agents hold this threat over the heads of those on probation, who can end up with a felony based on a minor offense and a probation violation.

One arrest can result in multiple charges, and typically does. This makes criminal charges look ominous, and gives the prosecutor leverage in negotiating a plea agreement. When a defendant looks at prison time possible for all alleged crimes, few have the nerve not to accept whatever the prosecutor offers, even if the penalty far outweighs the actual offense. Families, employers, or others who look at criminal records often don't realize that one act can carry multiple charges and that prosecutors have incentive to make charges look as serious as possible for purposes of promoting acceptance of a plea agreement.

Before we ostracize a felon, we should be aware that the same act can be a felony in one jurisdiction, a misdemeanor in another, and in yet another may result in free treatment. In the right jurisdiction, based on what they've admitted to doing, Bill Clinton, George W. Bush, and Barack Obama could as likely have been felons as presidents.

Felonies for low-level drug offenses explain the large percentage of people in the United States who now have a felony record. Research led by a University of Georgia sociologist estimates that eight percent of the total U.S. population now has a felony, and that 33 percent of African American males have felonies.[216] Felony convictions have quadrupled from 1980 to 2010. As of 2010, an estimated 20 million people in the United States had a current or prior felony conviction.[217]

If felony convictions helped to protect the public or helped those with substance use disorders to find recovery, perhaps the carnage could be justified, but that's not the case. An analysis of public health and state corrections data showed that punitive policies like felony convictions did nothing to positively impact drug use, overdose deaths, or future arrests for drug law violations.[218] Studies did show that the effects of felony convictions undermined public safety because of restrictions on ability to support themselves and their families using legal means.[219]

Felonies are also costly to taxpayers. Loss of opportunity leads to high unemployment rates and financial insecurity for felons. One study shows felony convictions in the United States leading to a loss of as much as $87 billion in annual GDP.[220]

Felony penalties vary from jurisdiction to jurisdiction. Some are permanent, while other rights may eventually be restored, but the process to restore rights can be long, costly, cumbersome, and tenuous. If you're "lucky" enough to have a felony in a jurisdiction that allows expungement, it might be possible to get the record expunged after a period of years, but many jurisdictions have age and other restrictions on expungement. With today's technology, even if the record is cleared, it'll likely still appear in internet searches. If you're in a jurisdiction where felonies cannot be expunged, the felony stays on the public record for life unless thousands of dollars are spent on attempts at receiving a presidential or governor's pardon, in states where the governor is willing to consider them.

In addition to fines, imprisonment, and issues inherent in having spent time behind bars, a felony conviction has a huge impact on nearly all aspects of life. As you review the following restrictions, ask yourself, "Is this a reasonable way to punish someone for having a substance in their pocket less than the size of a quarter? If the person does have a substance use issue that could be treated medically, does this punishment make sense?"

Following is a list of just some of the restrictions placed on felons:

Denial of Public Benefits: SSI/SSDI benefits may be denied to applicants whose substance use disorder contributed to their disability. The pertinent question: Is the medical condition for which the claimant alleges disability exacerbated or caused by alcohol or drug use? This is a subjective standard, and one that ignores current science and law recognizing addiction itself as a health condition. The Social Security Administration has the authority to use discretion in determining eligibility. Current law creates risk for patients to disclose addiction issues to physicians and other professionals due to fear of losing benefits.

21 U.S.C. § 862 lists federal benefits that are lost upon a state or federal felony drug conviction. The ban disqualifies offenders from benefits under the Temporary Assistance to Needy Families (TANF) program, as well as the federal food stamp program, which is now called the Supplemental Nutrition Assistance Program (SNAP). Lifetime disqualification for these benefits applies unless the state opts out of all or part of the ban. Some states have fully or partially opted out, but approximately three-quarters of all states still enforce the ban in full or in part.

This ban is imposed *only* for drug crimes. Other criminal activity— including violent crime—does not result in loss of these benefits. A rapist continues benefits, but the person with a pill in his pocket loses

them. These provisions were passed in 1996 after only two minutes of debate in the Senate. It appears that little thought was put into the true effect of this legislation, or to whether it would actually serve a purpose.

If the rationale was to minimize potential for welfare fraud, this legislation was unnecessary since federal legislation prohibiting that is already in existence. The benefit bans are especially harsh on women (and their children), on low-income individuals, and on those who've been incarcerated and need help when reentering society who are already dealing with the stigma of a felony conviction and being an ex-con. Having few options makes successful recovery and staying away from criminal activity more difficult for those being released from prison.

Denial of Access to Student Loans and Grants: If an individual is incarcerated in a federal or a state institution, he or she will not be eligible for Federal Pell Grants or federal student loans. Some progress has been made. Upon release, many of the limitations on eligibility will now be removed.

In 1998, the Higher Education Act was amended to prohibit anyone with a drug conviction from receiving federal financial aid for post-secondary education. In 2005, this ban was modified to apply only if the drug conviction happened while a student was receiving federal student aid in the form of grants, loans, and/or work-study. This ban continues today. Aid received after a conviction will be required to be repaid. It may be possible to reinstate eligibility by completing an acceptable treatment program that meets specific mandated requirements. Over 200,000 students have lost federal financial aid eligibility because of a drug conviction.[221]

Denial of Voting Rights: An estimated 6.1 million Americans are denied the right to vote because of felony convictions.[222] Some states deny voting rights for life, whereas others restore them after prison, probation, and/or parole have been completed. This can have significant implications. Those who are most impacted by archaic drug laws are denied the right to vote for reform.

Denial of voting rights due to drug felonies also has a racial component. With a third of black men having a felony conviction, even if voting rights are restored to some, there is still a huge impact on election outcomes because of voting restrictions. Whether voting privileges should be restored to violent felons is a different discussion, but denying voting rights to those whose felonies are based on drug charges is overly harsh, compromises elections that should be based on the opportunity of citizens to vote, and propagates a horrendously unfair and obsolete system.

Housing: As discussed earlier, housing alternatives are severely restricted for those with felony records, leaving those with felonies homeless in far too many instances.

Career Opportunities and Loss of Professional Licenses or Permits: A felony conviction severely restricts the ability to pursue many occupations and to obtain licenses for specific professions. With the increase in occupations that require licensing, this is increasingly problematic. Restrictions vary by state, but restrictions may deny licensing for many professions including the following, which means that those working in these professions will lose their jobs if they end up with a felony or will not be able to pursue these professions, limiting the ability to make a living.

In today's "gig" economy, those wanting to earn extra money often have opportunities ranging from Uber driving to shopping services, but nearly all of these companies deny applications from those with felonies. Employment recruiters typically refuse to represent felons in a job search.

When reviewing the following professions and/or licenses that are prohibited to felons, keep in mind that the felony may have been for possession of a substance smaller than the size of a penny. That "crime" keeps the individual from working in any of the following professions, in many cases, for life:

○ Academic staff or faculty member for public university

○ Architect

○ Armed Forces. A felony conviction causes ineligibility to enlist. "10 U.S.C. § 504. Persons not qualified: (a) Insanity, Desertion, Felons, Etc.—No person who is insane, intoxicated, or a deserter from an armed force, or who has been convicted of a felony, may be enlisted in any armed force. However, the Secretary concerned may authorize exceptions, in meritorious cases, for the enlistment of deserters and persons convicted of felonies."

○ Athlete agent

○ Barber

○ Business franchise registration

○ Burglar alarm installer

○ Casino work of any kind

○ Childcare worker

○ Chiropractor

○ Cigarette sales license

○ Commercial driver's license

○ Contractor

○ Cosmetologist

○ Day camper employee

○ Day care provider

○ Dentistry

○ Dietician/nutritionist

○ Driver's license instructor

○ Electrician

○ Elevator installer, repairer, or maintenance

○ Engineer

- Family support magistrate
- Federal spending and defense contracts; inability to participate
- Fire protection sprinkler system work
- Foster care; license or approval may be denied if any member of the household was convicted of certain crimes, including certain felonies
- Funeral director
- Gaming-related licenses
- Guard and patrol service worker
- Home inspector
- Insurance agent
- Interior designer
- Investment advisor
- Irrigation work
- Judge
- Landscape architect
- Law enforcement
- Lead abatement consultants, contractors, and workers
- License to sell, manufacture, or distribute non-intoxicating beverages
- Liquor or beer license/permit
- Nursing, including nurse's aides
- Manicurist
- Marital and family therapy
- Massage therapist
- Midwife
- Mortgage loan originator
- Optometrist

- Pawnbroker
- Pharmacist
- Physical therapist or physical therapist assistant
- Plumber or piping work
- Practice of medicine
- Practice of law
- Private detective
- Professional bondsman
- Public office or any other office of trust/profit or honor, and removal from office for anyone currently serving at time of conviction
- Public service gas technicians
- Psychologist
- Radiographer
- Real estate appraiser
- Sanitarian worker
- School bus driver
- Securities broker
- Security clearance; loss of ability to get clearance for many jobs
- Sheet metal work
- Social work or counseling
- Solar, heating, and cooling professions
- Teacher
- Tobacco distributor
- Veterinarian
- Watchman
- Wild animals; license to possess, exhibit, or sell
- Workers' compensation commissioner

Additionally, a felony conviction may result in loss of employment by the federal or state government, or by entities licensed by the government such as some jobs in casinos.

In addition to restrictions on career positions, a felony also restricts volunteer activities. A felony creates ineligibility to serve as an officer, director, or trustee of a charitable organization. Acceptance into advanced educational programs such as medical school is much more difficult, and sometimes impossible.

A felony conviction makes the road to recovery much more difficult, increases the risk of reoffending, and minimizes the chance that the individual will be self-supporting or will be able to successfully support his or her family.

Is there any legitimate way to justify these penalties for low-level drug users, particularly when studies show that they result in higher cost to taxpayers and higher rates of addiction and crime for those whose opportunities have been destroyed by these penalties?[223] Decades of evidence show that harsh punitive penalties increase recidivism for people who are at low risk to reoffend or have needs related to substance use disorder or mental health issues.[224]

States are beginning to recognize the harm caused and the wasted resources created by felony convictions for drug possession. In 2014, Proposition 47 in California reclassified drug possession from a felony to a misdemeanor and applied the new legislation retroactively, allowing those who'd received felonies for drug possession to apply for resentencing or reclassification.[225] In California, state and local prison populations have declined, saving an estimated $68 million in the first year alone.[226] Some of the savings were used to award grants to local governments for mental health treatment, crime prevention programs, and victims' services.[227]

Other states have also reclassified all drug possession from a felony to a misdemeanor, and it's likely that others will follow. Specific requirements vary from state to state ranging from weight thresholds on amount in possession to number of prior arrests.[228]

CHAPTER 17

BARGAINS OR BARS? THE WAR ON RIGHTS

"Our entire criminal justice system has shifted far away from trials and juries and adjudication to a massive system of sentence bargaining that is heavily rigged against the accused citizen."

—WILLIAM YOUNG, CHIEF JUDGE, U.S. DISTRICT COURT, MASSACHUSETTS, U.S. V. RICHARD GREEN (2004)

"A jury trial of your peers? The right to dispute evidence against you? The right to confront those accusing you? The right to show extenuating circumstances? Silly defendant. You obviously don't know how the system works. We don't have time for all of that. You do have the right to demand a trial, but did I mention that additional charges may be filed against you if you don't accept this plea agreement? Have you looked at the maximum penalty for what you're charged with? That pill in your pocket could carry seven years. If you go to trial, we'll convince that jury that you need to be behind bars for a long time. Do you really want to risk years in prison?"

Many U.S. citizens believe that when a citizen is accused of a crime, the case typically goes to trial, where facts and arguments are presented and a jury listens and then deliberates at length before making a decision based on evidence presented. We're told as young students in civics class that the law is structured to minimize risks of convicting the innocent. We hear about the presumption of innocence and the requirement of proof beyond a reasonable doubt in order to obtain a conviction.[229]

Approximately 97 percent of all criminal cases in the United States are the result of plea deals. An estimated 1.63 million arrests occur in the United States annually, with over 1.4 million of those arrests for drug possession.[230] If even a quarter of these cases required prosecutors to actually spend time reviewing facts in detail or preparing for trial to prosecute those charges, the court system would implode. Instead of focusing on reducing arrest rates, plea agreements have been used to quickly resolve cases and move onto the next one.

Defendants have a legal right to a trial. Why would so many put themselves in a position of accepting terms offered by a prosecutor instead of going to trial? If there's no trial, rights of due process like the right to a speedy trial, the right to cross-examine, and the right to apply the rules of evidence are lost.

The reason that nearly all defendants accept plea agreements is simple. If you were charged under a statute that carried a potential penalty of years in prison, would you risk taking the case to trial? In most cases, economics and risk make a plea agreement the only viable alternative. Prosecutors are given prosecutorial discretion, with few restrictions at the stage where they decide to bring charges. They want to move cases through quickly, so often charge harshly and then use those harsh charges to negotiate "reduced" penalties. Multiple crimes are often charged, and the criminal code allows for the same act to be charged in a variety of ways.[231] A defendant arrested for possession of one substance may end up being charged with several different counts for that one substance, and charges may be a laundry list of offenses that may, or may not, have occurred. Even a minor arrest can begin a life of being "in the system," with years of frustration, cost, and lost opportunity.

So how does this work in real cases? Police arrived at a home with a warrant for the individual who resided there. Paul was just visiting at the time, but was arrested and ultimately charged with multiple counts based on possession of seven Percocet and a small quantity of pot in his pocket. Charges included possession of methamphetamine, which Paul claimed he did not have. In reviewing the evidence, the defense attorney could find no trace of meth. The prosecutor's answer: "There was only enough on the outside of the bottle for our tests."

The fact that there was no longer any trace left for the defendant to test or any proof that the substance existed did not impact the charges filed. This reference to meth significantly increased risk if the defendant went to trial. Although this charge would likely not be provable at trial, having that charge appear could taint a jury. Would the jury believe that if a charge was included there must have been a reason for it? If that was the case, even if there was no conviction on that charge, chances of conviction on other counts would likely increase.

If Paul was convicted of possessing the seven Percocet, some pot, and a pipe (actions for which he was guilty), he could spend nine and a half years in prison. Per criminal statute, Paul risked five years in prison for possession of the seven Percocet, plus an additional four years due to a previous charge for possession of marijuana. The current marijuana charge added six months in jail, and paraphernalia charges added another 30 days. If the prosecution was able to convince a jury to convict on the alleged meth charges, another three and a half years in prison could be added, for total potential prison time of 13-plus years and total potential fines of $21,500. Would you turn down a plea? The incredibly harsh sanctions for drug offenses leave defendants little choice. These penalties fill our prisons, leave offenders at the mercy of the system for years, and wipe out opportunities for life.

Paul eventually entered into a plea, accepting seven misdemeanor counts, including two years of probation and several thousands of dollars in fines. Despite no proof whatsoever, the meth charge on the record likely impacted decisions later made by the probation officer. The meth charge will also appear on Paul's record, to be seen by potential employers and anyone else who accesses the internet. Many who see the charge will assume that he must be guilty, and will ignore the fact that he wasn't convicted.

The irony of this particular case was that appearances in the process of negotiations were delayed because one of the attorneys in the case had been in a car accident and was on pain medication, which happened to be Percocet, the exact same drug for which Paul was being prosecuted. In this case, Paul had been self-medicating chronic pain. Should Paul have seen a medical provider to obtain the pain medications that he needed instead of getting them on the street? Yes. Might his drug use indicate a substance use issue? Perhaps, but if that's the case, putting him into this system would only exacerbate the issue if there was one. Was it rational for Paul to suffer with threats of extended prison time, felony convictions, and years of probation for that lapse in judgment? As a citizen, a mother, an attorney, and a taxpayer, I don't think so.

In application, prosecutors and probation agents have much more power in our current criminal justice system than the courts, and there are few practical protections for the accused within this system. Resolution of criminal cases and the lives of those prosecuted are largely based on subjective decisions of prosecutors at the point that charges are filed and during plea negotiations.

Prosecutor tactics to obtain agreements can be harsh. Few citizens, until they're in the middle of a prosecutorial nightmare, realize that prosecutors regularly make serious threats as punishment for failure to accept the plea agreement offered. Prosecutors threaten to enhance charges to a higher level with more severe penalties. They threaten to seek more time behind bars for charges made. They threaten to add additional charges that would need to be defended at trial. Take-it-or-leave-it offers with short timelines put pressure on defendants to make fast decisions, sometimes before defendants have even had an opportunity to review evidence against them. Even if they are innocent, these tactics cause many defendants to accept the plea.

Unfortunately, use of these tactics is not the exception. They are used on a regular basis,[232] and have repeatedly been upheld by the courts.[233]

There are few rules that regulate prosecutors in regard to plea tactics.[234]

The U.S. Supreme Court has held that a guilty plea must be voluntary,[235] with the defendant knowing what (s)he's doing, acting freely and knowingly, and voluntarily waiving constitutional rights and pleading guilty.[236] Judges uphold these "rights" by asking, on the record, if the defendant understands the plea, if it was voluntary, and whether the defendant willingly accepts it. All of the risks and threats that led to acceptance of the plea result in "Yes, Judge" answers from defendants asked these questions. Judges have the authority to overrule a plea agreement, but judges understand the system, the glut of cases, and the need for pleas to resolve them. A judge who doesn't work with prosecutors by rubber stamping most plea agreements would be considered a pariah in a well-oiled system that simply processes cases as quickly as possible.

So what's the answer? Lawsuits can continue to debate the legality of harsh prosecutor tactics and potentially restrict use of the most egregious techniques, but the more rational solution is to end the millions of drug offense arrests to free prosecutors to focus on prosecution of rape, armed robbery, assault, murder, and other cases of violent crime where victims deserve resolution.

CHAPTER 18

YOU'D LIKE TO KEEP YOUR HOUSE? THE WAR ON YOUR ASSETS

"A society without the means to detect lies and theft soon squanders its liberty and freedom."

CHRIS HEDGES

The U.S. government seizes more assets under civil asset forfeiture law than ALL reported burglaries combined. 2014 was the first time that law enforcement officials took more property from American citizens than burglars did.[237] The trend continued. Forfeitures in 2017 reached an all-time record, with $8.2 billion in assets seized,[238] while victims of burglary lost an estimated 3.4 billion in assets in that same year.[239] When the risk of losing your assets to the government exceeds the risk of being burglarized, we obviously have a problem.

Your assets are at risk, **even if you've never been arrested or charged with a crime.** Under federal and most state civil forfeiture laws, law enforcement agencies can seize property simply suspected of involvement in criminal activity.

These laws were originally passed to allow for seizure of assets from drug kingpins, but have been applied large scale to individual citizens. Vehicles, cash, bank accounts, and real estate are just some of the types of assets that have been seized. Conviction is not required, nor is there even a requirement that criminal charges be filed to justify seizure in many jurisdictions.

In many cases, there is financial incentive for law enforcement agencies to seize property, since they get to keep a large percentage, supplementing their own budgets. In most states and on the federal level, law enforcement agencies that seize property are authorized to keep from 45 percent to 100 percent of the value of forfeited assets. According to the Institute for Justice report "Policing for Profit," from 2001 to 2014, the U.S. Department of Justice and Treasury Department Forfeiture Funds took in nearly $29 billion. Annual revenue for these funds grew 1,000 percent over the period from 2001 to 2014. Additionally, state and local law enforcement agencies have also seized billions of dollars of assets. A 2019 report assessing civil asset forfeiture solely in the State of Minnesota documented 8,091 forfeitures in 2018, with net receipts from the seized assets totaling $8.3 million.[240]

Could simply being in your car with some cash risk seizure of your car and the cash? Could an allegation of drug use on your rental property result in seizure of your real estate? If police suspect someone who's been in your home of drug possession, could authorities seize your home, force you out on the street, and turn off the power and screw the doors shut? Could this happen even if neither you nor your houseguest or child is ever convicted of a crime? The answer to all of these questions is "yes" in most jurisdictions.

If you own a business that handles cash, if you travel carrying cash, or if you have nice property that would help to supplement a police budget, it's important that you're aware of the risk of civil asset forfeiture and the incentives that are provided to law enforcement to confiscate assets, all authorized by federal and state law.

In most jurisdictions, the property owner does not have to be arrested, go through any legal procedure, or be charged with or convicted of a crime prior to seizure of property. Under federal and many state civil forfeiture laws, law enforcement agencies can seize property simply *suspected* of involvement in criminal activity. Under civil forfeiture law, it is the property itself, and not the owner, that is "charged" with involvement in a crime.

Worse yet, in some jurisdictions, the property is *presumed* to be guilty. It's up to the *owner* to prove that the property is innocent. It can be a tough job to prove innocence. How do you prove a negative? How do you prove that you had no knowledge of, or did not consent to, illegal activity connected to your property? There is no right to an attorney, and it can take years to get your day in court to attempt to get property returned. Paying for a personal attorney becomes more difficult when assets have been seized.

To get assets back, long legal struggles are often required, so in many cases, citizens accept return of half of the seized assets in lieu of the legal battle for return of all assets. Prosecutors also understand that the low burden of proof for civil forfeiture can be easier than pursuing a criminal conviction. In an Arizona case, a property owner was *acquitted* of criminal charges, but still lost her house based on civil forfeiture.[241]

Fortunately, public outcry about the egregious use of civil forfeiture is creating some positive change. There is a trend toward states changing law to require higher standards of proof, a few states have abolished civil forfeiture entirely, and a few states now require a criminal conviction for asset forfeiture.[242] In 2016 alone, at least eight states enacted statutory reforms, and a new case in Pennsylvania held that civil forfeiture is not authorized unless the state passes a statute authorizing continuation of their former practices. In California, effective January 1, 2017, conviction of a crime is now required before cash valued at under $40,000 or other property of any value may be permanently lost.[243]

Despite changes in state law, federal law is still a threat. Even if your state restricts civil forfeiture, state and local law enforcement can still seize property by partnering with federal law enforcement, where authority for seizure is under federal law, and where, in most jurisdictions, federal law enforcement shares the proceeds of assets seized with state or local agencies. This gives incentive for local law enforcement to make a seizure into a federal case. Some state legislatures are now directing where seized assets can go, restricting benefits for law enforcement to minimize conflicts of interest.[244] The new California legislation is a move in the right direction, requiring a conviction in a federal case before state law enforcement can receive a share of forfeited property (subject to the same "under $40,000" cash limit).

In 2019, the U.S. Supreme Court held that the Eighth Amendment barring "excessive fines" applies to state and local governments, and prohibits those entities from seizing assets that would be of greater value than the maximum fine that could be imposed.[245] Despite these positive changes, most citizens are still at risk of losing assets to civil forfeiture. All citizens should be aware of the devastating results of this policy.

The threat of civil forfeiture also increases addiction and overdose rates. The risk of losing their assets is a disincentive for parents or other family members to provide those struggling with substance use disorder with a place to live, or to even allow them to visit. This denies them emotional support that is incredibly important when moving from active addiction to recovery. In many cases, those with criminal records or just coming out of treatment programs, jail, or prison have no financial ability to live on their own—putting parents in the untenable position of turning their children away at a critical time of their lives, or putting their own assets at greater risk of seizure.

CHAPTER 19

WHY DOES THE WAR ON DRUGS CONTINUE?

THE BUSINESS & POLITICS OF PROHIBITION

"Change is never painful.
Only the resistance to change is painful."

THE BUDDHA

With the obvious ineffectiveness of the War on Drugs and the pain created, why does it continue? Unfortunately, the system and entrenched attitudes are difficult to change, particularly when gut reactions can easily lead in the wrong direction. When billions of dollars are at stake, profit and politics intersect to protect status quo, even when status quo is obviously wasting taxpayer money, escalating the issue, and killing people. Twelve primary obstacles block reform.

1. Political Fear

Many politicians are afraid they won't be re-elected if they're not tough on crime. They don't want to risk blame if they support change and something bad happens. Despite the passage of many years, politicians have not forgotten the famous Willie Horton ad that was a turning point in the Dukakis lost presidential bid for president in 1988. In that case, the furlough program under which Horton was released was highly successful. An issue arose with less than one inmate out of every 200 furloughed,[246] but Horton's crime after release was political suicide for Dukakis, who had supported the program. Ronald Welsh, who worked for the US Sentencing Commission in 1988, stated, "Clearly the Willie Horton ad was a very important lesson for politicians. They learned a bad lesson: not to go out on a limb."

Political fear of appearing soft on crime is bipartisan. The effects of bad drug policy including children without parents, trauma to individuals, taxpayer cost, civil liberties violations, and compromised health care for all are seldom reported in the news. Benefits of programs to keep people out of jail or to release them early get little coverage. The headline of one individual who fails is more compelling than all of those reunited with family, building careers, and succeeding. It only takes one individual to reoffend to hit the headlines and potentially compromise a political career or a beneficial program.

The economies of entire communities could be impacted if prisons located in a politician's jurisdiction aren't filled. Billions of dollars are at stake in the industries "serving" prison populations. It's simply easier to continue to use handcuffs and bars instead of evidence-based treatment. It's difficult to stop a moving train, even when it's killing people who step in its path.

Most voters don't realize that punitive policies are much more expensive than health-based treatment, are often ineffective, and exacerbate the issues. They don't realize that prosecution and incarceration or threats of incarceration make those needing help hesitant to come forward. Voters don't hear about the risk of transforming nonviolent drug offenders into lifelong wards of the state either in prison or financially due to lack of opportunity. Voters don't know that this "War" compromises their safety and puts them in danger due to escalation of drug cartels and other crime related to sale of illegal drugs.

Messages from constituents who often don't have the benefit of expertise on a topic are typically mixed and based on emotion. Politicians can always find constituents who want a tough-on-crime approach, and historically, that has been the safest position for legislators. Unfortunately, this continues incredibly bad policies that escalate, rather than solve, issues of addiction and overdose.

2. Prosecutor Lobbies

In many jurisdictions, prosecutors are elected, so the same political pressures that apply to other politicians apply to them. Additionally, severe penalties make prosecutors' jobs easier, promoting acceptance of plea agreements that eliminate work and wipe out the risk of loss at trial. Threats of additional drug charges provide leverage to negotiate harsh plea agreements. Long sentences and the potential for mandatory minimum sentences make the risk and cost of trial prohibitive for most defendants, making is easier for prosecutors to get the plea and move onto the next case.

Prosecuting attorneys associations on the state and federal levels are powerful lobbying groups. When prosecutors lobby to maintain harsh sentencing, they're typically not interested in the appropriate sentence for a specific crime, but rather penalties giving them room for bargaining to incentivize "successful" plea agreement negotiations. These organizations have historically been powerful and successful opponents to criminal justice reform, including lobbying against reduction or termination of mandatory minimum sentencing.[247]

In the book *Prisoners of Politics: Breaking the Cycle of Mass Incarceration*, author Rachel Elise Barkow states, "So criminal statutes become like sticker prices on cars. No one thinks of them as the real price; they are just there to start the bargaining. But for that dynamic to work, prosecutors need to get legislators to set the initial price high."[248] This tactic may make sense for the prosecutor, but as a family member who has read the maximum penalties for minor drug offenses with a sinking heart, and as a mother who lost sleep worrying about losing a son to prison for having a few pills in his pocket, the downside of these tactics are personal to me. The anxiety levels of individuals already struggling with health and other issues skyrocket while the criminal justice system sluggishly plays with their lives. These practices are inhumane, ineffective, and unfair.

Resolution can vary greatly from person to person. Those with mental health issues or who simply aren't likeable or aren't effective on a witness stand can be at a disadvantage. Low-level offenders also have little information to use in leveraging negotiations, so low-level offenders sometimes receive harsher sentences than those more heavily involved who can provide evidence on suppliers or others.

The trauma and stress involved for a defendant can also trigger relapse in individuals who are in successful recovery, but are being subjected to charges from an earlier time due to prosecutorial delay in bringing charges.

There are exceptions. Some prosecutors understand the long-term damage that can be created by our system of dealing with drug prosecution, particularly with low-level possession cases. They see the revolving door of prosecution, incarceration, release, and then return to the system. The recidivism rates have been attributed by many to the stigma, trauma, and lost opportunities that come with time behind bars and a criminal record.

Some prosecutors go out of their way to work with defendants to find treatment in lieu of criminal charges, giving them opportunity without the obstacles of criminal records. Adam Foss, a former criminal prosecutor in Boston and TED speaker[249], founded the nonprofit organization Prosecutor Impact to support prosecutors in improving community safety by working with individual defendants and ending the revolving door that so often happens with a strictly punitive approach. Other prosecutors, including the prosecuting attorney in King County, Washington, which includes Seattle, have stopped filing criminal charges in personal drug possession cases. (See # 24—De Facto Decriminalization—Some Police Know Best)

Many other groups have vested interests in maintaining the War on Drugs and the mass incarceration it creates.

3. Law Enforcement Lobbies

Law enforcement lobbies have actively promoted continuation of the War on Drugs.[250] Fourth amendment protections against search and seizure are largely extinguished by the War on Drugs. An assertion of the smell of cannabis allows police to search your vehicle or to knock on your door and then break it down if they hear noise that could be deemed to be hiding evidence. The Supreme Court upheld these practices in a 2011 case.[251] For as long as drug possession is illegal, law enforcement's authority of search and seizure is broad. It's no surprise that they would like to retain this power.

Monetary considerations also promote law enforcement's desire to maintain current drug policy. Prison guard and other law enforcement unions support continuation of harsh drug policy and building more prisons to protect members' jobs. In 2018, the New York State Correctional Officers and Police Benevolent Association mounted an ad campaign against criminal justice reform in that state. The New York City Patrolmen's Benevolent Association campaigned against parole reform.[252] The California Correctional Peace Officers Association spends approximately $8 million annually on lobbying to defeat criminal justice reform, ranging from opposition to reform of three strikes laws to prison expansion.[253]

The total amount spent on lobbying by law enforcement is difficult to track. There are more than 18,000 different police departments in the U.S. alone, and records for lobbying are different for public unions vs. other organizations. It is clear that law enforcement exerts power over legislators, through lobbying and using other methods including providing expert opinions to politicians. Legislators are sometimes afraid of political backlash if they vote against measures not supported by law enforcement. What politician doesn't like standing on a stage surrounded by officers in uniform?

4. Government Contracts with Private Prisons

Criminal justice reform threatens private prisons and other businesses profiting from mass incarceration. Privatization, in many instances, is a good way to bypass the costs of government bureaucracy and to minimize costs to taxpayers. Privatizing prisons is not one of those instances. When privatization results in incentives to put people behind bars in order to fill beds, and then prisons operate from exclusive contracts creating monopolies victimizing people who are literally held captive, privatization is immoral.

State and federal government contracts with private prison companies offer guaranteed minimum occupancy rates, often from 85 to 100 percent, for extended numbers of years.[254] If occupancy rates are not met, government bodies incur fines. The same bureaucrats responsible for meeting these minimum occupancy rates also have influence over law enforcement decisions made by police and prosecutors. This conflict of interest and these contracts create significant disincentives for criminal justice reform, particularly when that could mean reductions in our current mass incarceration rates. Direct financial penalties exist if prisons are *not* filled. Not only are private prison lobbies involved in promoting the status quo, but those who are lobbied have a direct conflict of interest based on the penalties faced by the government if prison populations are reduced.

The level of money involved in the business of incarceration also increases the risk of corruption. Just one example is the "Kids for Cash" scandal in Pennsylvania, the basis for a 2013 documentary film. In that case, two judges were convicted of taking millions of dollars of kickbacks from the builder of two private juvenile detention centers. They were paid for contracting with the facilities and imposing harsh sentences on juveniles for minimal infractions to fill the private detention centers. That case resulted in at least one suicide by a minor who was incarcerated for a minor offense.

Although Kids for Cash was an especially grievous case, the potential for payoffs to make the "right" decision to incarcerate defendants exists because of the high profits involved, and the low risk of getting caught for decisions that are deemed to be discretionary. The judges in the Kids for Cash scandal were extreme, but we'll never know how many individuals end up behind bars because decisions are tainted by opportunities for profit—legal or otherwise.

The challenges with use of private prisons were so egregious that, in 2016, the U.S. Department of Justice issued a memo to the acting director of the Bureau of Prisons directing "as each private prison contract reaches the end of its term, the bureau should either decline to renew that contract or substantially reduce its scope." Unfortunately, in 2017, the Justice Department announced that it would once again use private prisons. Only six percent of the 2.2 million federal prison population is held in private prisons on the federal level, but prisoners are still impacted, and this policy reversal indicates unwillingness on the part of the federal government to correct issues with this policy.

When profit motive enters the field of incarceration, incentives for quality are upside down, with cheap food, poor medical care, low-paid and untrained staff, and overall substandard conditions benefiting the providers. Those profiting from the business of incarceration have good reason to lobby for mass incarceration. Massive profits allow for fee sharing with those awarding the contracts or establishing mandates requiring inmates and their families to use their services if families want to maintain contact and support. Prison privatization is a recipe for human rights violations.

CoreCivic and the GEO Group are two of the largest private companies now running prisons, responsible for operating more than 170 prisons and detention centers. CoreCivic was previously Correction Corporation of America (CCA), and rebranded itself amid growing scrutiny of the private prison industry. According to *Mother Jones*, as of 2013, CCA's revenues increased 500 times in the last two decades. A report prepared for the 2011 Congressional Black Caucus[255] reveals that these two corporations cumulatively realized 2009 gross earnings of $2.9 billion.[256]

Private prison corporations are also hedging their bets. Seeing public sentiment changing, CoreCivic and GEO Group both publicly supported passage of the First Step Act, which was signed by President Trump in 2018 and which authorizes $375 million in expanded post-prison services. Perhaps it's possible that they truly want prison reform, but the more likely motivation is their entry into the business of post-prison rehabilitation. In 2017, GEO bought one of the largest providers of residential re-entry centers (halfway houses) in the U.S., and CoreCivic owns dozens and has told investors that they will be buying more.

Should we be thankful that the private prison industry is on the right side of reducing mass incarceration, or should we be wary of housing those released in facilities owned by those who've profited from the incarceration of those same individuals? It will be interesting to see if past citations for cutting costs and quality of care continue in re-entry housing. It will also be important to assess the impact of government contracts with re-entry providers. Will government guarantees or other contract terms impact the quality of services or lengths of stays required in transitional housing to assure profits for these companies?

5. Private Probation Companies

Over 1,000 courts in the United States contract with for-profit companies to supervise those on probation. This sounds like a great deal for the courts. Probation companies offer their services at no cost to the court, county, or municipality in exchange for the right to collect fees from the probationer, on the condition that incarceration is a penalty for nonpayment. Probationers are required to pay the companies for their services with little oversight by the courts. Most courts don't track fee collection, and have no idea how much probation companies collect in fees from those they supposedly "supervise."[257]

Many of the "offenders" are guilty of minor misdemeanors that have no threat of jail time for the offense itself, but risk jail every month if they can't afford to pay fines or the fees charged by the probation company. There are constitutional restrictions on this, but in practice they often do little to protect the probationers. (See # 15 The Ultimate Nanny State—The War on Freedom.) A report done by Human Rights Watch[258] described patterns of abuse by private probation companies, ranging from acting like abusive debts collectors to escalating fees until payment is impossible and results in incarceration or an extension of probation, resulting in yet more fees. An inherent conflict of interest exists. Companies have incentive to keep individuals on probation for as long as possible to continue the company's income stream.

Georgia is the U.S. state with the largest number on private probation. According to calculations made in the Human Rights Watch Report[259], estimated minimum total annual revenue collected by probation companies in Georgia alone is approximately $40 million.

The most egregious aspect of probation fees that result in incarceration for nonpayment is that these fees and the threats and criminal sanctions that result from inability to pay are essentially a tax on the poor, backed by the power of the criminal justice system.

6. Bail Bond Companies

Most people believe that, to be put behind bars, you must be convicted of a crime. In truth, hundreds of thousands of Americans are incarcerated simply because they're too poor to pay bail. If paid, while awaiting processing of a charge, they are released. If not paid, they sit in jail. This often leads to loss of jobs, further financial and family hardship, and overall trauma. It also leads to waiver of rights and guilty pleas in exchange for immediate release, regardless of actual guilt.

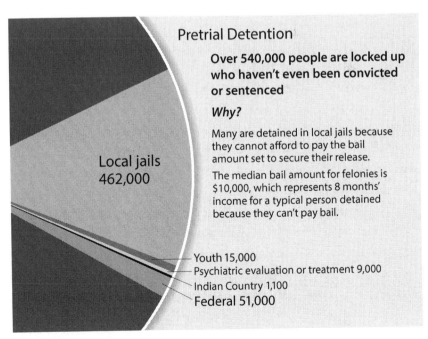

Pretrial Detention

Over 540,000 people are locked up who haven't even been convicted or sentenced

Why?

Many are detained in local jails because they cannot afford to pay the bail amount set to secure their release.

The median bail amount for felonies is $10,000, which represents 8 months' income for a typical person detained because they can't pay bail.

Local jails
462,000

Youth 15,000
Psychiatric evaluation or treatment 9,000
Indian Country 1,100
Federal 51,000

Reproduced/adapted with permission from Prison Policy Initiative [260]

On average, each day one-fifth of the U.S. jail population is behind bars awaiting trial without having been convicted of a crime because they can't financially pay their bail or afford to pay a bail bondsman. Arguments have been made that bail is necessary to ensure that defendants return to court, but studies have found no evidence to support this argument.[261]

States are finding other alternatives, or are completely eliminating cash bail. Unsecured bonds that would be due if a defendant failed to appear have proven to be as effective as traditional bail bonds.[262] Simple reminders have been more effective than bail bonds in promoting court appearances. Text messages have reduced failures to appear by close to 50 percent, saving millions in taxpayer dollars otherwise spent in holding people behind bars.[263]

Bail policies continue partly because of lobbying by the profitable bail bond industry, which underwrites tens of billions of dollars in bail bonds each year.[264] The bond company agrees to pay the full cash bond amount if the defendant fails to appear in court, for which defendants are charged a fee (typically 10 percent of the full bond amount). The fee is non-refundable, even if charges are dropped and regardless of whether the defendant is ultimately convicted of a crime or is innocent.[265]

As states begin to reform bail bond laws, the bail bond industry has fought back. The American Bail Coalition has used the services of the American Legislative Exchange Council (ALEC), an organization composed of lawmakers and corporations that drafts state legislation to serve their members' interests. ALEC has promoted legislation throughout the United States to protect and expand the bond industry and the bail bond companies. The American Bail Coalition has lobbied for multiple model bills, including one that would authorize some courts to require bond as a condition of early release from prison.[266]

Financial interests often create a one-step-forward, two-steps-back scenario. As legislation recognizes the issues of mass incarceration, the failure of the War on Drugs, and the unfairness and ineffectiveness of specific policies like bail bond, the companies that have been built on these horrific policies put great effort into protecting their turf.

7. Drug Testing Companies

Drug testing is far more prevalent in the U.S. than in other countries, largely because of an executive order signed by President Ronald Reagan in 1988 leading to legislation requiring federal employees and some federal contractors to be drug tested. Large companies followed suit, with the trend continuing to medium to smaller companies.

This, in turn, created a new industry and the economic and political pressures inherent with that, made up of drug test manufacturers, consulting and law firms specializing in development of drug testing policies and procedures, and labs carrying out testing. These companies serve a legitimate purpose, as do companies supplying services as part of the criminal justice system. It's important, though, that economics don't control public policy when science and historical results don't support that policy. Hopefully, as a society, we will continue to objectively assess best practices and act based on those findings. (See # 14, Liquid Gold—The War on Dignity.)

As drug testing has expanded to be required by treatment facilities, sober housing, physicians, and many levels of criminal justice, the market has grown to include companies offering drug testing services. As discussed in Chapter 14, approximately $8.5 billion is spent on urine screens and related tests annually. Annual revenues of $8.5 billion[267] can taint decision making and finance lobbying for policies to protect revenues and escalate the demand for services, obscuring rational analysis of the degree to which testing actually achieves goals.

8. Lobbying from Other Businesses Profiting from Mass Incarceration and the Continued War on Drugs

According to a 2018 report by the Corrections Accountability Project[268], over 3,100 corporations profit from the jail and prison system in the United States.

Eight percent of the U.S. prison population is held in private prisons, but private companies have found other ways of profiting from mass incarceration including provision of medical care, transportation, phone and communication services, and money exchanges. These services are offered in public prisons and jails, as well as part of private prisons.

According to the Corrections Accountability Project, the entire prison industry including food service, canteen and commissary sales, financial transactions, inmate health care, phone service, transportation, and other services because of incarceration generates $34.4 billion in annual revenues for private companies.[269] Lobbying, delay in criminal justice reform, and economics and politics of the drug war can seem theoretical. For me, it's personal. I've felt, firsthand, the impact of businesses whose profit centers are based on keeping sufficient numbers of people behind bars.

Services Connecting Families with Those in Jail or Prison

PHONE SERVICES

I thought my son was on his way home from work. I'm sleeping when the phone rings. It's a recording, telling me I have two minutes to insert a credit card number if I want to speak with him. My mind goes blank, as I race down the stairs in hopes that I can grab my purse, find the card, and insert it before my time expires. Although this sounds like a kidnapping scene out of a bad movie, it was reality for me—and the call was from an auto-dialer—operated by a company subcontracting with the county jail.

After the initial shock of this experience dissipated, my thoughts went to those parents who don't have a credit card, or don't have credit available—and thus have to ignore that phone call while they worry about their child behind bars, and the fact that finances prevented them from speaking with them, being able to tell them they're loved, or at least finding out why they're locked up. Even more importantly, that missed call may have been a plea for help because a medical condition was being ignored.

For the companies profiting from the War on Drugs, this is just business. For individuals and those who love them, it's agonizing pain—and sometimes, financial torture. Parents choose between maintaining their own financial security and speaking with their children or making sure they have ibuprofen, toilet paper, deodorant, or shampoo. These costs often follow legal fees, fines, and/or costs of medical treatment for substance use or other ongoing medical issues that frequently accompany or lead to addiction.

FCC regulations that limit exorbitantly priced prison phone calls went into effect in 2016, but after five prison phone providers filed petitions challenging the FCC decision to cap the rate charged for phone calls, the ruling was overturned, leaving the companies free rein to charge whatever they want to.

FAMILY VISITATION

Studies have consistently shown that continued contact with family significantly lowers recidivism rates and increases success rates of transitioning back into normal life after release. A 2012 study by the Vera Institute reported, "Incarcerated men and women who maintain contact with supportive family members are more likely to succeed after their release. . . . Research on people returning from prison shows that family members can be valuable sources of support during incarceration and after release. Prison inmates who had more contact with their families and who reported positive relationships overall are less likely to be re-incarcerated."[270]

With these studies in mind, it would be beneficial public policy to promote inmates' continued relationships with family. In reality, the system makes continued contact difficult in many ways. Some jurisdictions allow only one visit per week. Others limit time of any one visit to a half hour or less, which is particularly problematic if the inmate is placed in a prison far away from the family's location. According to the October 20, 2015 Prison Policy Initiative, 63 percent of inmates in state prison were incarcerated over 100 miles from their families. It would be nice if this would change based on provisions of the First Step Act, which requires the bureau of prisons to try to place prisoners within 500 driving miles of their primary residences. For many families, however, 500 miles might as well be 50,000, especially when combined with other prohibitions on visitation, ongoing expense of supporting their loved ones behind bars, and living without income generated by the incarcerated family member.

Some jurisdictions require visitors to provide their social security numbers, and still others charge fees for background checks run on visitors. In most jails and prisons, anyone with a felony is prohibited from visiting. These rules can isolate already traumatized inmates. With drug possession charges, these aren't hardened criminals. In many cases, they're scared young adults who desperately need emotional support from family and other loved ones.

While monitoring visitors is necessary for security purposes, many of the restrictions appear to simply be based on historical procedures, established prior to studies proving the importance of contact. For-profit service providers have huge motivation to maintain these rules, to keep inmate numbers high, and to promote methods of family contact requiring their services. Contracts with government entities sometimes provide for kickbacks to the jail or prison. This incentivizes policy decisions that favor the private service providers.

Families are significantly impacted by inmate services provided by private companies. Fees for phone calls, electronic messages (similar to email, but with restrictions), video visits, canteen, or other services can be enormously expensive, to the point that cost can be a disincentive for families to keep in contact with inmates. For some families, cost can simply make continued contact on a regular basis impossible.

BANKING SERVICES

Private companies managing canteen funds charge for each deposit made into an inmate's account. Many jails and prisons limit weekly amounts that may be deposited, ensuring payment of the minimum percentage due with each deposit. In some cases, after the fee paid to the "management" company, the state may take another percentage for court fees. In some cases, a percentage will be placed in a mandatory savings account that will be given to inmates upon release, but all interest generated from accounts during the period of incarceration goes to the state. The overall result can leave families paying large fees just to get a percentage of what's paid to the inmate. In many cases, fees punish families rather than inmates. Due to the exorbitant costs paid to "prison bankers," family finances are put at risk, or families limit contact or support of their incarcerated family members.

In 12 years, JPay, a private company based in Florida, says it has grown to provide money transfers to more than 1.7 million offenders in 32 states, or nearly 70 percent of the inmates in U.S. prisons. *Time* magazine, in its September 2014 article entitled "Meet the Prison Bankers Who Profit from the Inmates," reported, "For the families of nearly 40 percent of those prisoners, JPay is the only way to send money to a loved one. Others can choose between JPay and a handful of smaller companies, most of them created by phone and commissary vendors, to compete with the industry leader. Western Union also serves some prisons. JPay handled nearly 7 million transactions in 2013, generating well over $50 million in revenue. It expects to transfer more than $1 billion this year."[271] In a document obtained by *The Huffington Post*, JPay reported total revenue increasing from $30.4 million in 2011 to over $70.4 million only three years later.[272]

Profit motive creates important incentive and competition in areas of society where consumer choice is an option. Incarcerated individuals and their families have no choice, and are forced to pay whatever private companies demand. The only option available is to lose contact with one another—a result that has proven to increase recidivism rates and issues with re-entry into society. Our current system is trading profit for public safety and human rights.

E-MESSAGING SERVICES

Electronic messaging services are similar to email with the exception of the poor quality, restrictions, and lines to use services. There are no caps on fees that can be charged for video or electronic messaging services. In a letter to the FCC concerning profit-based prison communication services, the Human Rights Defense Center disclosed that Securus, one of the three biggest companies that provides these services to prisons and jails, boasted in its 2015 prospectus to investors that it is "expanding into unregulated areas of prison and jail communications in order to increase its profits."[273]

In normal life, email services are free. It's understandable that access to outside email could create challenges within a prison setting and that some cost may be required for secure systems and for monitoring. What actually happens has become a huge and highly lucrative business, not only for service providers but for jails and prisons as well. In 2014, more than 14.2 million messages were sent over JPay's service. Many prisons receive in the range of five percent as a commission. This would generate $710,000 in revenue from electronic messaging alone.[274]

JPay, the largest prison services company, charges a fee not only based on each email, but for each page of writing. Pictures and videos create an additional charge. Charges fluctuate, with fees typically increasing prior to events like Mother's Day. With no competition, inmates and their families typically pay whatever is required if they want to stay in contact.

Prison e-messaging services have also paved the way for barriers for other options. Some jails and prisons no longer allow greeting cards or other forms of mail, requiring e-messaging instead.

Service companies benefit from policies that cut families off from traditional visits and other ways of connecting with their incarcerated loved ones, since that incentivizes those families to pay whatever is asked. Companies maintain their monopoly on whatever services are offered. If a family opts not to pay for e-messaging services, it's likely that they'll use phone services, for which they'll pay Securus, JPay's parent company.

VIDEO VISITATION

Video visitation has become popular, and in many county jails, is the only method of visitation allowed. In many facilities, even when parents visit the location, they see their son or daughter only through a video monitor. Inmates in these circumstances may not physically see their families for the entire period of their incarceration.

Setup for video visitation can also be cumbersome, and dependability can be tenuous. Missing scheduled visits due to technical issues can be distressing for families and inmates, and may "use" one of the visits allowed, regardless of whether it works.[275]

The ABA Journal, in an article entitled "Is Video Visitation Helpful or Harmful for Prisoners and Their Families?"[276], reports, "In tandem with contracts made with prison video companies, some jails have eliminated in-person visits, which risks disconnecting inmates from society even more. A 2011 Minnesota Department of Corrections report found that in-person visitation greatly decreased the risk of recidivism. Similarly, after an Austin, Texas, jail adopted a video-visitation-only policy, inmate-on-inmate assaults rose 20 percent and inmate-on-staff assaults doubled, according to the Texas Criminal Justice Coalition."

Slate.com conducted research on the impact of visitation on inmates. Several of the inmates interviewed for that research said that visitation was the first time in a long time that they'd interacted with loved ones while sober. The report concluded that visitation was not only beneficial for the inmate, but also for the family, since if the offender's mental health declines while incarcerated, it affects that individual's ability to one day be a better parent, spouse, or employee. Denying ongoing communication punishes the family as well as the inmate.

In addition to issues created by lack of personal contact, the quality of video visitation is also an issue. Audio through the phone set connected to the video monitor is incredibly poor in many cases, and is completely defective on some occasions. When Karen, a mother visiting her son, approached the jail employee responsible for monitoring video visitation and told her that the audio set didn't work, the jail employee shrugged and responded that she knew, and that it had been broken for weeks. When Karen requested a different monitor and phone set, her request was denied. Despite that, the visit was counted as one of her allowed visits.

The quality of the video itself is often very poor, and the background noise in the room filled with inmates waiting for video visits can make quality communication impossible. When this is the only means for families to connect with their incarcerated loved ones, the level of apathy, disdain, and sometimes hostility in staff responsible for those systems can be astounding.

CANTEEN

With no other alternatives available for access to snacks, toiletries, and other items, inmates and their families are at the mercy of private companies and the jail or prison, which typically receives percentages of canteen profits. Those funds, by law in most jurisdictions, must be used for inmate's benefit including maintaining libraries and educational and other programs, but in many jurisdictions, the definition of use of funds for the inmates' benefit has been stretched to include everything from Sheriff's Department retirement parties to golf tournaments.[277]

Upcharges on canteen items can lead inmates and their families to feel like subjects of a shakedown to simply get basic necessities. Jurisdictions vary in regard to what is supplied and what must be purchased. In some jurisdictions, even toothpaste must be purchased, so if canteen funds aren't available, those basic necessities aren't accessible. Some jurisdictions provide the basics, with fees assessed against the inmate, with payment required after release. In some jurisdictions, fees to pay for inmates' incarceration or funds toward restitution to victims are deducted from canteen fees, so, in order to get some funds to an inmate, in many cases, already financially strapped families end up being the ones to pay these fees.

BLATANT CONFLICTS OF INTEREST

Sometimes profits aren't to private companies, but to law enforcement officials themselves. While inmates and their families struggled to cover fees and to forward canteen funds to supplement food available behind bars, in the state of Alabama, sheriffs legally took money budgeted to feed inmates as personal profit.[278] In 2018, the Birmingham News reported that Alabama Sheriff Todd Entrekin took more than $750,000 out of the inmate food budget, and then purchased a $740,000 beach home for himself.[279] According to investigative reporter Conner Sheets (who ultimately won the 2019 Goldsmith Prize for Investigative Reporting on the story) Entrekin "definitely personally pocketed more than $2.42 million since 2011."

The Entrekin finances were exposed by Matt Qualls, a young man who mowed the Sheriff's lawn and noticed that the check in payment was from the "Sheriff Todd Entrekin Food Provision Account". Four days after publication of a news story about the Alabama law allowing sheriffs to keep "excess" funds from the inmate food fund and quoting Qualls, he was arrested on drug trafficking charges based on an anonymous call and was detained in a jail overseen by Entrekin. An arrest warrant signed by Entrekin stated that over 1,000 grams of cannabis were found in Quall's apartment. Police actually found a container of homemade cannabis-infused butter.[280] The Sheriff's office denied involvement in Quall's case.

This story highlights the insanity of the War on Drugs. The Alabama Ethics Commission cleared Entrekin, (who prioritized his own gain over food for inmates and usurped millions of dollars) citing insufficient evidence of a violation since the practice was legal.[281] Quall ultimately accepted a plea deal that included mandatory drug court, random drug screenings and completion of substance abuse classes (regardless of whether he had a substance use disorder).[282] Whether Quall's case was retribution or coincidental, the penalties or lack thereof in these two cases certainly don't match the degree of harm caused. The War on Drugs is rampant with opportunities for corruption or for overly harsh penalties for actions that hurt no one.

Entrekin ultimately lost his re-election. Civil rights groups are currently suing 49 Alabama sheriffs who have refused to turn over records of jail food funds.[283] Shortly after this story broke, the governor of Alabama announced that jail food funds would no longer be given personally to sheriffs,[284] but there are many ways that mass incarceration created by the War on Drugs benefits law enforcement or their departments.

OTHER PRODUCTS AND SERVICES

The list of items for which prisoners and their families are charged goes far past those listed here. Imagine something needed by an inmate, and there's likely a company selling it to them at highly inflated prices.

Businesses profit from the War on Drugs and the mass incarceration it has created in many cases without competition. This is the essence of corporate welfare. These profits are based on lobbying for beneficial treatment, monopolistic contracts, and maintaining policies that destroy lives, on the backs of families already suffering and in financial distress. The War on Drugs, the profits made from it, and the disincentives to resist change are not just unethical. They are unconscionable.

After being required to overpay for daily necessities, inmates spend their time working for pennies an hour, creating further profits for those who are incentivized to maintain this system that's so lucrative for them.

9. Cheap Inmate Labor Provides Financial Incentives for Incarceration

Department of Corrections business deals based on prison labor are a billion-dollar industry.[285]

Prisoner work is not the issue. Learning skills, staying busy, and earning money all make sense for those behind bars and may reduce recidivism rates. The low pay, safety concerns, and overall lack of basic employee rights are problematic. When government and private entities profit from what some call "prison slavery," there's little incentive to end the ongoing supply of cheap labor through criminal justice reform. Using prison labor to cook, clean, and perform other tasks to operate the prisons themselves also helps to fund those workers' continued incarceration.

Some argue that learning skills in prison leads to employment upon release. This may be true in some cases, but in others, restrictions deny employment to released prisoners due to criminal records. For example, in 2018, 2,000 inmate firefighters helped to battle wildfires in California, for which they were paid $2/day. Upon release, these same individuals will be barred from becoming firefighters because of their criminal records.[286]

Inmates working (sometimes by mandate) have no sick pay, vacation, maximum work hours, or safety requirements.[287] Prisoners work for an average of 86 cents per hour,[288] while many families compromise their own financial security simply to continue contact with inmates. Family finances are further impacted to assure basic medical care and availability of personal hygiene items for loved ones behind bars. These policies take advantage of the most vulnerable, while creating profit for the government that holds those prisoners, and for the companies that purchase products and services based on prisoner labor. Additionally, small companies that don't benefit from government contracts are forced to compete with cheap labor available to large companies under contract with the government, but on a practical level, not available to them if they can't afford to retain lobbyists.

Safety issues are also a factor with prison labor since inmates have little power to refuse to perform, even if they see dangerous situations or unsafe working conditions. Cases vary on whether prisoners injured while working with defective equipment have an Eighth Amendment claim for cruel and unusual punishment.[289]

Availability of Workers' Compensation also varies widely from state to state. So, working conditions can be unsafe, and then medical care can sometimes be tenuous. Protections normally offered to typical employees may not be available to prison workers, who are barely compensated for that work.

UNICOR, the trade name for Federal Prison Industries, is the government-owned corporation that employs federal inmates. In 2017, UNICOR employed almost 17,000 federal inmates and sold $453.8 million in goods. UNICOR also employed nearly 4,500 federal prisoners in state settings, selling over $126 million of products generated by prison labor in those settings.[290]

The National Correctional Industries Association (NCIA) employs prisoners serving time on state charges. On the state level, compensation ranges from no pay at all in some states[291] to a maximum of $2/hour in Minnesota and New Jersey.

In 1979, the government created the Prison Industry Enhancement Certification Program (PIECP), which allows some prisoners to work for private companies. Although these prisoners are paid better, costs for room and board in prison are extracted from their pay, so many still receive little for their labor.[292]

The Work Opportunity Tax Credit (WOTC), passed in 2013, gives employers a tax credit of $2,400 for every work-release prisoner they employ. This may sound like an altruistic program that gives prisoners experience and a way to fill time, but it's also a source of cheap labor, with employees who are easier to control, who don't demand health insurance, sick days, vacation time, raises, or days off for leisure or family. Should businesses be blamed for taking advantage of a tax benefit? Probably not, since if they don't benefit, their competitors likely will. The "villain" is the legislation itself, which further entrenches mass incarceration into all facets of economics and society, and increases the numbers of those who would lose money if the prison population declines. This creates incentives to lobby to preserve the War on Drugs, a source of unending supplies of prisoners.

10. Pharmaceutical Lobbies Spend Big Money to Protect Their Interests

Those funding opposition to criminal justice reform have huge financial interests. When you hear a message, consider the source. Pharmaceuticals haven't historically made money from natural plants. Legalization of cannabis could leave pharmaceutical companies on the outside of a profitable business category, while reducing sale of their own manufactured drugs. They're well aware of this fact and have taken steps to protect their interests.

In 2011, pharmaceutical company Insys Therapeutics wrote to the DEA to express opposition to loosening restrictions on natural cannabis.[293] In 2016, Insys' donated half a million dollars to the organization working to defeat cannabis legalization in Arizona. This was one of the largest individual contributions to an anti-legalization campaign in history.[294] The effects of pharmaceutical money can't be ignored. Arizona was the only state with a legalization initiative on the ballot that failed in 2016.

While financing the organization arguing that legalization of cannabis "enriches dispensary owners at a dramatic cost to the rest of the state," Insys developed Syndros, a synthetic THC formulation, patented it, and, in 2017, obtained government approval to sell it.[295]

The issue is not FDA approval of medications if they pass appropriate testing, but the hypocrisy of pharmaceuticals funding campaigns to defeat cannabis reform while creating synthetic versions for their own profit. Parents hearing the ads touting fear if cannabis is legalized don't realize that the source of those messages is not objective science, but pharmaceutical companies whose motivations are based on profits of selling their own drugs.

Government agencies favor pharmaceutical companies over growers of natural plants who don't have deep pockets for lobbying. Syndros is categorized as a DEA Schedule 2 drug, while the plant form of cannabis remains as a Schedule 1. Marinol, another synthetic version of THC, is now a Schedule 3 drug.

Could the variations in treatment of plant forms of cannabis vs. synthetic THC be explained by proof that synthetic THC is somehow better or safer? That is not the case. Synthetic drugs, particularly in the case of cannabis, may be less effective and bring higher risk to patients. The website for Marinol, synthetic THC created by big pharma, states that THC is a natural compound found in cannabis. Marinol's sole ingredient is THC after synthesis in a lab. No CBD, which tends to help to counteract the psychoactive effects of THC, is included in Marinol. Marinol is taken orally, which can also increase the psychoactive effects of the drug.[296] So, after spending money touting the dangers of natural cannabis, pharmaceutical companies profit from sale of synthetic alternatives with no proof of increased safety and indications of potential greater risk and lower effectiveness. The motivations aren't a mystery to ascertain.

The federal government has allowed pharmaceutical companies to create medicine derived from a plant deemed illegal by that same government. While individual lives are destroyed through incarceration and criminal records for smoking a joint, pharmaceutical companies continue to create profit centers by selling those same drugs. Despite legalization in multiple states, 659,700 people were still arrested for possession of cannabis in 2017. That's not just a statistic. Each of those arrests impacted real people and real families. Arrest is an emotional, traumatic, and destructive event, uprooting lives every day.

Cannabis is not the only drug where this kind of hypocrisy exists.

The DEA has recently threatened to categorize kratom, a drug that has shown some success in detox from heroin, as a Schedule 1 drug. (Doing so would not only put more people behind bars, but would minimize research on medicinal uses of kratom.) At the same time, three synthetic drugs have been synthesized using the exact ingredients in the kratom plant, for sale by pharmaceutical companies.

It's not a surprise that the cost of lobbying and of promoting the "evils" of cannabis and kratom are a good investment for pharmaceutical companies.

Pharmaceutical companies have entered the business of addiction treatment as well. While it may seem wrong that the very companies whose marketing put massive amounts of opioids into this market are now profiting from offering solutions to the addiction and overdose epidemic, medications work in treatment and they need to be available. However, even with these positive developments, lobbying and huge pharmaceutical money spent on public relations sometimes overrides individual patient needs when determining treatment protocols.

Alkermes, the manufacturer of Vivitrol (trade name for injection form of naltrexone), has invested heavily in lobbying government to use Vivitrol in lieu of other medications available, in treating prisoners and those under supervision in the criminal justice system. While Vivitrol has saved lives and worked for many, as with other medical conditions and medications, one-size-fits-all is typically a recipe for disaster for those for whom that one size doesn't fit. It appears that the lobbying worked. President Trump's 2018 national strategy to combat the opioid crisis included provisions for expansion of Vivitrol in federal criminal justice settings, excluding other medication alternatives.[297]

Giving preference to pharmaceutical grade medications over other alternatives increases costs and reduces alternatives available to patients. This is one of many examples of the harm created by drug policy based on emotion, money, and politics.

We are beginning to see change. As public opinion favors legalization of at least some drugs, some politicians are gaining confidence in promoting reforms. As potential for legalization becomes more accepted, financial interests favoring those policies may appear. It is essential, as we assess policies, that motivations on all sides are considered. Legislation should focus on solving issues without creating new ones, and must avoid influence by lobbyists and others with financial interests.

11. Resistance from Traditional Treatment Centers and Others Structured to Provide Services Based on Old Models

Addiction treatment is a $35 billion industry. The vast majority of treatment facilities use 12-steps recovery, shown to have success rates of between five and seven percent.[298] Less than half of all treatment facilities in the United States allow use of medications in treatment[299]—the protocol with the highest success rate of all techniques.[300]

With passage of the Affordable Care Act in 2010, more patients with substance use disorder were able to get treatment. The ACA and the Mental Health Parity and Addiction Equity Act of 2008 cover young adults under their parents' insurance plans until age 26, provide coverage for behavioral health, and prohibit denial of coverage for pre-existing conditions, including past detox and treatment. While these provisions were helpful in many ways, they also opened opportunities for abuse and fraud to benefit from insurance dollars now available.[301] Patient brokering, where a third party is paid to bring a patient to a treatment establishment, grew as if on steroids. With families desperate to find help with fast placement, either because of fears of overdose or fear that the alternative will be prison if treatment is delayed, they become easy prey to unscrupulous providers. Relief of finding a bed often overshadows focus on the quality of the provider or matching treatment to the individual needs of the patient.

When huge profits are available, the scenario can become even darker. Unconscionable patient "brokers" have waited for those in sober houses to relapse or in some cases, helped them to relapse, in order to then refer them to a provider to be paid the commission. A few treatment providers have been prosecuted for using treatment facilities and sober houses to keep patients impaired, while selling them as prostitutes.[302]

With the War on Drugs still alive and well, substance use patients who are abused have little recourse. Who will believe them? Even family is told not to believe those with addiction issues, and that advocating for them is harmful "enabling." If they relapse based on poor care or absence of care despite payments made to treatment providers, they're more likely to end up in jail or prison on drug charges than in court testifying against those who abused them. When patients are in fear of law enforcement, they become easy prey, to be taken advantage of by *real* criminals.

12. Those Who Would Typically Advocate for Change Are Silenced

Perhaps the biggest tragedy in the War on Drugs is the silencing of families and others who care about the direct victims of this war. Parents are told that advocating for their children is harmful enabling. Calls to jails or prisons by parents are cut off, sometimes with angry admonishments that the inmate "is an adult." In no other setting does being an adult prohibit others from objecting when human rights are at issue. The deals behind the scenes, the profits, the living conditions, and the lack of humanity occur primarily behind closed doors.

The disabilities of many of the "offenders" prosecuted in this war makes it even more difficult for them to advocate for themselves or for those who care about them to determine what's true and what's not. In many cases, complaints are simply ignored, assumed to be untrue. If families are involved, finances have many times already been decimated by costs of legal defense, fines, fees, and treatment so the time and money required to fight the criminal justice system are hard to come by.

We hear about cult communities who won't allow members to have contact with outsiders. These structures typically make us nervous, with good reason. When those outside of a system aren't allowed to see what goes on "on the inside," potential for abuse is high. This is exactly what's happened with the criminal justice system and some of the treatment industry as it relates to substance use disorder. Parents and other loved ones who ask questions are often shut down, ostracized for "helicopter parenting" or "enabling," with the message that if you ask questions or advocate for someone you love, you could be harming them. And too often, we believe it.

It's true that if we assume all responsibility for another person, it can destroy our own lives and prevent a loved one from building the confidence that managing their own life brings. However, in the same way that someone battling cancer wouldn't benefit from family pulling back and requiring them to find alternatives for their own care, when an individual is in active addiction, asking them to accept responsibility for sifting through and setting up treatment is asking for failure. Whether addiction is involved or not, leaving someone on their own to battle a criminal justice system that is clearly out of control is a recipe for failure that can lead to death, long-term incarceration, or a criminal record that compromises opportunities for life.

If the War on Drugs had been successful, we would have to consider whether, even if harsh, it was the best approach. The reality is that the current epidemic has been *fueled* by the War on Drugs and other government policies. As we shame parents who advocate for their children by telling them enabling is harmful, the government, the giant "enabler," controls every aspect of life for those arrested on drug offenses. These horrible results of the 50-year War on Drugs, combined with what we now know about substance use disorder and how to treat it, clearly shows that the War on Drugs has been a colossal failure.

As I entered the interior of this world through personal and professional experience, the level of destruction became more and more unbelievable, and I became more astounded that these policies have continued for as long as they have. If we, in the United States, saw the impact of these policies in other countries, we would be crying out about human rights violations. Here, they've been right under our noses—but those who truly understand either have no voice, or simply can't walk away from the enormous profit their silence generates.

PART 2

Finding the Fix

CHAPTER 20

CHANGE IS POSSIBLE

"Be the change that you wish to see in the world."

MAHATMA GANDHI

It's apparent that current policies aren't working and that change is essential, but what change would be effective? What *would* work, to help those with substance use issues, to protect the public, and to save taxpayer funds? The short answer is "End the War on Drugs." We're beginning to hear this argument more often. Stating "End the War on Drugs" is now politically correct. What we don't often hear said out loud is exactly what that means. Legalize or decriminalize all drugs. That statement can get funding pulled from your organization. (See # 22, Running the Roadblocks.) That statement could lose you re-election. That statement will raise eyebrows, and whether stated out loud or through looks on peoples' faces, the response is often "Are you insane?"

Albert Einstein's wisdom applies here. "The definition of insanity is doing the same thing over and over again, but expecting different results." It's time we listened to Albert's genius. The carnage of the War on Drugs has been severe. It's time to end it. It's time to recognize that stigmatizing people, denying medications, and filling our prisons has escalated the issue, leaving bodies and destroyed lives in its path. It has destroyed hope and wasted funds that could have been used to provide medical care or been retained by taxpayers to benefit their own families. It has decimated communities, and has made too many parents bury their children. It's time to surrender—and to begin repairing the damage done by these policies.

We're at a unique moment in history. Medical advances have given us answers never before available. Technology now allows immediate sharing of information. Countries worldwide are reassessing overall drug policy. We have long-standing drug policy reform in multiple countries, giving a roadmap to what has worked and what hasn't.

If there's a benefit to the carnage caused by this half century of "War," it's that the public can no longer ignore the destruction. As the misery lands on more doorsteps, public awareness has increased and has begun to open minds. Few believe the War on Drugs has worked. The only questions remaining are when and how to end it, and what policies are needed for the smoothest transition possible.

Will ending the War on Drugs solve all issues and create a utopia? No. If ended with consistent, comprehensive, science-based, and evidence-based policies, will it end the suffering of hundreds of thousands of people, allow those who need help to come forward to get it, and replace fear and threats with compassion and medical care? Yes. If ended by replacing supply from drug cartels with regulated supply from the state, will it minimize use of tainted street drugs and reduce overdose rates? Yes.

Will ending the War on Drugs save taxpayer money and generate new tax revenues while providing much needed medical services to those with substance use disorders? Yes. Will it allow families to focus on helping loved ones to find the best treatment, and to experiment with various treatments to determine what works best? Yes. Will it free pain, substance use, and other patients and their physicians to determine what medical care and what medications work best for that patient, and free pharmacists or other suppliers to fill those prescriptions based on orders from the medical provider who knows the patient the best? Yes.

Will it expand drug research on substances on which research is now prohibited, and find new uses of medications to treat medical issues? Yes. Will police be able to more effectively focus on solving violent crime like rape, murder, armed robbery, and assault? Yes. Will it return freedom and personal choice to citizens? Yes. Will it reduce the power of drug cartels and minimize the destruction they cause? Yes.

Change is never easy, but we've reached the point where the pain of maintaining status quo—literally the death of hundreds of thousands and the compromised quality of life for millions—is more painful than the pain of change.

To move forward, it's important to assess what's worked and what hasn't and to review obstacles that stand in the way of change. It's essential to anticipate potential issues during transition and thereafter, and to design policies to minimize them.

That roadmap is the goal of Part 2 of this book.

CHAPTER 21

LEGALIZATION OR DECRIMINALIZATION?

"Would you tell me, please, which way I ought to go from here?" "That depends a good deal on where you want to get to," said the Cat.

LEWIS CARROLL, ALICE IN WONDERLAND

As jurisdictions have begun to reform drug policies, some have used legalization and some have used decriminalization.

Decriminalization continues to make substances illegal, but eliminates or significantly reduces criminal penalties for drug use and possession. Civil fines, court-ordered therapeutic responses, or other mandates continue to be used in many jurisdictions where decriminalization has been implemented, but jail time and criminal records are avoided.

Legalization makes the use, possession, manufacture, and supply of substances legal, treated like alcohol and tobacco with supply controlled through regulation, rather than by criminal law. Which approach makes the most sense, and which approach is most viable?

Decriminalization is less scary than legalization for many since it only addresses drug use and possession. It doesn't change laws dealing with drug distribution. Decriminalization may be easier to implement than legalization since its scope is narrower, and because fewer legal restrictions block passage. (See # 22, Running the Roadblocks.) As we continue to destroy the lives of drug users through arrest and incarceration while denying medical treatment to many, timing is important. Every day reform is delayed is another day of destruction. If decriminalization can be instituted more quickly, it may be a wise first step.

Decriminalization has one primary and serious flaw. As stated by *The Economist*, "[decriminalization] does nothing to undermine the criminal monopoly on the multi-billion-dollar drugs industry."[303] Not only does this flaw continue to support drug cartels, but it continues the high risk of impurities in street-level drugs, leading to overdose and other health issues. Decriminalization continues to keep drug users in the shadows when they purchase substances. Decriminalization continues much of the stigma that has caused misery for millions of pain and substance use patients and their families. Making possession of a substance legal while continuing to make the transaction to obtain that substance illegal is inconsistent and ripe for legal issues for consumers confused by these inconsistencies.

Some of these challenges have been addressed in proposals to include decriminalization of low-level sale of substances as part of decriminalizing use and possession. This protects the college student handing a substance to a friend from being swept back into the criminal justice system, but doesn't address the more pressing inconsistency and practical issue. If use and possession are legal but distribution is illegal, how do users obtain pure substances with consistent strength, and avoid having to deal with the criminal element in obtaining supply? Street drugs and laws that promote them have been key factors in the overdose epidemic.

If substances are legalized (as opposed to decriminalized), purchase and sale of those substances is also legal, subject to inspection and regulation to maintain substance integrity and safety. Drug legalization can be similar in process to the sale of whiskey. After prohibition, impure moonshine was replaced with alcohol that was and still is licensed, inspected, regulated, and taxed. Do minors sometimes get their hands on whiskey? Yes, and that will continue to happen with drugs, but when legal and regulated, the whiskey and the drugs are from sources without dangerous additives or inconsistencies in strength. In many cases, the impurities in the drugs cause or significantly increase the mental and physical damage. The impurities that exist because of illegal distribution channels, including addition of fentanyl to other substances, is the primary reason for the overdose epidemic.

Evidence indicates that legalization does not increase drug use by minors or adults. Multiple studies have shown that countries with less punitive drug policies had lower rates of drug use than those with harsher penalties.[304] It's apparent that under our current system, minors already have access to drugs, but to obtain them they become criminals and deal with drug dealers who sell impure and uninspected product.

Regulations ranging from age restrictions and use in public to potency and quality standards on distribution can all be considered as part of legislation. Regulations may vary depending on quantities and types of substances, ranging from licensing of distributors to distribution more closely resembling pharmacies.

Tax revenue from legal sale of drugs could be used for services to enhance medical care for all citizens, whether for pain, substance use disorder, mental health issues, or other medical needs.

Many jurisdictions have decriminalized. In regard to cannabis, some have legalized. In some jurisdictions, de facto decriminalization has taken place through non-enforcement of criminal laws, even though laws technically remain in force.

When drug policy doesn't threaten incarceration and other penalties, those with substance use disorders are more likely to come forward to ask for help. Recreational drug users are no longer swept up in criminal sanctions that can compromise opportunities for life. Billions of dollars are no longer spent on punitive, ineffective policies.

For those not involved in drug policy or not suffering at the hands of those enforcing it, legalizing or decriminalizing drugs may seem like a radical idea. The reality is that the horrific effects of drug prohibition have now created widespread support for ending the War on Drugs on an international level. The addiction and overdose epidemic and the apparent role that the War on Drugs has taken in creating it is also causing interesting discussion and developments in international law.

Obsolete policies have lingered far longer than logical, and have stymied implementation of better policies. Tradition and attitudes developed prior to current science and medicine are well entrenched. Change comes slowly, particularly when worldwide politics and policy is involved. Rising death tolls, mass incarceration, and other human rights violations and the overall impact on society are now forcing reassessment of outdated policies. When status quo becomes more painful than moving forward, doors are open to progress.

CHAPTER 22

RUNNING THE ROADBLOCKS

"A long habit of not thinking a thing wrong, gives it a
superficial appearance of being right, and raises at first a
formidable outcry in defense of custom. But the tumult
soon subsides. Time makes more converts than reason."

THOMAS PAINE, COMMON SENSE

The real basis for decriminalization vs. legalization in many countries
has been fear of being in violation of three United Nations treaties
(also referred to as Conventions)[305] that, among other things, prohibit
legalization as an alternative in drug policy reform. These treaties ob-
ligate member countries to establish criminal offenses for production,
possession, and trafficking of psychoactive substances.

The treaties were an initiative of the United States, and followed the
U.S. history of punitive drug policy attempting to control drug supply.
That 50-year experiment has failed, resulting in the outcomes described
in Part 1 of this book, but changing or revoking a U.N. treaty is no small
task. In an in-depth analysis of the Conventions by the international
research organization Transnational Institute[306], researchers concluded,
"Although many government officials admit in private that the
conventions are inconsistent and outdated, they hesitate to do so

190

publicly because of the potential political costs that open dissent could imply for their countries. Thus, debate on the conventions has become a taboo issue. As most countries take their international law obligations seriously, including those derived from the drug control treaty regime, the conventions do represent an obstacle for alternative drugs policies that fall outside of the conventions' limited flexibility and room for manoeuvre."

Countries find themselves choosing between the risk of violating a United Nations treaty or watching drug policy continue to destroy health care, economics, freedom, and safety in their countries. This concern was apparent in a statement by Jamaica's justice minister when he felt the need to justify Jamaica's reformed ganja laws.

He stated: "Jamaica is a small independent country that believes in the rule of law. Given our size and limited resources, our national security and territorial integrity depend on upholding the rule of law in the international sphere, and we have always respected and complied with our international obligations, just as we expect others to do the same. Therefore, in considering any change to the law relating to ganja, it is critical that regard must be had to obligations under the relevant international agreements to which Jamaica is signatory. These agreements place certain limitations on the changes that can be made to our domestic law without violating our international obligations. [It] is important to note that the relevant conventions recognise the supremacy of the constitutions of member states—the obligation to control, restrict and impose sanctions in respect of prohibited activities relating to drugs is expressly stated to be subject to the constitutional principles of member states. This, we submit, provides some flexibility in the treatment of the use and possession of ganja in our local context."[307]

The Conventions do provide various "escape" routes. The 1988 U.N. treaty requires countries to impose criminal sanctions on drug production, possession, and trafficking, but there is no specific obligation in any of the treaties to make drug *use* a criminal offense. The conventions don't require countries to prohibit substances. Commentary to the 1988 conventions[308] clarifies that the intention is not to require drug *use* to be a criminal offense. "It will be noted that, as with the 1961 and 1971 Conventions, paragraph 2 does not require drug consumption as such to be established as a punishable offence." The 1988 Convention does say that member states should consider possession for personal use as a crime.[309] This leaves the question of how one is to use a drug without possessing it, but that is only one of many inconsistencies in treaties, their application, and opinions of U.N. agencies and leadership. The 1988 treaty also provides that member states should consider possession for personal use as a crime but that the provision is "subject to [a member state's] constitutional principles and the basic concepts of its legal system." The 1988 Convention itself included reservations noted by individual countries, exempting themselves from specific provisions.[310]

As the issues with punitive drug policies have become more apparent and created more and more issues, an increasing number of countries have begun to reform policies. Some of the reforms, including use of medications in treatment and other shifts from punitive to health care models, have been justifiable within the treaties. There are, however, limits to the extent to which interpretation of the treaties can be stretched. Legalization and regulation of substance sales by member states typically fall into this category. For legalization to comply, treaty amendments will likely be required, or specific countries will need to claim exceptions based on special circumstances. Simply disagreeing with the punitive approach of the Conventions would not support an exception.[311]

It's possible that the U.N. treaties could be amended. In 1997, the first U.N. World Drug Report[312] stated, "Laws—and even the International Conventions—are not written in stone; they can be changed when the democratic will of nations so wishes it." For many years, even discussing reform was taboo, but as issues have escalated, there appears to be more potential for amendment.

The legalization of cannabis in Uruguay and Canada are likely technical breaches of the treaties. After cannabis legalization in each of those countries, the Vienna-based International Narcotics Control Board (INCB) that monitors treaty compliance issued statements to both Uruguay and Canada that their drug reform was incompatible with U.N. treaties.[313]

Challenges and claims of exemptions have become more prevalent. Harm reduction policies like needle exchanges and safe injection sites, decriminalization of various drugs in multiple countries, shifting from punitive measures toward social and health care responses to drug use, and moves toward sentencing reform and other reforms to protect human rights could all technically be considered breaches of treaties.[314]

Legalization in some U.S. states may avoid treaty violation since the federal government is the signatory on the U.N. treaties, and the U.S. constitution authorizes states' rights. Treaties may be a bigger factor in U.S. federal legislation on cannabis, but if federal law simply defers to individual state law, a valid claim may exist if the policy falls under the provision that treaty provisions are "subject to [a member state's] constitutional principles." The United States carries a lot of weight in the United Nations. The challenge faced by the U.S. with individual state legalization of cannabis could be an impetus for the U.S. to promote treaty amendment or revocation.

If treaties aren't revoked or amended to more closely conform to rational drug policy, tensions could be created between the treaties and the practices of individual countries, causing political friction. This flies in the face of U.N. goals of unity among nations. These concerns, major changes in public opinion on drug policy worldwide, and the extent of issues demanding reform may incentivize amendment of the U.N. Conventions.

There are risks to countries in breach of Conventions. Member states technically risk losing access to international drug supply as a sanction for breach of a treaty. It is unlikely that the U.N. would apply these sanctions since it would create obvious human rights violations, but those sanctions are available under the drug policy treaties. International isolation, trade sanctions, and removal of financial assistance are all risks.

Another driving factor for amendment is that the U.N. drug control treaties are in conflict with other U.N. policies including the Universal Declaration on Human Rights,[315] putting countries in the position of choosing which U.N. policies and agreements to violate. In practice, international drug policy has resulted in human rights violations worldwide ranging from state-sanctioned military operations, death penalties for drug offenses[316], long-term incarceration far out of proportion to offenses, and racial inequities in law enforcement. If countries are unable to comply with conflicting U.N. dictates, as punitive drug policy creates greater and greater issues, it's likely that countries will choose to challenge drug policy treaties instead of breaching human rights declarations.

United Nations' messages on drug policy reform are themselves contradictory. While the U.N. treaties remain in place, various U.N. boards and agencies have called for major drug policy reform. The Scientific Consultation Working Group on Drug Policy, Health and Human Rights of the UNODC, released a 2014 report[317] stating that criminal sanctions are not beneficial and discouraging criminal sanctions for drug use. Nora Volkow, head of the U.S. National Institute on Drug Abuse (NIDA), was part of that group. These recommendations are consistent with a broad and respected group of people calling for drug decriminalization, including the International Federation of Red Cross and Red Crescent Societies, American Public Health Association, the Organization of American States, Human Rights Watch, the NAACP, the American Civil Liberties Union, and the National Latino Congreso.[318]

Calls for drug policy reform have been in place long term. The Vienna Declaration, a human rights declaration adopted by the World Conference on Human Rights, called for drug policy reform in 1993[319], stating, "The criminalization of illicit drug users is fueling the HIV epidemic and has resulted in overwhelmingly negative health and social consequences. A full policy reorientation is needed." The Declaration calls for governments and international organizations, including the United Nations, to decriminalize drugs.

The 2016 United Nations General Assembly Special Session (UNGASS) on Drugs offered an opportunity to amend treaties to replace failed punitive approaches with evidence-based, scientific policies, but they fell far short of that. Despite much discussion and despite support for reform from high-level members, UNGASS failed to make necessary changes.[320]

In 2017, the World Health Organization (WHO), in conjunction with the United Nations, entered into a joint statement expressing support of repeal of laws that discriminate in health care settings. The statement [321] includes a call for "reviewing and repealing punitive laws that have been proven to have negative health outcomes and that counter established public health evidence. These include laws that criminalize or otherwise prohibit . . . drug use or possession of drugs for personal use."

In 2019, the United Nations Chief Executives Board (CEB), which represents 31 agencies of the United Nations including the U.N. Office on Drugs and Crime (UNODC), unanimously endorsed decriminalization of drug possession for personal use, stating that member states should pursue science-based, health-oriented drug policies.[322] The Directions for Action contained in the report address and solve many of the issues highlighted in this book. Recommendations include "a rebalancing of drug policies and interventions towards public health approaches," "providing equal access for people who use drugs to public services, including housing, health care and education," and " the decriminalization of drug possession for personal use."

The U.N. secretary general chaired the meeting. Endorsement for decriminalization of possession and use of drugs was unanimous, making decriminalization the common position for the entire U.N. group of agencies. The endorsement for decriminalization did not extend to legalization or the ability of member countries to regulate substance sales, leaving the criminal element to supply the substances for which possession and use would be decriminalized. Despite that, this endorsement is a huge step toward serious drug policy reform.

The Directives for Action do not override restrictions in treaties, so until treaties are amended or replaced, directives are conflicting, but it is becoming more apparent that the treaties will ultimately either be amended or, with the strong support for decriminalization, more countries may do legal gymnastics to justify pursuing drug policy reform in their own countries.

United States' Prohibitions on Legalization

In the United States, another huge roadblock to legalization exists. Saying "legalize it" out loud, or even suggesting that it should be talked about, can get funding pulled from your organization. It could put you in the crosshairs of the Office of National Drug Control who are directed, per 21 U.S.C § 1703(b)(12), to "take such actions as necessary to oppose any attempt to legalize the use of a substance." This law also places absolute restrictions on funding for any contract or any study that "relates" to legalization. Per this law, studies not biased against legalization are prohibited from being funded.[323]

These provisions jeopardize the objectivity of data collected at taxpayer expense, as well as outcomes that should be based on unbiased research and assessment. In an August 2018 letter to the acting director of the Office of National Drug Control Policy (ONDCP), Senator Mike Bennet (D-Colorado) expressed concerns that the administration was "cherry-picking data to support pre-ordained and misinformed conclusions on marijuana." The director, James Carroll, responded, "You have my full and firm commitment that ONDCP will be completely objective and dispassionate in collecting all relevant facts and peer-reviewed scientific research on all drugs, including marijuana."

That would be a logical way for government to approach data, except that an even-handed approach is illegal under the 21 U.S.C. § 1703(b) (12) requirement that the director shall "take such actions as necessary to oppose any attempt to legalize the use of a substance" listed in Schedule 1 of the Controlled Substances Act. That includes marijuana at this time.

Mandating the director of a government agency to "oppose any attempt" or to pull funding from organizations that are open to a discussion of best drug policy practices would appear to be a blatant infringement on constitutional free speech (in addition to being horrifically bad policy). A country whose foundation is built on free speech, per its own statute, suppresses conversation that includes an obvious alternative on drug policy reform that would reduce street drugs that are killing tens of thousands every year in the U.S. alone. Restricting discussion on studies to include all possibilities is a huge roadblock to stopping the carnage created by current policies. Why is fear so great that we legislatively silence discussion and analysis? These provisions should make citizens suspect the objectivity of government reports on drugs or drug policy.

In researching this book, I found a bewildering vacuum of discussion on the pros and cons of legalization vs. decriminalization. This statute explains that. If I were an organization hoping for funding or simply wanting to avoid the wrath of the Office of National Drug Control, I would stay away from the topic as well. That is the epitome of restrictions on free speech. It's a sad restriction on discussion leading to the best ideas and the best foundation for moving forward to correct bad policy responsible for hundreds of thousands of deaths over the past half century. Until distribution of substances can be regulated, criminal elements will control supply and impurities and inconsistent potency of drugs will continue to kill.

Alcohol is more addictive than many of the drugs to which these treaties and statutes apply. Prohibition to control supply of alcohol resulted in organized crime and in deadly moonshine. The end of prohibition and instituting state-regulated supply saved lives. Tobacco kills many more people than heroin ever will. Our approach to drug policy has been emotional, political, and inconsistent. Status quo is radical. Change is not.

Due to U.N. treaties, we don't have the benefit of comparing results of legalization vs. decriminalization of all substances in various countries. Despite the challenges with inability to control and regulate supply, even decriminalization has proven to be a very positive move forward.

CHAPTER 23

DECRIMINALIZATION
—A WORLDVIEW

"The decriminalization of drug use needs to
be considered as a core element in any public
health strategy."

ORGANIZATION OF AMERICAN STATES, 2013

Change began slowly, but momentum for change is escalating. At this
time, approximately 30 countries have implemented some form of decriminalization. The exact number of countries to be counted depends on
the definition used. Some countries officially continue to criminalize, but
don't enforce their law. Other countries claim decriminalization, but use
other penalties so harsh that there's little distinction between criminal and
non-criminal sanctions. Vietnam, for example, claims decriminalization
while forcibly detaining drug users in prison-like "drug detention centers,
which have been associated with serious human rights violations."[324]

Removing criminal sanctions does not prevent other penalties that can
continue the stigma and the harm. Types of penalties that have survived
decriminalization vary greatly including fines, mandatory treatment or

education programs, driver's license suspensions, community service mandates, travel bans, property confiscation, mandatory reporting and/or drug testing, and termination of public benefits. Statistics on success may be tainted for jurisdictions that have decriminalized, while retaining many of the penalties that occurred when substance use and possession were criminal.

The definition of decriminalization is the absence of jail time, but decriminalization does not guarantee that an offender won't end up behind bars if he or she is unable to pay fees and fines. Decriminalization may also increase the number of guilty pleas since, in the United States, right to counsel does not apply if jail time isn't a potential sanction for an offense, so indigent offenders will likely not have access to counsel.

Decriminalization of cannabis will be discussed under # 25, The Cannabis Experience. First, let's look at the world's experience with decriminalization of other drugs. Drug policy changes constantly, but the following is an overview of some of the policies throughout the world. Clearly, the worldwide trend is toward relaxing drug policy. Decriminalization is no longer an unusual or radical idea.

What's Working? Decriminalization Around the World:

Portugal: In 2001, Portugal became the first country in the world to decriminalize the consumption of all drugs.

After Portugal's liberation from dictatorship in 1974, drug use became a crisis. Portugal initially followed the punitive, criminal approach to the War on Drugs used by so many countries. By 1999, nearly one percent of Portugal's population was addicted to heroin, and drug-related AIDS deaths in the country were the highest in the European Union. A new approach was needed, leading to decriminalization in 2001.

When Portugal decriminalized all drugs including heroin and cocaine, many predicted disaster. Now, nearly two decades later, Portugal's drug policy continues to be an astounding success on many levels, and has become increasingly popular in the country since it passed. Since decriminalization, both the liberal and conservative parties have been in power, and both parties have retained decriminalization because it works.

The contrast between results of drug policy in the United States and Portugal sends a clear message. The United States faces an escalating addiction and overdose crisis that killed over 72,000 in 2018 alone. At the same time, Portugal's drug-induced death rate per capita is 1/50th that of the United States (and five times lower than the European Union average).[325] Drug use has remained approximately the same overall, but has declined among the 15- to 24-year-old population. HIV rates went from 104.2 new cases per million in 2000 to 4.2 cases per million in 2015. Drug prohibition-related crime has dropped drastically.[326]

Portugal's drug policy prior to reform looked a lot like the United States today. Drugs were denounced as evil, users were stigmatized, and criminal punishment was the norm. Nearly half the people in prison were there for drug-related charges. Doctors, psychiatrists, and pharmacists attempted to deal with the flood of drug-related issues that came in their doors, with the professionals risking arrest or scorn for trying to help their patients.

Today, in Portugal, consumption, acquisition, and the possession of less than 10 daily doses of narcotic drugs and psychotropic substances for personal use are punished with seizure of the substance, potential fines, and a visit before a local "dissuasion commission" managed by the Ministry of Health. The commissions are made up of one legal professional and two health or social services professionals. Individuals meeting with the commission can be honest because regardless of the answers, they won't be incarcerated, punished, or end up with a criminal record. This gives authorities the opportunity to share safety information without fear or defensiveness on the part of drug users. The commissions have the authority to refer individuals to voluntary treatment programs or to impose minor fines or other administrative sanctions. The number of people in treatment in Portugal increased by over 60 percent from 1998 to 2011, with nearly three-quarters of them receiving medication as part of treatment.[327]

The foundation of the Portuguese drug policy reform was movement away from the punitive criminal model to focus on public health. João Goulão, the architect of Portugal's revolutionary drug policy, stated. "We realized we were squandering resources. It made much more sense for us to treat drug addicts as patients who needed help, not as criminals."[328]

The foundation upon which Portugal's policy rests would be wise for any drug policy:

1. There is no such thing as a soft or a hard drug—only healthy and unhealthy relationships with drugs.

2. An individual's unhealthy relationship with drugs often conceals relationship difficulties with loved ones, with the world around them, and with themselves; and

3. The eradication of all drugs is an impossible goal.[329]

Decriminalization was part of a larger shift to address drug use through the public health system rather than the criminal justice system. It included a major expansion of treatment and harm-reduction services ranging from access to medications used in treatment, access to sterile syringes, and greater access to vital services.[330] These expanded services were funded through reallocation of funds from criminal justice to public health. In the U.S., approximately 90 percent of funding is allocated to punishment and attempting to curb supply of drugs. Only 10 percent is allocated to treatment and prevention. In Portugal, these numbers are reversed, with the primary focus and funding on treatment and prevention.[331]

Based on Portugal's statistics, approximately 10 percent of individuals attending a dissuasion commission meeting have drug addiction issues, and funding is prioritized to help these individuals, while leaving recreational users alone. For those with substance use disorders, treatment is recommended but not mandated. Free treatment can begin that day, and may last for about a year and a half. Portugal also gives a one-year tax break to any employer who hires someone in recovery from addiction to help them in integrating into society and to increase success rates, with nearly all of these employees retained past the initial year—indicating that rehabilitation is working, creating productive citizens.

For those who don't choose treatment programs, methadone is made available to help them stay off of heroin and to reduce risk of overdose or of contracting a disease from dirty needles. Because individuals don't have to worry about punishment for their addictions, drug users no longer run from authorities since they no longer see the police as enemies. This makes investigating other types of crime easier, leaves resources available to go after real criminals, and enhances the day-to-day experience of police officers.

There have been some criticisms of Portugal's policy. Portugal decriminalized rather than legalized drugs (likely based on U.N. treaty restrictions). Sale of drugs is still illegal and dealers still exist, creating a strange combination since those possessing obviously have to buy drugs somewhere. This policy continues the illegal drug trade and the issues that accompany it.

Additionally, decriminalization didn't segment less harmful substances from others, so distribution of cannabis is still criminal. Despite being ahead of its time on decriminalization of all substances, as reforms regarding cannabis use and distribution have developed, Portugal is now more stringent than some other countries in regard to distribution of cannabis.

Norway: Norway appears to be following Portugal's lead in moving drug policy from the criminal justice sector to the health sector. The Norwegian Parliament authorized the minister of health to appoint a commission to determine how this can be implemented. Target for negotiation and implementation is 2020. Since the health sector is unable to punish people criminally, this means that the intention is for drug possession and use to be decriminalized.[332] At this time, however, drug possession in Norway is still a criminal offense.

Mexico: Possession of small amounts of drugs were decriminalized in Mexico in 2009, but quantities constituting small amounts are low and ambiguous, leading to accusations of police corruption.[333] In 2019, Mexico released a five-year policy document[334] including a plan to decriminalize all drugs, saying that lifting prohibition is the only way to curb drug use and admitting that the current "War on Drugs" is endangering public safety. Under the plan, substances would not be legal, but arrests would be replaced by medical treatment with resources redirected from law enforcement to medical treatment. Location between Canada, where cannabis was legalized nationally in 2018, and Mexico where legalization is in planning stages. may make U.S. lawmakers feel more pressure for reform.

United States: Decriminalization has not happened on the federal level in the United States. However, on the federal level, possession of any drug for personal use is a misdemeanor, provided the offender does not have a prior drug-related offense, in which case it can still be charged as a felony.[335] No drug weight restriction is included in the statute or guidelines.[336]

Several states and Washington, D.C. also treat possession of any drug for personal use as a misdemeanor. Beginning with California's Proposition 47 in 2014, a trend toward defelonization began. These laws continue to change, but possession of any drug for personal use (subject to various requirements and restrictions) is now a misdemeanor in California, Utah, Connecticut, Alaska, and Oklahoma. Laws in these states apply to all controlled substances, and all provide for misdemeanor charges for possession up to the third conviction. All of these state laws prohibit those convicted solely of drug possession from state prison sentences.[337]

The trend toward defelonization continues. In May 2019, Colorado Governor Jared Polis signed a law that will be effective in 2020 that defelonizes drug possession for Schedule 1 and 2 substances.[338] In assessing this bill, the Colorado Joint Budget Committee predicted cost savings from $8.6 million to $13.7 million over five years. Money saved will be used for a grant program to fund new treatment centers.[339] Although defelonization still leaves drug users with stigma and criminal penalties, it is far superior to the use of felonies. (See # 16, The Scarlet "F.")

U.S. jurisdictions with reduced penalties do not have higher rates of drug use. In fact, many states that treat possession as a misdemeanor have slightly lower rates of illicit drug use and higher rates of admission to drug treatment than states that consider it a felony.[340]

Switzerland: In Switzerland, doctors prescribe drugs, and various programs are offered to help those with substance use issues. Free methadone and clean needles are provided. Seventy percent of the 20,000-30,000 opiate or cocaine users in Switzerland now receive treatment. The number of HIV drug users and injector overdose mortality rates have been reduced by 50 percent in the last 10 years.[341]

Czech Republic: Possession of all drugs in the Czech Republic was decriminalized in 2010. [342]

Spain: Following a 1974 Supreme Court ruling, Spain decriminalized possession and private use of small amounts of drugs in 1982.[343]

Italy: Drug possession has been decriminalized since 1975 in Italy, but penalties have varied from harsh to lenient since then.[344]

Germany: Application of law varies between German states, but in 1994 the Federal Constitutional Court held that drug addiction and possession and personal use of small amounts of drugs are not crimes.[345] In 2000, supervised injection rooms became legal in Germany.

Armenia: As of 2008, small quantities of drugs in Armenia are punished with administrative penalties rather than with criminal penalties. However, Armenia is a good example of challenges with decriminalization. Although drugs are decriminalized, fines, even for first time offenders, are 100-200 times the minimum wage, and those who are unable to pay may still be incarcerated.[346]

Latvia, Estonia, and Slovenia all allow possession of small amounts of drugs for personal use, with fines as the only sanctions.[347]

Chile decriminalized possession in 2007, but the law fails to define a personal quantity, so many people continue to be criminally charged for possession of small quantities of drugs.[348] Chile is assessing full decriminalization.[349]

In **Argentina**, in 2009, the Supreme Court ruled that prison sentences for small amounts of drugs for personal use are unconstitutional.[350]

Costa Rica decriminalized all personal drug possession in 1988.

In **Uruguay**, the law does not criminalize drug use or possession of drugs for personal use. (See more in-depth discussion of Uruguay's cannabis policies in # 25 The Cannabis Experience.)

Ecuador's drug policy was impacted by the Andean Trade Promotion and Drug Eradication Act (ATPDEA). In entering into this act in the early 1990s, parties promised to adopt prohibitionist drug policies in exchange for tariff exemptions from the United States. (The logic was to strengthen legal industries as incentive to replace income generated by drug production.)

Ecuador decriminalized drug use in 1991, but continued to prosecute drug possession, leading to significant increases in prison populations. In 2009, clear distinctions on treatment of quantities of drugs were established. In 2013, Ecuador left the Andean Trade Promotion and Drug Eradication Act (ATPDEA), and the act, which initially included Bolivia, Columbia, Ecuador, and Peru expired.

Columbia decriminalized consumption of drugs in 1994, which was reaffirmed by the Supreme Court in 2011. Possession of up to 20 grams of cannabis and up to a gram of cocaine is allowed for personal use, but possession and trafficking is still illegal. Colombia's current president signed a decree in 2018 allowing police to confiscate even small quantities of cannabis or other substances, even if legal, unless the citizen can prove an addiction. Civil liberties groups have objected to these new policies.

Paraguay allows possession of a maximum of two grams of cocaine or heroin, and 10 grams of cannabis for personal possession.[351]

In **Peru**, personal drug possession has been decriminalized since 2003, but harsh police practices in Peru make drug possession risky.[352]

Venezuela allows up to 10 grams of marijuana and up to two grams of cocaine for personal use.

The worldwide trend is certainly toward liberalization of drug policy on all drugs. Decriminalization ends the cycle of incarceration, which can lead to trauma, opportunity-killing criminal records, and overall misery. It's a great start.

Decriminalization leaves many inconsistencies and challenges. What's the threshold between a user and a distributor? How does a legal user acquire the substance without dealing with criminal suppliers? Stigma still applies to drug use, since, despite omitting incarceration as a penalty, drug use continues to be a crime, handled by criminal justice authorities. Drug cartels still control supply, and users are still put in contact with criminals for supply. Users are still at risk of tainted drug supply with no assurances of consistent quality or concentration—the number one reason for drug overdose.

Funds previously used for prosecution and incarceration of small-time users can be reallocated for medical treatment, but the benefit of taxing sale of substances, along with denying profits to drug cartels, is lost. Unfortunately, changing long-held assumptions, defying billion-dollar industries built on the drug war, and establishing logical policies and changing laws takes time. Legalization is the most consistent and rational long-term policy, but a series of steps may be required to implement change. Decriminalization is a legitimate first step.

In some jurisdictions, until the law is changed, it is simply not enforced. In these jurisdictions, drugs have, in a practical sense, been decriminalized. Let's look at this de-facto decriminalization.

CHAPTER 24

DE FACTO DECRIMINALIZATION —SOME POLICE KNOW BEST

"Just Do It"

NIKE SLOGAN[353]

During U.S. prohibition, my Uncle John, the sheriff in a small county in Wisconsin, routinely warned the farmers when the feds would be coming to raid their barns looking for stills. Sheriff John understood that less harm would arise from notifying the farmers than potential confrontations between them and federal agents. He also knew that prohibition would never successfully control supply of alcohol.

History is repeating itself. In more and more jurisdictions, law enforcement is simply not applying what they know to be bad law. In practice, this is the equivalent of decriminalization.

Most people are supportive when they hear about police finding treatment for those with substance use disorder in lieu of putting them behind bars. For years, those same people may have rejected the idea of decriminalizing drugs. Legalization or decriminalization somehow sounds frightening, whereas police who find treatment for those who need it sounds compassionate and effective. Decriminalization is simply putting into law what police are already doing in some jurisdictions. If police compassion is acceptable, legislative policy reforms should be as well. Seeing the benefits of decriminalization is eye-opening, whether based on legislation, court rulings, or law enforcement simply being "done" with enforcing ineffective and harsh law.

As casualties have increased and as the effects of drug policy have entered more of our lives, we're asking the important questions. Public officials are beginning to hear those questions and to look for solutions. One of the most immediate solutions is for the warriors on the front lines to lay down their weapons and begin helping those who are suffering, including the public, substance use patients, and the warriors themselves. Police who've worked in enforcement of the punitive War on Drugs are now helping in applying de facto decriminalization and seeing real progress, and once again feeling like "peace officers" who make a real difference in their communities.

So, how does de facto decriminalization work, and who has taken that approach? Since many instances of de facto decriminalization are not codified and can change based on sentiment of law enforcement, prosecutors, and the public, a complete list of jurisdictions using this approach is not feasible, but here are a few examples of how these policies work.

Netherlands: Contrary to public perception, all drugs are illegal in the Netherlands. In application, de facto decriminalization has been applied since passage of the Opium Act of 1976,[354] which differentiated cannabis from other drugs and reduced penalties to a minor infraction. Despite technically being criminal, possession of up to five grams of cannabis (30 grams prior to 1996) or "one dose" of any other drug for personal use is not prosecuted.[355] Technically, coffee shops commit a crime when they sell cannabis because the sale and possession of quantities for sale are prohibited by the Opium Act, but the Code of Criminal Procedure allows the prosecutor to refrain from prosecution of offenses if that's deemed to be in the public interest. [356]

The U.N. Conventions pose a challenge for the Netherlands. The International Narcotics Control Board states that the Dutch policy of tolerance in regard to coffee shops is not in compliance with U.N. treaties.[357] In response, the Netherlands made an official "reservation" to the treaties, stating, "The Government of the Kingdom of the Netherlands accepts the provisions of [U.N. treaties] only in so far as the obligations under these provisions are in accordance with Dutch criminal legislation and Dutch policy on criminal matters."[358]

The Netherlands has persisted in their drug policy despite U.N. and other pressure, although they have moved in the direction of more restrictive policy over the years.[359] A 1996 change in quantities of cannabis allowed without intervention may provide insight into the effectiveness of de facto decriminalization. The traditional perception of hundreds of coffee shops where cannabis was smoked in public in the Netherlands is no longer accurate. The government now requires coffee shops to choose between selling alcohol or marijuana, and new laws target marijuana growers, creating issues with supply for coffee shops. Growers risk losing access to government housing where more than 50 percent of citizens live. The result has been price increases in marijuana, rise in street dealers and criminal organizations, and decrease in quality and purity of marijuana.

The Netherlands was one of the first countries to use heroin-assisted treatment and safe injection sites, which may be why they have fewer drug-related deaths than anywhere else in Europe. The U.N. Board took issue with safe injection rooms established in the Netherlands, stating that such policies promote social and legal tolerance of drug abuse and drug trafficking, thereby contravening the international drug control treaties.[360] In practice, safe injection sites save lives and protect the public from witnessing injections and finding used needles in public places.

Local municipalities have a lot of discretion in whether to allow coffee shops and their rules of operation, but must file an enforcement plan, so everyone is informed about the local policy and knows what to expect.[361]

As with any decriminalization, whether de facto or by legislative action, the contradiction in allowing use, but not providing for supply, is an issue in the Netherlands. Although policy makers in the 1970s preferred legalization of cannabis, this was not feasible within the U.N.

Conventions, and "reservations" to the treaties were not considered to be an option in regard to supply. The Netherlands anticipated that the treaties would ultimately be amended to give member states the freedom to determine their own policies in regard to cannabis and cannabis cultivation,[362] but to date, that hasn't happened. The issue of legalization and regulation of cannabis cultivation remains an issue in the Netherlands.

Poland: Since 2011, prosecutors in Poland have had discretion not to prosecute small-scale possession offenses or cases where an individual is judged to have a substance use disorder.[363]

United States: Numerous police departments in the United States have begun de facto decriminalization with programs to coordinate treatment for substance use disorder in lieu of making drug arrests.

PAARI—In 2005, the Police Assisted Addiction and Recovery Initiative (PAARI; www.paariusa.org) was created in Gloucester, Massachusetts, to bridge the gap between the police department and those with substance use issues seeking recovery. The Gloucester initiative began changing the relationship between substance users and the police, putting the police in a helping, rather than a punitive role. Under this initiative, anyone who walks into a police station with the remainder of their drug equipment and asks for help is not criminally charged, and will instead be walked through the process to get immediate treatment. Treatment providers have partnered with PAARI to make treatment available. Additionally, PAARI has negotiated agreements with pharmacies to make nasal Narcan, a spray to counter overdose effects, available without a prescription and at little or no cost.

The PAARI program has now spread to police departments across the United States. It costs nothing for police departments to join PAARI, and PAARI offers resources, funding, recovery programs, and information and support for departments who join.[364]

LEAD—In 2011, the Law Enforcement Assisted Diversion (LEAD) program began in a suburb of Seattle, Washington. In a LEAD program, police officers have discretionary authority to avoid booking, detention, prosecution, conviction, and incarceration. Instead, the officer has the option of referring individuals into a program where they meet with a social worker to develop a plan that may include low-income assistance programs, help in locating housing, and medical care including addiction treatment. A study found that LEAD participants were 60 percent less likely to be arrested within six months than a control group of those not participating in LEAD. Over two years, LEAD participants were still 58 percent less likely to be arrested. Additionally, LEAD participants were 39 percent less likely to be charged with a felony.[365]

The LEAD program has now expanded to be the largest organization of its kind, helping police departments throughout the United States to offer community care in lieu of arrest.[366]

Policies described above were instituted by police who were on the front lines of the drug war, and saw that policies weren't working and needed to be changed. If these policies make sense, then isn't it time to consider changing law to institute these policies on a larger scale—where lives of those struggling with substance use disorder don't depend on what jurisdiction they happen to reside in or are arrested in? Changing drug policy away from the punitive model where focus is on law enforcement and incarceration to a treatment-based model would not be a new experiment. The PAARI and LEAD programs as well as actual decriminalization in multiple jurisdictions provide examples of policies that have proven to be successful.

Challenges with De Facto Decriminalization

De facto decriminalization is a huge accomplishment and a testament to the determination of professionals who stepped forward to solve issues that were not otherwise being solved. The beauty of de facto decriminalization is that it can be instituted quickly to save lives and prevent more destruction by obsolete policies.

There are challenges with de facto decriminalization. As long as something is illegal, the risk of selective prosecution always exists, leaving citizens uncertain about the level of security in officially breaking a law that is still in force. A change in police chief or prosecutor could end or change these programs that aren't based on statute or other formal law.

De facto decriminalization continues to put law enforcement officers at the forefront of dealing with substance use issues. It's now indisputable that substance use disorder is a medical issue that should be treated medically. Co-existing health issues further complicate diagnosis and determination of best treatment protocols for each individual. De facto decriminalization programs that allow police to refer individuals to other service providers including medical professionals are a huge step forward. Removing drug policy from law enforcement and criminal justice and officially putting it under the umbrella of public health would reflect the fact that addiction is a treatable health issue. It would remove the stigma that accompanies engagement with law enforcement, it would put medical professionals in the position to treat medical issues, and it would allow law enforcement to focus on violent crimes or crimes with an immediate victim.

In 2018, King County, Washington (where Seattle is located) took a step further than the LEAD program, formally announcing that they would no longer criminally charge for drug possession of under a gram of any drug. Instead, they offer assistance. Individuals are not mandated to accept it, but relationships are built, not out of fear, but based on continued offers of help.

Dan Satterberg, the King County prosecuting attorney who initiated the program, had spent years prosecuting drug cases. He also watched his sister battle a heroin addiction. As he learned more about the science of addiction and looked at his office budget, in 2018, he decided to end the $3 million annual expense of prosecuting 800-1,000 drug possession cases. He'd seen the same people arrested, prosecuted, and then repeatedly recycled through the system. Now, those same people are offered help and the expense of prosecution is saved. Police work in conjunction with the LEAD program is providing needed services. The distraction and expense of criminal defense and the risk of time behind bars is replaced with services that can break the pattern and move individuals toward hope in the future.

The program has critics, particularly since Seattle's homeless population is third in the U.S., behind New York and Los Angeles. Unless the alternative is incarcerating all of the homeless, it would appear that programming to help with medical and drug treatment, as well as aid in finding housing options, would do more to solve the housing issue than money spent on arrest, prosecution, and incarceration. Many housing issues in the U.S. are the result of long-term punitive approaches to addiction and mental health.

CHAPTER 25

THE CANNABIS EXPERIENCE

"Even if one takes every reefer madness allegation
of the prohibitionists at face value, marijuana prohibition
has done far more harm to far more people than
marijuana ever could."

WILLIAM F. BUCKLEY, JR.

The standard for drug policy reform has been decriminalization—until cannabis. Most cannabis reform has been legalization, allowing governments to set up and regulate distribution channels and to tax substance sales. This provides guidance for other jurisdictions in cannabis reform, as well as a foundation for assessing policy for legalization of other substances in the future.

The speed with which public opinion supporting cannabis reform has developed in the United States is nothing short of astounding. According to a 2019 CBS News Poll, 65 percent of Americans now support legalization, including 56 percent of Republicans.[367] This is similar to a 2018 Gallup Poll showing 66 percent support[368] and a 2018 Pew Research Poll that indicated 62 percent approval, compared with 31 percent approval in 2000.[369] In 1969, just 12 percent of those polled supported cannabis legalization.[370] A 2017 Quinnipiac poll indicates

214

that 93 percent of voters support legalization of medical marijuana.[371]

Prior to 2012, marijuana was decriminalized in some states[372] with Oregon the first to decriminalize in 1973. The trend toward legalization of medical marijuana began in 1996 when California passed Proposition 215,[373] but no jurisdiction legalized recreational marijuana until 2012, when Colorado and Washington State began an unstoppable trend. As of 2019, 11 states and Washington D.C. have fully legalized possession and personal use of cannabis, 10 states have both decriminalized marijuana and allow medical use, 16 states allow medical use but have not yet decriminalized, and three states decriminalized but do not specifically allow medical use. Marijuana is fully illegal in only 10 states, and many of them are considering reform. Links and information on the current state of cannabis and other drug policy reform can be found at www.WarOnUs.com.

Drug policy reform can build on itself. As states legalized medical marijuana, predictions of disaster didn't come true. That made politicians more comfortable with supporting reform. Economics played a role too, as state budgets needed tax dollars. Taking those dollars from illegal suppliers and putting them into state funds offered compelling incentives. The cannabis business presented economic advantages to both public and private beneficiaries, with business and job opportunities created. Positive developments with medical marijuana opened minds to legalization for recreational use, which offers many of the same benefits as medical marijuana but on a larger scale. It avoids expense of physicians and solves mass incarceration and other issues inherent with criminalization of cannabis.

Technology and the ability to quickly share information may have helped to escalate cannabis reform. As millennials replace baby boomers in the voting booths, reform becomes easier to pass, and voter pressure on politicians increases. With 72 percent of young adults aged 18-34 in favor of legalization, the trend is clear.[374]

Additionally, the overall topic of drug policy reform reached the forefront as a response to mass incarceration and the addiction and overdose epidemic. Use of cannabis as an alternative to opioids in treating pain and as a method of treating opioid addiction increased public interest and demand.

CBD

The Farm Bill[375] signed by President Trump in 2018 removed hemp-derived CBD from the U.S. Controlled Substances Act, and legalized the cultivation and sale of hemp at the federal level effective January 1, 2019. This legislation makes CBD, an extract from the hemp plant that has few, if any, intoxicating properties, legal in all 50 U.S. states and on the federal level. The bill opened doors to large-scale marketing of hemp-based CBD products. (In 2017, the year prior to passage of the Farm Bill, retail sales for products containing hemp reached $820 million,[376] so markets were already in place.) Forecasters project hemp and CBD to be a $1 billion industry by 2020.[377]

The FDA has not yet approved CBD for medical use. If manufacturers and marketers claim that CBD-infused food, beverages, creams, and dietary supplements are effective in treatment and prevention of specific medical conditions, the products are subject to regulation as drugs. That classification requires prior FDA approval based on clinical trials to establish product safety. Marketers should stay clear of aggressive health-related marketing, and consumers should be aware that the FDA has not approved CBD products for medical use. FDA warning letters have been issued to a number of vendors for making claims, but no enforcement actions have been taken to date.

CBD derived from cannabis, rather than hemp, is still illegal on the federal level and in states that haven't legalized either medical or recreational marijuana. The variation in hemp vs. cannabis CBD and the law surrounding them can be confusing. The difference is based solely on the amount of THC in the plant. Both plants are varieties of the same species. Legally, hemp must contain no more than 0.3 percent THC, the substance with psychoactive properties.

Reports vary on the effectiveness of hemp CBD vs. cannabis CBD, but criminal policies against THC still prohibit patients from determining what is most effective for them. Those on probation who could potentially benefit from CBD are often afraid to try even hemp CBD out of fear that traces of THC could show up on drug tests and cause a probation violation. The result is prohibition of a non-addictive, non-psychoactive substance that could, in some cases, replace stronger, addictive prescription medications used in treating pain and other issues.

Medicinal Benefits and Restrictions on Studies of Medicinal Uses of Cannabis

According to a recent Gallup poll, 86 percent of those who support cannabis legalization say the primary reason for their support is the medicinal benefit.[378] As the addiction and overdose epidemic makes patients more wary of pharmaceutical medications or makes access to other medications more and more difficult, interest in cannabis as an alternative has grown. There is ongoing evidence that cannabis is an effective treatment for pain, chemotherapy-related nausea, and multiple sclerosis-related muscle spasms.[379] Cannabis has been used to treat Alzheimer's, appetite loss, eating disorders such as anorexia, insomnia, anxiety, spasticity, pain, treatment of epileptic seizures, cancer, Crohn's disease, glaucoma, schizophrenia, posttraumatic stress disorder, muscle spasms, and tremors due to Parkinson's disease.[380]

Opinions differ as to the extent to which cannabis effectively treats these medical issues, but evidence is compelling. The challenge is that drug policy has restricted studies on medicinal uses. As a Schedule 1 drug, the U.S. Drug Enforcement Administration (DEA) classifies cannabis as a drug likely to be abused and lacking in medicinal value.[381] Due to that classification, researchers need a special license to study it, minimizing studies. Opponents of drug policy reform then cite lack of studies as a reason not to decriminalize cannabis.

Cannabis is the only Schedule 1 drug that the DEA prohibited from being produced by private laboratories for scientific research. Until 2016, all tests were required to use product from one facility at the University of Mississippi, which is under contract with the National Institute on Drug Abuse (NIDA), an agency mandated to study the harms of cannabis and not its potential medical benefits.[382] In 2016, the Obama

Administration lifted some of the barriers on marijuana research, but the DEA has failed to implement the policy, effectively maintaining the old restrictions on research to date. The DEA has indicated that they intend to increase availability of cannabis for research.

Using only one source of cannabis for research has restricted research data. When the only federal source of cannabis for research purposes is solely from one grow room at one university, research could be tainted by outdated product or product that does not reflect what's available to potential users or patients. Access to product has also significantly delayed research. For example, a project funded by the Colorado Health Department to test potential of cannabis in treating PTSD was delayed by seven years before DEA approval was granted.

Congress is aware of the issue. A bipartisan congressional group sent a letter to the attorney general and the DEA asking that they "speed research on the medicinal benefits of cannabis."[383] The DEA created an application process for that purpose, but has failed to act on applications submitted, and has not yet responded to a lawsuit claiming that it has failed to act on research applications submitted as far back as 2016.

The bipartisan congressional group also introduced the Medical Marijuana Research Act of 2019.[384] If passed, this bill would expedite and simplify registration processes for cannabis research, make it easier for researchers to obtain cannabis for research purposes, and allow for private manufacturing and distribution of cannabis for research purposes.

Despite restrictions on funding of studies, searching online for Pub-Med and typing in "Marijuana" provides over 22,500 citations to peer-reviewed scientific papers on cannabis. Links to over 250 clinical trials and pretrial studies on cannabis are listed on the NORML (National Organization for the Reform of Marijuana Laws) website.[385] We do have a body of evidence with strong support for medicinal uses of cannabis despite DEA roadblocks.

The FDA has approved two pharmaceutical forms of cannabinoid medications to treat two forms of epilepsy, and has approved two medications to treat nausea and vomiting from chemotherapy. (Remember the Chapter 19 discussion about the pharmaceutical company funding opposition to medical marijuana in Arizona, while creating their own pharmaceutical version of THC for sale?) FDA approval makes these substances eligible for insurance coverage.

Insurance Coverage

Until the FDA approves CBD and/or cannabis for medical use and until the DEA removes marijuana from classification as a Schedule 1 controlled substance, insurance coverage is not available other than for those pharmaceutical versions approved by the FDA. This leaves patients in the untenable position of having insurance coverage for harder, more addictive drugs while having to pay out of pocket for cannabis, even when medical marijuana is legal in their jurisdiction.

In May 2019, the FDA held a public hearing to gather information on cannabis and cannabis-derived compounds including safety and experiences, for use in the agency's development of future strategy in regard to these substances.[386] Discussion on these topics is a positive development, but potential for change in the near future is doubtful as long as cannabis continues to be classified as a Schedule 1 drug, and because it typically takes years for processing of FDA approval.

Successes of Cannabis Legalization

In addition to support for legalization due to medical benefits, surveys listed other motivations for legalization. Motivations include ending mass incarceration and respecting personal freedom, freeing up police resources to focus on other crimes, and generation of tax revenue. It appears that these goals are being accomplished in states that have legalized.

Most importantly, cannabis legalization has prevented lives from being destroyed through arrest, incarceration, probation, and opportunity-killing criminal records. According to a 2016 report by the Colorado Department of Public Safety, in the three years following legalization in 2012, marijuana-related court filings in Colorado declined by 81 percent, and marijuana possession charges declined by 88 percent. Numbers in other states that have legalized have been similar.[387]

Consider the degree of misery that was avoided by these reductions in arrests and prosecutions. These percentages represent thousands of people who are no longer handcuffed. People no longer sit in jail hoping their lives aren't destroyed by criminal records or wondering what the impact of this arrest will be on their children. People no longer have to lose work hours to appear in court, and people no longer build resentments against law enforcement and the criminal justice system because of arrests for possession of cannabis.

Hundreds of millions of taxpayer dollars that would have been spent on law enforcement and the judiciary have been saved by discontinuing these practices.[388] Additionally, allowing citizens to continue to work and to support their families without the disruption caused by an arrest for cannabis possession minimizes public benefit costs to taxpayers. Cannabis businesses have also stimulated economies of states that have legalized, creating hundreds of thousands of new jobs. Estimates are that, as of 2017, the legal cannabis industry had already created between 165,000 to 230,000 full- and part-time jobs.[389]

Cannabis legalization has saved taxpayer dollars previously spent on law enforcement and criminal justice when possession of cannabis was a crime. Additionally, tax revenues on cannabis sales create a significant income for states, funding various programs and minimizing cost to taxpayers. Tax revenues generated are often applied to education and public health programs including school construction, overall public school costs, and drug prevention and substance use treatment. Legalization has begun to solve issues created by earlier policies.[390] For each cannabis possession arrest not made, law enforcement can focus on preventing and on prosecuting violent crime. For each possession case not heard, prosecutors and judges can take the time needed to process cases in front of them, rather than rubber stamping plea agreements that may, or may not, represent fair resolution.

Another benefit of cannabis legalization has been minimizing drug cartel profits from cannabis. David Bier, in a Cato Institute policy analysis entitled "How Legalizing Marijuana Is Securing the Border," reports, "Marijuana legalization starting in 2014 has cut marijuana smuggling between ports of entry . . . [by] 78 percent from 114 pounds per agent in 2013 to just 25 pounds per agent in 2018. . . . Since marijuana is the primary drug smuggled between ports of entry, the total value of all drugs seized by the average Border Patrol agent fell 70 percent from 2013 to 2018." This minimizes drug cartel involvement in U.S. cannabis markets, and frees border agents for other priorities.

Cannabis legalization has begun the transition of moving substance use considerations from the criminal system to the public health system. This includes optimizing benefits of cannabis for medical purposes. Multiple studies have shown 44-64 percent reductions in chronic pain with use of cannabis.[391] Studies have also shown that some patients are either supplementing cannabis with opioids to lower opioid usage or are replacing opioid usage with cannabis altogether.[392] Overdose mortality rates are nearly 25 percent lower in medical marijuana states as opposed to states where use of cannabis is still criminal.[393]

Social Impact of Legalized Cannabis—Have Concerns Been Alleviated?

Polls indicate that the primary concerns of Americans who oppose cannabis legalization is driver safety and whether legalization may escalate cannabis used by teens.[394] Data is now available with which to assess these concerns.

Does Cannabis Affect Driving Ability?

Studies to determine the extent to which cannabis use impairs driving ability are inconsistent, but do indicate that DUI issues are not significant. Simulator studies have found that drivers affected by THC may have slower reaction times, impaired route planning, and impaired cognitive performance. Other studies have found no negative effects in response to hazards, sudden lane change, or sign detection.[395] A study by the National Institute on Drug Abuse (NIDA) indicated that both alcohol and THC caused increases in lane weaving, but only alcohol increased the number of times the driver left the appropriate lane when weaving and the speed of weaving. The NIDA study indicated that when alcohol and THC were both present, impairment increased.[396] However, a later study using the same simulator found that THC reduced the time spent driving above the speed limit, actually mitigating some of the negative effects of alcohol.[397]

It is illegal to drive while impaired by cannabis in all 50 states. The challenge is in determining impairment. State definitions and procedures vary. Colorado, Washington, and Nevada rely on blood tests to check THC levels. Other states use drug recognition experts (DRE's) to assess driver impairment.[398]

Testing THC levels (patterned after tests for alcohol in the blood) can punish drivers who are not impaired. THC metabolizes differently than alcohol. It may be present in blood for weeks after use, long after any impairment would be present.[399] While sobriety tests by DREs may be preferable to blood tests, the ability of Standard Field Sobriety Test techniques to detect impairment on cannabis is not well established at this time.[400]

Studies by the National Highway Transportation Safety Administration (NHTSA) stated that, unlike alcohol, "there are currently no evidence-based methods to detect marijuana-impaired driving" and as a result, "the scope and magnitude of the marijuana-impaired driving problem in this country can't be clearly specified at this time."[401] A report by the AAA Foundation for Traffic Safety pointed out that THC tests are so unscientific that they can over-punish some drivers and under-punish others by failing to detect those who are actually impaired.[402]

These issues with testing and the fact that THC may stay in the blood long after impairment ends make it difficult to determine whether legalization increases the number of impaired drivers. Statistics in various states have also been inconclusive. Cannabis-related DUIs have decreased in Colorado since legalization, but have increased in Washington State.[403]

Laws in all jurisdictions give police authority to pull a driver over for inattentive driving, crossing the center line, or other obvious illustrations of driver impairment. If jurisdictions determine that methods of predicting impairment other than actual driver performance are necessary, further study will be important to create tests that accurately indicate impairment.

Legalization of cannabis appears to have reduced the overall number of DUI arrests, including those for alcohol and other substances.[404] Despite the issues with blood testing for THC, very few drivers arrested for DUIs in Colorado and Washington since legalization have tested positive solely for THC. Studies indicate that some people use cannabis as a replacement for substances like opiates or alcohol that have historically been more closely associated with driver impairment.[405] That may explain reductions in DUI arrests in some states with legal cannabis.

Does Teen Drug Use Increase When Cannabis Is Legalized?

One of the primary fears of legalization of cannabis has been a concern that drug use would increase, particularly in youth. A surprising statistic is that, in states where cannabis is legal, youth report that it is more difficult to access the substance.[406] Upon consideration, this data makes sense. Street-level dealers are equal-opportunity suppliers regardless of age. Legal distributors check identification and risk loss of licenses if sales are made to minors. Although street-level dealers may still exist, their numbers and accessibility are reduced as competition from legal distributors cuts into their customer base.

These conclusions are supported by research published in JAMA Pediatrics in July, 2019[407] that reported declines in underage cannabis use in states with recreational cannabis.

The 2018 National Survey on Drug Use and Health produced by the U.S. Substance Abuse and Mental Health Services Administration (SAMHSA)[408] reports that past month cannabis use by ages 12-17 remained stable from 2017 to 2018. Use by that age group continued to be lower than in years prior to state legalization of cannabis.

The SAMHSA report also showed a decline in cannabis use disorder in the 12-17 age group, continuing a seven-year decline in misuse in that age group as shown in the chart below.

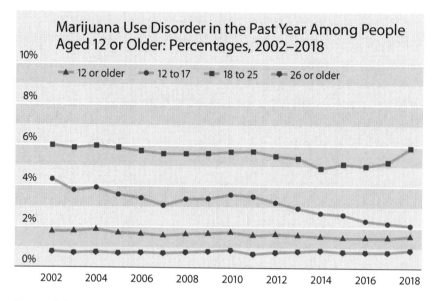

Source: Substance Abuse and Mental Health Services Administration[409]

Issues Created by Inconsistencies Between U.S. Federal and State Law

In 2019, cannabis is still illegal on the U.S. federal level, classified as a Schedule 1 drug[410]. The dynamics between the U.S. federal government and the states have been confusing for most people, and the inconsistencies are mind-boggling. Citizens acting legally under state law risk arrest, prosecution, and incarceration based on violation of federal law. Cannabis consumers in states where the substance is legal may be barred from public housing or federal financial aid because use is illegal under federal law. Cannabis businesses may lose assets to asset forfeiture and may be jailed. Additionally, as long as cannabis is a Schedule 1 drug, insurance coverage won't apply to the substance.

Cannabis customers and business owners can hopefully be free of federal raids for the time being. Current Attorney General Barr says that he does "not intend to go after parties who have complied with state law in reliance on the Cole Memorandum." That memorandum directed federal prosecutors not to interfere with state cannabis legalization laws. Legislation to guarantee this policy would eliminate insecurities created by changes in attorneys general or changes in their opinions. Movement is underway to do just that.

In June 2019, the U.S. House of Representatives passed a bipartisan bill that would prevent the Department of Justice from spending money to intervene in state and territory cannabis policies, as well as cannabis policies on tribal lands. The bill applies to use, distribution, possession, and cultivation of marijuana.[411] Passage by the Senate is undetermined at this time.

Banks don't want to risk doing business with a cannabis business handling a substance classified as a Schedule 1 Controlled Substance by the federal government since that could be deemed to be money laundering. Under federal law, the FDIC cannot insure money obtained from illegal transactions, and banks are required to include all deposits under FDIC insurance. On top of that, the IRS has put pressure on banks to refrain from opening accounts for cannabis businesses. Some regional banks and credit unions reportedly offer banking services, but thousands of dollars in additional monthly fees are charged for those services and services may be terminated at any time.[412]

Lack of banking services, requiring cannabis businesses to operate with cash, can lead to risks to public safety, issues with tax collection, and financial accountability for owners and employees. Mandating cash operations can make monitoring cannabis businesses more difficult, incentivizing underground operations. From a law enforcement and tax perspective, this makes no sense. Cash from cannabis businesses is used to pay employees, landlords, vendors, and others, further increasing safety and other risks.

Cash payments to the IRS for tax liability create issues for the IRS, so taxpayers foot the $1.7 million bill for the IRS to outsource processing of cash payments from cannabis businesses.[413] (Legislators: Please consider this my application for that job!) Banking restrictions leave cannabis businesses little choice but to pay taxes in cash, requiring delivery of bags of cash to IRS offices. Is this reality, or the script of a very bizarre and poorly written comedy? The contradictions and the results of drug policy can make a head spin.

The Internal Revenue Code (26 U.S. Code § 280E)[414] denies business expense deductions to taxpayers whose business consists of trafficking in a Schedule 1 or 2 controlled substance. On the federal level, this applies to cannabis, subjecting cannabis businesses to tax on gross income with no business expense deductions or tax credits. Tax planning, including dividing cannabis and non-cannabis related activities into separate businesses, can minimize some of these issues. However, requiring cannabis businesses to jump through more hoops than other businesses increases overall tax liability, leaves greater risk if tax planning is not properly completed, and compromises legal distribution systems.

The Secure and Fair Enforcement (SAFE) Banking Act, currently pending in the U.S. Congress, would protect U.S. banks working with cannabis companies from criminal scrutiny by regulators, so would resolve the banking issues described above.[415] Hopefully, sanity will prevail and this act will become law.

Most Americans oppose the federal government taking action to stop cannabis sales in states that have legalized or decriminalized it. Multiple legislative proposals currently being considered are reflecting that.

U.N. Policy and Its Impact on Cannabis Reform

As discussed earlier, U.N. treaties are a potential barrier to drug legalization. How do jurisdictions in the United States avoid issues with the U.N. treaties? The federal government, but not state or local governments, are signatories to the treaties. The U.S. Constitution provides states rights independent of the federal government, so local actions fall within the provisions that treaties are "subject to [a member country's] constitutional principles and the basic concepts of its legal system."[416]

U.S. federal legislation legalizing cannabis nationally would create greater consistency and could streamline programs for distribution of legal cannabis. States could still opt out and establish their own regulatory requirements as Canada did in their federal legislation. Federal legislation, however, could be more problematic in regard to U.N. treaties.

The U.S. was integral in initial adoption of the treaties, and should be a leader in promoting revocation or amendment of the treaties based on the failures that have resulted from this punitive approach to drug policy. If treaties cannot be revoked or amended, complying with human rights mandates of the U.N. should be the priority, even if drug policy treaties are not followed. Human rights mandates, as well as directives from all agencies of the U.N. and its secretary general, would put the United States in a strong position to proceed with legalization.

Federal Cannabis Legalization in Other Countries

Only two countries have legalized cannabis on the federal level to date. Uruguay legalized in 2017, followed by legalization in Canada in 2018.

Uruguay

In response to drug cartel violence and growth of local mafia benefiting from supplying cannabis, in December 2013, Uruguay became the first country in the world to completely legalize marijuana. Smoking pot has been legal in Uruguay for decades, but it was illegal to grow it or to buy it. Former president Jose Mujica stated that the law is simply "regulation of a market that already exists."

Driving while high or smoking on the job continues to be illegal in Uruguay. Pharmacies are allowed to sell cannabis to people over 21 who produce an ID, and customers are restricted to buying 40 grams monthly. Crops are grown legally in the country and taxed. Each home is allowed to grow up to six plants for personal use, and can belong to private grow clubs that can produce up to 99 plants. Legal access to cannabis applies only to Uruguayan citizens. There have been some arrests of locals who were selling to tourists.

A huge issue for Uruguay is that few pharmacies have cannabis available. Despite a 2017 agreement between the Uruguayan government and 16 drugstore chains to sell the product, pressure from the banks makes it difficult for pharmacies to participate. Most banks in Uruguay route their international transactions through U.S. banks, so they refuse to work with pharmacies acting as distributors out of fear of international sanctions because of the USA Patriot Act[417] and U.N. treaties.[418] One of the goals of the Patriot Act was to prevent terrorists from using the international banking system to launder profits from heroin and other illegal substances. The result in Uruguay is benefit to drug cartel suppliers who fill the void caused by lack of product in pharmacies, defeating the primary purpose of legalization. If the Secure and Fair Enforcement (SAFE) Banking Act, which is currently pending in the U.S. Congress, passes, this may alleviate these issues.

Another issue with the Uruguayan legislation is that all customers are required to register with a database run by the Ministry of Health. This creates one of the largest objections to the legislation, particularly for those who've previously lived under dictatorships and are hesitant to be part of a government database identifying themselves as a drug user.

Uruguay's current president and the Ministry of Public Health are much less supportive of cannabis legalization than was the prior president.

Canada

Canada is the largest country in the world to legalize cannabis nationally, providing a beneficial blueprint for other countries assessing benefits and processes of legalization. The Cannabis Act[419] legalized cannabis in Canada as of October 17, 2018.

Canada's Cannabis Act is a broad federal law, but allows provinces and territories to dictate variations in regulations including where cannabis can be sold and consumed. For example, Ontario allows purchase only from an online store run by the government, whereas Saskatchewan allows purchase only from licensed private retail stores. Individual jurisdictions in Canada also have the ability to ban recreational use, but residents of those provinces still have the legal right to purchase cannabis from online government stores, eliminating the need for illegal suppliers.

Taxes on cannabis in Canada are modest, minimizing the risk that black market suppliers will undercut government distribution, and incentivizing legal purchase so taxes are paid. Canada also set its legal age to purchase at 18 years, minimizing the risk of a black market to supply ages 18-21. Structuring law to reduce opportunities for black market suppliers also reduces the likelihood of access for those under age 18.

To minimize the stigma, to increase opportunity, and to treat those convicted prior to changes in law, Canada has sealed marijuana conviction records without fees or waiting periods. Canada has not yet dealt with individuals currently incarcerated for actions that are now legal.

Other Jurisdictions

In addition to countries that have decriminalized cannabis and all drugs, a few countries have decriminalized only cannabis, including Belgium, which decriminalized small-scale cannabis possession in 2003,[420] and Jamaica, where two grams of marijuana is allowed for personal use. [421]

Moving Forward

Cannabis has been the ultimate political football. Fear, rather than facts, has driven policy for far too long. There is no possible justification for classification of marijuana as a Schedule 1 drug, the same classification as heroin, LSD, and ecstasy. Oxycodone, fentanyl, and morphine are Schedule 2, supposedly with less potential for abuse than cannabis. Continuing to classify cannabis as a DEA Schedule 1 narcotic flies in the face of scientific research about its medical uses, with no factual basis for its initial scheduling on Schedule 1 to begin with.

Prohibitions on medical studies have likely delayed or lost opportunities for medical solutions that may have benefited many citizens. Arrests and fear of arrest for cannabis possession have created adversarial relationships between police and citizens. There is no basis for incarcerating people for years, and in some cases decades, on marijuana charges. Cannabis can create issues, but those challenges don't approach the harm that's been created by cannabis prohibition.

Bill Murray says it well: *"I find it quite ironic that the most dangerous thing about weed is getting caught with it."*

Our children are not fools. They see obvious lies. Fear tactics on pot have compromised the credibility of adults in the eyes of youth. If our politicians are dishonest about cannabis, why should they be trusted about warnings of the dangers of other drugs?

The movement for cannabis legalization has been a valuable learning experience. What we've learned can be used as legislation develops in regard to cannabis, as well as drug policy on other substances.

We've seen the bizarre results of inconsistencies in federal vs. state law. We've learned that the sky doesn't fall when patients and recreational users are provided with product choices and markets, and are allowed to make decisions on their own behalf. We've learned that rules applied to alcohol shouldn't automatically be applied to other drugs that impact our bodies in different ways.

With opioid use and overdose declining in states where legal cannabis is available, indications are that most people, including drug users, act in their own best interest in selecting less risky substance alternatives when given the choice. We've learned that law enforcement and tax dollars can be successfully reallocated to much more productive purposes than prosecuting and incarcerating masses of cannabis users. And we've learned that public sentiment can make a difference, and can quickly bring change.

Change may be scary for some, but as a mother who's lost sleep worrying about drug use in my own family and as a researcher reviewing the effects of our cannabis policies, I can confidently say that legalization is a tremendously positive development. Legal cannabis will make your children safer, our society more compassionate, and our policies more honest, consistent, and respected.

"I mistakenly believed that the Drug Enforcement [Administration] . . . must have quality reasoning as to why marijuana is in the category of the most dangerous drugs that have 'no accepted medical use and a high potential for abuse.' They didn't have the science to support that claim, and I now know that when it comes to marijuana neither of those things are true."—Dr. Sanjay Gupta

Should we consider legalizing cannabis, while continuing criminalization of other drugs? Would using drug courts to minimize incarceration and utilize medical solutions make sense? Let's take a look at that policy.

CHAPTER 26

ARE DRUG COURTS THE ANSWER?

"One of the concerns we have is that drug courts are basically a way for policymakers to make it look like they're doing something on the War on Drugs without actually addressing the War on Drugs."

TRACY VELASQUEZ, JUSTICE POLICY INSTITUTE

Drug court programs were designed in an attempt to minimize drug use, save money, and reduce incarceration rates of those charged with nonviolent drug-related crimes. A team including judges, prosecutors, defense attorneys, corrections personnel, social workers, and treatment professionals work with participants who agree to undergo treatment and comply with other drug court requirements in lieu of incarceration. This sounds like a positive approach. Could drug courts be a shortcut to helping those struggling with addiction and ending mass incarceration without going through the challenges of full drug policy reform?

Many believed that to be the case. Since the first U.S. drug court in Miami-Dade County, Florida, in 1989, drug courts have grown dramatically. All 50 U.S. states now have drug courts, and drug courts exist in Australia, Canada, New Zealand, and the United Kingdom.

Drug courts offer treatment in lieu of incarceration. How could that possibly be anything but positive? There's no doubt that some individuals have benefited. For those able to comply perfectly with drug court mandates, the treatment offered can be a turning point toward sobriety and a productive life. Within our current system, many of these individuals would be unable to afford other treatment options, so drug court offers the opportunity for treatment services that would otherwise be unavailable to them.

So, What's Not to Like?

"Failing" Drug Court Is a Huge Risk

Unfortunately, participants who aren't successful in drug court—meaning they haven't perfectly complied with every requirement, are often punished with incarceration. This is different than the LEAD program where compliance is voluntary and where there are no criminal charges. Failure in drug court could be due to a relapse, missing, or being late for *even one* appointment, or not following every individual mandate of the program.

Requirements are subjective, and may include onerous written homework and other assignments—even for those with learning disabilities, making compliance difficult. Mandates often include many hours of meetings, classes, and counseling sessions, adding to the burden of defendants who may already be required to perform many hours of community service, and who are already under pressure to keep jobs to create income with which to pay ongoing fees for the drug court "services." We now know that stress and anxiety exacerbate addiction. These programs increase stress and anxiety of participants and their families, particularly when the threat of incarceration is ever present.

Drug court success statistics are based *only on those who successfully complete the program*, ignoring those who are kicked out or end up behind bars because they didn't meet the perfection model. Even when counting only those who complete the program, less than half are deemed to be successful.[422] Statistics are also based on drug court tendencies to "cherry-pick" those who qualify. To boost their success rates, drug courts routinely allow individuals with simple drug possession charges to participate, while keeping those with serious substance use issues out of the program.[423]

Penalties Are Often More Severe for Drug Court "Failure" Than Without Drug Court

Penalties for not meeting the perfection standard are severe. In many cases, the amount of time spent behind bars is significantly longer for those who "fail" drug court than would have been the case if they hadn't agreed to drug court in the first place. The price of entering drug court is a guilty plea in most jurisdictions, with the defendant waiving the right to a trial, to discovery, or to contesting the circumstances of the arrest. The guilty plea usurps the opportunity for a plea agreement. In some drug courts, if drug court is successfully completed, records are expunged, but in other jurisdictions, the guilty plea will remain on the defendant's permanent record.

The concern about the potential for more jail time after agreement to drug court than without it was expressed by the Drug Policy Alliance in its report on drug courts: "Not only will some drug court participants spend more days in jail while in drug court than if they had been conventionally sentenced, but participants deemed "failures" may actually face longer sentences than those who did not enter drug court in the first place (often because they lost the opportunity to plead to a lesser charge)."[424]

Those who understand the risks and opt not to participate in drug court may be punished by prosecutors who are unhappy about the defendant's unwillingness to participate in the program.

Some drug courts incarcerate offenders for a short time for an initial act of non-compliance, and some courts immediately trigger the full sentence for any infraction. Every drug court that receives federal funding is *required* to use jail as a penalty.[425] Either short- or long-term incarceration can create serious medical issues related to limited medical care and withdrawal from medications prohibited in many jails and prisons, significantly increasing risks of overdose when released.[426]

There have been multiple lawsuits for wrongful detention without a hearing or due process, federal civil rights violations, and unauthorized arrests and searches of drug court participants.[427] Some drug court participants were held pending placement in treatment, but when no placements were available, they were kept in jail with no hearing and no due process.[428]

Treatment Services May Be Compromised and Are More Expensive Than Non-Court Related Treatment:

Treatment services offered by drug court are restricted only to specific treatment mandated by the court, regardless of whether it's the best fit for the individual. Treatment services are often based on contracts negotiated with a particular provider, and many are faith-based programs that have been ruled unconstitutional as a violation of the Establishment Clause of the First Amendment.[429] "Offenders" are in a poor position to assert their constitutional rights.

Counselors with whom defendants are supposed to build trust report directly to court personnel who have the power to put the defendant in jail. This incestuous relationship between treatment providers and courts can significantly compromise trust and severely minimize benefits of treatment. Drug court participants (and those on probation or parole) are typically required to sign release forms to allow counselors to share information, and if they don't sign, they risk incarceration.

Drug Court Threats May Be Triggers for Relapse

Feeling overwhelmed, stress, and an inability to trust others can be triggers for relapse. The standard of perfection required by drug courts would be unrealistic for anyone, let alone individuals struggling with substance use issues (and often mental or physical health issues and financial challenges). Would any of us be willing to enter an agreement stating that if we were late for or missed an appointment or a payment in the period of a year or more, we would be put behind bars? The stress created by daily fear and the isolation caused by the risks involved in trusting others is the exact opposite of what experts recommend for recovery.

Drug Court May Mandate Treatment for Those Without Substance Use Disorder, While Those Who Need Services Sometimes Can't Get Them

As discussed earlier, less than 20 percent of drug users suffer from substance use disorder. Drug courts don't verify that someone arrested for drug possession is addicted. Unlike other "crimes," drug possession arrests don't require an overt criminal act. The arrest is solely based on possession of a drug. When thousands who want treatment can't get it, mandating treatment for those who don't need it is unproductive and expensive, as well as potentially damaging to the individual.

Structure Is Rampant for Abuse

Drug court participants have little control over their own lives, and are sometimes subjected to humiliation and abuse on a daily basis for a year or more. Treatment providers' financial survival depends on catering to the court—their referral source—more than their actual client, and have financial incentives to keep defendants in the system for as long as possible. While some providers can withstand these incentives and serve their true clients well, this structure is ripe for abuse and overreaching. Defendants have no power, and risk incarceration if they rock the boat in any way, so are very unlikely to complain regardless of what may occur in the treatment setting.

Judges (and Prosecutors, Probation Agents, etc.) Are Dictating Medical Decisions

Daniel N. Abrahamson, former director of legal affairs and senior legal advisor at the Drug Policy Alliance, and a law school lecturer on drug law and policy, points out that in "recent years, reports from the Government Accountability Office, the Justice Policy Institute and the Legal Action Center have found that drug court procedures contradict accepted medical practices."

As discussed previously, medications have proven to be a viable method of treatment for substance use disorder, and can reduce relapse rates by over 50 percent. Additionally, medical providers prescribe medications to their patients for a variety of physical and mental health reasons. Some drug court judges mandate that defendants go off of their medications to be in compliance with drug court.

A 2015 survey by SAMHSA (the Substance Abuse and Mental Health Services Administration) indicated that less than 20 percent of drug courts allow treatment using medications. Some progress is being made. In February 2015, the Office of National Drug Control Policy announced that it would refuse to fund drug courts that apply for grants if they do not allow medications to be used in treatment.[430] However, most drug courts are funded primarily by states or other local governments, so that announcement has not created broad change.

Most jails ban medications including Suboxone and methadone, and some ban naltrexone or the Vivitrol injection as well. This puts those on probation or parole who are being treated with medications at risk of cold-turkey withdrawal behind bars if they're incarcerated due to a drug court, probation, or parole violation. Patients are punished for drug use, and then denied the very treatment that has proven to be the most effective in treating substance use disorder.

Judges, who are trained on legal matters but have no medical training, should NEVER have the authority to put a defendant in the position of going to jail for refusing to terminate prescription medications. Judge's orders to end medications used in treatment have been directly linked to several defendants' deaths due to overdose after being forced to terminate medications that had been working successfully for them.[431]

"Offenders" are sometimes given short jail sentences due to noncompliance with drug court mandates. Going through withdrawal behind bars with no medical help is the norm and has resulted in numerous deaths. Individuals are at significantly heightened risk of overdose upon release because drug tolerance levels are reduced if they go for periods of not using while incarcerated. A short jail stay can become a death sentence. Compromising body chemistry and impacting physical and mental health by denying prescription medications is inhumane, and increases the risk of addiction and other medical issues.

Drug Court May Jeopardize Defense

Defense attorneys are part of the drug court "team" when the client is agreeing to drug court, and most withdraw from cases upon a client's entry into drug court, so are unaware of issues arising after the client's agreement to become part of a drug court program. Additionally, defense attorneys need to have positive relationships with prosecutors and judges, and failure to recommend drug court to their clients can put them at risk of jeopardizing those relationships.

Elizabeth Kelley of the National Association of Criminal Defense Attorneys expressed concern that, in many drug courts, the defense attorney is asked to forfeit the traditional role of being the zealous advocate of the client to be part of the team. Federal drug court guidelines direct defense attorneys to explain all of the rights that the defendant will temporarily or permanently relinquish, and then to work with prosecutors "to build a sense of teamwork and to reinforce a non-adversarial atmosphere." A non-adversarial atmosphere does not protect the rights of a defendant who fails drug court.

Drug Courts Don't Solve the Issues Inherent with the War on Drugs

Drug courts are simply an attempt at a less expensive way of enforcing the War on Drugs. They do nothing to solve the problems with it.

"In terms of the politics," says Tracy Velasquez of the Justice Policy Institute, "one of the concerns we have is that drug courts are basically a way for policymakers to make it look like they're doing something on the War on Drugs without actually addressing the War on Drugs."

It's important that we take a broader view of public policy as it's applied to addiction, and to take steps to end the War on Drugs as we know it. When offers of drug court are made, defendants frequently agree to the offer with little understanding of the pros and cons or on how this agreement will truly impact their day-to-day life or their risk of incarceration. Unfortunately, options are often so horrendous that this bad alternative seems preferable to other choices.

According to the Drug Policy Alliance, approximately 95,000 drug offenders fail U.S. drug court *every year*. Anyone considering drug court should be aware that, statistically, only about half of those entering drug court successfully complete it, and those who don't successfully complete the program pay a high price for failure.

Multiple government agencies recognize substance use disorder as a health condition. It's time to stop hiding behind drug courts as a façade for a solution. It's time to allow medical professionals to treat a medical issue, and to remove treatment for substance use disorder from the criminal justice system.

CHAPTER 27

IMMEDIATE STEPS TO END THE CARNAGE

"If I had to design a system that was intended to keep people addicted, I'd design exactly the system that we have right now."
Dr. Gabor Maté

Full drug policy reform takes time. While reform is assessed, negotiated, drafted, and passed, people are dying, being put behind bars, and living lives of quiet desperation because of obsolete, punitive policies entrenched before we had the benefit of today's science and medicine. To reduce the damage, some policies need to end immediately and others need to be instituted.

Are there ways that we can *immediately* reduce the harm? Can we save lives through immediate action? Are there things we can do today?

Harm reduction practices focus on saving lives and reducing suffering. These policies are compassionate, while applying common sense for the most practical and cost-effective solutions. Products and strategies help those with addiction issues to survive and to move forward in their lives. That, in turn, reduces the damage to communities. Policies reduce the prevalence of used needles in public areas, minimize the risk of children witnessing public drug use, reduce spread of infectious disease, expand medical services for all patients, and save taxpayer dollars.

Harm reduction acknowledges that a drug-free world is neither practical nor achievable. It focuses on minimizing the harm associated with drug use rather than prevention of the use itself. This may seem counterintuitive. Some resist these techniques, believing that reducing harm will somehow incentivize drug use, but there is no evidence to support that belief. There *is* verification of many lives saved through these protocols.[432] Supporting these policies could save your life or the life of someone you love. As long as there's life, there's hope for recovery.

Let's begin with policies that are particularly egregious and need to end. Then, we'll discuss policies that, when implemented, immediately save lives.

"Drugs are infinitely more dangerous if they are left solely in the hands of criminals who have no concerns about health and safety. Legal regulation protects health."—KOFI ANNAN, FORMER SECRETARY GENERAL OF THE UNITED NATIONS

CHAPTER 28

END DEBTORS' PRISON

"If court decisions are based on revenue generation, not the advancement of justice, the right to due process is imperiled."

MIRIAM ARONI KRINSKY

Debtors' prisons are alive and well in the United States. Those who can't pay fines and fees assessed by the criminal justice system are arrested and jailed daily.[433] Fees include charges for public defenders, probation supervision, court administration, and jail operating costs. Fines can be in the thousands of dollars, even for minor drug possession charges.

People who fall behind on their payments may be arrested with no hearing to assess ability to pay or an offer of alternatives or methods to satisfy the debt. Penalties for nonpayment of fees and fines can exceed punishment for the initial "crime." Nonpayment can also result in an extension of probation, creating yet more fees and a never-ending downward spiral. Failure to pay drug court or other fees may cause a defendant to be removed from drug court and be deemed to be a probation violation, punishable with incarceration.

Debtors' prisons were outlawed in the U.S. nearly 200 years ago, but the 1983 U.S. Supreme Court case, *Bearden v. Georgia*[434], held that if a defendant has the ability to pay but "willfully" refuses, the defendant can be imprisoned for nonpayment. The court failed to define a standard for determining "ability to pay." An investigation by National Public Radio found sweeping discrepancies on how judges determined ability to pay, including assumptions that tattoos, smoking, or a nice jacket indicates ability to pay.[435] Other judges have simply told defendants that they must ask family members for money with which to pay. Every day, people are put behind bars because they are unable to pay court debts.

The amount of court fees and costs assessed to individuals is high, and often leaves defendants on a revolving wheel where they simply have no hope of getting out from under the financial burden of the fees and costs, plus added penalties for past payment or fees that accumulate during periods of incarceration. Parents' finances are frequently drained in efforts to keep their children out of jail for nonpayment. These are the same parents who have likely already been hit financially by paying for treatment and medical care for their child, and are now further drained in efforts to prevent the criminal justice system from reversing progress from programs they've already paid for.

These onerous policies attack the most vulnerable in society and often force funds to be used to pay the court instead of paying for medical care and medications. Arresting an individual on a small drug possession charge, applying huge fines, mandating long-term supervision through probation, and then prosecuting them for nonpayment of the fees to pay for that mandated supervision is harmful, destructive, and unconscionable. These tactics cannot be justified as beneficial to recovery or to rebuilding productive, successful lives. There is no evidence indicating that these policies are productive in any way.

These policies can put individuals in a position where job opportunities are unavailable due to criminal records, leaving them with two choices. Do they wait for the arrest warrant to take them to jail for nonpayment of fees, or do they deal drugs or commit other crimes to generate cash with which to pay the fees and fines? Going to jail for nonpayment will, in most cases, result in a never-ending cycle, generating yet more fines and fees. At least 45 states authorize fees for room and board in jail.

Inmates are charged some form of fee in 90 percent of jails.[436]

Some argue that offenders should pay the fees incurred to avoid taxpayer expense for their criminal act. In reality, these policies increase costs to taxpayers, who pay the costs of incarceration. Even assuming fees are eventually paid, costs of incarceration typically exceed the amounts collected.

Locking people up for unpaid fees increases taxpayer cost in many other ways. Punitive criminal penalties for minor drug offenses combined with assessments to pay the costs of administering those penalties creates second-class, vulnerable citizens at the hands of the State. It also minimizes the chance that those individuals will have the opportunity to move past the minor offense and end up as successful, taxpaying citizens. As individual opportunity is decreased, potential for more cost to taxpayers increases. Assessing unconscionable fines and fees is morally wrong and it's expensive to more than just the individual.

Fines and fees don't only compromise offenders' budgets for other expenses. Unpaid fines and fees can negatively impact credit scores, compromising employment, housing, and the ability to access loans. A credit report with outstanding debt to a criminal court can also be a red flag to employers and potential landlords that a criminal conviction exists.

The question shouldn't be who pays the expense of prosecution, incarceration, and supervision. The question is why we're mandating these abusive, punitive policies that create the expense in the first place.

"Being unable to pay can result in a range of penalties, including jail time and a suspended license." —Jessica Brand

---

Total Amount Due: **$1446.00**

In accordance with your payment plan agreement, you must make up all missed payments immediately upong receipt of this notice or one or more of the following enforcement actions will be taken:

- arrest and commitment to the county jail.
- suspension of your driving privileges.
- a civil judgment entered against you.
- referral to a collection agency.
- certification to the Department of Revenue for interception of your tax refund.

FINAL NOTICE

Return this notice with payment to: **County Circuit Court**
Clerk of Court

CHAPTER 29
END ARRESTS FOR LOW-LEVEL OFFENSES

"An unjust law is itself a species of violence.
Arrest for its breach is more so."

MAHATMA GANDHI

According to the journal *Pediatrics*, in the U.S., 41 percent of young adults in the United States have been arrested for something other than a minor traffic violation by the time they're 23 years old.[437]

Not all who are arrested end up behind bars, but most jurisdictions allow a two- to three-day hold upon arrest, until charges are assessed or a determination is made not to file charges at that time. Until charges are filed or an arrestee is released, bail is not available since bail amounts are determined by the charges filed.

Criminal justice professionals who work in the system can become desensitized about what they consider to be minor charges and short jail stays. When expressing concerns to prosecutors, a comment of "It's only a few days" is not uncommon. For those arrested and/or put behind bars, even a short stay can be life changing, and not in a positive way.

Trauma behind bars can lead to anxiety, depression, phobias, and PTSD in those who previously had no serious mental health issues. For those who begin with some of those issues, time behind bars can seriously escalate mental health challenges.[438]

The isolation of incarceration can create trauma. Contact with family, with the exception of one phone call, is nonexistent during the initial few days behind bars, and severely restricted after that. Other inmates are focused on their own safety and issues. This is typically not an atmosphere to receive social support. Jail populations are transient with inmates ranging from those picked up with a joint to those in transit to prison for violent crime. These populations aren't conducive to connection and friendship. According to experts, isolation can increase a person's risk of mental health issues such as depression and anxiety as well as increasing the risk of addiction or relapse.[439]

Being booked and treated as a criminal can change an identity, particularly for a young adult. A criminal record and a period of probation further establishes an identity as a criminal. Isolation can minimize social confidence, and may incentivize making friends who are also on probation, increasing the risk of association with criminals. A naive kid arrested with a pill in his pocket can end up going down a path far different than a similar individual who had the pill but who didn't get arrested.[440] Jails can become "criminal universities" for those who had no interest in that element prior to the arrest for minor drug possession.

Jails are not equipped to provide medical care, whether for physical or mental health care needs. Staff nurses are overwhelmed, leading to lack of compassion and care. Depending on the size of the facility, medical providers may only visit periodically, and will only see inmates if orders are submitted before deadlines prior to the visit. Nearly two million people with mental health issues are booked into U.S. jails annually.[441] Sixty-five percent of inmates have a substance use disorder[442], and those who are on medications for treatment are often forced off of those medications, leading to withdrawal behind bars and increased risk of overdose upon release. Medical services in jail and prison are simply not available to deal with these issues.

Suicide is the leading cause of death in county jails, and suicide rates are increasing.[443] Suicide rates for those in jail prior to convictions are seven times higher than for convicted inmates.[444] Twenty-seven percent of jail suicides occur two to 14 days after arrest.[445]

The following chart shows rates of suicide for local jail inmates and U.S. residents, per 100,000.

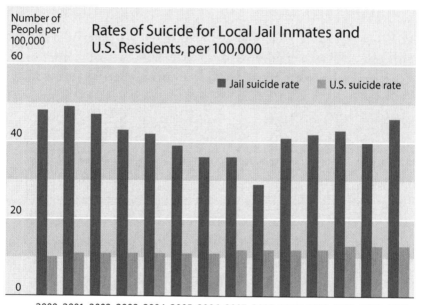

Source: Bureau of Justice Statistics, Deaths in Custody Reporting Program and Centers for Disease Control and Prevention

Reproduced/adapted with permission from The Marshall Project[446]

Many also believe that small jails are somehow less traumatic than large ones. The nation's smallest jails have a suicide rate more than six times as high as the largest jails.[447]

In what universe could it possibly make sense to arrest someone for minor drug possession and then subject them to these risks and conditions? Arrest for minor drug offenses needs to end.

CHAPTER 30

END LATE NIGHT RELEASE FROM JAIL

"Compassion is the basis of morality."

ARTHUR SCHOPENHAUER

It's winter in Wisconsin. "I'll be released at 4 a.m., Mom. Could you pick me up?" This *had* to be a mistake, Meg thought. Who would consider releasing an inmate in the middle of the night, with no verification that anyone would pick them up, with little or no money, and with or without a jacket? Could this possibly be the same system that had arrested her son, ostensibly to "protect" him from his drug use? Could this system that spends money on studies to determine what could minimize the recidivism rate and permanently keep people out of jail or prison really be this inept?

Release from jail in the middle of the night is standard procedure in many jurisdictions. Immediately after release can be a very vulnerable time for people incarcerated for drug use, and risk of overdose skyrockets due to reduced tolerance if drug use ended while incarcerated or if medications used to treat the substance use disorder were denied by the jail. Release late at night or in the middle of the night creates multiple issues including lack of transportation if bus service has ended, inability to enter treatment or access to other social services if facilities are closed, and overall temptation as well as security issues. Something as simple as the cost of an Uber ride is often prohibitive to those just released who may have no funds or active cell phones with which to call or pay.

Family members may not be willing or able to pick up in the middle of the night. Even if family can make themselves available, the message continues to be clear. Because you or a family member had a pill in a pocket (or a joint in some jurisdictions), you're a second-class citizen unworthy of basic respect. Is making an inmate feel stigmatized, scorned, uncared for, alone, and desperate in anyone's best interest?

Middle-of-the-night releases are most often done before shift changes based on convenience for jail personnel. Late-night releases are reportedly done because paperwork processing is delayed, and law in some jurisdictions requires release before midnight on the designated "day" of release, so release is near midnight in cases where paperwork wasn't completed earlier.

Time of day of release is only one issue. If any part of incarceration is actually to minimize the chance of reoffending, then pre-release planning and coordination with families would be worthwhile. If minimization of re-offense isn't a goal, then we should stop giving lip service to that objective and admit that incarceration is solely to punish. If punishment is the rationale, the overall drug policy debate needs to acknowledge that. Science and medicine dictates an end to these egregious policies.

Adjustment in jail policies could prevent time of release issues. When amending policies, it's important that the jail stays are not inadvertently extended because a deadline on filing a piece of paper is missed.

If jails weren't overcrowded due to arrest for minor drug possession offenses, jail personnel would be less overwhelmed and issues like these would be significantly reduced.

CHAPTER 31

LOSE A SATELLITE SIGNAL —GO TO JAIL

"It has become appallingly obvious that our technology has exceeded our humanity."

ALBERT EINSTEIN

Think of the number of times you've lost service on your cell phone or a GPS signal halted for a moment. Then consider what it would be like if, each of those times, you were at risk of being jailed because of that technical blip. That's life with an electronic monitor.

Use of electronic monitors by law enforcement rose by 140 percent in the decade from 2005 to 2015, tracking more than 125,000 people on probation, parole or pretrial release by 2015.[448] Monitors are sometimes perceived as "no big deal" by authorities. They see the ankle accessories as a simple alternative to incarceration. For those living with them, they can be a very big deal.

Electronic monitoring is another way of dehumanizing, stigmatizing and punishing those with substance use disorder or casual users in possession of a substance. Techniques used for violent criminals are easily transferred to all individuals when substance use is deemed to be a crime.

As technology advances, it becomes easier for prosecutors to feel good about using methods of "minimizing incarceration", while they continue to extend the arm of the law to increasing numbers of offenders.

Emma, discussed in chapter 13 when drivers' licenses were discussed, had been arrested dozing in her car in a parking lot five days after release from the hospital following surgery. She was charged with driving under the influence because prescription medications were found in her blood. In an attempt to avoid having to go to trial, she entered into discussions with the prosecutor for a plea agreement. She expressed concern about any agreement that would include jail time because that would, once again, force her off of the medications that helped her in recovery from substance use disorder and put her through withdrawal behind bars.

The prosecutor's answer was use of an ankle monitor for the 30-day sentence being proposed. For Emma, that electronic monitor could present a major health risk. Her health issues included an autoimmune disease that caused swelling of her joints. If a monitor was on when swelling occurred, it could be life threatening. She found herself being presented with the decision of either going off of her prescription medications and going to jail, or putting her life in danger with a metal monitor attached to her ankle. This choice was all because she'd appropriately used her prescription medications in the first place and had the audacity to nap in a parking lot while waiting for a friend. She'd been fatigued because of her recent surgery.

This may be a unique example, but the cascade effects of criminalizing a health condition aren't unique. Even for those whose life isn't threatened by electronic monitoring, wearing a monitor IS a "big deal". These monitoring techniques may make sense for true criminals who need to be tracked for public safety. That is not the case for low level drug offenders who so often find themselves caught in this net.

Fees for monitors are paid by the offender, and can range from $5 to $25 a day.[449] Unpaid fees can lead to incarceration. Skin irritations from the devices are common, and removal or tampering with the monitor in any way can also lead to incarceration. Most programs have no clear policy or fast technique for removal of a device in case of an emergency. Medical procedures including MRIs, x-rays, CT scans and mammograms cannot be done with a monitor on.[450]

The risk of lost service is a constant threat. A dead battery, walking to the other side of a garage and losing connection, or a power outage can all lead to jail time, even when the lost service had nothing to do with an offender's actions. Departments of Corrections have the authority to hold offenders in jail for up to three work days while they investigate violations. If the offender is unlucky enough to encounter a loss of service at the beginning of a weekend, he or she will likely be held through the weekend and up to three additional days. This can lead to loss of jobs, family stress, missed events, and potential medical issues, particularly if medications are denied while behind bars. Putting people in constant stress worrying about technical issues, with the potential of jail time for reasons completely beyond their control is completely unwarranted when the "crime" is minor drug possession where the individual poses no threat. As discussed previously, the isolation and stress created also increase the risk of relapse.

Loss of service and other technical issues are not unusual. They are the norm. An audit of monitors in Los Angeles County, California found that one in four had defective batteries or excessive false alerts.[451] Massachusetts replaced all of its monitors in 2016 due to poor cell coverage.

A 2017 assessment of monitors in Wisconsin found that the state monitoring center lost cell connection an average of 64 times per offender and that multiple offenders had been jailed between one and three times for what Department of Corrections records showed were because of technical malfunctions. Wisconsin is notorious for issues with electronic monitoring devices, and for ignoring those issues. In 2013, the Wisconsin Center for Investigative Journalism documented serious problems with monitoring systems including false alerts that resulted in jail time, lost jobs and disrupted lives. Five years later, issues remain, but monitoring continues. As of January, 2018, Wisconsin monitored 1,258 offenders with GPS devices at an annual cost of 9.7 million dollars.[452]

Electronic monitoring and accompanying issues apply worldwide. Australian National University and University College London reviewed 33 studies on electronic monitoring and found repeated issues with equipment malfunction, battery failure, inadequate broadband capacity and loss of signal or power.[453]

The editor of the Journal of Offender Monitoring expressed concern about the impact of incarceration based on technical issues with monitors, stating " "If [offenders] are trying to reintegrate themselves … to suddenly find yourself carted back to prison for something that is in no way your fault seems to me to be quite an unnecessary disruption in the life of an offender—and quite at odds with good practice in reintegrating them."

Constitutional issues may exist with use of GPS monitoring for drug possession cases. In 2015, the U.S. Supreme Court ruled that GPS constitutes a fourth amendment search, but did not define whether the search in that case was unreasonable and therefore unconstitutional. The Department of Corrections spokesperson in that case stated, "While GPS monitoring may pose an 'inconvenience' to these offenders, the state Legislature or DOC have determined that these tools enhance public safety and protect victims." This may be the case with some types of crime, but applying that logic to victimless drug possession cases is a broad stretch.[454]

The availability of technology may make it easier to use electronic monitoring in cases where, without this technology, individuals would be left to rebuild their lives without dealing with the issues discussed here. In cases where public safety is at risk, the benefits may outweigh the detriments, but in drug possession cases, the trauma created by issues with electronic monitoring is clearly not justified.

CHAPTER 32

END DRUG-INDUCED HOMICIDE LAWS

"F.E.A.R. has two meanings—Forget Everything
and Run OR Face Everything and Rise."

UNKNOWN

Will this person save a life, or run out of fear of being prosecuted for manslaughter?

There is a recent trend in drug-induced homicide laws which define delivering drugs that result in a death as a homicide. Several states[455] currently have drug-induced homicide laws on the books, and a number of states without specific statutes still charge defendants alleged to have delivered drugs resulting in death with felony-murder or involuntary or voluntary manslaughter.

We all worry about our loved ones. It's natural to want to blame someone when we lose someone we love to overdose, but these laws increase the risk that overdose will end in death.

Issues with drug-induced homicide laws include the following:

1. These penalties make it much more likely that someone suffering an overdose will be left to die while those worried about prosecution flee.

2. Your naïve son or daughter who stupidly shares a drug with a friend (or is accused of doing so) can be caught up in prosecution under these laws and spend life in prison.

3. Prosecutors use drug-induced homicide laws to frighten defendants into harsh plea offers to avoid even a threat that a defense against a homicide charge would be required. This can result in guilty pleas by innocent defendants, as well as plea agreements that are much harsher than is warranted for the crime committed.

Studies have consistently shown that punitive sentences for drug offenses have no deterrent effect. They simply don't accomplish the goal, but do cause significant harm.[456]

Good Samaritan laws shield individuals calling for emergency medical help or administering medications that can save the life of an overdose victim, from civil liability. These laws also prevent criminal prosecution for drug possession, possession of paraphernalia, and/or being under the influence for people who overdose or who seek medical help for someone else overdosing. These laws have proven to be effective in providing incentives for bystanders or others to call for help and to stay with someone in medical trouble. The trend toward drug-induced homicide laws counteracts the benefits of Good Samaritan laws.

CHAPTER 33

PROHIBIT LEGAL PROFESSIONALS FROM PRACTICING MEDICINE WITHOUT A LICENSE

"Overconfidence is the most dangerous
form of carelessness."

STAR WARS: THE CLONE WARS

Law is complicated. That's why attorneys are licensed to practice law. Medicine is also complicated. Medical providers are trained and licensed to practice medicine. The War on Drugs has created an absurd system. Physicians are now raided under suspicion by the DEA, essentially restricting their ability to use their best medical judgment to treat their patients. At the same time, judges, prosecutors, probation agents, and corrections officers make medical judgments, mandating medical treatment and denying other medical treatment.

Medications prescribed by professionals whose expertise is addiction medicine are denied to patients because legal or criminal justice professionals with no medical training and no personal medical information on individual patients believe they know more about treatment than the physician. Then, when the patient is put behind bars, they lose access to that personal physician, and are restricted to a general jail doctor for medical needs, if they are allowed to see that provider. That practitioner will almost certainly not be trained in addiction or pain management medicine, and will almost certainly not be certified to prescribe medications that are essential for substance use patients.

As an attorney, if a medical provider began giving legal advice to a client, and particularly if that provider denied my access to the client, I would consider filing an action for unauthorized practice of law against that medical professional. I would also be concerned for my client. In that case, though, my client's life would not be at stake. When attorneys replace their judgment for the medical professional's medical diagnosis and treatment plan, they are putting lives at stake.

Any action by legal professionals to deny prescription medications to a patient must end. Any directive mandating a patient to undergo a treatment protocol not selected by the patient with advice from medical professionals of that patient's choice must end. Restrictions on a patient's right to pursue treatment based on advice from that patient's medical advisors must end.

The logical way to do this is simply to stop arresting those with substance use disorder. In lieu of criminal justice involvement, referrals could be made to organizations providing services similar to LEAP, as discussed in Chapter # 23. Offering help in locating treatment is beneficial, but mandating or prohibiting specific types of treatment is inappropriate, has led to death in multiple cases, and has done immense harm in others.[457]

CHAPTER 34

UNCUFF THE JUDGES— END "THREE STRIKES" AND MANDATORY MINIMUMS

"Mandatory minimum sentences for drug offenses are the prime reason that the U.S. prison population has ballooned since the 1980s to over 2.5 million people, a nearly 300% increase."

PIPER KERMAN

One of the most dangerous and frightening aspects of criminal law are federal and state mandatory minimum and three-strikes statutes, which increase penalties for those deemed to be repeat offenders.

Mandatory minimum sentences are established by Congress or by state legislatures, and remove discretion on sentencing from the judge who can otherwise take individual circumstances into consideration. Mandatory minimum sentences apply primarily to drug offenses.

One of the challenges for patients with substance use disorder is that until they get help, they will likely continue to use drugs. This makes them prime candidates to get caught in repeat offenses, which can result in decades-long sentences.

These laws have devastating consequences. In numerous cases, court transcripts show judges apologizing and frustrated that the law mandates that they apply penalties that far exceed what the judge believes is appropriate.

Unfortunately, rather than getting drug kingpins and high-level dealers off the streets, many low-level, nonviolent offenders are caught by the provisions of these statutes and serve inordinately long sentences. These defendants often have no information to exchange for special consideration by prosecutors who decide what charges are to be filed, so are in a disadvantageous negotiating position. Patients with substance use disorder, those with poor communication skills, or who have mental health issues are at a particular disadvantage.

National Public Radio discussed mandatory minimums with federal judge Mark Bennett of Iowa, who stated, "These mandatory minimums are so incredibly harsh, and they're triggered by such low levels of drugs that they snare at these nonviolent, low-level addicts who are involved in drug distribution mostly to obtain drugs to feed their habit. They have a medical problem. It's called addiction, and they're going to be faced with five- and 10- and 20-year and sometimes life mandatory minimum sentences. I think that's a travesty."[458]

In recent years, the trend has been to reduce mandatory minimums under these statutes and to increase judges' discretion in sentencing. Reforms have occurred based on the devastating effects, not only for the prisoners but also for the taxpayers who have carried the burden of the huge expense of long-term incarceration. The First Step Act adjusted sentences from life to 25 years, increased judge discretion in some cases, and increased the threshold for prior convictions that trigger higher mandatory minimum sentences. It's a start, but the risk for low-level drug users to end up behind bars for years remains.

Three-strikes laws mandate incredibly long sentences for "repeat offenders" who may find themselves under the umbrella of these policies based on two minor drug possession felonies and one bar fight or other crime involving violence. While a violent action may warrant punishment, most people would agree that decades in prison is excessive.

In some cases, the "violent crime" was a woman sitting in a car while her boyfriend committed an act that she may have been unaware of. The First Step Act resolved some of these issues by changing the definition of felonies for three strikes law purposes from any felony drug offense to "a serious drug felony or serious violent felony."[459] That is a good first step, but we have a long way to go.

The First Step Act only applies to federal cases. State law varies considerably from jurisdiction to jurisdiction. Families Against Mandatory Minimums[460] has excellent, current information on each state's statutes as well as federal law and recent legal developments.

Decriminalization or legalization of drugs would solve the issue with these statutes. Mandatory minimum and three strikes laws may make sense for repeat offenders committing violent crime, but mixing drug possession into the mix has created heartbreaking and unjust results.

CHAPTER 35
A NASAL SPRAY FOR LIFE

"Maybe I couldn't help everyone survive,
but I could, at least, save this one life."

TIANA WARNER, ICE CRYPT

Opioids including heroin, morphine, oxycodone, methadone, hydroco-done (Vicodin), codeine, tramadol, and other prescription pain medica-tions can slow or stop a person's breathing, which can result in death or brain damage. If you see someone whose breathing is slowed or cannot be woken up, a simple nasal spray can save that life. Naloxone (trade name Narcan) is available in an easy-to-use nasal spray. Naloxone is also available under the trade name Evzio as an epi-pen, similar to those used for allergic reactions, which can be administered into the upper arm muscle or the outer thigh.

If all EMTs and other medical personnel, criminal justice professionals, teachers, parents, and concerned citizens carried naloxone, there is no doubt that many lives would be saved. Despite some who've suggested that the life of a patient with a substance use disorder is not worth saving, it's important to understand that 10 percent of the U.S. population reports having had a substance use issue at some point in their life.[461] Many have gone on to make significant contributions to society. Having this simple nasal spray on hand could also save the life of a first-time user. It may be a teen simply experimenting. One-time experimentation can be fatal.

You may be familiar with Narcan, but if you don't have it in your possession, you could miss an opportunity to save a life. Could you access it *right now* if it was needed? Does your son or daughter have it available for immediate access if a friend or acquaintance overdoses? Statistics on overdose death make it important for as many people as possible to have this life-saving drug on hand.

If you see someone whose breathing is slowed or cannot be woken up, naloxone should be administered. Within two to five minutes, the overdose victim should wake up. Rescue breathing should be done while waiting for naloxone to take effect to get oxygen to the brain.

Administering naloxone may cause uncomfortable withdrawal symptoms, but these symptoms are not fatal. Naloxone can reverse the effects of the opioid overdose and block the opioid for 30 to 90 minutes. After that time, the person may stop breathing again unless more naloxone is available. Calling 911 to access more advanced medical care after administering naloxone is recommended.

If a response doesn't happen within two to three minutes, administer a second dose. Reports that fentanyl does not respond to naloxone are not true, but multiple doses of naloxone may be required if fentanyl is involved. Reports that fentanyl can be fatal to police or other first responders is also a myth, and unfortunately could be deadly if a first responder fails to act based on fear perpetuated by that myth. It's a good idea to wear gloves and to use water to wash skin exposed to fentanyl, but reports of first responder overdoses ended up being untrue, and toxicology experts confirm that for fentanyl to cause an overdose, it must be inhaled, ingested, or delivered by a syringe.[462] Dermal patches can be used for delivery of fentanyl, but those take several hours to absorb.

According to a report from the Centers for Disease Control and Prevention, naloxone was used by lay people to save nearly 27,000 lives from 1996 to 2014.[463] Many instances go unreported and use of naloxone has increased significantly since that report, so it's likely that the number of lives saved is far greater.

Even if an overdose victim's "drug of choice" is not an opioid, administering naloxone may still be beneficial. Fentanyl, which is an opiate, is added to other non-opioid drugs such as methamphetamine or cocaine. Naloxone won't help with an overdose on non-opioids, but *can* reverse an overdose due to fentanyl within another drug. Naloxone is not addictive, and it does not create a "high." If naloxone is administered to someone who doesn't use opioids, unless there's an allergic reaction or unless it's a pregnant or nursing woman, it is not dangerous. Generally, it's much safer to err on the side of administering naloxone rather than delaying.

To protect high-risk family members, or simply to make sure your community is using current harm-reduction methods, check with local police departments and first responders to determine whether they carry naloxone, and to verify that the jail has it available on site. Emergency medical personnel have been using naloxone to save overdose victims for decades, but with increasing overdose rates, many states are expanding training and access to the medication to increase use by law enforcement and first responders.

If your local police and first responders don't carry naloxone, advocating that they begin having it available may be instrumental in saving a life. Even if first responders and police in your area carry naloxone, it's still important to personally have it on hand. Even a five-minute delay, waiting for emergency personnel to arrive, could be the difference between life or death or brain damage or full recovery.

Unfortunately, legal access to naloxone does not guarantee actual availability. An essential first step in harm reduction is for government entities to make this medication available to anyone who wants it. As more people became aware of its effectiveness and as the overdose rates climbed over the years, it has become easier to access, but in some locations, it still takes diligence to get access to this important medication and it can be prohibitively expensive.

After newspaper and internet articles reported that naloxone without a prescription was available at pharmacies, I visited two major chains to obtain naloxone and to experience the process needed to get it. CVS didn't require a personal prescription, but did require extensive paperwork. They said their supply was on backorder, and recommended that I check back at a later time to see if any came in. It was fortunate that I didn't have an immediate need.

At Walgreens, the pharmacist informed me that they had none available, and that I would need a prescription to order any. As I exited the Walgreen's pharmacy and walked toward my car, a young man who'd overheard my conversation with the pharmacist approached me and offered one of the two doses of naloxone that he carried. Although the interesting 45-minute conversation that followed was inspiring, the fact that getting a legal, life-saving drug required a chance meeting in a parking lot for "contraband" naloxone is an example of the dysfunction and utter insanity of our current system. Had I been a parent still in the depths of dealing with a child's active addiction, the lack of access may have made me simply give up at that time, resulting in not carrying a life-saving medication.

The difficulty of obtaining naloxone can make parents feel dirty, as if they're trying to score illegal drugs. The stigma involved with obtaining this medication can make a desperate situation even more difficult for those simply trying to prepare to save the life of their child or others. The experience of obtaining this important medication left me seriously questioning our priorities. We spend billions of dollars arresting, prosecuting, and incarcerating people with substance use disorders, yet policy and lack of funding make it difficult to obtain a life-saving nasal spray.

Some object to making access to naloxone easier under the mistaken belief that this could increase drug use. There is no evidence to support this objection.[464] Even if that objection could somehow be supported, letting someone die when that life could be saved with a simple nasal spray is inhumane.

Some states have developed workarounds to make naloxone access easier, using a "standing order" that authorizes a pharmacist to distribute it without a patient-specific prescription from the patient's personal medical provider. This may be easier than a full appointment with a practitioner to get a prescription, but still entails significant paperwork at the pharmacy, including answering a lot of questions. There may be cost savings if a personal prescription is obtained to benefit from potential insurance coverage, to obtain discounts given to insurers, or to use discount coupons that only apply to medications purchased with a prescription. Unfortunately, many drug users and their parents are either embarrassed to complete paperwork at the pharmacy or to request a prescription from their medical provider, or are afraid to do so in fear of being identified as a drug user, increasing the risk of arrest and prosecution.

In 2018, the U.S. Surgeon General issued an advisory calling for wider distribution of naloxone to opioid users and those who are close to them. To accomplish this, the U.S. Food and Drug Administration (FDA) should reschedule naloxone to make it an over-the-counter drug. Lives would be saved, and those who want to have it available could simply check it out at the counter without answering questions or risking stigma from the pharmacist. That would also likely reduce cost, making it more economically feasible for many to carry it.[465] Naloxone has been available over the counter in Italy for over 20 years, and Australia made it over-the-counter in 2016.[466]

CHAPTER 36

IS A LIFE WORTH TWO DOLLARS?

"An ounce of prevention is worth a pound of cure."

BENJAMIN FRANKLIN

It's not unusual for a parent to have the talk with their teen saying, "Please don't drink, but if you find yourself in a negative situation, even if you've been drinking, call us and we'll pick you up." The priority is on safety. Lessons in social and personal responsibility may come later, but that knowledge is irrelevant if the teen doesn't make it home.

Test strips that indicate whether fentanyl is present in a drug utilize the same rationale. These strips are available for approximately two U.S. dollars. It's counter-intuitive to hand a loved one a test strip that would only be used if they're in active drug use, but whether we want to face it or not, if a person is in active addiction, they will use drugs anyway. The question is whether we can keep them alive until they reach a point where help is available or accepted. Until then, is it worth a $2 test strip to potentially save a life? A test strip that shows whether fentanyl is present in the drug may keep someone you know from becoming a statistic.

Fentanyl is a synthetic opioid that can be 50 to 100 times more potent than morphine, and is increasingly used by drug dealers to cut their drug supplies. Researchers at Rand Corporation pointed out that the fentanyl crisis is different because "the spread of synthetic opioids is largely driven by suppliers' decisions, not by user demand. Most people who use opioids are not asking for fentanyl and would prefer to avoid exposure."[467] The fentanyl crisis is a direct result of drug prohibition, which incentivizes drug dealers to concentrate substances for easier smuggling.

Overdose deaths from synthetic opioids, particularly fentanyl, increased from approximately 3,000 in 2013 to over 30,000 in 2018 in the U.S. alone, now causing twice as many deaths as heroin.[468] Death rates are likely higher. The National Institute on Drug Abuse reported that in gathering their statistics, 15 to 25 percent of death certificates analyzed did not indicate the type of drug involved in the overdose because drug tests were not conducted or test results were not recorded.

Synthetic opioids, primarily Fentanyl, were involved in 19,413 reported overdose deaths in 2016, comprising nearly 50 percent of opioid-related overdose deaths.

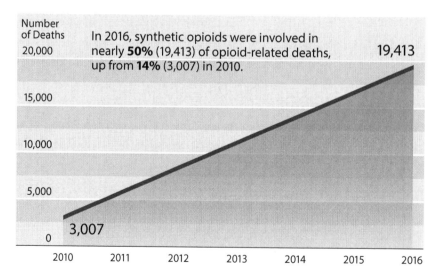

Source: National Institute on Drug Abuse[469]

When fentanyl is added to other drugs, it's typically not mixed evenly, so content of one side of a baggie may contain none while the other side of the baggie is deadly. Therefore, testing the drug to be consumed, rather than just representative samples from a baggie, is essential. Fentanyl may be in heroin, methamphetamine, cocaine, MDMA, and many other drugs. Test strips could have saved Prince or Tom Petty. They may save your child.

Will use of test strips convince a person addicted to a drug not to use it? There's no guarantee that it will, but if the strips don't convince them not to use the drug, a positive test may convince them to use a reduced amount, or to at least use with someone nearby who has Narcan available. This is a depressing picture, but is still better than receiving a call about a fatal overdose.

Misuse of prescription drugs is dangerous when used in a manner other than medically directed or when mixed with other drugs, but at least prescription drugs are manufactured under FDA guidelines. Dosage is consistent and content is controlled. Illegal drugs are manufactured in unknown, uncontrolled conditions. Users have no way of knowing potency or actual ingredients. For this reason, the War on Drugs has created results similar to incidents of alcohol poisoning from moonshine during the prohibition era, but multiplied many times in death and tragedy created.

Would it be preferable for loved ones to never use an unprescribed drug? Yes. But if the multiple-choice options don't include "drug-free" but do include test strips vs. fatal overdose, I know which alternative many will select if they're aware of that alternative.

CHAPTER 37

PUBLIC RESTROOMS OR SANITARY CARE?

"Studies from other countries have shown that supervised injection facilities reduce the number of overdose deaths, reduce transmission rates of infectious disease, and increase the number of individuals initiating treatment for substance use disorders without increasing drug trafficking or crime in the areas where the facilities are located."

AMERICAN MEDICAL ASSOCIATION

Safe consumption sites (SCS), also appropriately referred to as "Overdose Prevention Sites," are legally sanctioned locations where people can inject drugs under medical supervision. The sites provide sterile equipment, information about reducing the harm of drugs, health care, treatment referrals, and access to medical staff. Some offer other services like condom distribution and counseling services.

There are approximately 120 legally sanctioned safe consumption sites worldwide. Locations include Australia, Canada, Denmark, France, Germany, Luxembourg, the Netherlands, Norway, Spain, and

Switzerland. There are currently no authorized safe consumption sites in the United States. One unsanctioned site in the United States has been reviewed and found to have beneficial outcomes.[470]

Many of the most effective methods in combatting addiction and in sound drug policy are counterintuitive. (That helps to explain our tendency to hold onto failed policies, even after more than half a century of failure.) Safe consumption sites are no exception. How can providing a place to inject heroin possibly be good policy, and how could it help someone who is addicted to drugs?

Based on the history of existing sites worldwide, evidence is conclusive that these programs are successful from a public health perspective. Hundreds of peer-reviewed studies have assessed these sites and analyzed the results of their use.[471] Evidence is clear that safe consumption sites prevent the spread of infectious disease including HIV and hepatitis, and increase access to social services and treatment for substance use disorder. These programs also protect the public, including reduction in use of public restrooms for drug injection and reduction in the number of used needles left in public places.[472]

There have been no overdose fatalities in any safe injection site worldwide, and overall overdose rates of areas in which sites are located have been significantly reduced. The fatal overdose rate in Vancouver, Canada's downtown Eastside decreased by 35 percent after opening of Insite, a safe injection site.[473]

Barriers to safe consumption sites are high, however, largely based on lack of information, emotion, fear, and stigma. In the United States, Safehouse, a nonprofit organization, was set to open a safe consumption site in Philadelphia. The Philadelphia mayor had announced that the city would not stand in the way of opening the site. Then, the U.S. attorney for the Eastern District of Pennsylvania filed an action to prevent opening of the site. In the Complaint, the federal government cites no evidence-based rationale for prohibiting the site. The basis for the prohibition is 21 USC § 856, the so-called 'crack house statute', a provision of the Controlled Substances Act that makes it illegal to "knowingly open, lease, rent, use, or maintain any place . . . for the purpose of . . . using any controlled substance." This puts property owners at risk of prosecution if they rent to or allow safe consumption sites to operate on their property.

Legally, states and some municipalities have the power to authorize safe injection sites under state law, but, as with cannabis issues discussed earlier, federal authorities may interfere. Attorneys general from seven states and the District of Columbia filed a brief in the Safehouse case in support of supervised injection sites, framing it as a states-rights issue. More than five dozen current and former state and federal prosecutors and some police chiefs also joined in support of Safehouse.

In October, 2019, the U.S. vs. Safehouse case was decided in favor of Safehouse. U.S. District Court Judge Gerald McHugh ruled that the safe consumption site planned by Safehouse does not violate the Controlled Substances Act because "The ultimate goal of Safehouse's proposed operation is to reduce drug use, not facilitate it . . ." This decision allows the nonprofit to open the safe injection site. However, the case will be appealed, and a state senator plans to propose Pennsylvania state legislation that would prohibit safe injection sites. If Safehouse is able to open its doors, it's likely that it will serve as a model for other U.S. cities.

In 2018, California's Governor Jerry Brown vetoed a bill that would have allowed San Francisco to open the first safe injection site in the United States, stating "enabling illegal and destructive drug use will never work." Brown has now been replaced by Governor Gavin Newsom, who stated when campaigning that he was open to the idea of safe injection sites. A bill very similar to the one vetoed by Brown has been introduced and passed by the California Assembly.[474]

Despite the stigma and disdain often directed at drug users, their lives are important. They can recover and can be important members of society. They are sons, daughters, husbands, wives, parents, and friends. They're human beings struggling with a health issue for which our society offers little help and has historically ignored standard medical practices. Evidence tells us that safe injection sites are beneficial to the public as well as to patients utilizing the sites. The American Medical Association states, "Studies from other countries have shown that supervised injection facilities reduce the number of overdose deaths, reduce transmission rates of infectious disease, and increase the number of individuals initiating treatment for substance use disorders without increasing drug trafficking or crime in the areas where the facilities are located."[475]

One of the reasons for the success of safe consumption sites and the increase in willingness to accept treatment is that these sites provide medical resources without judgment, treating drug users with respect, as human beings. This environment is one which is seldom available to those with substance use disorder. Not only are safe consumption sites beneficial for individuals and for the public; They are simply the most humane and moral approach available.

Heroin-assisted treatment (HAT) is used in conjunction with safe consumption sites in Europe and Canada. In countries that allow safe consumption sites but not HAT, patients bring their own substances to the site, where at least clean syringes and Narcan are available. In countries allowing HAT, providing the medical grade drug reduces risk of overdose, disease and other issues caused by adulterated street drugs. Patients are also often prescribed oral methadone to stem cravings to move toward recovery.

A study by the Rand Corporation concluded that the success of HAT and safe consumption sites in Europe and Canada suggests that clinical trials for HAT and safe consumption sites in the United States would be worthwhile.[476] The report found that HAT, combined with oral methadone, can be more beneficial than methadone alone. It also found that HAT successfully reduces exposure to tainted street drugs, and reduces the criminal activity of people seeking drugs on the street. Before these techniques can be used in the United States, however, several legal hurtles need to be addressed. Heroin is a Schedule 1 drug, complicating the ability to conduct clinical trials and prohibiting writing of prescriptions.

Needle exchange programs are sometimes used in conjunction with safe injection sites and sometimes as separate programs. They allow people to exchange used needles for clean ones, preventing sharing of needles and transmission of disease. Needle exchange programs have been proven to decrease HIV rates and other blood-borne viruses. Many needle exchange programs also provide public health services ranging from referral to treatment to HIV counseling and testing and other health care.

U.S. federal law prohibits use of federal funds to support needle exchange programs.[477] Despite that, state, local, or privately funded programs operate in 38 states in the U.S. An average city spends approximately $160,000 to run a program. This is cost-effective, since one syringe-infected AIDS patient will require in excess of $120,000 annually in public health costs.[478] Needle exchange programs create a reduction in risk behaviors as high as 80 percent according to a study by the National Institutes of Health.[479] The Centers for Disease Control and Prevention also found that needle exchange programs resulted in an 80 percent lower incidence of HIV among those who inject drugs.

CHAPTER 38

RECRUIT, TRAIN, AND RESPECT THE DOCS

*"An investment in knowledge always
pays the best interest."*

BENJAMIN FRANKLIN

As we move away from using punitive measures through the criminal justice system toward a public health approach in addressing concerns with substance use, the need for professionals with specialized training in addiction medicine becomes essential. The ability of family medicine practitioners to diagnose substance use disorder and to either treat or refer cases appropriately also becomes incredibly important.

General practitioners and emergency room medical professionals are in unique positions to begin treatment or to make appropriate referrals at a time when the patient may be open to help. Most of those with substance use disorders ultimately end up in the emergency room. This offers opportunities to get them immediate treatment, including beginning medications when appropriate. This is often a time of crisis, when they may be open-minded to treatment if it is offered and available. Until recently, the extent of addiction treatment in the ER was being sent home with a Narcotics Anonymous flyer. That has begun to change.

Dr. Zachary Dezman, an emergency room physician in Baltimore, Maryland, stated, "These patients are marginalized from the health care system. We see people every day who have nowhere else to go. If they need addiction medicine—and many do—why wouldn't we give it to them in the ER? We give them medicine for every other life-threatening disease."[480] This is not yet the norm, but incorporating addiction treatment into emergency room practices is the trend, and initial results are promising.

Researchers at Yale School of Medicine, in a 2017 study, reported that patients with opioid use disorder who were given an initial dose of buprenorphine in an emergency room were twice as likely to be in treatment a month later as compared to those who were only given a referral to an addiction treatment specialist.[481]

2018 legislation in Massachusetts requires most hospitals and ERs in the state to offer medications to treat substance use disorder to patients who may need it. The Massachusetts Health and Hospital Association (MHA) issued guidelines to help medical professionals to work through the maze that can arise when treating substance use patients including special requirements to write scripts for buprenorphine and coordination of follow-up care. The MHA guidelines are being used to begin programs in other locations in and outside of Massachusetts. These practices are still the exception rather than the rule. A 2017 survey by the American College of Emergency Physicians reported that only five percent of emergency physicians work in hospitals where either buprenorphine or methadone are offered.

One of the barriers to administration of initial addiction medications in the emergency room is the special waiver requirement for physicians to write buprenorphine prescriptions. There is a three-day rule that allows doctors without the special DEA license to administer a single day's dose of the medication to be taken within 72 hours.[482] This is a workaround. Restrictions on prescribing medications to treat substance use disorder should be eliminated to allow ER and other medical professionals to treat this deadly health issue.

As ERs become more aware and engaged in addiction treatment including use of medications, follow-through after discharge is essential. Otherwise, use of medications for a short time may simply lower tolerance levels, increasing risks of overdose if the patient resumes drug use at levels comparable to those used prior to the initial ER visit. Referral to physicians licensed to continue prescriptions for buprenorphine are typically made.

In addition to changes in emergency room practices, education, support, and incentives for physicians and other health care professionals to practice in areas treating addiction and pain management are desperately needed.

Medical providers may have justifiable reservations about serving patients with substance use issues or patients struggling with chronic pain. These areas of practice are often less lucrative than other specialties, patients can be difficult to work with, and diagnosis can be challenging with multiple issues often overlapping. On top of that, practitioners have become fearful of DEA raids and criminal and civil liability related to prescribing medications. Insurance companies are sending directives to providers encouraging changes in prescribing practices, and prior approval requirements cause delay and sometimes denial of treatment prescribed. Out of frustration and fear, physicians and other health care providers have left areas of practice treating pain patients or addiction patients, and fewer new medical professionals are focusing on these areas.[483]

Pain management specialties overlap with addiction services not because most pain patients are addicted, but because medications used to treat pain have received a reputation for being dangerous. While it's important to be aware of potential for addiction during treatment for pain, it's also important for medical professionals to be legally allowed to prescribe pain medications without undue risk of liability.

Steps to minimize risk and to reduce stigma and potential liability for medical professionals in these areas would go a long way to saving lives, providing medical care for medical issues, and minimizing costs to society of active addiction. Government incentives to attract physicians to these areas of practice including satisfaction of outstanding medical school loans and tax incentives could help in filling the huge void that currently exists for qualified physicians to treat the hundreds of thousands of patients needing medical care in these specialty areas.

Drew E. Altman, PhD[484], when discussing the issues with lack of health care treatment for substance use disorder, stated, "In homes, doctors' offices, hospitals, schools, prisons, jails and communities across America, misperceptions about addiction are undermining medical care. Although advances in neuroscience, brain imaging and behavioral research clearly show that addiction is a complex brain disease, today the disease of addiction is still often misunderstood as a moral failing, a lack of willpower, a subject of shame and disgust. . . . The medical system, which is dedicated to alleviating suffering and treating disease, largely has been disengaged from these serious health care problems. The consequences of this inattention are profound."

A study by Columbia University[485] concluded that only about one in 10 people with addiction involving alcohol or drugs other than nicotine receive any form of treatment. They further concluded: "Of those who do receive treatment, few receive anything that approximates evidence-based care. This compares with 70 percent to 80 percent of people with such diseases as high blood pressure and diabetes who do receive treatment. This report exposes the fact that most medical professionals who should be providing addiction treatment are not sufficiently trained to diagnose or treat the disease, and most of those providing addiction care are not medical professionals and are not equipped with the knowledge, skills or credentials necessary to provide the full range of effective treatments. Misunderstandings about the nature of addiction and the best ways to address it, as well as the disconnection of addiction medicine from mainstream medical practice, have undermined effective addiction treatment."

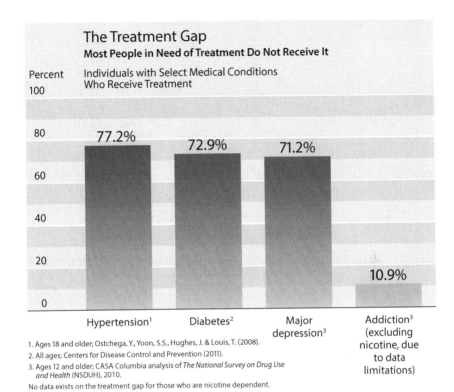

The Treatment Gap
Most People in Need of Treatment Do Not Receive It

Percent — Individuals with Select Medical Conditions Who Receive Treatment

1. Ages 18 and older; Ostchega, Y., Yoon, S.S., Hughes, J. & Louis, T. (2008).
2. All ages; Centers for Disease Control and Prevention (2011).
3. Ages 12 and older; CASA Columbia analysis of *The National Survey on Drug Use and Health* (NSDUH), 2010.
No data exists on the treatment gap for those who are nicotine dependent.

Reproduced/adapted with permission from National Center on Addiction and Substance Abuse at Columbia University[486]

The role of traditional health care professionals in treatment of substance use disorders has been minimal at best. Funding and training for addiction services has been woefully absent when compared to other medical treatment and the numbers of people impacted. United States spending statistics illustrate how incredibly underfunded addiction treatment is in relationship to other medical issues.

Disease	# of People Affected	Funding Provided
Cancer	19 million	$86.8 billion
Diabetes	25.8 million	$43.8 billion
Heart Condition	27 million	$107 billion
Addiction	40.3 million	$28 billion

Reproduced/adapted with permission from National Center on Addiction and Substance Abuse at Columbia University[487]

Even more distressing is the fact that, of the $28 billion in funding, 95.6 cents of every dollar has been allocated to pay for consequences and attempts at controlling supply (including prosecution and incarceration), with only 1.9 cents of every dollar spent on any type of prevention or treatment.[488]

The Columbia report[489] states, "There is no other disease that affects so many people, has such far-reaching consequences and for which there is such a broad range of effective interventions and treatments that is as neglected as the disease of addiction."

An understanding of substance use disorder impacts all areas of medical practice. Addiction seldom exists in a vacuum. It's often combined with attention deficit, depression, anxiety, physical pain, and/or other physical or emotional issues.[490] This can create a vicious cycle in diagnosis and treatment. What came first—the underlying issue or the addiction? Was the drug use an attempt to self-medicate the initial condition, or did the addiction and the lifestyle that accompanies drug use create or exacerbate the other physical or emotional condition?

The "Just Say No" culture also reduces societal resolve to find solutions, and is likely the reason for the underfunding of medical treatment in this area. We are beginning to understand the medical basis for substance use disorder and the impact of other medical issues on the addiction and overdose epidemic.

The long medical history that can be a result of addiction can overwhelm families and medical professionals and cloud diagnostic focus. Symptoms may be mistakenly attributed to the effects of drug use or the unhealthy lifestyle that often accompanies addiction. The same symptoms presented by a patient without substance use issues may be taken more seriously or may be easier to spot than when presented in a substance use patient, since symptoms aren't camouflaged by drug use.

Many in the medical profession are distrustful of patients exhibiting signs of addiction. Recently, this suspicion has expanded to pain patients with no history of substance use disorder. Patients complaining of pain may simply not be taken seriously. The medical provider may believe that the patient is exaggerating pain simply in an effort to get a prescription. Although there may be legitimate basis for the distrust of those in active addiction (providers are "conned" by those attempting to get prescriptions), this can also create challenges for those who have medical issues, whether addiction-related or otherwise. Pain patients are sometimes treated like drug-seekers, required and charged for ongoing drug tests, and denied medications that have worked for them long term or that are necessary for their comfort and health.

For addiction patients, emotional issues, especially combined with drug use, make communication more difficult, and may make the patient less willing to participate in his or her own therapeutic treatment. Medical issues combined with addiction also add to risk of relapse. If physical and/or emotional pain led to addiction in the first place, how can that be controlled without using narcotics? No medical provider wants to be accused of writing prescriptions when there's a history of addiction, and those with substance use disorder have to be more careful than the general population about taking addictive medications, but a diagnosis of addiction should not permanently deny patients access to medications that could be beneficial in medical treatment.

Determining appropriate medications and finding other ways of controlling health issues can be a greater challenge when addiction is a factor. Many of the more holistic approaches—counseling, yoga, physical therapy, massage, chiropractic, and other types of complimentary care can be helpful, but also may not be covered by insurance. For those with significant pain, being told to use yoga in place of medications can be infuriating, and can seriously jeopardize quality of life.

Not getting appropriate medical treatment can lead to use of potentially tainted street drugs as a last effort for control of physical or emotional pain if it can't be achieved through legal methods, potentially creating ongoing criminal justice issues and increasing overdose risks.

Historically, medical and nursing schools have provided very little training on addiction. Medical and nursing school curriculum is beginning to include more training on substance use disorder, and students are more aware of the need for information. In 2015, the American Board of Medical Specialties recognized addiction medicine as a bona fide subspecialty that, in turn, allowed for approval of addiction fellowships.[491] There are now approximately 60 fellowships in addiction medicine.

The American Institute of Health Care Professionals, Inc. (AIHCP) offers a "Substance Abuse Practitioner Certification" program.[492] The University of Seattle offers a Master of Science in Nursing/Psychiatric Mental Health Nurse Practitioner with Addictions Focus Specialization.[493] These and other programs will be pivotal in converting substance use policy from a punitive, criminal justice approach to a compassionate, science-based medical approach.

Medical schools are becoming more aware of the need for more extensive training on addiction for all specialties, to allow general practitioners and physicians practicing in all areas to recognize signs of substance use disorder, and to understand the interactions of addiction with their respective areas of practice. This education has centered heavily on opioids and prescribing of opioids, but hopefully training will develop to include broader-based training on all substance use disorders.

Stanford's medical school has broken substance use training into a separate unit (no longer just included as part of the psychiatry unit), and clinical rotations will also now include training on substance use disorder.

Part of the reason for minimal training on addiction in medical schools is that medical faculties, like the general public, historically looked at it as a result of poor choices rather than a medical issue. Stigma and outdated attitudes about addiction are present in the medical community as they have been in society at large. Those attitudes can be life threatening, and can create immense pain for patients as well as their families.

More extensive training on the medical causes and treatments of addiction will minimize stigma that some patients feel from their physicians or other medical professionals who may treat them. Judgments and attitudes impact the level of medical care. Demands on emergency room medical providers leave them little time to get personal histories, increasing the risk that harmful judgments may be made. An understanding of the trauma experienced by patients at the hands of the criminal justice system is important to give medical professionals insight into emotional and physical responses the patient may present because of that trauma.

As addiction treatment services are expanded and include medical services, taxpayers may have legitimate concern about taxpayer cost, whether in the emergency room or through traditional medical care. However, treatment could be provided to patients with NO additional cost simply by converting focus from punishment to medical care. If the money spent on punitive measures including law enforcement, prosecution, incarceration, long-term probation or parole, and other criminal justice expenses related to possession of drugs was reallocated to funding treatment, we would see much greater progress in minimizing the addiction and overdose epidemic, with no additional cost to taxpayers.

Cost savings will also be achieved by ending the waste that occurs because of the impact of punitive drug policy on medical care. The prevalence of drug testing and the impact that prescription drugs can have in causing false negatives for illegal drugs may cause patients who are on probation or parole to be afraid to take prescription drugs even when those drugs are medically indicated. Attitudes of many within the criminal justice system as well as the general population that the only viable alternative to addiction is total abstinence from all drugs can make it more difficult to treat patients with substance use disorders.

In many cases, the patient may not disclose their reasons for failing to follow through with recommendations, further frustrating medical professionals who are trying to adequately treat patients. It's important that physicians and other medical professionals are aware of the reasons that these patients may avoid some forms of medical care. Legal professionals including judges, prosecutors, and defense attorneys, as well as other court personnel such as probation agents, should understand that abstinence-only attitudes and reliance on drug tests that can give false positives due to legitimately prescribed medications can seriously jeopardize overall medical treatment.

Medical professionals have a difficult job. Not only have they received little training in regard to substance use disorder, but they are typically under tight time constraints for how much time they can allocate to a patient. This, combined with challenges with communication and multiple medical issues typical when working with patients with substance use disorder, make good medical treatment a challenge. When looking at all of the challenges faced by trained medical professionals in diagnosis of addiction and accompanying disorders, it is astonishing that our current system assigns these tasks to peer support groups and legal professionals with no medical training who apply one-size-fits-all "treatment," and then punish the patient when that treatment is ineffective.

Pain patients, addiction patients, and others are finding it more and more difficult to obtain the medications needed for their personal health care. Ongoing issues with lapses in prescriptions, forced taper off of medications that were working, and requirements of refill every few days compromise overall health. If drug policy is to protect individual health, it is doing just the opposite. Going on and off of meds, changing dosages, and the stress of worrying about lack of access to needed medications and professional medical care all compromise health and make the lives of patients and their physicians very difficult.

Drug policy reform must prohibit criminal justice professionals from dictating treatment and overruling medical professionals. This would be a positive development, but would also require changes within the medical field to assume responsibility for treating patients if funding and authority are moved from criminal justice to medical and public health arenas. It's important that reform includes funding and structure to build these services.

"Take care of the patient and everything else will follow."
—Thomas Frist, M.D.

CHAPTER 39

COULD LUCK BE THE BASIS OF DRUG POLICY?

"Nobody gets justice. People only
get good luck or bad luck."

ORSON WELLES

A Facebook post says: "Feeling proud tonight. Two years ago on this night I made a total ass out of myself in front of some old friends and my fiancé. The next day I actually started medications that helped me to turn my life around. It really doesn't seem like two years have gone by. Life is great now. Has been for a while. Pretty solid. I'm married to my beautiful, wonderful, and patient wife. She's been with me through some of the worst days of my addiction. She decided I was worth staying with, never gave up. We have a beautiful 3-month old baby girl. She is beyond my words of explanation. She is the best thing I've ever had a chance to be part of. My career is going strong. Bills are paid. Savings in the bank, which never mattered to me before. My credit has been rebuilt. We're actually able to live a normal life." [Photo of baby followed.]

Reading this type of post gives us hope, and warms the heart. It's the result we all want. I'm thankful that this individual was allowed to move on to fully live his life, to support his family, to contribute to society, and to reap the benefits of his hard work in recovery. Unfortunately, the exact same story ends much differently for many.

On that night when he "made a total ass of himself" or on many other nights during his active addiction, based on our criminal justice system, he was committing the crime of drug possession. Had he been arrested and charged, it's likely that, about the time that he was getting his life together, he would have been put behind bars. At a minimum, he would have been faced with the demands and costs of years of probation, severe fines, and the stigma of a criminal record, minimizing career and other opportunities. This, in turn, would have minimized his chances of turning his life around. That baby girl may still have been born, but may have become one of the 2.7 million children under the age of 18 who have a parent in jail or prison.[494] And the cycle may have continued.

"Luck" Based on Status, Race, and Economics

The stories of celebrity addiction are plentiful, and jokes about drug use are typical at social gatherings. According to the National Survey on Drug Use and Health (NSDUH), 19.7 million Americans aged 12 or older battled a substance use disorder in 2017.[495] That included 38 percent of American adults.[496] About 10 percent of American adults over the age of 18 say they are in recovery from a substance use disorder.[497] Each of these patients, according to U.S. drug policy, could be deemed to be a criminal.

Looking at these statistics, it becomes very apparent that those who are arrested for drug possession and whose lives are often destroyed, or at best sidetracked, are severely punished for actions that many others do on a regular basis with no punishment. When a felon is stigmatized, it may be much more about whether he or she happened to be arrested than for the "criminal activity" engaged in.

The issue is not that all drug users should be punished equally. It's that punishing drug possession with criminal sanctions is destructive, and is unfair in its application. Arrests and prosecution are more prevalent against those with mental health issues, those who cannot economically afford to get good legal defense, have severe addiction issues, or simply don't have the social skills to be able to "work the system" or to make themselves sympathetic to prosecutors.

The number of people affected is staggering. In 2017 someone in the United States was arrested for drug possession every 23 seconds.[498] Incarceration for drug offenses has increased 11-fold from 40,000 in 1981 to over 450,000 in 2017. In 2017, over 1.6 million people were arrested for drug law violations and 85 percent were for possession only.[499] It's not surprising that law enforcement, courts, jails and prisons, and probation and parole systems are overwhelmed and dysfunctional.

"Luck" Based on Geography

The geographic location where an "offense" occurs also plays a huge part in outcomes, and is largely based on luck. Cannabis use is now legal, either recreationally or medicinally, for a majority of the U.S. population, yet in states like my home state of Wisconsin, the first offense of possession of marijuana in any amount can currently include up to six months in jail, with a second offense a felony with 3.5 years in prison and up to a $10,000 fine.[500] Full sanctions may not be enforced, but these penalties give prosecutors broad license to force harsh plea agreements since going to trial could result in application of maximum penalties. And, of course, in any state, federal prosecution is still a risk.

Dirty little secrets abound when addiction is involved and a system is based on punishment. How many suffer in silence, attempt detox without medical care, or reject treatment out of fear of prosecution or of being railroaded into one-size-fits-all treatment that doesn't fit? Threats or the reality of being locked in a cage create fear and silence—recipes for corruption, bullying, and propagation of obsolete policies.

What human being will complain of horrendous living situations or abuse when the individuals accused have complete control over that inmate, resident, or probationer's daily life and safety? What family has the courage to challenge or reject court-ordered treatment, even if that treatment is not appropriate for their loved one? How many parents are silenced from openly discussing issues and potential solutions when a family member has substance use issues out of fear of being accused of enabling or bad parenting? Silence by those directly impacted is the fertilizer of bad policy.

Each of us has the ability to lend our voices to create badly needed change and to truly make a difference.

CHAPTER 40

THREE STEPS TO SOLUTIONS THAT ARE IN YOUR POWER

"Justice will not be served until those who are unaffected are as outraged as those who are."
Benjamin Franklin

How can each of us personally make a difference? How can we affect drug policy so it's in line with current evidence, based on science and medicine and what's been proven to be successful? How can you protect yourself and those you love if the War on Drugs lands on your doorstep?

1. Advocate and Offer Opportunity

Protecting the rights of another person, particularly when faced with highly dysfunctional, unfair, and inconsistent policies, is never harmful. Standing up for an individual with mental or physical health issues should never be discouraged. The fear of enabling has paralyzed parents who would otherwise never stand by while their children endured the treatment forced on them by our current criminal justice policy, or by one-size-fits-all treatment mandates. If advocacy or shining a light on policies is discouraged, it should be a red flag that perhaps that light is badly needed.

Lives can be saved simply by a kind word to a person who has been stigmatized by everyone else. Challenging ignorant statements that assume those with substance use disorder chose that life and should be punished could give hope to someone desperately in need of it.

During a busy day, it can be easy to hit "share" on the Facebook post comparing the cost of Narcan with insulin without considering that the message is telling parents that their child's life isn't worth the cost of a nasal spray. It's easy to make or listen to comments about a lazy criminal who's been in the system most of his life. I hope that the information in this book will lead readers to question whether that happened partly, or largely, because the system wouldn't allow an exit out of that system or did so much damage that hope for the future was destroyed. Many people don't realize that the person sitting next to them or listening to that conversation may be living the tragedies outlined in this book that very day. More than two-thirds of American families have been impacted by addiction or overdose.[501] One little sentence of support can change a life.

Making local law enforcement aware of programs like the Seattle LEAD program could save the life of someone you love, or could protect your community from the fallout inherent with punitive policies. LEAD and other similar programs help other law enforcement organizations to integrate effective policies, converting criminal enforcement to health-driven initiatives.

If you're an employer or a landlord, there can be benefits of asking more than just the one "Have you been convicted of a crime?" question. This person may contribute to your business or your community. Some amazing and very appreciative people might walk in when doors are opened. You could save a life, or give hope and opportunity to someone who simply wants a chance, and when given that chance may be a long-term, loyal tenant or employee.

Speaking out, talking about the addiction epidemic, the horrific results of drug policy, and the issues facing pain patients who are unable to obtain their medications is the first step to ending stigma. Each of us can have a hand in ending the addiction and overdose epidemic and restoring dignity and individual rights. Giving a voice to those who have none is the first step. Your voice is needed, whether talking to neighbors or speaking with representatives.

2. Be Aware of Language

Junkie. Dopehead. Druggie. Drug addict. When addiction is involved, we can likely add *felon, inmate,* and *ex-con* to the lexicon. Language and attitudes make a huge difference. Benjamin Lee Whorf, an American linguist, said, "Language shapes the way we think, and determines what we can think about." It can also bring hope or create despair.

Terminology used in the past had a part in promoting poor assumptions and poor policy that's led to the current epidemic. Language can support, or language can destroy. Sometimes, we use destructive language without even being aware of it. Is it possible that, even when we're referring to our own loved ones or speaking directly to them, our language may unintentionally be sending messages that can be harmful? Could our references unknowingly support lingering policies that have been proven ineffective and harmful long ago? Two of the most common stigmatizing terms are "clean" and "addict". The terms "enabling" and "co-dependent" can also be very stigmatizing, and lead parents and others to make decisions out of shame and fear.

Clean. Isn't this a compliment? It refers to someone in recovery. The challenge is that the implication is that someone not "clean" is "dirty". When we acknowledge that addiction is a treatable health condition, a reference to a person with that health condition as being dirty is not helpful.

Additionally, use of the word *clean* adds to the total abstinence model, which contradicts best medical practices for many patients who need medications to combat substance use disorder and other medical issues.

Addict. We don't refer to someone as "a cancer." A person is not the equivalent of their health condition. Motivational speakers don't generally tell us to stand up and state, "I'm (name). I'm a loser." Requiring people to define themselves in negative ways or with negative labels is counterproductive. It makes that label part of their identity, which can make the path to recovery more difficult. Recognizing that addiction is a treatable health condition and not a moral failing can give hope and change lives.

The 12-steps tradition of introductions including "I'm (name) and I'm an alcoholic (or addict)" began as a method to help those struggling with addiction to acknowledge that they have a problem. Having said that, many groups have converted this introduction to "I'm (name), a member of AA" or "I'm (name), and I'm in recovery."

Dropping this term in general conversation can be difficult. Referring to "a person with a substance use disorder," although more accurate and less judgmental, is long and can be cumbersome. Despite that, it's worth being aware of the potential negative impact and minimizing use of this term to the extent possible. In many contexts, the term "patient" makes sense and has far less stigma.

Political correctness and over-sensitivity to language can restrict conversation, but the stigma surrounding addiction is so destructive that it's worth increased awareness.

Enabling & Co-Dependent. Parents are constantly told that "enabling" is bad. Many have already convinced themselves that their child's addiction is their fault. Daily crisis may include dealing with a family member with a substance use disorder including physical and emotional issues, trying to find treatment alternatives, preserving personal financial security, and dealing with a punitive criminal justice system. Parents feel beat up emotionally, financially, and sometimes legally, are often exhausted, and everyone seems to have an opinion. Most opinions—even well meaning ones—imply parental guilt or harsh judgment of our child or of our parenting. Then, we're told that helping our child is enabling that could be harmful, and that caring about our child or being pre-occupied with their well-being is the forbidden 'co-dependency'.

Misunderstandings of the terms "enabling" and "codependency" have cost lives, and have created immense misery. Unfortunately, many believe that any help or support provided to an individual struggling with substance use is enabling. This is not the definition of enabling, but misinterpretation has led to parents holding back from advocating for a child or providing much-needed emotional support at a time when it is essential. Misinterpretation of this term has created untold misery.

Codependency is another term that is sometimes misinterpreted. Concern about codependency sometimes causes parents to back away, worried that *they* now have a "disease". After all, it's not uncommon to live with a sick feeling in the gut and ongoing emotional and physical pain.

As with enabling, the term tugs at truths. It's not healthy to live our lives on the basis of another person's actions over which we have no control. It's important to know, though, that there is no official disease of codependency, and telling a parent that they're sick because they're impacted by watching their child disintegrate can be harmful. Maia Szalavitz (author of the book *Unbroken Brain*), in her article 'Why the Codependency Myth of Drug Addiction Needs to Die',[502] quotes Carrie Wilkens, PhD., co-founder and clinical director for the Center for Motivation and Change: "There is no disease of codependence. It's not in the DSM [psychiatry's diagnostic manual], you can't diagnose and get reimbursed for it. It doesn't exist."

Knowledge, love, compassion, and expert help should prevail over stigmatizing terms that can result in guilt, shame and poor decisions. Hopefully, the information in this book can help. If you're a parent needing additional information, visit www.WarOnUs.com for information on online courses available.

3. Vote Strategically

You can impact decisions made by government. For any policy considered, before supporting a politician or program, ask yourself, "Is this policy further punishing those struggling with addiction?" "Increased funding" might simply mean more prisons. A proposal to "Expand drug courts" escalates the power of lawyers and one-size-fits-all treatment with prison as a threat, while restricting individualized medical care by health professionals. Proposals can *sound* good, yet simply be disguised ways to spend taxpayer dollars to threaten, intimidate, or imprison yet more people. For any policy, simply ask, "Will this lead to more punishment and destruction, or to individual success and reuniting of families?" Does the proposal lead to health-based, individualized treatment based on science and evidence and administered by medical professionals?

Our tax dollars, wasted on the War on Drugs, support the systemic destruction of human beings struggling with substance use disorder and the denial of medications to pain patients in need of them. As taxpayers, we have purchased the addiction and overdose epidemic, and we have purchased the restrictions on health care that are now affecting millions of pain patients. Help your politicians, on either side of the aisle, to clean up the mess that past policies have created by showing them that you support an end to the War on Drugs and re-establishment of physician-patient relationships in regard to prescription medications. Your support will give them the courage to make necessary changes. Public opinion is the driving force for change, as evidenced by the cannabis revolution.

CHAPTER 41

REPLACE THE CARTELS & PROTECT OUR KIDS

"The cost of the drug war is many times more painful, in all its manifestations, than would be the licensing of drugs combined with intensive education of non-users and intensive education designed to warn those who experiment with drugs."

—WILLIAM F. BUCKLEY, JR.

Let's be honest about the War on Drugs. When we make a drug illegal, we are saying "Lock them up." If a drug is illegal and someone uses it, they may end up in a cage. The results of these policies have escalated drug use, overdose deaths, and incarceration rates. *This* is radical policy. Craig McClure, former executive director of the International AIDS Society, states, ". . . the prohibitionist model is the radical approach, in that it is based exclusively on a moral judgment against drug use and drug users and not on an evidence-based approach to reducing drug-related harms."

Still, it's natural to worry about the effect of drugs on our children, on ourselves, or on our communities. Might our children harm themselves through experimentation? Could they be at risk from someone else under the influence? Could citizens find themselves footing a huge bill to care for people who become addicted?

It's apparent that the War on Drugs has failed, but our guts may still lead us to wonder whether change could make things worse. Won't drug use increase if drugs are legal?

These are legitimate questions. For real change to happen, we need to know that ending the War on Drugs will benefit and protect us and those we love. To be motivated to take the risk of change, we need to know that the risk of harm is greater if we don't change.

What's Safest for Our Kids?

In November 2018, Davonte Friedman stood in front of the Baltimore City Council and described his research on teens who lack opportunity. When asked what he wanted for his 18th birthday, he replied that he didn't want a big celebration. He responded, "I'm glad I made it to see 18." Less than a week after his 18th birthday, he was shot and killed. Davonte was a casualty of the War on Drugs.[503] He was innocently caught in the crossfire. Other teens end up dead because, in their neighborhoods, being a street dealer is the only opportunity they see.

Regardless of the neighborhood we live in, when challenges arise for our kids, most parents want to be in a position of weighing options, getting help, and getting their son or daughter back on track. In past generations, parents had the opportunity to guide a child through rebellious years. Now, the state often usurps that power from parents. After arrest, parental influence is restricted. If addiction concerns exist (and often even if they don't), courts often dictate types of "treatment." For teens or young adults, early experimentation with drugs or initial stages of substance use disorder can escalate because of the stigma, isolation, and lost opportunities created by an arrest.

Twenty-three percent of young adults in the U.S. are now arrested before age 23, largely due to the War on Drugs. In 2017, there were 1,632,921 drug law violations in the United States, with 85.4 percent of those for possession only.[504] Your child is more than three times more likely to be arrested than previous generations.[505] Over 70 million

Americans, or one in three adults, have an arrest or conviction record, with the majority related to drug possession.[506]

The arrest itself may be more harmful than drug use itself. A University of Michigan study surveying 35,000 participants showed that being arrested during childhood or young adulthood was associated with an $11,000 decrease in earnings every year as an adult, and a 3.5 percent drop in likelihood of eventual marriage.[507]

An arrest is far from a learning experience. Overwhelmed court systems and "tough on drugs" policies have turned minor arrests into life-changing and opportunity-killing sagas. If you're a parent, you have a legitimate reason to worry that your child, or you, could be a casualty of the War on Drugs, even if drug use is minimal. Years of probation and being treated like a criminal for a minor offense doesn't shape young minds. It creates trauma, isolation, and an identity as a criminal. It destroys opportunity, and it increases the risk of addiction and overdose. With risks of planted evidence or of items like cotton candy mistaken for drugs justifying arrest and jail, some are casualties despite no drug use at all.

As Kofi Annan, former U.N. secretary general, stated, "We all want to protect our families from the potential harm of drugs. But if our children do develop a drug problem, surely we will want them cared for as patients in need of treatment and not branded as criminals."

Even if our son or daughter is never arrested, would we rather have police focused on searching cars because they smelled pot and breaking down doors because they received a drug tip, or would removing pedophiles, rapists, burglars, and murderers from the streets be a better priority for public safety?

Will Legalization Increase Drug Use?

Do you use heroin? If it became legal today, would you run out, buy some, and stick a needle in your arm? That's unlikely, for you and for the vast majority of people. Drinking bottles of cough syrup, sucking in large doses of helium, or sniffing glue or gasoline are all ways of getting high with legal products, but most people would never consider doing this. Larry Elder says it well: "The War on Drugs is wrong, both tactically and morally. It assumes that people are too stupid, too reckless, and too irresponsible to decide whether and under what conditions to consume drugs."

Most people want to protect their own health. The path to addiction is typically self-medicating emotional or physical pain, and is often intensified by impure street drugs and the stigma of criminal records and having to hide in the shadows to obtain substances. Legalization eliminates these triggers.

For those who currently choose to use illegal drugs, they are readily available. The difference between legalization and current policy isn't in increased use, but in whether users have access to substances that are regulated, where content is pure and potency is consistent. The difference is whether users are in contact with and create profits for street dealers employed by drug cartels, or access substances through safe, legal channels.

We're not guessing about the effects of legalization on drug use. Since Portugal decriminalized all drugs, drug use has stayed essentially the same overall, but has declined among 15- to 24-year-olds. HIV rates, addiction rates, and drug-related crime all dropped significantly.[508] In Colorado, youth reported that cannabis was more difficult to access after legalization when street dealers were less plentiful and legal distributors checked identification. In states legalizing cannabis, reports to date show that use either remained stable or decreased.[509]

If Drugs Are Legal, Will Taxpayers End Up Footing a Big Bill?

Over a trillion U.S. dollars have been wasted on the War on Drugs, with dismal results. Jeffrey Miron of the Department of Economics at Harvard University analyzed the financial impact of legalizing and taxing all currently illegal drugs. He concluded that, if taxed at rates comparable to those on alcohol and tobacco, tax could generate $58 billion annually. An additional $47 billion in annual savings in law enforcement and judiciary spending could be saved.[510]

Miron's calculations show potential savings and tax revenue of $105 billion annually, which could be used to provide health care, substance use treatment including medications, re-entry services for those who had been incarcerated on drug charges, and other social services. Funds spent could be applied to solving issues, to moving people forward, and to offering opportunity in lieu of destructive, punitive, revolving door tactics of our current system. Miron's calculations didn't include lost revenue from incarcerating individuals and wiping out career opportunities and tax payments from lost earnings, nor savings on public costs of supporting families of individuals who can no longer provide for their families due to incarceration or criminal records.

Legalization is the only way to minimize the control of the cartels while funding services to provide medical treatment to attack the addiction and overdose epidemic, offering opportunity and future success instead of punishment. That is safer and less expensive for all of us.

Ending the War on Drugs has many facets, and it would be easy to assume that taking it one step at a time would be the most prudent approach. The challenge is that, when politics are involved, it's typical to take one step forward and then two steps back. For example, as we've begun to legalize cannabis, the War on Drugs has expanded to include legal prescriptions. Pain patients are denied medications that have been used successfully for years, and are treated as drug-seeking criminals. Progress in using Good Samaritan laws to incentivize help for those who may be overdosing has been overshadowed by recent felony homicide statutes.

While we think about changes in drug policy, more individuals are sentenced to jail and to prison, more felony convictions are entered, and more low-level drug offenders enter a system that increases their chances of becoming another casualty of the War on Drugs. Funding remains focused on law enforcement and incarceration, and the vast majority of those needing treatment for substance use disorder are still not getting it in a timely manner or based on sound medical protocols. Pain patients are deprived of medications because their physicians and pharmacists are afraid of DEA raids and other cascade effects of the War on Drugs. Real lives are destroyed every day.

Had we attempted to end U.S. alcohol prohibition in phases, it's likely that it would still be with us, leaving more death and despair in its tracks. If we attempt to unravel the mess created by the War on Drugs incrementally, people will die and lead lives of misery and desperation for no reason while years pass as political maneuvering continues.

The degree to which government has grown and usurped citizens' individual rights is illustrated by comparing alcohol prohibition with the War on Drugs. In 1920, before prohibition began, legislators acknowledged that denying citizens the choice of what to put in their own bodies required a constitutional amendment. Nothing in the U.S. Constitution gives the government the right to restrict those freedoms. Supreme Court Justice Thurgood Marshall once reminded the other justices that "there is no drug exception to the Constitution."[511] This fact has been ignored throughout the entire War on Drugs.

When it became obvious that alcohol prohibition was a dismal failure, the failed experiment was ended with 176 words—the 21st Amendment to the Constitution,[512] which repealed the 18th Amendment and ended prohibition.

Legislation creating the War on Drugs has no constitutional foundation. While we don't have a constitutional amendment to repeal, it is time to repeal the unconstitutional legislation that created this "War."

The United States was the architect of punitive drug policy and was instrumental in exporting that policy worldwide through promotion of U.N. treaties. It's time to admit that mistake and to correct it. Treaty revocation will be expedited when U.S. support is added to worldwide sentiment, the pain of status quo felt by individual countries, and unanimous support already in place by U.N. agencies and leadership. It's time for the U.S. to take a leadership role and to advocate for revocation or major amendment to U.N. treaties to allow countries to determine their own drug policy.

The United States should immediately implement harm-reduction policies discussed in this book and begin steps to full legalization. The losses of life, of health, and of freedom are too high to delay. Most drugs are already legal. Comparatively speaking, drugs deemed as illegal by DEA drug schedules[513] are a small percentage of substances, yet making these drugs illegal has been the source of untold agony, death, and mass incarceration. Howard Wooldridge, a retired police detective and founder of Citizens Opposing Prohibition (COP),[514] describes this well: "There are 1000's of drugs in America, and all of them are legal, regulated and taxed, except for five categories. We understand that these drugs are dangerous—Government should take control and regulate them. The drug dealer is now completely in control of these drugs."

We all use drugs. Coffee, tea, sugar, alcohol, tobacco, over-the-counter-medicines, prescription medications . . . The question is not whether drugs should be legal. The question is whether it is rational to make subjective decisions about which ones should be legal and which should be deemed to be illegal. Which ones do authorities determine should put you behind bars or destroy opportunities for life? How do those authorities make those decisions? Who and what influences those decisions?

Throughout history, these decisions have not been based on evidence, fact, or rational assessment. Drugs deemed to be criminal have not been based on the degree to which they're addictive, or the extent to which they negatively impact health. If that were the case, tobacco would certainly be a Schedule 1 drug. They haven't been deemed to be criminal based on the degree to which they can be fatal. Alcohol and tobacco kill more than all other drugs combined.[515] Is criminality dependent upon the degree to which they have medicinal qualities? If that were the case, cannabis would certainly not have been deemed to be a Schedule 1 drug.

Why have we persecuted all drug users? Does it really have anything to do with addiction? How can prosecution be justified against a recreational drug user who continues to be productive in life and hurts no one? How can prosecution of those who have a substance use disorder be rationalized when the same government that incarcerates these patients defines addiction as a disease, and when we now have medical proof that the condition can be treated with medications and other medical protocols?

Actual harm is sometimes based on the type of substance, but more often, the actual harm depends on the way the drug is acquired and the social environment of the individual.

Methamphetamine is created in unsanitary labs with no regulation or control. Pharmaceutical amphetamines are successfully used to treat ADHD, narcolepsy, and other medical issues. The components are very similar. Much of the harm is based on the stigma and the societal punishment surrounding use of a medication, as well as impurities in the street versions of the substances. Crime, HIV and other blood-borne infections, violence, incarceration, and death are all fueled by punitive and ineffective government policies.

Heroin is typically purchased in the back alley. Hydromorphone is administered in the hospital. The compounds are nearly identical, yet heroin has a much higher overdose and addiction rate.[516] The likely reason is additives and impurities in the street drug. Addiction is also based on social circumstances. According to studies authorized by the Nixon administration, 34 percent of U.S. servicemen in Vietnam used heroin, and 20 percent had symptoms of addiction. In the first year after returning home, 10 percent tried heroin, but only one percent became re-addicted.[517] Extensive review showed that the studies were accurate, and that the low relapse rates were the change from fighting in a jungle to returning home with goals and hope for the future. Perhaps, if our policies changed from being locked in a cage to medical help and hope for the future, our success rates would change as well.

Drug distribution and safety, under our current system, remain under the direction of drug cartels. Then we add social stigma, fear, and lack of opportunity to complete the recipe for failure. Making all drugs legal takes decision-making from bureaucrats and drug cartels and puts it under the discretion of individuals and their medical professionals. It replaces fear with hope, and stigma with opportunity. Legalization would also open research opportunities to fully and objectively study benefits of substances in treating various medical conditions.

Three outcomes are essential to sound drug policy:

1. Minimize tainted street drugs sold by drug cartels and their deputies to reduce overdose rates and the reign of drug cartel terror.

2. Open access to medical solutions to all patients, whether suffering from chronic pain, addiction, or other health issues, including funding of medical care without increasing cost to taxpayers and ending restrictions on medical research.

3. End mass incarceration and mass arrest, restore individual rights, and allow police to focus on violent crime.

There is only one way to achieve these results. End the War on Drugs. Legalize, regulate, and tax all drugs. Decriminalization doesn't provide for control of substance distribution, so anything short of full legalization leaves cartels as distributors. Without legalization, cartel profitability continues to finance terrorism and increase crime. Without legalization, taxes on substances to fund medical care and other taxpayer needs is not possible.

If the U.S. federal government does not act, it's likely that individual states and cities will. Cannabis legalization is unstoppable. Denver, Colorado, and Oakland, California have already decriminalized psilocybin mushrooms. A 2020 ballot initiative may make psilocybin legal in Oregon under licensed, therapeutic conditions.

As the failure of punitive drug policy becomes more apparent and more painful, change will occur. The question is whether it will occur in haphazard ways or whether federal leadership will admit the failure of current policy and, in conjunction with states, develop sane, effective policy including broad-based distribution channels, rational regulation, and sound tax policy.

The United States has had a history of leadership and was built on principles of individual freedom. Thoughtful legalization would be a shining light to the rest of the world, minimizing ongoing human rights violations and applying science and medicine to enhance health and reduce crime in the United States and worldwide.

"How many ears must one person have, before he can hear people cry? How many deaths will it take til he knows that too many people have died?"—Bob Dylan, "Blowin' in the Wind"

CONCLUSION

There was a time when I assumed that if someone was incarcerated, they must have done something worth punishing. There was a time when I believed that a felon must be dangerous or dishonest, and was likely a danger to society. There was a time that, as an attorney, I thought I understand our criminal justice system. There was a time when I was simply uninformed and very wrong.

Then, nearly two decades ago, addiction hit our family, and I began my journey in learning the truth about substance use and the impact of drug policy on addiction, substance users, and those who love them. I began my journey into understanding why the War on Drugs has not only failed, but has been a direct cause of the addiction and overdose epidemic. More recently, I saw the impact of the War on Drugs on pain patients, in agony every day and treated like criminals simply because they need medications, of which they are often deprived.

As I researched drug policy and saw its impact on real people, real families, and real communities, I began to realize that this War has no foundation in evidence, and has been a heartbreaking failure. I began to understand that assumptions, judgment, and repetition of bad policy over many years are the basis for a system that literally kills people and destroys lives every day.

Research was straightforward. There are medical answers to addiction. We have solutions. The challenge is that nearly all of those solutions are directly rejected by drug policy, which does exactly the opposite of what has proven to be successful in minimizing drug use and addiction. I began my research suspecting that the system was flawed. What I found shocked me. The system is so horrific that criticisms are often discounted as over-statements. No system could be *that* horrific. Unfortunately, it is. Addiction expert Dr. Gabor Maté expressed, "If I had to design a system that was intended to keep people addicted, I'd design exactly the system that we have right now."

Initially, I wondered why professionals didn't see the mayhem being created, but then I realized that each professional is doing their job and seeing only one small aspect of the overall system. Until our family was personally impacted by the many facets of the system and experienced the true consequences, I truly had no idea of the application of this atrocious system to those entwined in it. And therein lies the issue.

Typically the only people seeing the outcomes of the entire system are those arrested and prosecuted for drug crimes. Those who would be in the best position to expose the horrors of this system are criminals by the War's own definition. Those who would typically object can be locked in cages in retaliation if they speak out. The credibility of those who do have the courage to speak is highly questioned. Many aren't even allowed to vote, so politicians have little motivation to protect the interests of those enmeshed in a dysfunctional system. Family members who may be aware of injustices are told that advocacy is "enabling" and may be harmful.

Those prosecuted by this system are left with no support system, years of onerous mandates, and a lifetime of stigma. They are denied housing, careers, and basic human rights, in many cases because they had a pill is their pocket, no different than presidents, actors, business leaders, and millions of others who did the same thing, but just didn't happen to get arrested. Forty percent of drug arrests are for a quarter of a gram (less than the size of a penny). Less than one percent are for a kilogram or more, and more than 80 percent of drug violation arrests are for possession alone. The vast majority of those whose lives are turned upside down by drug arrests are not hardened criminals.[518]

The United States was founded on the principal of personal freedom. In the case of drug policy, we have been instrumental in denying personal freedom to hundreds of thousands of people, and have exported our punitive policies worldwide. At best, initial goals were noble, designed in a naive attempt to rid the world of harmful drugs and to protect people from themselves. At worst, it's all been based on politics and power. Either way, there is no way to justify its continued existence.

It's likely that you or someone you love has already been impacted by addiction, overdose, or the War on Drugs. If it hasn't happened yet, sadly, it's likely that it will. An August 2017 Pew Research study reported that nearly 46 percent of Americans have a family member or close friend who's been addicted to drugs.[519] Many more have no substance use disorder, but are arrested for minor drug possession. May we all remember that it could be us, or someone we love, behind bars for self-medicating a health issue, or left for dead because those able to call for help were afraid of prosecution.

This book is the result of over a decade of research and experience. More importantly, it's a plea from a mother who nearly lost her son to the War on Drugs. No child, no parent, no family, no human being should go through what we did. No individual should be in fear of not receiving a medication that allows him or her to live his or her best life. No parent should be told that advocating for a child against a dysfunctional system is wrong. No individual should be put through withdrawal behind bars, or denied housing, career opportunities, or other benefits because of a criminal record for drug possession. No human being should be handcuffed and humiliated because of a pill in a pocket.

We are at a critical time in the world of addiction and drug policy, with new science giving new hope and improved results. Attitudes are evolving. I envision a world where all people are respected and treasured, including those with medical challenges, and where the stigma we now encounter will end. I envision a criminal justice system focused on real crime, with drug policy acknowledged as a public health matter and treated with compassion and science, without destructive punishment and fear. Knowledge is the beginning of change, for our children, for us, and for our society.

Sharing the knowledge I gained over more than a decade of research is my goal for this book. Enough lives have been sacrificed. Too many people have died. Too many lives have been destroyed. It's time to move past old assumptions, and to accept what science has proven. It's time to treat addiction as a public health issue and to remove it from the criminal justice system. It's time to restore the physician-patient relationship where doctors advise and treat their patient based on one-on-one confidential conversations.

It's time to return to constitutional freedoms where an allegation of the smell of cannabis doesn't wipe out Fourth Amendment protections against unlawful search and seizure. It's time to end citizens' fear that police will arrest them, not for hurting someone or something, but for possessing a substance. It's time to end the assault on individual civil liberties and to regain the freedom to control our own bodies. Most importantly, it's time to return to a time of compassion, hope, and opportunity.

There will be a time when we will look back at the era of the War on Drugs as a dark blight on history. The questions are: How long will this failed War go on? How many people will die or sit in cages as their lives pass? How many families will grieve the fatalities and the waste of life created by this War?

It's time to end the War on Drugs. Let's do it now. Please share the knowledge. Together, we can make a difference.

Drug policy & the science
impacting addiction
change constantly.

To receive free, current information on
developments including free updates to this book,
visit www.WarOnUs.com.

Are you or someone you care about personally impacted by substance use disorder?

Online Course Available

A Parents' Guide to Addiction: Moving Past Punishment

Learn why forced meetings, punishment, 'letting them hit bottom' and other traditional techniques often fail, and what to do instead.

Learn how conventional 'wisdom' IS sometimes wise, and other times, is based on politics, profit and history.

Topics include:

- Is there anything I can do to minimize the risk of overdose?

- How do medications used in treatment work? Are they appropriate for our situation? What are the benefits and the downsides?

- What treatment has the best chance of working, and how do we persuade our child to accept help? Can insurance or other resources cover some of the costs?

- How do we protect all family members, from siblings to grandchildren?

- What do we do if our son or daughter is arrested?

- How do we protect *ourselves*, financially, emotionally, and legally?

This 20-hour course (done on your own time or used as a resource) includes video, audio, text, graphics, checklists, worksheets and downloadable legal and other documents on these topics and more. The goal of the course is to minimize the pain that families experience and to improve outcomes for those suffering from substance use disorder or enmeshed in a dysfunctional criminal justice system.

Whether a loved one's addiction is a new challenge or one you've been dealing with for years, this course offers sanity, guidance and resources to parents who are casualties of a time in history where judgment and punishment are too often more plentiful than medical treatment or support.

Visit www.WarOnUs.com for detailed course content, videos, and more.

ACKNOWLEDGMENTS

Thank you to all of those who shared their stories openly and honestly, helping me to understand the vast scope of the pain created by this War. Your perspective, heart, determination, and commitment to family motivated me to share those stories and to help those not yet directly impacted to understand the trauma and to see that we can do better.

I'm grateful for the many supportive, nonjudgmental friends and family who allowed me to process ideas and arguments, never outwardly saying, "Please shut up about drug policy!' Special thanks to those who gave direct feedback on the manuscript, and who were there throughout our family's experiences with this War. I have great appreciation for warrior cousins who created a protective shield when stigma hit our son at the height of his challenges, and who so effectively chewed up and spit out those attacking him on social media. Don't mess with the cousins!

My respect and gratitude goes to fellow advocates who have inspired my path, and who have given me perspective and courage in fighting for rational, compassionate and effective policy.

Special thanks to Gretchen Burns Bergman, Howard Wooldridge, Susan Prince and Cassandra Clinton for their early and ongoing feedback on the book, and for the many others who read the book and commented on it in ways that made it better.

I'm grateful to Steve Harrison and the Quantum Leap coaches and QL group for providing a tribe with whom to share victories and challenges, and for giving me a roadmap to share my message. Special thanks goes to Martha Bullen for her insight and incredible ability to transform this path into achievable daily steps.

Most importantly, I am thankful for family. My husband, who has lived this journey with me and been a full partner in this book and other adventures has propped me up when needed, kept me fed, proofed citations, and stepped up on every occasion. My grandchildren have made me laugh and provided perspective while writing about a very serious topic, and made me determined to protect them from being casualties of this crazy "War on Us" as they grow up. Special thanks to my sons and daughter-in-law for their love and support, for wisdom and perspective from a different generation's point of view, and for allowing me to share some of their stories.

Gratitude goes to those who read this book and apply it to help in replacing stigma, fear and incarceration with hope, health and freedom.

MEDICATIONS FOR USE IN TREATING SUBSTANCE USE DISORDER

Multiple types of medications are available for use in treatment of substance use disorder. There are pros and cons to each. It's important that the most appropriate medication and other services are coordinated for each patient.

The three medications most frequently used in treatment of opioid addiction are:

1. Naltrexone (in pill form, or trade name Vivitrol in monthly injectable form)

2. Buprenorphine (trade name Suboxone when buprenorphine is combined with naloxone; trade name Subutex® when buprenorphine alone), and

3. Methadone

Alternative methods for taking various medications ranging from pills, films, injections, and implants have been developed over the years.[520] Other medications are available to treat addiction to other substances, as well as underlying disorders that can lead to or accompany addiction.

Let's begin with the three most frequently used medications in the treatment of substance use disorder.

Naltrexone/Vivitrol:

Naltrexone, available as a tablet or as an injection, is used in treatment of opioid or alcohol addiction. The extended-release monthly injection is sold under the trade name **Vivitrol.** The pill form of naltrexone is sold under the trade names ReVia and Depade.

Naltrexone pills have been used successfully in treatment of alcohol without total abstinence. Taking a pill an hour before a drink can be very effective in curbing drinking. A documentary film, *One Little Pill*,[521] describes this technique known as the Sinclair Method. Those with traditional biases that total abstinence is the only way to combat addiction have been defensive about sharing knowledge and use of this technique with the public. Lives have been sacrificed as a result.

For treatment of opioid addiction, naltrexone works by blocking the effects of narcotic drugs. While using naltrexone, if the patient relapses on opiates, naltrexone prevents any feeling of getting high. *One huge benefit to naltrexone is that* **there is no abuse potential, and when naltrexone is discontinued there's no withdrawal since this drug does not include opioids.**

Naltrexone is not a narcotic so there's less stigma with its use, although even this is prohibited in many state jails and prisons, as well as in some sober houses and treatment centers. There are fewer challenges with drug testing, which can show positive for narcotics with other forms of medications used in addiction treatment. The Vivitrol injection can be a life-changer for those for whom it works.

One of the biggest issues with naltrexone is that it will trigger severe withdrawal symptoms if opioids have been used in the prior seven to 14 days (dependent upon what type of drugs were in use). For some, this period of abstinence is simply not feasible. Another issue, particularly for patients on injectable Vivitrol, is that if pain medications are needed in the event of an emergency, they cannot be used without creating severe withdrawal symptoms. Patients typically wear a medical alert bracelet to notify medical personnel that they're on the medication. These issues need to be considered before selecting the appropriate medication, particularly for patients who have a history of pain, or who are at higher risk of needing surgery or other medical procedures where pain medications may be required.

Some have reported that Vivitrol caused depression. Nausea, headache, insomnia, and muscle or joint aches can also be side effects. In some cases, these subside after a period of time. If a patient attempts to override the naltrexone by taking opiates, the effects of the opiates won't be felt, but can still cause overdose.

Some jurisdictions have begun mandating a Vivitrol shot upon release from jail.[522] The swings of government from total prohibition to mandate should be cause to question the basis upon which any of these decisions are made. Mandating shots can be dangerous if patients aren't in a position to continue the treatment. Periods of abstinence while on the shot or while incarcerated lower tolerance levels, putting patients at a much higher risk of overdose if a relapse occurs. Liver damage and other side effects could impact some patients.

While release from jail is a good time to administer Vivitrol if there's a period of abstinence while incarcerated, mandating anyone to take a medication crosses the line of basic civil liberties, particularly when one medication is selected, not based on individual patient needs, but on blanket policies dictated by lobbying and other political factors.

There have been reports that the manufacturer of Vivitrol has taken part in lobbying efforts for these mandates, and to promote legislation that makes other forms of medications to treat substance use disorder more difficult to obtain.[523] Access to whatever medication and treatment may be best for an individual should be the priority. The alternative of Vivitrol is a positive one, but access to other alternatives that may be more appropriate for some should not be restricted, and medications should not be mandated.

Buprenorphine/Suboxone:

Buprenorphine partially binds onto the same brain receptors that heroin, oxycodone, and other opioids do, reducing cravings and withdrawal symptoms, and preventing the patient from feeling the effects of other opioids. Like naltrexone, buprenorphine blocks the high from heroin and other narcotics, but because it's an opiate, it can replace heroin and other opiates without a period of abstinence.

The most popular buprenorphine medication is a combination of buprenorphine and naloxone (trade name **Suboxone**). This combination decreases the potential for abuse and deters intravenous injection.

Basically, Suboxone replaces the opiate that creates a high with one that does not, so converting from drugs like heroin or oxycodone to Suboxone does not entail withdrawal, yet allows the patient to live a normal life. For those who were self-medicating to alleviate pain or other physical or emotional medical issues, buprenorphine is a way to treat those medical issues without using dangerous and illegal street drugs. This medication can be abused since it is an opiate, but can also be very effective.

One of the disadvantages of buprenorphine vs. naltrexone (Vivitrol) is that ending use of buprenorphine creates severe withdrawal symptoms. Naltrexone has none. However, in the same way that we wouldn't approach treatment for other medical issues by limiting the duration of treatment, it's important to acknowledge that medications used in treatment may be necessary long term. Concern about withdrawal is legitimate, but shouldn't prevent use of this medication if it's indicated for overall medical care.

Buprenorphine and Suboxone are less expensive than Vivitrol, but, as discussed earlier, regulations make finding a physician to prescribe more difficult. Whereas any physician licensed to prescribe can write a prescription for Vivitrol (or pill form naltrexone), special requirements apply to medical professionals writing prescriptions for buprenorphine in any form. Restrictions make it more difficult for patients to find providers, increases expense of office visits, and limits access to a physician to obtain those prescriptions. While waiting for access to a physician, the patient remains at risk of overdose or other issues faced by a patient in active addiction. Research by Michelle Lofwall, an associate professor at the University of Kentucky College of Medicine's Center for Drug and Alcohol Research[524], indicated that some people buy buprenorphine on the street to self-medicate to wean themselves off of opiates because they can't find a doctor to prescribe it legally. This increases risk of overdose significantly.

Methadone:

Methadone has been used for decades to help reduce or end use of heroin or other opiates. Like buprenorphine, it reduces withdrawal symptoms and blocks the euphoric effects of opiates.

Although methadone is a strong drug, when taken as prescribed, it allows people to lead active and meaningful lives. If not taken per prescription, methadone can be very addictive and has a high risk of abuse. Suboxone is considered safer than methadone because it's less likely to cause an overdose, but for some patients, methadone may work better.

Methadone's effects last at least 24 hours, and build up in body tissue and the bloodstream during the "induction phase" as the dose is slowly increased, causing it to act somewhat like a time-release drug. When stabilization is reached for the consistent dose, the methadone utilizes the body's opiate receptors, so there's no room for heroin or other narcotics to "sit." Methadone must be taken *every* day, and dosages are specifically structured for each individual, monitored and adjusted as needed. Methadone may interact with other medications and cause heart conditions. If a patient doesn't initially feel the effects of the methadone, it's imperative that more isn't taken since it remains in the body for an extended time and additional doses can cause overdose.

These concerns have been the basis for strict prescribing rules. Methadone is dispensed only by state-licensed clinics. Initially, patients are required to go to the state-licensed center daily for dosage. While this precaution may be beneficial for some, the need to go to the clinic daily is one of the disadvantages. Eventually, patients may be allowed to take methadone at home with less frequent visits to the clinic.

Methadone has been used for pregnant or breastfeeding women, helping them to convert from illegal opiate use to methadone without the risk of miscarriage or premature birth that can result from outright withdrawal from opiates.

Other Alternatives

Each medication alternative has pros and cons. To determine which medication is appropriate for a specific patient, individual medical assessment is important.

Sometimes, as with other medical issues, various treatment alternatives need to be tested to find the one that works best for an individual. Unfortunately, drug policy complicates this standard medical procedure since if one treatment is ineffective and a patient relapses, even if it's a one-time occurrence, the risk that medical treatment will end and be replaced by criminal prosecution and potential incarceration is high. This leaves many at risk of failure. If the first medication isn't successful, they may be punished, or be too afraid to risk trying other alternatives.

Prescribing medications that treat the underlying symptoms for which the patient may be self-medicating can be very effective, yet many physicians are concerned about potential liability for doing so, and patients risk suspicion and sometimes prosecution simply for utilizing medications for an underlying medical condition. For example, amphetamines used to treat ADHD and narcolepsy have been successful in treating methamphetamine addiction.[525] The compounds are similar, but amphetamines, when properly prescribed, help patients with symptoms of attention deficit, while avoiding potential impurities in street-level meth that can be deadly. Adderall provides treatment for ADHD and replacement of self-administered meth, avoiding the horrific mental and physical health issues created by meth.

It's not uncommon for a patient who begins one of the medications used to treat opioid addiction to then relapse on methamphetamine, leading to potential overdose or incarceration. Adding other medications like prescription amphetamines can treat these issues. Medical professionals often begin with one medication first, to allow for assessment of how each medication works for the patient, but using this logical medical protocol puts the patient at risk of arrest before the correct combination of medications can be ascertained.

Incarceration can be a threat to overall health, so minimizing the risk of arrest is an additional health benefit of these medications. Amphetamines can be abused, but are also a viable alternative in treating serious symptoms. Prescription amphetamines are much safer than street-level methamphetamine.

Buprenorphine and methadone are only effective in treatment of opiate addiction, and naltrexone is used solely for opiate and alcohol addiction. Amphetamines may be used in treating methamphetamine addiction. Other medications have shown success in treatment of other substances. Ibogaine, a substance found in an African shrub, has been used for treatment of multiple drugs. This treatment is illegal in the

U.S. and some other countries, but treatment clinics operate in Mexico, Canada, the Caribbean, South Africa, New Zealand, the Netherlands, and across Central and South America.

Research and personal testimonials support the claim that ibogaine reduces cravings and risk of relapse for alcohol, cocaine, methamphetamine, and nicotine, as well as opiates. Treatment is typically one-time use. If ibogaine is used where it is legally available, it's essential that it be done under close supervision at a credible clinic. There are efforts to promote legalization in the United States. It's effectiveness against methamphetamine might provide motivation. Forms of ibogaine that do not cause the hallucinogenic experience are being tested. Opinions differ as to whether these formulas will be effective.

Kratom (Mitragyna speciosa) is an evergreen tree native to Southeast Asia that has been used to relieve pain for hundreds of years. Kratom is not derived from opium, but has similar effects. It's the only substance outside of the opioid family that affects opioid receptors in the brain. The effects of kratom are more subtle than opioids, but kratom provides similar results that minimize cravings for opiates. It's been used for pain relief, to increase appetite, to stabilize mood including relief from depression and anxiety, and in treatment of opiate addiction. Reports of use of kratom as a replacement for opium go back as far as 1836.

Traditionally, kratom leaves were chewed. It's now commonly made into a tea or taken in a condensed powder form because of its bitter taste when just chewed. The powder can be mixed into a drink, taken in capsule, tablet or liquid form. In low doses, kratom acts as a stimulant. In large amounts, it acts as a sedative. Kratom takes effect within 30 minutes of ingestion and lasts anywhere between two to eight hours depending on amount taken and tolerance.

As with any drug, kratom can be dangerous, and can be psychologically addictive. There will be withdrawal symptoms if kratom is used habitually and then stopped abruptly. Side effects when taking it can include nausea and vomiting. The DEA considered scheduling kratom as a Schedule 1 drug in 2016, but based on public backlash (including a rally in front of the White House and a petition against scheduling with 142,000 signatures), the DEA has not implemented that classification.

There continue to be some who promote DEA scheduling of kratom. One of the issues with classifying a drug as Schedule 1 is that it minimizes the ability to study potential medical uses. The DEA has asked the FDA to speed up a scientific and medical evaluation of kratom, as well as a scheduling recommendation. At this time, kratom is legal in the United States (although some individual states have banned it). It is currently legal in all countries except Australia, Denmark, Finland, Israel, Lithuania, Malaysia, Myanmar, Poland, Romania, South Korea, Sweden, Thailand, and the United Kingdom.[526]

A 2016 study by Susruta Majumdar, PhD, a researcher at Memorial Sloan Kettering Cancer Center in New York[527] found that unlike morphine, a synthetic compound derived from kratom (mitragynine pseudoindoxyl) does not lead to harmful side effects like respiratory depression (the slowed breathing that causes most opioid overdose deaths), constipation, and physical dependence. Walter C. Prozialeck, PhD, chairman of the Department of Pharmacology at Midwestern University in Illinois, analyzed about 100 studies on kratom. His review found that in almost every case of reported kratom side effects, other factors were involved, like other drugs or other health conditions. Prozialeck says that a big outstanding question remaining is "How addictive is Kratom?" He believes that, at a minimum, kratom should be researched as a potential alternative to opioids for use in pain control.

Over the past 20 years, clinical research has been done on use of psychedelics in treatment of alcohol and other substance use disorders. MDMA has been successfully used to treat substance use disorders as well as treating PTSD.[528] Pilot studies have shown promising success rates for use of psilocybin (sometimes referred to as "magic mushrooms") in treatment of tobacco, alcohol, cocaine, and opioid addiction.[529]

Legalization and decriminalization of cannabis in several countries and in several U.S. states has provided data with which to assess pros and cons of cannabis and its use in treating substance use disorder. (See # 27, The Cannabis Experiment—What We've Learned.) Expanded use of CBD oils for treatment of various medical conditions has also provided valuable data and opportunity.

GLOSSARY & TERMINOLOGY

DRUGS/ALCOHOL: References to drug or drug use encompass alcohol as well.

SUBSTANCE USE DISORDER: Throughout this book, the terms "substance use disorder" and "addiction" have been used interchangeably. In the *DSM-5: Diagnostic and Statistical Manual of Mental Disorders*, a handbook used by health care professionals and much of the world, the classifications "substance abuse" and "substance dependence" have been eliminated, with the broader term "substance use disorder" now used. The term "addiction" continued to be used for brevity and variety. Where studies were done prior to the terminology change, original terminology was used for accuracy.

OPIATE/OPIOID: These terms sometimes confuse people. So, here's the difference: Opiates are created by the poppy plant. Opiates include opium, morphine, and codeine—made directly from poppy plants. Opioids are synthetic or partly synthetic. They're created chemically, but act just like opiates because of similar molecules. Common opioids are fentanyl, oxycodone, and hydrocodone. Despite these differences, many references now use the term "opioid" to include both opiates and opioids.

CANNABIS/MARIJUANA: When possible, the term "cannabis" has been used instead of the term "marijuana." Cannabis is the accurate scientific name. The term "marijuana" was used in a political PR campaign to connect the substance to fear of Hispanic migrant workers.

CANNABIS/CANNABINOIDS/THC/CBD: Cannabis is also referred to as marijuana. The cannabis plant contains over 480 natural components, of which 66 have been classified as "cannabinoids." Cannabinoids interact with specific brain receptors. Two of the most well-known cannabinoids are THC (which creates a high) and CBD (which does not).

LEGALIZATION/DECRIMINALIZATION: Legalization completely removes criminal sanctions from the use of a drug—provided it doesn't conflict with other laws, such as using in public. If a drug is decriminalized, it continues to be illegal but no longer carries criminal charges or incarceration. Typically, under decriminalization, fines are assessed. In some countries, other penalties or requirements still exist (e.g., Portugal has the right to require classes; Italy may confiscate driver's licenses for marijuana offenses). The challenge with decriminalization vs. legalization is that decriminalization still incentivizes drug cartels and other black market suppliers.

MEDICATION-ASSISTED TREATMENT: This term, or MAT, has been the standard term used to describe medications used in treatment (e.g., naltrexone, buprenorphine, methadone). The terminology "medication-assisted treatment" has come under criticism because, by its name, it presumes that medications only "assist" treatment, and cannot be treatment in and of themselves. For this reason, in most places within this book, the term "medications" has been used. Where the term needed to be clarified, we attempted to do so without using "medication-assisted treatment." Am I arguing that other forms of treatment should not be used in conjunction with medications? Absolutely not. However, it is important for all of us to be aware of opinions and assumptions tied to terminology. I have made every attempt to avoid using terminology that implies conclusions or judgments or in any way restricts discussion on all possible paths to stopping the demon of substance use disorder. Therefore, the term "medications," in lieu of medication-assisted treatment, seems more appropriate.

Endnotes

1   "U.S. Jails Are Killing People Going Through Opioid Withdrawals." HuffPost. Huff-
     Post, December 7, 2017. https://www.huffpost.com/entry/us-jails-are-killing-people-
     opioid-withdrawals_b_9563940.

2   https://paruresis.org. According to the International Paruresis Association, approxi-
     mately 21 million Americans (220 million worldwide) may suffer from paruresis, a social
     anxiety disorder recognized as a disability by the Americans with Disabilities Act.

3   Mitchell, Jerry. "'Protection Money' Common for Inmate Families." *The Clarion Ledger*,
     October 5, 2014. www.clarionledger.com/story/news/2014/10/04/protection-mon-
     ey-common-inmate-families/16654743/.

4   Mate, Gabor. *In the Realm of Hungry Ghosts*, North Atlantic Books, 2010.

5   "When Addiction Treatment Is One-Size-Fits-All." *Psychology Today*. www.psychology-
     today.com/us/blog/inside-rehab/201302/when-addiction-treatment-is-one-size-fits-
     all.

6   Gomez, Alan. "'El Chapo' Arrest Sparks Homicide Surge as Factions Fight to Fill Vacu-
     um." *USA Today*, March 31, 2017. www.usatoday.com/story/news/world/2017/03/31/
     el-chapo-guzman-arrest-sparks-homicide-surge-in-mexico/99833240/.

7   Ho, Jessica. *Population and Development Review*, February 2019, (https://onlinelibrary.
     wiley.com/doi/full/10.1111/padr.12228, February 20, 2019.

8   Vchangul. "World Drug Report 2019: 35 million people worldwide suffer from drug use
     disorders while only 1 in 7 people receive treatment," United Nations Office on Drugs
     and Crime. https://www.unodc.org/unodc/en/frontpage/2019/June/world-drug-re-
     port-2019_-35-million-people-worldwide-suffer-from-drug-use-disorders-while-only-
     1-in-7-people-receive-treatment.html.

9   "Drug and Opioid-Involved Overdose Deaths—United States, 2013-2017 | MMWR."
     Centers for Disease Control and Prevention. https://www.cdc.gov/mmwr/volumes/67/
     wr/mm675152e1.htm.

10   Correctional Populations in the United States, 2013 (NCJ 248479). Published Decem-
     ber 2014 by U.S. Bureau of Justice Statistics (BJS). By Lauren E. Glaze and Danielle
     Kaeble, BJS Statisticians. See appendix table 5 on page 13, for "Estimated number of
     persons supervised by adult correctional systems, by correctional status, 2000-2013."

11   Western, Bruce and Becky Pettit. "Collateral Costs: Incarceration's Effect On Economic
     Mobility." Pew Charitable Trusts, 2010. https://www.pewtrusts.org/~/media/legacy/
     uploadedfiles/pcs_assets/2010/collateralcosts1pdf.

12   "Americans with Criminal Records." The Sentencing Project. http://www.sentencing-project.org/wp-content/uploads/2015/11/Americans-with-Criminal-Records-Poverty-and-Opportunity-Profile.pdf.

13   "Nicholas Kristof Interview." InterviewCelebrity.com, September 25, 2014. https://www.interviewcelebrity.com/interview/2014/9/nicholas-kristof.html.

14   Alexander, Michelle. The New Jim Crow: Mass Incarceration in the Age of Colorblindness. The New Press, 2010.

15   "Criminal Justice Facts." The Sentencing Project. https://www.sentencingproject.org/criminal-justice-facts/.

16   "Criminal Justice Facts." The Sentencing Project. https://www.sentencingproject.org/wp-content/uploads/2019/05/US-prison-pop-1925-2017.png.

17   Ye Hee Lee, Michelle. "Does the United States Really Have 5 Percent of the World's Population and One Quarter of the World's Prisoners?" The Washington Post, April 30, 2015. https://www.washingtonpost.com/news/fact-checker/wp/2015/04/30/does-the-united-states-really-have-five-percent-of-worlds-population-and-one-quarter-of-the-worlds-prisoners/.

18   "Criminal Justice Facts." The Sentencing Project. https://www.sentencingproject.org/criminal-justice-facts/.

19   Overdose Death Rates. NIDA, January 29, 2019. https://www.drugabuse.gov/related-topics/trends-statistics/overdose-death-rates.

20   https://www.cdc.gov/nchs/images/databriefs/301-350/db329_fig2.png.

21   Miron, Jeffrey. "The Budgetary Effects of Ending Drug Prohibition." Cato Institute, July 23, 2018. http://www.cato.org/publications/tax-budget-bulletin/budgetary-effects-ending-drug-prohibition#full.

22   "Drug War Statistics." Drug Policy Alliance. http://www.drugpolicy.org/issues/drug-war-statistics.

23   "More Imprisonment Does Not Reduce State Drug Problems." The Pew Charitable Trusts, March 2018. https://www.pewtrusts.org/en/research-and-analysis/issue-briefs/2018/03/more-imprisonment-does-not-reduce-state-drug-problems.

24   Friedersdorf, Conor. "Ben Carson: Intensify the War on Drugs and Keep Marijuana Illegal." The Atlantic, October 23, 2015. https://www.theatlantic.com/politics/archive/2015/10/ben-carson-intensify-the-war-on-drugs-and-keep-marijuana-illegal/411868/. Ben Carson, the current United States secretary of housing and Urban Development, in an interview with Glenn Beck in October 2015.
Glenn Beck: Do you continue the War on Drugs?
Ben Carson: Absolutely.
Beck: You do?
Carson: I intensify it.
Beck: Let me ask you a question. I mean, it doesn't seem to be working now.
Carson: Yeah, well, go down to the border in Arizona like I was a few weeks ago. I mean,

it's an open highway. And the federal government isn't doing anything to stop it.
Beck: Okay. Legalize marijuana?
Carson: I disagree with it.

25   "How Effective Are Medications to Treat Opioid Use Disorder?" NIDA. https://www.
      drugabuse.gov/publications/research-reports/medications-to-treat-opioid-addiction/
      efficacy-medications-opioid-use-disorder?fbclid=IwAR1yHTKMlC6RJd3YRVc9pk-
      P2yVrmXW8tZdFwbG 4D2dq45dHLSCjx-i2KBb4.

26   "WHO Model List of Essential Medicines." World Health Organization. www.
      who.int/medicines/publications/essentialmedicines/EML_2015_FINAL_amend-
      ed_NOV2015.pdf?ua=1; "Guidelines for the Psychosocially Assisted Pharmacological
      Treatment of Opioid Dependence," World Health Organization. https://apps.who.
      int/iris/bitstream/handle/10665/43948/9789241547543_eng.pdf;jsessionid=D-
      CAA9850E9A72E37DBB5272034912E8A?sequence=1.

27   "New U.S. Drug Overdose Data Show Treatment Still Too Elusive." The Pew Charita-
      ble Trusts, December 13, 2018. https://www.pewtrusts.org/en/research-and-analysis/
      articles/2018/12/13/new-us-drug-overdose-data-show-treatment-still-too-elusive.

28   Borwick, Kim. "Myths Fueling the Stigma of Medication-Assisted Treatment." Drug
      Rehab, https://www.drugrehab.com/featured/the-myths-and-misconceptions-of-med-
      ication-assisted-treatment/.

29   "Principles of Adolescent Substance Use Disorder Treatment: A Research-Based
      Guide", National Institute on Drug Abuse, https://www.drugabuse.gov/publications/
      principles-adolescent-substance-use-disorder-treatment-research-based-guide/intro-
      duction

30   "Is It Possible for Someone to Become Addicted to Marijuana? | FAQs | Marijuana |
      CDC." Centers for Disease Control and Prevention, https://www.cdc.gov/marijuana/
      faqs/marijuana-addiction.html; Lopez-Quintero, C, et al. (2011). Probability and
      predictors of transition from first use to dependence on nicotine, alcohol, cannabis, and
      cocaine: results of the National Epidemiologic Survey on Alcohol and Related Condi-
      tions (NESARC). Drug Alcohol Depend. 115(1-2): p. 120-30.

31   "Opioid Addiction 2016 Facts & Figures" American society of Addiction Medicine,
      https://www.asam.org/docs/default-source/advocacy/opioid-addiction-dis-
      ease-facts-figures.pdf; "Drug Facts, What is Heroin?" National Institute on Drug Abuse,
      https://www.drugabuse.gov/publications/drugfacts/heroin.

32   Patterson, Eric, "Meth Facts, History and Statistics: Dangers and Legality." DrugAbuse.
      com, December 4, 2018. https://drugabuse.com/methamphetamine/history-statistics.

33   Terminology and standards vary between studies. Dependence is defined in some circles
      as physical dependence, which is less severe than addiction, but in other usage the terms
      dependence and addiction were used interchangeably. Substance use disorder is now the
      preferred term in the scientific community.

34   "Is It Possible for Someone to Become Addicted to Marijuana? | FAQs | Marijuana |
      CDC." Centers for Disease Control and Prevention, https://www.cdc.gov/marijuana/
      faqs/marijuana-addiction.html; Lopez-Quintero, C, et al. (2011). Probability and

predictors of transition from first use to dependence on nicotine, alcohol, cannabis, and cocaine: results of the National Epidemiologic Survey on Alcohol and Related Conditions (NESARC). Drug Alcohol Depend. 115(1-2): p. 120-30.

35   Hari, Johann. *Chasing the Scream*. London: Bloomsbury, 2016, 172.

36   Alexander, Bruce. "Addiction: The View from Rat Park," 2010. https://www.bruce-kalexander.com/articles-speeches/rat-park/148-addiction-the-view-from-rat-park.

37   Hari, Johann. *Lost Connections: Uncovering the Real Causes of Depression and the Unexpected Solutions*. Bloomsbury, 2019.

38   Mate, Gabor. *In the Realm of Hungry Ghosts*. Vermillion, 2018.

39   "Drugs in Prison: The Record." The Marshall Project. www.themarshallproject.org/records/1422-drugs-in-prison.

40   Zhao, Christina. "Former Florida Sheriff Deputy Caught Planting Drugs on at Least 10 Innocent People." *Newsweek*, July 12, 2019. www.newsweek.com/former-florida-sheriff-deputy-caught-planting-drugs-least-10-innocent-people-1448860.

41   "Contrary to a common misperception, methamphetamine is not 'instantly addictive' for most people who use it. Most people who use methamphetamine do not develop an addiction. . . . 10.3 million Americans have tried methamphetamine at least once. Of those 10.3 million, only 1.3 million used methamphetamine in the last year; and only 512,000 used it within the last 30 days." "Methamphetamine Facts." Drug Policy Alliance, www.drugpolicy.org/drug-facts/methamphetamine-facts.
     At a U.S. Conference on Methamphetamine, HIV and Hepatitis, a speaker from RTI international stated that an estimated 12.3 million Americans, or 5 percent of the adult population, have used methamphetamine at least once, and an estimated 600,000 people are weekly meth users. Citing World Health Oganization data, the same speaker stated that 35 million use methamphetamine worldwide. Roehr, Bob. "Half a Million Americans Use Methamphetamine Every Week." *BMJ (Clinical Research Ed.)*, BMJ Publishing Group Ltd., September 3, 2005, www.ncbi.nlm.nih.gov/pmc/articles/PMC1199019.

42   Knox, Liza. "Drugs in Ancient Cultures: A History of Drug Use and Effects." Ancient Origins, June 9, 2016. www.ancient-origins.net/opinion-guest-authors/drugs-ancient-cultures-history-drug-use-and-effects-006051.

43   "War on Drugs." History.com, May 31, 2017. www.history.com/topics/crime/the-war-on-drugs.

44   "Chapter 8. The Harrison Narcotic Act (1914) ." DrugLibrary. www.druglibrary.org/schaffer/library/studies/cu/cu8.html.

45   Libby, Ronald T. "The DEA's War on Doctors: A Surrogate for the War on Drugs," 2004, http://www.aapsonline.org/painman/paindocs2/libbystatement.pdf.

46   Hari, Johann. *Chasing the Scream*. Bloomsbury, 2016.

47   "Marijuana Tax Act Law and Legal Definition." USLegal, Inc. definitions.uslegal.com/m/marijuana-tax-act /.

48   Downs, David. "The Science behind the DEA's Long War on Marijuana." *Scientific American*, April 19, 2016. www.scientificamerican.com/article/the-science-behind-the-dea-s-long-war-on-marijuana/.

49   Firestone, David. "Let States Decide on Marijuana." *New York Times*, July 26, 2014.

50   Baum, Dan, Rich Cohen, Rachel Poser, Chris Rush, and Sean Williams. "[Report]: Legalize It All, by Dan Baum." Harper's magazine, March 31, 2016. https://harpers.org/archive/2016/04/legalize-it-all/.

51   Coughlin-Bogue, Tobias, et al. "The Word 'Marijuana' Versus the Word 'Cannabis.'" The Stranger, April 13, 2016. www.thestranger.com/news/2016/04/13/23948555/the-word-marijuana-versus-the-word-cannabis.

52   Nellis, Ashley. "The Color of Justice: Racial and Ethnic Disparity in State Prisons." The Sentencing Project, June 14, 2016. http://www.sentencingproject.org/publications/color-of-justice-racial-and-ethnic-disparity-in-state-prisons/.

53   "About the Drug War." Drug Policy Alliance. www.drugpolicy.org/issues/about-drug-war.

54   "War on Drugs." History.com, May 31, 2017, www.history.com/topics/crime/the-war-on-drugs.

55   "Criminal Justice Facts." The Sentencing Project. https://www.sentencingproject.org/wp-content/uploads/2019/05/drug-offenses-prison-jail-alt.png.

56   Ostrow, Ronald. "Casual Drug Users Should Be Shot." *Los Angeles Times*, September 6, 1990.

57   In the book *Outgrowing Addiction* (Upper Access Books, 2019), Stanton Peele and Zach Rhoads state: "DARE . . . is the standard, abstinence-only, police-based approach used throughout the United States, despite never having been shown to be effective, and in fact often resulting in more drug use. This is because DARE doesn't address—cannot even conceive—that children are able to expand their experiences and meet their basic responsibilities, and smart enough to know that the answers are more complex than just whether or not they are doing drugs." Also see Stanton Peele's book *Addiction-Proof Your Child*.

58   "UN Convention against Illicit Traffic in Narcotic Drugs and Psychoactive Substances." UN International Narcotics Control Board, 1988. https://www.incb.org/incb/en/precursors/1988-convention.html.

59   Johnson, Carrie. "20 Years Later, Parts Of Major Crime Bill Viewed As Terrible Mistake." NPR, September 12, 2014. www.npr.org/2014/09/12/347736999/20-years-later-major-crime-bill-viewed-as-terrible-mistake.

60   Riggs, Mike. "Obama's War on Pot." *The Nation*, June 29, 2015. www.thenation.com/article/obamas-war-pot/.

61   Lopez, German. "The First Step Act, Explained." Vox, February 6, 2019. www.vox.com/future-perfect/2018/12/18/18140973/state-of-the-union-trump-first-step-act-criminal-justice-reform.

62   Ibid.

63   Ellis-Petersen, Hannah. "Duterte's Philippines Drug War Death Toll Rises above 5,000." *The Guardian*, December 19, 2018. www.theguardian.com/world/2018/dec/19/dutertes-philippines-drug-war-death-toll-rises-above-5000.

64   Lopez, German. "Why You Can't Blame Mass Incarceration on the War on Drugs." Vox, May 30, 2017. www.vox.com/policy-and-politics/2017/5/30/15591700/mass-incarceration-john-pfaff-locked-in. This article also has good discussion of prosecutorial discretion.

65   Wilson, B. "Alcoholics Anonymous in its third decade." Presented to the New York Medical Society on Alcoholism, April 28, 1958.

66   Ibid.

67   "That Time When a Devastating Attack on a Seminal Controlled Drinking Study Set Us Back Decades." Overcome Addiction—Life Process Program, October 22, 2018. lifeprocessprogram.com/seminal-controlled-drinking-study-set-us-back-decades/.

68   Szalavitz, Maia. "After 75 Years of AA, It's Time to Admit We Have a Problem." *Pacific Standard*, June 14, 2017. psmag.com/social-justice/75-years-alcoholics-anonymous-time-admit-problem-74268.

69   Ibid.

70   DeFulio, Anthony, et al. "Criminal Justice Referral and Incentives in Outpatient Substance Abuse Treatment." *Journal of Substance Abuse Treatment*, July 2013. www.ncbi.nlm.nih.gov/pmc/articles/PMC3645315/.

71   Knudsen, Hannah K, Amanda J Abraham, and Paul M Roman. "Adoption and Implementation of Medications in Addiction Treatment Programs." Journal of addiction medicine. U.S. National Library of Medicine, March 2011. https://www.ncbi.nlm.nih.gov/pubmed/21359109.

72   The Business of Recovery, www.thebusinessofrecovery.com/.

73   "How Obamacare Created Massive Addiction-Treatment Fraud." Foundation for Economic Education, June 3, 2019. fee.org/articles/how-obamacare-created-addiction-treatment-fraud/.

74   "How Obamacare Created Massive Addiction-Treatment Fraud." Foundation for Economic Education, June 3, 2019. fee.org/articles/how-obamacare-created-massive-addiction-treatment-fraud/; Lurie, Julia. "A Disturbing New Phase of the Opioid Crisis: How Rehab Recruiters Are Luring Recovering Addicts into a Deadly Cycle." Mother Jones, July 8, 2019. https://www.motherjones.com/crime-justice/2019/02/opioid-epidemic-rehab-recruiters/.

75   Wine, F. H. "Report on the defective, dependent and delinquest classes of the population of the United States," 1888. U.S. Government Printing Office.

76   Aufderheide, Dean. "Mental Illness In America's Jails And Prisons: Toward A Public

Safety/Public Health Model." *Health Affairs*, April 1, 2014. https://www.healthaffairs.org/do/10.1377/hblog20140401.038180/full/.

77   Fischer, Wyman E. and Donald L. Barnes. *Tackling the Issues: Critical Thinking About Social Issues* . J. Weston Walch, 1994.

78   Lamb, Richard, Linda Weinberger, Jeffrey Marsh, and Bruce Gross. "Mentally Ill Treated in Jail, Not Community." Mental Illness Policy, January 23, 2019. https://mentalillnesspolicy.org/crimjust/mental-illness-jail.html.

79   U.S. Dept of Justice Bureau of Justice Statistics Report, 2006. https://www.bjs.gov/content/pub/pdf/mhppji.pdf.

80   Sarah Liebowitz, et al. "A Way Forward: Diverting People With Mental Illness Away From Inhumane and Expensive Jails Into Community-Based Treatment That Works." American Civil Liberties Union of Southern California, July 2014. https://www.prisonlegalnews.org/media/publications/A%20Way%20Forward%20-%20Diverting%20People%20with%20Mental%20Illness%20from%20Inhumane%20and%20Expensive%20Jails%20into%20Community-Based%20Treatment%20that%20Works%2C%20ACLU%20%26%20Bazelon%2C%202014.pdf.

81   Torrey, E. F., et al. "Criminalizing the seriously mentally ill." National Alliance for the Mentally Ill and Public Citizen Health Research Group, 1992, p. 43.

82   Rich, B A. "Physicians' Legal Duty to Relieve Suffering." The Western journal of medicine. Copyright 2001 BMJ Publishing Group, September 2001. https://www.ncbi.nlm.nih.gov/pmc/articles/PMC1071521/.

83   Baker, David. The Joint Commission's Pain Standards: Origins and Evolution. https://www.jointcommission.org/assets/1/6/Pain_Std_History_Web_Version_05122017.pdf.

84   "Pharma Lobbying Held Deep Influence over Opioid Policies." Center for Public Integrity, September 18, 2016. http://www.publicintegrity.org/2016/09/18/20203/pharma-lobbying-held-deep-influence-over-opioids-policies.

85   Van Zee, Art. "The Promotion and Marketing of Oxycontin: Commercial Triumph, Public Health Tragedy." American Journal of Public Health, February 2009. www.ncbi.nlm.nih.gov/pmc/articles/PMC2622774/.

86   Based on 2012 estimates, the adult population (ages 18 and older) of America was 240,291,024. "Data Access and Dissemination Systems (DADS)." American Fact Finder —Results. https://factfinder.census.gov/faces/tableservices/jsf/pages/productview.xhtml?src=bkmk.

87   "Drugs Most Frequently Involved in Overdose Deaths: United States, 2011-2016." National Vital Statistics Reports. https://www.cdc.gov/nchs/data/nvsr/nvsr67/nvsr67_09-508.pdf.

88   Evans, William N., and Ethan Lieber. "How the Reformulation of OxyContin Ignited the Heroin Epidemic." Cato Institute, August 15, 2018. https://www.cato.org/publications/research-briefs-economic-policy/how-reformulation-oxycontin-ignited-heroin-epidemic.

89   Singer, Jeffrey. "Scapegoating Opioid Makers Lets True Offender Get Away." UPI. UPI, April 24, 2019. https://www.upi.com/Top_News/Voices/2019/04/24/Scapegoating-opioid-makers-lets-true-offender-get-away/6371556106270/.

90   Nicholson, Kate, Diane Hoffman, and Chad Kollas. "How the CDC's Opioid Prescribing Guideline Is Harming Pain Patients." STAT, May 1, 2019. https://www.statnews.com/2018/12/06/overzealous-use-cdc-opioid-prescribing-guideline/#targetText=There's

91   Dasgupta, Nabarun, Michele Jonsson Funk, Scott Proescholdbell, Annie Hirsch, Kurt M Ribisl, and Steve Marshall. "Cohort Study of the Impact of High-Dose Opioid Analgesics on Overdose Mortality." Pain medicine (Malden, Mass.). U.S. National Library of Medicine, January 2016. https://www.ncbi.nlm.nih.gov/pubmed/26333030.

92   Singer, Jeffrey A., and UPI. "Scapegoating Opioid Makers Lets True Offender Get Away." Cato Institute, April 24, 2019. http://www.cato.org/publications/commentary/scapegoating-opioid-makers-lets-true-offender-get-away.

93   Ibid

94   Kertesz, Stefan, and Kate Nicholson. "No More 'Shortcuts' in Prescribing Opioids for Chronic Pain." STAT, May 1, 2019. http://www.statnews.com/2019/04/26/no-shortcuts-prescribing-opioids-chronic-pain.

95   "How the Reformulation of OxyContin Ignited the Heroin Epidemic." MIT Press Journals, March 4, 2019, www.mitpressjournals.org/doi/abs/10.1162/rest_a_00755.

96   2017 death rates in the U.S. declined for heroin (4.9 per 100,000) and for prescription opioids (4.4 per 100,000), but rates of overdose deaths from synthetic opioids, primarily fentanyl, rose from 1 per 100,000 individuals in 2013 to 9 per 100,000 in 2017. Brauser, Deborah. "Ten-Fold Rise in Deaths from Fentanyl, Other Synthetic Opioids." Medscape, September 5, 2019. https://www.medscape.com/viewarticle/917794; "Fentanyl and Other Synthetic Opioids Drug Overdose Deaths." National Institute on Drug Abuse (NIDA), May 29, 2018. https://www.drugabuse.gov/related-topics/trends-statistics/infographics/fentanyl-other-synthetic-opioids-drug-overdose-deaths.

97   Centers for Disease Control and Prevention.

98   Alpert, et al. "Supply-Side Drug Policy in the Presence of Substitutes: Evidence from the Introduction of Abuse-Deterrent Opioids." American Economic Journal. www.aeaweb.org/articles?id=10.1257/pol.20170082&&from=f.

99   "CDC Guideline for Prescribing Opioids for Chronic Pain United States," Centers for Disease Control and Prevention, 2016. https://www.cdc.gov/mmwr/volumes/65/rr/pdfs/rr6501e1er.pdf.

100 Dr. Deborah Dowell and Tamara Haegerich of the CDC and Dr. Roger Chou of Oregon Health and Science University.

101 Dowell, Deborah, Tamara Haegerich, and Roger Chou. "No Shortcuts to Safer Opioid Prescribing: NEJM." New England Journal of Medicine, June 13, 2019. http://www.nejm.org/doi/full/10.1056/NEJMp1904190?query=featured_home.

102 "Pain Management Best Practices Inter-Agency Task Force Report: Updates, Gaps, Inconsistencies, and Recommendations." U.S. Department of Health and Human Services, May 23, 2019. https://www.hhs.gov/sites/default/files/pmtf-final-report-2019-05-23.pdf.

103 In April 2019, the Washington State Department of Health issued a Notice of Adoption of an Interpretive Statement directing "... practitioners to not exclude, undertreat, or dismiss a patient from a practice solely because the patient has used or is using opioids in the course of normal medical care. While in most circumstances a practitioner is not legally required to treat a particular patient, the refusal to see or continue to treat a patient merely because the patient has taken or is currently using opioids is contrary to the clear intent of the Commission's rules governing opioid prescribing. Ending opioid therapy or initiating a forced tapering of opioids to a particular MED level for reasons outside of clinical efficacy or improvement in quality of life and/or function or abuse would violate the intent of the rules."; "Washington State Interpretive Statement: Opioid Prescribing & Monitoring for Allopathic Physicians and Physician Assistants," March 2019. https://wmc.wa.gov/sites/default/files/public/documents/OpioidINS2019-01.pdf. "Washington State Interpretive Statement: Opioid Prescribing & Monitoring for Allopathic Physicians and Physician Assistants," March 2019. https://wmc.wa.gov/sites/default/files/public/documents/OpioidINS2019-01.pdf.

104 "Sackler Family." *Forbes*, www.forbes.com/profile/sackler/#67f07c975d63.

105 Baker, David, The Joint Commission's Pain Standards: Origins and Evolution, PDF File, https://www.jointcommission.org/assets/1/6/Pain_Std_History_Web_Version_05122017.pdf.

106 State of Oklahoma vs. Purdue Pharma L. P. et al, August 26, 2019, PDF File, http://fm.cnbc.com/applications/cnbc.com/resources/editorialfies/2019/8/26/1044673351-20190826-151346-.pdf

107 State of North Dakota v Perdue Pharma, https://static.reuters.com/resources/media/editorial/20190516/northdakotavpurdue--dismissaldecision.pdf

108 Kline, Thomas. "SUICIDES Associated with Forced Tapering of Opiate Pain Treatments." Medium, June 12, 2019. https://medium.com/@ThomasKlineMD/opioidcrisis-pain-related-suicides-associated-with-forced-tapers-c68c79ecf84d.

109 "American Society of Addiction Medicine." ASAM Definition of Addiction, April 12, 2011. www.asam.org/resources/definition-of-addiction.

110 "Trends in Opioid Use, Harms, and Treatment. Pain Management and the Opioid Epidemic: Balancing Societal and Individual Benefits and Risks of Prescription Opioid Use," U.S. National Library of Medicine—National Academies of Science, July 13, 2017. www.ncbi.nlm.nih.gov/books/NBK458661/.

111 "Opioid Overdose Data." Centers for Disease Control and Prevention, October 3, 2018. www.cdc.gov/drugoverdose/maps/rxrate-maps.html.

112 "Overdose Death Rates." National Institute on Drug Abuse, January 29, 2019. www.drugabuse.gov/related-topics/trends-statistics/overdose-death-rates.

113 "Overdose Death Rates." National Institute of Drug Abuse, January 2019. https://www.drugabuse.gov/related-topics/trends-statistics/overdose-death-rates.

114 Kertesz, Stefan G, and Ajay Manhapra. "The Drive to Taper Opioids: Mind the Evidence, and the Ethics." Spinal Cord Series and Cases. Nature Publishing Group UK, July 27, 2018. https://www.ncbi.nlm.nih.gov/pubmed/30083393.

115 "DEA Proposes to Reduce the Amount of Five Opioids Manufactured in 2020, Marijuana Quota for Research Increases by Almost a Third." United States Drug Enforcement Administration, December 6, 2018. https://www.dea.gov/press-releases/2019/09/11/dea-proposes-reduce-amount-five-opioids-manufactured-2020-marijuana-quota?fbclid=IwAR2vSMvyMJXofPqkhaP_8c57a807Tc5shDXVwXVbjbrBJL_-6rkMPGfIrlc.

116 "FDA Drug Shortages." accessdata.fda.gov. Accessed September 19, 2019. https://www.accessdata.fda.gov/scripts/drugshortages/default.cfm?fbclid=IwAR3QgFbUS-3n9WNtvRLujShkgQV36Sris45A7VGMP4eoMy2Jg2KY1v9uTPHw#H.

117 "DEA Proposes to Reduce the Amount of Five Opioids Manufactured in 2020, Marijuana Quota for Research Increases by Almost a Third." United States Drug Enforcement Administration, September 11, 2019, https://www.dea.gov/press-releases/2019/09/11/dea-proposes-reduce-amount-five-opioids-manufactured-2020-marijuana-quota?fbclid=IwAR2vSMvyMJXofPqkhaP_8c57a807Tc5shDXVwXVbjbrBJL_-6rkMPGfIrlc.

118 "Opioid Overdose." Centers for Disease Control and Prevention, October 3, 2017. https://www.cdc.gov/drugoverdose/pdmp/states.html.

119 "Carpenter v. United States." American Civil Liberties Union. https://www.aclu.org/cases/carpenter-v-united-states.

120 "U.S. DOJ v. Jonas Amicus Brief." American Civil Liberties Union. https://www.aclu.org/legal-document/us-doj-v-jonas-amicus-brief-0.

121 "SUPPORT for Patients and Communities Act (2018 - H.R. 6)." GovTrack.us. https://www.govtrack.us/congress/bills/115/hr6.

122 Sanger-Katz, Margot and Thomas Kaplan. "Congress Is Writing Lots of Opioid Bills. But Which Ones Will Actually Help?" New York Times, June 20, 2018.

123 National Conference of State Legislators. Prescribing Policies: States Confront Opioid Overdose Epidemic. NCSL website. http://www.ncsl.org/research/health/prescribing-policies-states-confront-opioid-overdose-epidemic.aspx. Published October 31, 2018.

124 "Opioid Prescribing Limits Across the States." Pharmacy Times, February 5, 2019. https://www.pharmacytimes.com/contributor/marilyn-bulloch-pharmd-bcps/2019/02/opioid-prescribing-limits-across-the-states.

125 Scott, Jeff, "Florida's New Law on Controlled Substance Prescribing", flmedical.org, https://www.flmedical.org/florida/Florida_Public/Docs/HB-21_Highlights-secured.pdf; Miller, Naseem S. "Florida's New Opioid Law: What You Need to Know." orlandosentinel.com. Orlando Sentinel, December 13, 2018. https://www.orlandosentinel.com/health/os-florida-opioid-bill-doctors-20180803-story.html.

126 Davis, Corey, Amy Judd Lieberman, Hector Hernando-Delgado, and Carli Suba. "Laws Limiting the Prescribing or Dispensing of Opioids for Acute Pain in the United States: A National Systematic Legal Review." Science Direct, November 3, 2018. https://doi.org/10.1016/j.drugalcdep.2018.09.022.

127 "Corrupting Influence, Purdue & the WHO, Exposing Dangerous Opioid Manufacturer Influence at the World Health Organization", Clark, Kathrine, and Hal Rogers, May 22,2019, https://katherineclark.house.gov/_cache/files/a/a/aaa7536a-6db3-4192-b943-364e7c599d10/818172D42793504DD9DFE64B77A77C0E.5.22.19-who-purdue-report-final.pdf.

128 "US attack on WHO 'hindering morphine drive in poor countries'" Boseley, Sarah. The Guardian. September 18, 2019. https://amp.theguardian.com/society/2019/sep/18/us-attack-world-health-organization-who-hindering-morphine-drive-poor-countries?__twitter_impression=true&fbclid=IwAR0yeLcieFpAmhtlLuysAU-j4b7SQKQKofANwe9kdiuV7ZKQCdhS1gn9BDak; "Corrupting Influence, Purdue & the WHO, Exposing Dangerous Opioid Manufacturer Influence at the World Health Organization", Clark, Kathrine, and Hal Rogers, May 22,2019, https://katherineclark.house.gov/_cache/files/a/a/aaa7536a-6db3-4192-b943-364e7c-599d10/818172D42793504DD9DFE64B77A77C0E.5.22.19-who-purdue-report-final.pdf.

129 "60 Physicians and Pharmacists Charged in Federal Opioid Prescription Crackdown." Fox News. https://video.foxnews.com/v/6027338568001/#sp=show-clips.

130 "How Effective Are Medications to Treat Opioid Use Disorder?" National Institute on Drug Abuse. https://www.drugabuse.gov/publications/research-reports/medications-to-treat-opioid-addiction/efficacy-medications-opioid-use-disorder?fbclid=IwA-R1yHTKMlC6RJd3YRVc9pkP2yVrmXW8tZdFwbG4D2dq45dHLSCjx-i2KBb4.

131 "Mary Jeanne Kreek." https://www.rockefeller.edu/our-scientists/heads-of-laboratories/1198-mary-jeanne-kreek.

132 "Most People with Opioid Addictions Don't Get Medication-Assisted Therapy." STAT, June 24, 2018, https://www.statnews.com/2017/09/21/patients-opioid-addictions-dont-get-right-treatment-medication-assisted-therapy.

133 "How Effective Are Medications to Treat Opioid Use Disorder?" National Institute on Drug Abuse. https://www.drugabuse.gov/publications/research-reports/medications-to-treat-opioid-addiction/efficacy-medications-opioid-use-disorder?fbclid=IwA-R1yHTKMlC6RJd3YRVc9pkP2yVrmXW8tZdFwbG4D2dq45dHLSCjx-i2KBb4.

134 "World Drug Report 2015." United Nations, May 2015. https://www.unodc.org/documents/wdr2015/World_Drug_Report_2015.pdf.

135 "Let All Doctors Prescribe Buprenorphine for Opioid Use Disorder." STAT, May 1, 2019. www.statnews.com/2019/03/12/deregulate-buprenophine-prescribing/.

136 "MAT Statutes, Regulations, and Guidelines." SAMHSA, September 6, 2019. https://www.samhsa.gov/medication-assisted-treatment/statutes-regulations-guidelines#DATA-2000.

137 Confidentiality of Substance Use Disorder Patient Records regulations – 42 CFR Part 2 (Part 2)

138 Knopf, Alison. "SAMHSA Move Invites Law Enforcement 'Fishing Expeditions' for MAT Patients." Filter, August 29, 2019. https://filtermag.org/samhsa-law-enforcement-mat/?fbclid=IwAR3_GREGgGspRAqcRfImpk02R1YtgdPg-1k-0kz1iAI-j10TmfZ6xD_PW_gs.

139 Firth, Shannon. "HHS Proposes 'Part Two' Changes." MedPage Today: Medical News and Free CME. MedpageToday, August 23, 2019. https://www.medpagetoday.com/publichealthpolicy/opioids/81779.

140 Lenzer, Jeanne. "Physician Health Programs under Fire." The BMJ. British Medical Journal Publishing Group, June 30, 2016. https://www.bmj.com/content/353/bmj.i3568; Simmons-Duffin, Selena. "Treatment Limitations For Physicians With Opioid Addictions." NPR. NPR, September 5, 2019. https://www.npr.org/2019/09/05/758043712/treatment-limitations-for-physicians-with-opioid-addictions?fbclid=IwAR2UG9n-BCvYracs36oF5xlXfYskfzg606Jk6sw_Cw7kkp2aREsOAJaEcZA0.

141 The State of Pennsylvania has recently entered into an agreement with seven of the largest insurance payers to waive prior authorization requirements for addiction medications. The negotiation also included waiver of prior authorizations for opioid prescriptions when opioids are the appropriate medication for patients, minimizing days of pain while pain patients wait for medications. Statistics are not yet available, but representatives of the AMA and the Pennsylvania Medical Society asserted that this agreement "will be crucial to the fight against the opioid crisis." Johnson, Steven Ross. "Pennsylvania Health Insurers to End MAT Prior Authorizations." Modern Healthcare, October 12, 2018. https://www.modernhealthcare.com/article/20181012/NEWS/181019942/pennsylvania-health-insurers-to-end-mat-prior-authorizations.
   "AMA Calls to Eliminate Prior Authorization for MAT Patient Access." Xtelligent Healthcare Media, June 24, 2019. https://patientengagementhit.com/news/ama-calls-to-eliminate-prior-authorization-for-mat-patient-access.

142 Leshner, Allen, and Michelle Mancher. "Medications for Opioid Use Disorder Save Lives." National Academies Press. https://www.nap.edu/read/25310/chapter/1.

143 Associated Press. "A Peek into Opioid Users' Brains as They Try to Quit." NBCNews.com, July 9, 2019. https://www.nbcnews.com/health/health-news/peek-opioid-users-brains-they-try-quit-n1027911?fbclid=IwAR1GraXqGEYgMMcicMNengJ1KwovMx-RJJg5W9uTg-i3aBF4GWqgJOpmWo64.

144 "The Science of Drug Use and Addiction: The Basics." National Institute on Drug Abuse. https://www.drugabuse.gov/publications/media-guide/science-drug-use-addiction-basics.

145 "The Cost of Substance Abuse to America's Health Care System." The National Center on Addiction and Substance Abuse at Columbia University. file:///C:/Users/User/Downloads/The-cost-of-substance-abuse-to-americas-health-care-system-report-2-medicare-hospital-costs.pdf.

146 "Effects of Risky Drinking, Tobacco and Drug Use." Center on Addiction, April 14, 2017. https://www.centeronaddiction.org/addiction/effects-of-risky-substance-use.

147 "America's Need for and Receipt of Substance Use Treatment in 2015." Substance Abuse and Mental Health Services Administration. www.samhsa.gov/data/sites/default/files/report_2716/ShortReport-2716.html.

148 "Most Violent and Property Crimes in the U.S. Go Unsolved." Pew Research Center. http://www.pewresearch.org/fact-tank/2017/03/01/most-violent-and-property-crimes-in-the-u-s-go-unsolved/.

149 Hoerner, Emily. "Cops Across the US Have Been Exposed Posting Racist And Violent Things On Facebook. Here's The Proof." BuzzFeed News, July 23, 2019. https://www.buzzfeednews.com/article/emilyhoerner/police-facebook-racist-violent-posts-comments-philadelphia.

150 Mate, Gabor. In the Realm of Hungry Ghosts. Vermillion, 2018.

151 "Americans with Criminal Records." The Sentencing Project, 2014. https://www.sentencingproject.org/wp-content/uploads/2015/11/Americans-with-Criminal-Records-Poverty-and-Opportunity-Profile.pdf. Also National Conference of State Legislators. Barriers to Work: People with Criminal Records, NCSL website. http://www.ncsl.org/research/health/prescribing-policies-states-confront-opioid-overdose-epidemic.aspx. Published October 31, 2018. July 17, 2018

152 Lohr, David. "For Third Straight Year, Police Suicides Outnumber Line-Of-Duty Deaths." Huffington Post, January 2, 2019. https://www.huffpost.com/entry/for-third-straight-year-police-suicides-outnumber-line-of-of-duty-deaths_n_5c2d110de4b05c88b-70542fa.

153 Whitney, Brian. "On the Job and on Drugs: Police Officers Who Struggle with Addiction." The Fix, June 20, 2019. https://www.thefix.com/job-and-drugs-police-officers-who-struggle-addiction.

154 Coble, Christopher. "Are Cops Drug Tested?" Findlaw, August 4, 2016. https://blogs.findlaw.com/blotter/2016/08/are-cops-drug-tested.html.

155 Citizens Opposing Prohibition (COP). http://www.citizensopposingprohibition.org. Law Enforcement Action Partnership (LEAP). https://lawenforcementactionpartnership.org. Law Enforcement Leaders. http://lawenforcementleaders.org/.

156 Oxenham, Simon. "The Police Fighting To End The War On Drugs." Big Think, January 30, 2019. https://bigthink.com/neurobonkers/the-police-fighting-to-end-the-war-on-drugs.

157 "Mexican Drug Cartel." Arcgis.com. https://www.arcgis.com/apps/Cascade/index.html?appid=3ea52e1815524adfa8c69bddb50d056b.

158 Noel, Ted. "The Other Opiate Problem." American Thinker, March 3, 2019. https://www.americanthinker.com/articles/2019/03/the_emotherem_opiate_problem_comments.html.

159 Singer, Jeffrey A. "Scapegoating Opioid Makers Lets True Offender Get Away." Cato Institute, April 24, 2019. https://www.cato.org/publications/commentary/scapegoating-opioid-makers-lets-true-offender-get-away.

160 Ahmed, Azam. "El Chapo's Prosecution Has Fueled the Drug War in Mexico." *New York Times*, July 17, 2019. https://www.nytimes.com/2019/07/17/world/americas/el-chapo-mexico.html.

161 "New Annual Data Released by White House Drug Policy Office Shows Record High Poppy Cultivation and Potential Heroin Production in Mexico." The White House, July 20, 2018. https://www.whitehouse.gov/briefings-statements/new-annual-data-released-white-house-drug-policy-office-shows-record-high-poppy-cultivation-potential-heroin-production-mexico/.

162 "No Second Chance: People with Criminal Records Denied Access to Public Housing." Human Rights Watch, July 1, 2019. https://www.hrw.org/report/2004/11/18/no-second-chance/people-criminal-records-denied-access-public-housing.

163 "Punishing the Poorest." Coalition on Homelessness. http://www.cohsf.org/Punishing.pdf; Ruiz-Grossman, Sarah. "Homelessness Rises For Second Year In A Row In U.S. After Years Of Decline." HuffPost., January 22, 2019. https://www.huffpost.com/entry/homelessness-statistics-united-states-2018_n_5c1970a9e4b02d2cae8e322e.

164 Gorman, Anna, and Heidi de Marco. "'Medieval' Diseases Flare as Unsanitary Living Conditions Proliferate." Kaiser Health News, April 29, 2019. https://khn.org/news/medieval-diseases-flare-as-unsanitary-living-conditions-proliferate.

165 Bharel M., et al. "Health care utilization patterns of homeless individuals in Boston: preparing for Medicaid expansion under the Affordable Care Act." *American Journal of Public Health*. 2013;103:S311-S317.

166 Balko, Radley. "Shedding Light on the Use of SWAT Teams." *The Washington Post*, February 17, 2014. https://www.washingtonpost.com/news/the-watch/wp/2014/02/17/shedding-light-on-the-use-of-swat-teams/?utm_term=.64b99442191d.

167 "Children and Swat Raids: An Unintended Consequence." *Worcester Magazine*, March 1, 2018. https://www.worcestermag.com/2018/03/01/feature-children-swat-raids-unintended-consequence.

168 Ibid.

169 Livni, Ephrat. "Police in the US Shoot Dogs so Often That a Justice Department Expert Calls It an 'Epidemic.'" *Quartz*, December 23, 2016. https://qz.com/870601/police-killing-dogs-is-an-epidemic-according-to-the-justice-department/.

170 Meixler, Eli. "Mexico's Murder Rate in 2018 Sets a New Record." *Time*, January 22, 2019. https://time.com/5509216/mexico-murder-rate-sets-record-2018/.

171 "The Staggering Death Toll of Mexico's Drug War." Public Broadcasting Service, July 27, 2015. https://www.pbs.org/wgbh/frontline/article/the-staggering-death-toll-of-mexicos-drug-war.

172 Knox, Patrick. "Mexico Murder Bloodbath Spirals out of Control Reaching All-Time High with 94 Killings Every DAY." *The Sun*, July 7, 2019. https://www.thesun.co.uk/news/9446065/mexico-murder-rate-highest-ever-94-killings-each-day/.

173 Johansen, Ragnhild. "Drug Trafficking and the Financing of Terrorism." United Nations Office on Drugs and Crime. http://www.unodc.org/unodc/en/frontpage/drug-trafficking-and-the-financing-of-terrorism.html.

174 "The Day Police Told Parliament to End the War on Drugs." Politics.co.uk, March 14, 2016. https://www.politics.co.uk/comment-analysis/2016/03/11/the-day-police-told-parliament-to-end-the-war-on-drugs.

175 McCoy, Alfred W. "How the Heroin Trade Explains the US-UK Failure in Afghanistan." *The Guardian*, January 9, 2018. https://www.theguardian.com/news/2018/jan/09/how-the-heroin-trade-explains-the-us-uk-failure-in-afghanistan.

176 https://www.thenation.com/article/alfred-mccoy-washington-drug-war-ruining-world/.

177 Jones, Russell. "Six Reasons the Drug War Is Disastrous for Latin America." Witness for Peace, https://witnessforpeace.org/six-reasons-the-drug-war-is-disastrous-for-latin-america/.

178 Nazario, Sonia. "The Children of the Drug Wars." *The New York Times*, July 11, 2014. https://www.nytimes.com/2014/07/13/opinion/sunday/a-refugee-crisis-not-an-immigration-crisis.html?_r=0.

179 "Race and the Drug War." Drug Policy Alliance. http://www.drugpolicy.org/issues/race-and-drug-war.

180 "U.S. Incarceration Rates by Race." Prison Policy Initiative. https://www.prisonpolicy.org/graphs/raceinc.html.

181 "Punishment and Prejudice: Racial Disparities in the War on Drugs." Human Rights Watch. https://www.hrw.org/legacy/campaigns/drugs/war/key-facts.htm.

182 Alexander, Michelle. "Where Have All the Black Men Gone?" Huffington Post, May 25, 2011. https://www.huffpost.com/entry/where-have-all-the-black_b_469808.

183 "Criminal Justice Fact Sheet." NAACP. https://www.naacp.org/criminal-justice-fact-sheet/.

184 "Race and the Drug War." Drug Policy Alliance. http://www.drugpolicy.org/issues/race-and-drug-war.

185 "Criminal Justice Fact Sheet." NAACP. https://www.naacp.org/criminal-justice-fact-sheet/.

186 Ibid.

187 Kennedy, Joseph, Isaac Unah and Kasi Wahlers. "Sharks and Minnows in the War on Drugs: A Study of Quantity, Race and Drug Type in Arrests." *UC Davis Law Review*, 2018. https://lawreview.law.ucdavis.edu/issues/52/2/Articles/52-2_Kennedy.pdf.

188 Following is an example of proposed local regulations that can result in those with criminal records being shut out of housing. "Proposed Rental Housing Licensing Pro-

gram: Maplewood, MN." Maplewood, Minnesota. https://maplewoodmn.gov/1503/Proposed-Rental-Housing-Licensing-Progra.

189   "Office of General Counsel Guidance on Application of Fair Housing Act Standards to the Use of Criminal Records by Providers of Housing and Real Estate-Related Transactions", U.S. Department of Housing and Urban Development, April 4, 2016, https://www.hud.gov/sites/documents/HUD_OGCGUIDAPPFHASTANDCR.PDF

190   24 C.F.R. § 100.500; see also Inclusive Cmtys. Project, 135 S. Ct. at 2514-15 (summarizing HUD's Discriminatory Effects Standard in 24 C.F.R. § 100.500); id. at 2523 (explaining that housing providers may maintain a policy that causes a disparate impact "if they can prove [the policy] is necessary to achieve a valid interest."; https://www.thebalancesmb.com/renting-to-tenants-with-criminal-records-4149540

191   23 U.S.C. Sect; 159. This statute, also known as the "Solomon-Lautenberg Amendment," was part of the 1991 Department of Transportation and Related Agencies Appropriations Act (H.R. 5229). "23 U.S.C. § 159—U.S. Code Title 23. Highways § 159." Findlaw. https://codes.findlaw.com/us/title-23-highways/23-usc-sect-159.html.

192   Natapoff, Alexandra, et al. "Punishment Without Crime." *Motor Vehicle Affordability and Fairness Task Force Final Report.* Edward J. Bloustein School of Planning and Public Policy, Rutgers University, 2006, 38.

193   Aiken, Joshua. "Reinstating Common Sense: How Driver's License Suspensions for Drug Offenses Unrelated to Driving Are Falling out of Favor." Prison Policy Initiative. https://www.prisonpolicy.org/driving/national.html#recent_reforms.

194   "Woman Jailed for 3 Months Because Police Thought Her Cotton Candy Was Meth." WTVR.com, November 27, 2018. https://wtvr.com/2018/11/27/woman-jailed-for-3-months-because-police-thought-her-cotton-candy-was-meth/.

195   Lucas, Fred and Elizabeth Schulte. "Urine Screens Cost $8.5 Billion a Year—More than the Entire EPA Budget." Public Broadcasting Service, November 7, 2017. https://www.pbs.org/newshour/health/urine-screens-cost-8-5-billion-a-year-more-than-the-entire-epa-budget.

196   "Medicare Spending on Urine Drug Tests Has Quadrupled. Is That Protecting Patients—or Wasting Money?" Advisory Board Daily Briefing, November 10, 2017. https://www.advisory.com/daily-briefing/2017/11/10/urine-tests.

197   Lucas, Fred and Elizabeth Schulte. "Urine Screens Cost $8.5 Billion a Year—More than the Entire EPA Budget." Public Broadcasting Service, November 7, 2017. https://www.pbs.org/newshour/health/urine-screens-cost-8-5-billion-a-year-more-than-the-entire-epa-budget.

198   Laino, Charlene. "Drug Tests Often Trigger False Positives." WebMD. WebMD, May 28, 2010. https://www.webmd.com/drug-medication/news/20100528/drug-tests-often-trigger-false-positives#1.

199   "FAQ." International Paruresis Association (IPA), https://paruresis.org/faq/.

200   Legalization of medical marijuana (and recreational marijuana in some jurisdictions)

and the prevalence of use of legally prescribed drugs makes it much more difficult for an employer to act, even if a drug test is positive. Employers may actually lose more than is gained by testing. Testing can negatively impact employee morale and trust between management and employees. Additionally, recruiting may be negatively compromised. Many highly qualified and productive employees who are occasional, recreational drug users or who are on prescription drugs, which they don't care to disclose, simply don't apply at companies with mandatory drug testing policies.

201   Covert, Bryce and Josh Israel. "States Spend Millions to Drug Test the Poor, Turn up Few Positive Results." ThinkProgress, March 29, 2019. https://thinkprogress.org/states-spend-millions-to-drug-test-the-poor-turn-up-few-positive-results-81f826a4afb7/.

202   "Americans with Disabilities Act , Chapter 4, Substance Abuse under the ADA ", https://www.usccr.gov/pubs/ada/ch4.htm.

203   Wurman, Ilan. "Unconstitutional Conditions and Drug Testing Welfare Recipients." Jurist, March 13, 2013. https://www.jurist.org/commentary/2013/03/ilan-wurman-drug-testing.

204   Mazelis, Joan Maya. "Punishing the Poor Isn't Just Bad Policy, It's Wasting Taxpayer Money." The Hill, February 20, 2018. https://thehill.com/opinion/civil-rights/374700-punishing-the-poor-isnt-just-bad-policy-its-wasting-taxpayer-money.

205   Terry-McElrath, YM, et al. "Middle and high school drug testing and student illicit drug use: a national study 1998-2011." *Journal of Adolescent Health.* 2013 Jun; 52(6):707-15. doi: 10.1016/j.jadohealth. 2012.11.020. Epub, February 11, 2013.

206   Goldberg L. et al. "Outcomes of a prospective trial of student-athlete drug testing: the Student Athlete Testing Using Random Notification (SATURN) study." *Journal of Adolescent Health.* 2007 Nov;41(5):421-9. doi:10.1016/j.jadohealth, 2007.08.001.

207   Levy, Sharon, and Miriam Schizer. "Adolescent Drug Testing Policies in Schools." Pediatrics. American Academy of Pediatrics, April 1, 2015. https://pediatrics.aappublications.org/content/135/4/782.full.

208   Phelps, Michelle Suzanne. "Why Ending Mass Probation Is Crucial to U.S. Criminal Justice Reform." Scholars Strategy Network, September 14, 2018. https://scholars.org/brief/why-ending-mass-probation-crucial-us-criminal-justice-reform.

209   Quattlebaum, Megan, and Juliene James. "As Candidates Search for Criminal Justice Talking Points, Parole and Probation Reform Should Top List." USA Today. Gannett Satellite Information Network, July 4, 2019. https://www.usatoday.com/story/opinion/policing/2019/07/03/probation-parole-criminal-justice-candidates-policing-the-usa/1643628001.

210   "Probation and Parole Systems Marked by High Stakes, Missed Opportunities." The Pew Charitable Trusts, https://www.pewtrusts.org/en/research-and-analysis/issue-briefs/2018/09/probation-and-parole-systems-marked-by-high-stakes-missed-opportunities.

211   https://www.prisonpolicy.org/graphs/probation_and_correctional_control.html; Data Source: Compiled from Bureau of Justice Statistics' "Annual Probation Survey" and "An-

nual Parole Survey" data series and Prison Policy Initiative "Tracking State Prison Growth in 50 States." (Graph: Peter Wagner, 2015).

212 Sawyer, Wendy, and Peter Wagner. "Mass Incarceration: The Whole Pie 2019." Prison Policy Initiative, March 19, 2019. https://www.prisonpolicy.org/reports/pie2019.html.

213 "Risk/Needs Assessment 101: Science Reveals New Tools to Manage Offenders." Pew Center on the States, 2011. https://www.pewtrusts.org/~/media/legacy/uploaded-files/pcs_assets/2011/pewriskassessmentbriefpdf.pdf.

214 Kennedy, Joseph, Isaac Unah and Kasi Wahlers. "Sharks and Minnows in the War on Drugs: A Study of Quantity, Race and Drug Type in Arrests." *UC Davis Law Review*, 2018, https://lawreview.law.ucdavis.edu/issues/52/2/Articles/52-2_Kennedy.pdf.

215 "Race and the Drug War." Drug Policy Alliance. http://www.drugpolicy.org/issues/race-and-drug-war.

216 Shannon, Sarah K. S., et al. "The Growth, Scope, and Spatial Distribution of People with Felony Records in the United States, 1948–2010." SpringerLink, September 22, 2017. https://link.springer.com/article/10.1007/s13524-017-0611-1.

217 Elderbroom, Brian and Julia Durnan. "State Drug Law Reforms to Reduce Felony Convictions and Increase Second Chances." Urban.org, October 2018. https://www.urban.org/sites/default/files/publication/99077/reclassified_state_drug_law_reforms_to_reduce_felony_convictions_and_increase_second_chances.pdf

218 Adam Gelb (director, Public Safety Performance Project, The Pew Charitable Trusts), letter to Chris Christie (The President's Commission on Combating Drug Addiction and the Opioid Crisis), re. "The Lack of a Relationship between Drug Imprisonment and Drug Problems," June 19, 2017. http://www.pewtrusts.org/~/media/assets/2017/06/the-lack-of-a-relationship-between-drug-imprisonment-and-drug-problems.pdf.

219 Bucknor, Cherrie, and Alan Barber. "The Price We Pay: Economic Costs of Barriers to Employment for Former Prisoners and People Convicted of Felonies." Center for Economic and Policy Research, June 2016. http://cepr.net/publications/reports/the-price-we-pay-economic-costs-of-barriers-to-employment-for-former-prisoners-and-people-convicted-of-felonies.

220 Ibid.

221 "Injustice 101: Higher Education Act Denies Financial Aid to Students with Drug Convictions." American Civil Liberties Union. https://www.aclu.org/other/injustice-101-higher-education-act-denies-financial-aid-students-drug-convictions.

222 "6 Million Lost Voters: State-Level Estimates of Felony Disenfranchisement, 2016." The Sentencing Project, October 6, 2016. https://www.sentencingproject.org/publications/6-million-lost-voters-state-level-estimates-felony-disenfranchisement-2016/.

223 "After Prison: Roadblocks to Reentry." CSG Justice Center, August 28, 2019. https://csgjusticecenter.org/nrrc/publications/after-prison-roadblocks-to-reentry-2/.

224 "Alaska's Criminal Justice Reforms." The Pew Charitable Trusts, December 2016. https://www.pewtrusts.org/~/media/assets/2016/12/alaskas_criminal_justice_reforms.pdf.

225 The full text of Proposition 47 is available at https://oag.ca.gov/system/files/initiatives/pdfs/13-0060percent20percent2813-0060percent20percent-28Neighborhoodpercent20andpercent20Schoolpercent20Fundingpercent29percent29.pdf.

226 "Second Chances and Systems Change," Californians for Safety and Justice. https://safeandjust.org/wp-content/uploads/P47_Report_Final.pdf.

227 "Prop. 47 funding to fight criminal recidivism has finally arrived—right on time." *Los Angeles Times*, June 6, 2017. http://www.latimes.com/opinion/editorials/la-ed-prop-47-funding-20170606-story.html.

228 Subramanian, Ram, and Rebecka Moreno. "Drug War Détente? A Review of State-Level Drug Law Reform, 2009-2013." Vera Institute of Justice, April 2014. https://storage.googleapis.com/vera-web-assets/downloads/Publications/drug-war-d%C3%A9tente-a-review-of-state-level-drug-law-reform-2009-2013/legacy_downloads/state-drug-law-reform-review-2009-2013-v5.pdf.

229 Lynch, Tim. "The Devil's Bargain: How Plea Agreements, Never Contemplated by the Framers, Undermine Justice." Cato Institute, June 24, 2011. https://www.cato.org/publications/commentary/devils-bargain-how-plea-agreements-never-contemplated-framers-undermine-justice.

230 "Crime in the United States 2017." FBI Uniform Crime Report US Dept. of Justice, September 2018, p. 1, and Arrest Table: Arrests for Drug Abuse Violations. https://ucr.fbi.gov/crime-in-the-u.s/2017/crime-in-the-u.s.-2017.

231 42 C.J.S. *Indictments* § 204 (2016); James Austin et al., "Unlocking America: Why and How to Reduce America's Prison Population." The JFA Institute, 2007. http://www.jfa-as- sociates.com/publications/srs/UnlockingAmerica.pdf.

232 Herman, G. Nicholas. *Plea Bargaining*. Lexis Law Publishing, 1997.

233 *Brady v. United States*, 397 U.S. 742, 748, 751-52 (1970); *Bordenkircher v. Hayes*, 434 U.S. 357, 358-59, 365 (1978).

234 Bibas, Stephanos. "Regulating the Plea-Bargaining Market: From Caveat Emptor to Consumer Protection," 99 California Law Review. 1117, 1117–19 (2011) (cited in *Lafler v. Cooper*, 132 S. Ct. 1376, 1387 (2012)); Darryl K. Brown, Lafler, Frye *and Our Still-Unregulated Plea Bargaining System*, 25 FED. SENT'G. REP. 131 (2012).

235 *Brady v. United States*, 397 U.S. 742, 747 (1970).

236 *Boykin v. Alabama*, 395 U.S. 238, 242–43 (1969).

237 In 2014, U.S. Treasury and Justice Departments seized over $5 billion of assets; FBI reports show 3.5 billion in 2014 burglary losses. "Executive Summary." Institute for Justice. https://ij.org/report/policing-for-profit/executive-summary/.
   Jackson, Kerry. "Police Took More Of Other People's Stuff Than Burglars Did In 2014." *Investor's Business Daily*, November 19, 2015. https://www.investors.com/politics/commentary/cops-seize-more-in-assets-than-burglars-steal-in-2014/.

238 "Audit of the Assets Forfeiture Fund and Seized Asset Deposit Fund Annual Financial Statements Fiscal Year 2017." Office of the Inspector General U.S. Department of Justice, December 2017. https://oig.justice.gov/reports/2017/a1805.pdf.

239 "Burglary." FBI 2017 Crime in the United States, September 10, 2018. https://ucr.fbi.gov/crime-in-the-u.s/2017/crime-in-the-u.s.-2017/topic-pages/burglary.

240 Ferguson, Dana. "Minnesota Collected Nearly $8.9 Million in Civil Forfeitures Last Year." *West Central Tribune*, August 15, 2019. https://www.wctrib.com/news/government-and-politics/4613987-Minnesota-collected-nearly-8.9-million-in-civil-forfeitures-last-year; Nino, Jose. "Minnesota Is Making a Killing Off of Civil Asset Forfeiture." The Advocates for Self-Government, September 3, 2019. https://www.theadvocates.org/2019/09/minnesota-is-making-a-killing-off-of-civil-asset-forfeiture/?fbclid=IwAR3tt-SvgAB7I7PqScR2AddPNB9AHTcfGtSRA_imyIni0c2nsajImRYiuvA.

241 Smith, Kim. "Woman Must Forfeit Property." *Arizona Daily Star*, April 7, 2010. https://tucson.com/news/local/crime/woman-must-forfeit-property/article_26658120-3cf4-5535-bbd1-573d7a500021.html.

242 Teigen, Anne and Lucia Bragg. "Evolving Civil Asset Forfeiture Laws." National Conference of State Legislators, February 2018. http://www.ncsl.org/research/civil-and-criminal-justice/evolving-civil-asset-forfeiture-laws.aspx.

243 "California Governor Brown Signs Bill Protecting Californians from Civil Asset Forfeiture Abuse." Drug Policy Alliance, September 28, 2016. http://www.drugpolicy.org/news/2016/09/california-governor-brown-signs-bill-protecting-californians-civil-asset-forfeiture-abu.

244 Teigen, Anne and Lucia Bragg. "Evolving Civil Asset Forfeiture Laws." National Conference of State Legislators, February 2018 http://www.ncsl.org/research/civil-and-criminal-justice/evolving-civil-asset-forfeiture-laws.aspx.

245 Supreme Court of the United States, *Timbs v. Indiana*. https://www.supremecourt.gov/opinions/18pdf/17-1091_5536.pdf.

246 Thomas, Owen. "Easy Answer on Prison Furloughs Eludes Dukakis. Public Opinion Makes Bush's Job Easier." *The Christian Science Monitor*, September 8, 1988. https://www.csmonitor.com/1988/0908/afur.html.

247 Pfaff, John. "The Perverse Power of the Prosecutor." *Democracy Journal*, February 22, 2018.

248 Barkow, Rachel Elise. *Prisoners of Politics*. Belknap Press, 2019, 113.

249 Foss, Adam. "A Prosecutor's Vision for a Better Justice System | Adam Foss." TED on YouTube, April 12, 2016. https://www.youtube.com/watch?v=H1fvr9rGgSg.

250 Rucke, Katie. "The Law Enforcement Lobby's Heavy Hand In American Policy." *MintPress News*, June 2, 2014. https://www.mintpressnews.com/the-law-enforcement-lobbys-heavy-hand-in-american-policy/191557/.

251 "FindLaw's United States Supreme Court Case and Opinions." Findlaw, https://caselaw.findlaw.com/us-supreme-court/09-1272.html.

252 Lennard, Natasha. "Police Unions' Opposition to Prison Reform Is About More Than Jobs—It's About Racism." The Intercept, August 14, 2018. https://theintercept.com/2018/08/14/police-unions-prison-reform/.

253 Ibid.

254 Watson, Joe, et al. "Report Finds Two-Thirds of Private Prison Contracts Include 'Lockup Quotas.'" Prison Legal News, August 2015. https://www.prisonlegalnews.org/news/2015/jul/31/report-finds-two-thirds-private-prison-contracts-include-lockup-quotas/., 2019.

255 Sloan, Bob. "Prison Labor and Crime in the U.S.—Industry, Privatization, Inmate Facts and Stats." Prepared for the 2011 Congressional Black Caucus. phewacommunity.org/images/Presentation_to_the_Congressional_Black_Congress.pdf.

256 The full report, including a map of private prison locations, is available at http://www.phewacommunity.org/images/Presentation_to_the_Congressional_Black_Congress.pdf.

257 "Profiting from Probation: America's 'Offender-Funded' Probation Industry." Human Rights Watch, February 5, 2014. https://www.hrw.org/report/2014/02/05/profiting-probation/americas-offender-funded-probation-industry.

258 "Profiting from Probation: America's 'Offender-Funded' Probation Industry." Human Rights Watch, June 28, 2019. https://www.hrw.org/report/2014/02/05/profiting-probation/americas-offender-funded-probation-industry#d781ca.

259 Ibid.

260 Sawyer, Wendy, and Peter Wagner. "Mass Incarceration: The Whole Pie 2019." Prison Policy Initiative, March 19, 2019. https://www.prisonpolicy.org/reports/pie2019.html.

261 Wykstra, Stephanie. "Want to Fix the Criminal Justice System? Start by Getting Rid of Bail." Vox, October 17. 2018, https://www.vox.com/future-perfect/2018/10/17/17955306/bail-reform-criminal-justice-inequality.

262 "Unsecured Bonds: The Most Effective and Efficient Pretrial Release Option." National Institute of Corrections, October 5, 2018. https://nicic.gov/unsecured-bonds-most-effective-and-efficient-pretrial-release-option.

263 Tashea, Jason. "Text-Message Reminders Are a Cheap and Effective Way to Reduce Pretrial Detention." ABA Journal, July 17, 2018. http://www.abajournal.com/lawscribbler/article/text_messages_can_keep_people_out_of_jail.

264 Gupta, Arpit, and Ethan Frenchman. "The US Bail System Punishes the Poor and Rewards the Rich." Quartz, December 3, 2018. https://qz.com/900777/the-us-bail-system-punishes-the-poor-and-rewards-the-rich/.

265 Ibid.

266 "Bail Bond Industry Fights Back Against Moves To Limit Or End Cash Bail." Wisconsin Public Radio, January 22, 2019. https://www.wpr.org/bail-bond-industry-fights-back-against-moves-limit-or-end-cash-bail.

267   Schulte, Fred, and Elizabeth Lucas. "Urine Screens Cost $8.5 Billion a Year—More than the Entire EPA Budget." PBS, Public Broadcasting Service, November 7, 2017, https://www.pbs.org/newshour/health/urine-screens-cost-8-5-billion-a-year-more-than-the-entire-epa-budget.

268   Hackett, Ashley. "Thousands of Privately-Owned Companies Are Profiting From the U.S. Prison System." Pacific Standard, April 27, 2018. https://psmag.com/social-justice/thousands-of-privately-owned-companies-are-profiting-from-the-us-prison-system.
        "The Prison Industrial Complex: Mapping Private Sector Players." Corrections Accountability Project, April 2018. https://static1.squarespace.com/static/58e127cb1b10e31ed45b20f4/t/5ade0281f950b7ab293c86a6/1524499083424/The+Prison+Industrial+Complex+-+Mapping+Private+Sector+Players+percent28April+2018percent29.pdf.

269   Ibid.

270   Friedmann, Alex. "Lowering Recidivism through Family Communication." Prison Legal News, August 29, 2019. https://www.prisonlegalnews.org/news/2014/apr/15/lowering-recidivism-through-family-communication.

271   The company declined to provide any financial details; those included in this article are culled from public records and interviews with current and former employees. Wagner, Daniel. "Criminal Justice: States Profit from Prisoners, Families Pay." Time, September 30, 2014. https://time.com/3446372/criminal-justice-prisoners-profit.

272   Law, Victoria. "How Companies Make Millions Charging Prisoners to Send An Email." Wired, October 30, 2018. https://www.wired.com/story/jpay-securus-prison-email-charging-millions/.

273   Letter to the FCC. Human Rights Defense Center. https://www.humanrightsdefensecenter.org/media/publications/HRDC%20FCC%20Comment%20in%20response%20to%203rd%20FNPRM%20Monday%20011816%20FINAL%20Version.pdf.

274   Law, Victoria. "How Companies Make Millions Charging Prisoners to Send An Email." Wired, October 30, 2018. https://www.wired.com/story/jpay-securus-prison-email-charging-millions/.

275   Rabuy, Bernadette, and Peter Wagner. "Screening Out Family Time." Prison Policy Initiative, January 2015. https://www.prisonpolicy.org/visitation/report.html.

276   Gordon, Leslie A. "Is Video Visitation Helpful or Harmful for Prisoners and Their Families?" ABA Journal, October 1, 2015. http://www.abajournal.com/magazine/article/is_video_visitation_helpful_or_harmful_for_prisoners_and_their_families.

277   "Ripping off L.A.'s Inmates." Daily News, May 1, 2007. https://www.dailynews.com/2007/05/01/ripping-off-las-inmates/.

278   Littman, Aaron, and Frank Knaack. "Civil Rights Groups Sue 49 Alabama Sheriffs for Access to Public Records Showing How Sheriffs Personally Profit from Funds Allocated for Feeding People in Jail." Southern Center for Human Rights, January 8, 2018. https://www.schr.org/resources/civil_rights_groups_sue_49_alabama_sheriffs_for_access_to_public_records_showing_how.

279 Sheets, Connor. "Etowah Sheriff Pockets $750k in Jail Food Funds, Buys $740k Beach House." al, March 13, 2018. https://www.al.com/news/birmingham/2018/03/etowah_sheriff_pocketed_over_7.html.

280 Nobel, Carmen. "Alabama Reporter Investigates Story of Sheriff Who Pocketed Jail Food Funds." Journalist's Resource, March 11, 2019. https://journalistsresource.org/tip-sheets/reporting/connor-sheets-alabama-sheriff-pocketed-jail-food-funds-goldsmith/.

281 Sheets, Connor. "Alabama Ethics Commission Drops Case against 'Beach House Sheriff'." al, October 4, 2018. https://www.al.com/news/2018/10/alabama_ethics_commission_drop.html.

282 Sheets, Connor. "Man Arrested after Criticizing Etowah Sheriff Released from Jail, to Attend Drug Court." al, March 6, 2018. https://www.al.com/news/birmingham/2018/03/man_arrested_after_criticizing.html.

283 "Alabama Will No Longer Give Jail Food Funds To 'Sheriff's Personally.'" Alabama News, July 11, 2018. https://www.alabamanews.net/2018/07/11/alabama-will-no-longer-give-jail-food-funds-to-sheriffs-personally/.

284 Ibid.

285 "Prison Labour Is a Billion-Dollar Industry, with Uncertain Returns for Inmates." The Economist, March 16, 2017. https://www.economist.com/united-states/2017/03/16/prison-labour-is-a-billion-dollar-industry-with-uncertain-returns-for-inmates.

286 Sibilla, Nick. "Inmates Who Volunteer to Fight California's Largest Fires Denied Access to Jobs on Release." USA Today, August 20, 2018. https://www.usatoday.com/story/opinion/2018/08/20/californias-volunteer-inmate-firefighters-denied-jobs-after-release-column/987677002/.

287 Lafer, Gordon. "Captive Labor." The American Prospect, September 1999. https://prospect.org/article/captive-labor.

288 Sawyer, Wendy. "How Much Do Incarcerated People Earn in Each State?" Prison Policy Initiative, April 10, 2017. https://www.prisonpolicy.org/blog/2017/04/10/wages/.

289 Daugherty, Colleen. "The Cruel and Unusual Irony of Prisoner Work Related Injuries in the United States." University of Pennsylvania Journal of Business and Employment Law. https://scholarship.law.upenn.edu/cgi/viewcontent.cgi?article=1305&context=jbl.

290 "The Business of Reducing Crime." Unicor. https://www.unicor.gov/publications/reports/FY2017_AnnualMgmtReport.pdf.

291 Moritz-Rabson, Daniel. "Inmates in Government Prisons Are Paid Pennies to Manufacture Clothing, License Plates and Office Supplies." Newsweek, September 4, 2018. www.newsweek.com/prison-slavery-who-benefits-cheap-inmate-labor-1093729.

292 Moses, Marilyn, and Cindy Smith. "Factories Behind Fences: Do Prison Real Work Programs Work?" National Institute of Justice, June 1, 2007. https://nij.ojp.gov/topics/articles/factories-behind-fences-do-prison-real-work-programs-work.

293 Letter from Insys Therapeutics to the DEA. *Washington Post*, https://www.washing-tonpost.com/blogs/wonkblog/files/2016/07/Synthetic-Competitor-Objection-1.pdf?tid=a_inl.

294 Baca, Richard. "Marijuana's Biggest Enemy Is Not Jeff Sessions—It's Big Pharma." *Esquire*, October 5, 2017, www.esquire.com/lifestyle/health/a54160/big-pharma-against-legal-weed/.

295 Ingraham, Christopher. "A Pharma Company That Spent $500,000 Trying to Keep Pot Illegal Just Got DEA Approval for Synthetic Marijuana." *The Washington Post*, March 24, 2017, www.washingtonpost.com/news/wonk/wp/2017/03/24/a-pharma-compa-ny-that-spent-500000-trying-to-keep-pot-illegal-just-got-dea-approval-for-synthetic-marijuana/?utm_term=.6d34375c5738.

296 "What Is Marinol And How Does It Differ from Cannabis?" Royal Queen Seeds, July 27, 2017.   www.royalqueenseeds.com/blog-what-is-marinol-and-how-does-it-differ-from-cannabis-n579.

297 "Trump Opioid Plan Writes in Favoritism to Vivitrol over Other Medications." STAT, April 24 2018. www.statnews.com/2018/03/26/trump-opioid-plan-alkermes-vivit-rol/.

298 Dodes, Lance M., and Zachary Dodes. *The Sober Truth: Debunking the Bad Science behind 12-Step Programs and the Rehab Industry*. Beacon Press, 2015.

299 Nationally, less than half of all "residential facilities" allow people to be on opioid maintenance medications. (That number includes hospitals and other licensed institu-tional living facilities. But it excludes many recovery houses, which don't have licensing requirements and so aren't required to report to an oversight body.) Feldman, Nina. "Many 'Recovery Houses' Won't Let Residents Use Medicine To Quit Opioids." NPR, September 12, 2018. www.npr.org/sections/health-shots/2018/09/12/644685850/many-recovery-houses-wont-let-residents-use-medicine-to-quit-opioids.

300 In the first long-term follow-up of patients treated with buprenorphine/naloxone (Bp/Nx) for addiction to opioid pain relievers, half reported that they were abstinent from the drugs 18 months after starting the therapy. After 3.5 years, the portion who reported being abstinent had risen further, to 61 percent, and fewer than 10 percent met diagnostic criteria for dependence on the drugs. Sarlin, Eric. "Long-Term Follow-Up of Medication-Assisted Treatment for Addiction to Pain Relievers Yields 'Cause for Optimism.'" NIDA, November 30, 2015. https://www.drugabuse.gov/news-events/nida-notes/2015/11/long-term-follow-up-medication-assisted-treatment-addic-tion-to-pain-relievers-yields-cause-optimism.

301 "How Obamacare Created Massive Addiction-Treatment Fraud." Foundation for Eco-nomic Education, June 3, 2019. fee.org/articles/how-obamacare-created-massive-ad-diction-treatment-fraud/.

302 Mower, Lawrence. "Police Reports Link Sober Home Operator to Prostitution, 'Flop' Houses." *The Palm Beach Post*, September 4, 2016. www.palmbeachpost.com/arti-cle/20151219/NEWS/812069235.

303 "The Difference between Legalisation and Decriminalisation." *The Economist*, June 18,

2014. www.economist.com/the-economist-explains/2014/06/18/the-difference-between-legalisation-and-decriminalisation.

304 A study of European Union member-states showed that countries with less punitive drug polices had lower rates of drug use than countries with more punitive policies. Vuolo, Mike. "National-Level Drug Policy and Young People's Illicit Drug Use: A Multilevel Analysis of the European Union." *Drug and Alcohol Dependence*, 131. No. 1-2 (2013) 149-56. See also Degenhardt, Louisa, et al. "Towards a Global View of Alcohol. Tobacco, Cannabis, and Cocaine Use: Findings from the WHO World Mental Health Surveys." *PLoS Medicine*, 5. No. 7 (2008). http://journals.plos.org/ plosmedicine/ article/ le?id=10.1371/journal.pmed.0050141&type=printable. Room, Robin, et al. *Cannabis Policy: Moving Beyond Stalemate*. Oxford University Press, 2010. Reinarman, Craig, et al. "The Limited Relevance of Drug Policy: Cannabis in Amsterdam and in San Francisco." *American Journal of Public Health*, 94. No. 5 (2004). Hughes, Caitlin Elizabeth and Alex Stevens. "What Can We Learn from the Portuguese Decriminalization of Illicit Drugs?" *British Journal of Criminology*, 50. No. 6 (2010). Single, Eric W. "The Impact of Marijuana Decriminalization: An Update." *Journal of Public Health Policy*. (1989). MacCoun, Robert J. and Peter Reuter. *Drug War Heresies: Learning from Other Vices, Times, and Places*. Cambridge University Press, 2001. Vuolo, Mike. "National-Level Drug Policy and Young People's Illicit Drug Use: A Multilevel Analysis of the European Union." *Drug and Alcohol Dependence*, 131. No. 1-2 (2013).

305 The three United Nations treaties that are the cornerstones of international drug policy are the Single Convention on Narcotic Drugs of 1961, as amended by the 1972 protocol [https://treaties.un.org/Pages/ViewDetails.aspx?src=TREATY&mtdsg_no=VI-18&chapter=6&clang=_en], the Convention of Psychotropic Substances of 1971 [https://www.unodc.org/unodc/en/treaties/single-convention.html], and the United Nations Convention against Illicit Traffic in Narcotic Drugs and Psychotropic Substances of 1988 [https://www.unodc.org/pdf/convention_1988_en.pdf].

306 The Transnational Institute (TNI) is an international research and advocacy institute committed to building a just, democratic, and sustainable world. For more than 40 years, TNI has served as a unique nexus between social movements, engaged scholars, and policy makers. TNI has a reputation for well-researched analysis on key global issues long before they become mainstream concerns. As a non-sectarian institute made up of researchers, scholar-activists, and movement-builders, TNI uniquely combines a "big picture" analysis with proposals and solutions that are both just and pragmatic.

307 "Ganja Laws: The Government's Case for Reform." *Jamaica Observer*, June 15, 2014. www.jamaicaobserver.com/columns/Ganja-laws--The-Government-s-case-for-reform_16895074.

308 WOLA Advocacy for Human Rights in the Americas. Annotated relevant quotes from the UN Conventions and the official Commentaries. https://www.wola.org/sites/default/files/downloadable/Drug%20Policy/2010/notes%20for%20editors_pr240210.pdf.

309 "UN, United Nations, UN Treaties, Treaties." United Nations, November 11, 1990. treaties.un.org/Pages/ViewDetails.aspx?src=TREATY&mtdsg_no=VI-19&chapter=6&clang=_en.

310 Ibid.

311   Bolivia was granted an exception allowing its traditional domestic coca market to be maintained. There were objections to that exception, but the United Nations did grant it.

312   "United Nations Office on Drugs and Crime." WDR 1997. www.unodc.org/unodc/en/data-and-analysis/WDR-1997.html.

313   "International Narcotics Control Board Expresses Deep Concern about the Legalization of Cannabis for Non-Medical Use in Canada." International Narcotics Control Board, June 21, 2018. www.incb.org/incb/en/news/press-releases/2018/incb-expresses-deep-concern-about-the-legalization-of-cannabis-for-non-medical-use-in-canada.html.

314   "The UN Drug Control Conventions." United Nations. https://www.tni.org/en/publication/the-un-drug-control-conventions#11.

315   "Universal Declaration of Human Rights." United Nations. www.un.org/en/universal-declaration-human-rights/.

316   "The Death Penalty for Drug Offences." Harm Reduction International. www.hri.global/the-death-penalty-for-drug-offences.   PDF   File.   https://www.hri.global/files/2012/11/13/Death_penalty_2012_Tipping_the_Scales_Web.pdf.

317   "Annual Report 2014." United Nations Office on Drugs and Crime. https://www.unodc.org/documents/AnnualReport2014/Annual_Report_2014_WEB.pdf.

318   "United Nations: Criminal Sanctions for Drug Use Are 'Not Beneficial.'" Drug Policy Alliance, March 12, 2014. www.drugpolicy.org/news/2014/03/united-nations-criminal-sanctions-drug-use-are-not-beneficial.

319   "The Vienna Declaration: A Global Call to Action for Science-Based Drug Policy." Harm Reduction International, July 4, 2010. www.hri.global/contents/628.

320   The Outcome Document of that Session states: "We recognize that civil society, as well as the scientific community and academia, plays an important role in addressing and countering the world drug problem, and note that affected populations and representatives of civil society entities, where appropriate, should be enabled to play a participatory role in the formulation, implementation, and the providing of relevant scientific evidence in support of, as appropriate, the evaluation of drug control policies and programmes."
      Unfortunately, reaffirming the treaties, the Outcome Document also states: "We reaffirm the principal role of the Commission on Narcotic Drugs as the policy-making body of the United Nations with prime responsibility for drug control matters, and our support and appreciation for the efforts of the United Nations, in particular those of the United Nations Office on Drugs and Crime as the leading entity in the United Nations system for addressing and countering the world drug problem, and further reaffirm the treaty-mandated roles of the International Narcotics Control Board and the World Health Organization." https://www.unodc.org/documents/postungass2016//follow-up/18-01924_UNGASS_eBook_002.pdf.

321   "Joint United Nations Statement on Ending Discrimination in Health Care Settings." World Health Organization, June 27, 2017. www.who.int/en/news-room/detail/27-06-2017-joint-united-nations-statement-on-ending-discrimination-in-health-care-settings.

322   United Nations, Chief Executive Board for Coordination, January 18, 2019. https://www.unsceb.org/CEBPublicFiles/CEB-2018-2-SoD.pdf.

323   21 U.S. Code § 1703 (b) (12) provides that the Director or Deputy Directors "shall ensure that no Federal funds appropriated to the Office of National Drug Control Policy shall be expended for any study or contract relating to the legalization (for a medical use or any other use) of a substance listed in schedule I of section 812 of this title and take such actions as necessary to oppose any attempt to legalize the use of a substance (in any form) that (A) is listed in schedule I of section 812 of this title; and (B) has not been approved for use for medical purposes by the Food and Drug Administration."

324   "Assessment of compulsory treatment of people who use drugs in Cambodia, China, Malaysia and Vietnam: An application of selected human rights principles." Manila: WHO Western Pacific Region. www. wpro.who.int/publications/docs/FINALfor-Web_Mar17_Compulsory_Treatment. pdf . "The Rehab Archipelago: Forced Labor and Other Abuses in Drug Detention Centers in Southern Vietnam." New York: Human Rights Watch. http://www.hrw.org/reports/2011/09/07/rehab-archipelago-0.

325   "Trends and Developments, 2015." European Monitoring Centre for Drugs and Drug Addiction.   http://www.emcdda.europa.eu/attachements.cfm/att_239505_EN_TDAT15001ENN.pdf

326   Ibid.

327   Laqueur, Hannah. "Uses and Abuses of Drug Decriminalization in Portugal." Law & Social Inquiry, 2014. https://www.law.berkeley.edu/ les/Laqueur_percent-282014percent29_-_Uses_and_Abuses_of_Drug_Decriminalization_in_Portugal_-_LSI.pdf. Domoslawski, Artur. Drug Policy in Portugal: The Benefits of Decriminalizing Drug Use. Open Society Foundations, 2011. https://www.opensociety-foundations.org/sites/default/les/drug-policy-in-portugal-english-20120814.pdf.Hughes, Caitlin Elizabeth and Alex, Stevens. "What Can We Learn from the Portuguese Decriminalization of Illicit Drugs?" The British Journal of Criminology, 50, 6 (2010) 999-1022. Andrade, Paula Vale de and Ludmila Carapinha. "Drug Decriminalization in Portugal." The BMJ, 2010.

328   "Want to Win the War on Drugs? Portugal Might Have the Answer." Time, August 1, 2018. www.time.com/longform/portugal-drug-use-decriminalization/.

329   Ferreira, Susana. "Portugal's Radical Drugs Policy Is Working. Why Hasn't the World Copied It?" The Guardian, December 5, 2017. www.theguardian.com/news/2017/dec/05/portugals-radical-drugs-policy-is-working-why-hasnt-the-world-copied-it.

330   Stevens, Alex. "Portuguese Drug Policy Shows at Decriminalisation Can Work, but Only Alongside Improvements in Health and Social Policies." London School of Economics Blog, 2012. Domoslawski, Artur. Drug Policy in Portugal: The Benefits of Decriminalizing Drug Use. Open Society Foundations, 2011. Hughes, Caitlin Elizabeth and Alex Stevens. "What Can We Learn from the Portuguese Decriminalization of Illicit Drugs?" British Journal of Criminology, 50, 6, (2010) 999-1022. De Andrade, Paula Vale and Ludmila Carapinha. "Drug Decriminalisation in Portugal," The BMJ, 341, 2010. c4554. Berger, Lisa. "Drug Policy in Portugal: An Interview with Helen Redmond, Lcsw, Cadc," Journal of Social Work Practice in the Addictions 13, no. 2 (2013). Queiroz, Mario, "Q&A: In Portugal, We Fight the Illness, Not the People Who Suffer from It."

Inter-Press Service, 2012. In addition, other indirect factors such as an aging population of people who use heroin may account for some of the declines in problematic drug use and associated health consequences.

331 Ferreira, Susana. "Portugal's Radical Drugs Policy Is Working. Why Hasn't the World Copied It?" *The Guardian*, December 5, 2017. www.theguardian.com/news/2017/dec/05/portugals-radical-drugs-policy-is-working-why-hasnt-the-world-copied-it.

332 Daly, Max. "Is Norway Set to Spark a Drug Policy Revolution?" *Vice*, August 3, 2018, www.vice.com/en_uk/article/594wkb/is-norway-set-to-spark-a-drug-policy-revolution.

333 Hernández Tinajero, Jorge and Carlos Zamudio Angles. "Mexico: The Law Against Small- Scale Drug Dealing," Transnational Institute Series on Legislative Reform of Drug Policies No. 3, October 2009. http://www.tni.org/ les/down- load/dlr3.pdf.

334 Presidencia de la Republica Mexico, Plan Nacional de Desarrollo 2019-2024. https://lopezobrador.org.mx/wp-content/uploads/2019/05/PLAN-NACIONAL-DE-DE-SARROLLO-2019-2024.pdf.

335 21 U.S.C. § 844. A conviction that occurs after a prior drug-related offense has become final triggers a mandatory minimum of not less than 15 days in custody, raises the maximum available penalty to two years, and increases the fine to a minimum of $2,500. If the conviction occurs after two or more prior convictions for drug-related offenses have become final, the mandatory minimum penalty becomes 90 days in custody, the maximum available penalty is three years, and the minimum fine is $5,000. In order for the enhanced felony penalties to apply, the government must meet the procedural requirements set forth in 21 U.S.C. § 851 (proceedings to establish prior convictions).

336 Neither the statute (21 U.S.C. § 844) nor the guideline (USSG §2D2.1) specify a drug weight for this offense.

337 California Proposition 47; Utah House Bill 348, 2015; Connecticut House Bill 7104, 2015; Alaska Senate Bill 91, 2016: and Oklahoma ballot initiative State Question 780.

338 State of Colorado, House Bill 19-1263. https://leg.colorado.gov/sites/default/files/documents/2019A/bills/2019a_1263_01.pdf

339 State of Colorado, House Bill 19-1263. https://s3.amazonaws.com/cordillera-network/wp-content/uploads/sites/11/2019/04/02114809/Joint-Budget-Committee-Memo-on-HB-19-1263.pdf.

340 "More Imprisonment Does Not Reduce State Drug Problems." The Pew Charitable Trusts, March 8, 2018, https://www.pewtrusts.org/en/research-and-analysis/issue-briefs/2018/03/more-imprisonment-does-not-reduce-state-drug-problems.

341 Nebehay, Stephanie. "Swiss Drug Policy Should Serve as Model: Experts." Reuters, October 25, 2010. https://www.reuters.com/article/us-swiss-drugs/swiss-drug-policy-should-serve-as-model-experts-*idUSTRE69O3VI20101025*.

342 "New Drug Guidelines Are Europe's Most Liberal." Drugs-Forum. https://drugs-forum.com/ams/new-drug-guidelines-are-europes-most-liberal.10270/.

343 Barriuso, Alonso M. "Cannabis social clubs in Spain: A normalizing alternative underway." Amsterdam: Transnational Institute. https://pdfs. semanticscholar.org/6098/6091c2bd24009fa550aabc8bcbfd08cee809.pdf?_ ga=2.241965888.317174989.1567096960-1779835326.1567096960.

344 Solvetti, L.M. "Drug Use Criminalization v. Decriminalization: An Analysis in Light of the Italian Experience." Report prepared for the Swiss Federal Office of Public Health. http://www.antoniocasella.eu/archila/solivetti_2001.pdf.

345 "Germany Drug Report 2019." European Monitoring Centre for Drugs and Drug Addiction, 2019. http://www.emcdda.europa.eu/countries/drug-reports/2019/germany/ drug-laws-and-drug-law-offences_en.

346 National Programme on Combating Drug Addiction and Illicit Traffic in Narcotic Drugs in the Republic of Armenia in 2009-2012, draft, 12.

347 Penalties for Drug Law Offences at a Glance. www.emcdda.europa.eu/publications/ topic-overviews/content/drug-law-penalties-at-a-glance_en.

348 Law 20.000, Article 4, 2007, Library of the National Congress of Chile. http://www. leychile.cl/Navegar?idNorma=235507&buscar=Ley+20.000.

349 elsma, M. "Drug Law Reform Trend in Latin America." Amsterdam: Transnational Institute, 2, 1990. http://www.druglawreform.info/images/stories/documents/country_overview_drug_laws_ nal.pdf.

350 Touzé G. "Argentina: Reform on the way?" Amsterdam: Transnational Institute, 2009. http://www.tni.org/sites/www.tni.org/ les/download/dlr6.pdf. Cozac. D. "Rulings in Argentinian and Colombian courts decriminalize pos- session of small amounts of narcotics." *HIV/AIDS Policy & Law Review* Vol. 14, No. 2, December 2009.

351 Law N° 1.340, Art. 30: "Whoever possesses substances detailed in this Law, prescribed by a doctor, or whoever possessed them exclusively for personal consumption, will be exempted from punishment." Transitional Institute, June 30, 2015. https://www.tni.org/en/publication/about-drug-law-reform-in-paraguay.

Drug users' exclusive personal use will be determined by the amount of substance in possession equivalent to what is considered a daily dosage, as determined by the forensic doctor and a specialized doctor designated by the Social Welfare and Public Health Ministry and another by the defendant, at his/her own cost, if so requested. In the case of marijuana this shall not surpass 10 grams and in the case of cocaine, heroine, and other opiates, 2 grams.

352 Garrido, R. S. "Legislation on drugs and the prison situation in Peru." Transitional Institute, 71. https://www.wola.org/sites/default/files/downloadable/Drug%20Policy/2011/TNIWOLA-Systems_Overload-def.pdf -peru.

353 This quote fits a chapter about police and prosecutors who've taken it upon themselves to stop the damage of the War on Drugs. It's also fitting that Nike's slogan was created from a combination of Nancy Reagan's "Just Say No" campaign and "Let's Do It," the final words of prisoner Gary Gilmore prior to his execution. https://www.wbur.org/ onlyagame/2018/11/23/just-do-it-nike-gilmore.

354 Gesley, Jenny. "Decriminalization of Narcotics: Netherlands," July 1, 2016, www.loc.gov/law/help/decriminalization-of-narcotics/netherlands.php.

355 EMCDDA. "Threshold quantities for drug offences." European Monitoring Centre for Drugs and Drug Addiction. http://www.emcdda.europa.eu/html.cfm/index99321EN.html%20Accessed%205%20June%202012.

356 Art. 167, lid 2, Sv. (Neth.); Art. 242, lid 2 Sv. (Neth.)

357 Kort, Marcel de. Tussen patiënt En Delinquent: Geschiedenis Van Het Nederlandse Drugsbeleid = (Between Patient and Delinquent, the History of Drug Policy in the Netherlands). Hilversum: Verloren, 1995.

358 P.H.P.H.M.C Van Kempen and M. I. Dedorova. Internationaal Recht En Cannabis: Een Beoordeling Op Basis V An Vn-Drugsverdragen En Eu- Drugsregelgeving Van Gemeentelijke En Buitenlandse Opvattingen Pro Regulering Van Cannabisteelt Voor Recreatief Gebruik [International Law And Cannabis: An Assessment Of Municipal And Foreign Views In Favour Of Regulating Cannabis Cultivation For Recreational Use Based On Un Narcotic Drugs Conventions And The Eu Legal Instruments In Anti-Drugs Policy] 71 (2014).

359 Margriet Van Laar, et al. Scheiding Der Markten En Beleid Ten Aanzien Van Coffeeshops, Separation Of Markets And Policy With Regard To Coffee Shops, In EVALUATIE VAN HET NEDERLANDSE DRUGSBELEID, EVALUATION OF THE DUTCH DRUG POLICY, 109, 147; Van Laar Et Al., Supra Note 11, At 120; Marianne Van Ooyen-Houben & Edward Kleemans, Drug Policy: The "Dutch Model," 44 CRIME & JUST. 213 (2015).

360 Rep. of the Int'l Narcotics Control Board for 2011, U.N. Doc. E/INCB/2011/1, 283 (2012). Note that the Netherlands also has a policy of tolerance with regard to drug injection rooms. These reflect, like the coffee shops, the national health oriented and risk-reducing drug policy.

361 Arnt Mein & Marianne Van Ooyen-Houben, Bestuurlijke Rapportage Coffeeshop Checkpoint [Administrative Report Coffee Shop Checkpoint] 10 (2011).

362 A.C.M. Jansen, Hasj-coffeeshops als experiment, 19 JUSTITIËLE MARCEL DE KORT, TUSSEN PATIËNT EN DELINQUENT, GESCHIEDENIS VAN HET NEDERLANDSE DRUGSBELEID [BETWEEN PATIENT AND DELINQUENT, THE HISTORY OF DRUG POLICY IN THE NETHERLANDS] 253 (1995) (with a report summary in English).

363 "Polish President approves new drug law." International Drug Policy Consortium. May 27, 2011. http://www.idpc.net/alerts/polish-president-approves-new- drug-law.

364 www.paariusa.org.

365 Collins, Susan E., et al. "Seattle's Law Enforcement Assisted Diversion (LEAD): Program Effects on Recidivism Outcomes." Evaluation and Program Planning, U.S. National Library of Medicine, October 2017. www.ncbi.nlm.nih.gov/pubmed/28531654.

366 "LEAD National Support Bureau: About LEAD." LEAD. www.leadbureau.org/about-lead.

367 "Support for Marijuana Legalization Hits New High, CBS News Poll Finds." CBS News, April 19, 2019. www.cbsnews.com/news/support-for-marijuana-legalization-hits-new-high-cbs-news-poll-finds/.

368 McCarthy, Justin. "Two in Three Americans Now Support Legalizing Marijuana." Gallup.com, August 5, 2019. https://news.gallup.com/poll/243908/two-three-americans-support-legalizing-marijuana.aspx.

369 "62% Of Americans Favor Legalizing Marijuana." Pew Research Center, October 8, 2018. www.pewresearch.org/fact-tank/2018/10/08/americans-support-marijuana-legalization/.

370 McCarthy, Justin. "Two in Three Americans Now Support Legalizing Marijuana." Gallup.com, August 5, 2019. news.gallup.com/poll/243908/two-three-americans-support-legalizing-marijuana.aspx.

371 "QU Poll Release Detail." Quinnipiac University Poll, February 23, 2017. poll.qu.edu/national/release-detail?ReleaseID=2432.

372 In 1973, Oregon became the first state to decriminalize cannabis, and Texas law was amended to make possession of four ounces or less a misdemeanor. In 1975, Alaska, Maine, Colorado, California and Ohio decriminalized, and Minnesota decriminalized in 1976. In 1977, Mississippi, New York, North Carolina, and South Dakota decriminalized, but South Dakota repealed decriminalization shortly after it was passed. In 1978, Nebraska decriminalized. No other state would decriminalize until Nevada's decriminalization in 2001.
"NORML—Working to Reform Marijuana Laws." The National Organization for the Reform of Marijuana Laws. norml.org/news/2001/06/07/nevada-defelonizes-pot-possessionstate-eliminates-jail-criminal-record-for-minor-offenders-legalizes-medical-marijuana-for-seriously-ill.

373 Balzar, John. "Voters Approve Measure to Use Pot as Medicine." *Los Angeles Times*, November 6, 1996.

374 "Support for Marijuana Legalization Hits New High, CBS News Poll Finds." CBS News, April 19, 2019. www.cbsnews.com/news/support-for-marijuana-legalization-hits-new-high-cbs-news-poll-finds/.

375 H.R.2—115th Congress (2017-2018): Agriculture Improvement Act of 2018, Congress.gov (2018).

376 Prince, Jennifer." U.S. Hemp, CBD Product Sales Reach $820 Million in 2017." Nutritional Outlook, June 2018. http://www.nutritionaloutlook.com/herbs-botanicals/us-hemp-cbd-product-sales-reach-820-million-2017.

377 "Hemp CBD Production Projected to Become Billion Dollar Market by 2020." MarketNewsUpdates.com., November 2, 2017. www.prnewswire.com/news-releases/hemp-cbd-production-projected-to-become-billion-dollar-market-by-2020-654675053.html.

378 Jones, Jeffrey M. "In U.S., Medical Aid Top Reason Why Legal Marijuana Favored." Gallup.com, August 5, 2019. news.gallup.com/poll/258149/medical-aid-top-reason-why-legal-marijuana-favored.aspx.

379 "Therapeutic Effects of Cannabis and Cannabinoids. (The Health Effects of Cannabis and Cannabinoids: The Current State of Evidence and Recommendations for Research)". U.S. National Library of Medicine, January 12, 2017. https://www.ncbi.nlm.nih.gov/books/NBK425767/.

380 Grinspoon, Peter. "Medical Marijuana." Harvard Health Blog, June 25, 2019. www.health.harvard.edu/blog/medical-marijuana-2018011513085.

381 "Clinical Implications and Policy Considerations of Cannabis Use," American Medical Association. https://assets.ama-assn.org/sub/meeting/documents/i16-resolution-907.pdf.

382 "Challenges and Barriers in Conducting Cannabis Research." "The Health Effects of Cannabis and Cannabinoids: The Current State of Evidence and Recommendations for Research." National Center for Biotechnology Information, U.S. National Library of Medicine, January 12, 2017. www.ncbi.nlm.nih.gov/books/NBK425757/.

383 Letter from Members of Congress to the Attorney General, May 2019. https://mjbizdaily.com/wp-content/uploads/2019/05/LettertoDOJDEAreCannabis-Barr-May-2019.pdf.

384 "H.R.601—116th Congress (2019-2020): Medical Cannabis Research Act of 2019." Congress.gov, March 4, 2019. www.congress.gov/bill/116th-congress/house-bill/601?q=percent7Bpercent22searchpercent22percent3Apercent5Bpercent-22medical cannabis research actpercent22percent5Dpercent7D&s=5&r=1percent2.

385 "NORML—Working to Reform Marijuana Laws." The National Organization for the Reform of Marijuana Laws. norml.org/component/zoo/category/recent-research-on-medical-marijuana.

386 "FDA Regulation of Cannabis and Cannabis-Derived Products: Q&A." U.S. Food and Drug Administration, April 2, 2019. www.fda.gov/news-events/public-health-focus/fda-regulation-cannabis-and-cannabis-derived-products-questions-and-answers.

387 "Marijuana Legalization in Colorado: Early Findings, A Report Pursuant to Senate Bill 13-283." Colorado Department of Public Safety, March 2016. http://cdpsdocs.state.co.us/ors/docs/reports/2016-SB13-283-Rpt.pdf.

388 Egan, Daniel and Jeffrey Miron. "The Budgetary Implication of Marijuana Prohibition." In *Pot Politics: Marijuana and the Costs of Prohibition*. Edited by Earleywine M. Oxford University Press, 2006.

389 McVey, Eli. "Chart: Cannabis industry employs 165,000 plus workers." *Marijuana Business Daily*, June 26, 2017. https://mjbizdaily.com/chart-cannabis-industry-employs-165000-plus-workers/.

390 Colorado is a good example, since their distribution and taxation system has been in effect longer than states legalizing more recently. Of the approximate $600 million in receipts for the state of Colorado from 2014-2018, $230 million was distributed to the Colorado Department of Education to fund school construction, behavioral health programs, bullying prevention, and early literacy. Revenues from a 15 percent excise tax on marijuana sales are allocated to public schools and other education in Colorado. The 15 percent sales tax on cannabis is divided, with 10 percent to the local government and the 90 percent

balance split, with $30 million to the Public School Fund, 28.15 percent to the general fund, and the 71.85 percent balance to the Marijuana Tax Cash Fund to pay for health care, monitoring health effects of marijuana, and substance use disorder prevention and treatment. "From Prohibition to Progress: A Status Report on Marijuana Legalization." Drug Policy Alliance. www.drugpolicy.org/legalization-status-report,2018.

391 Boehnke, Kevin F. and Evangelos Litinas and Daniel J.Clauw. "Medical Cannabis Use Is Associated With Decreased Opiate Medication Use in a Retrospective Cross-Sectional Survey of Patients With Chronic Pain." *The Journal of Pain: Official Journal of the American Pain Society, 17,* No. 6 (June 2016): 739-744. https://doi.org/10.1016/j.jpain.2016.03.002. Haroutounian, S., et al. "The Effect of Medicinal Cannabis on Pain and Quality-of-Life Outcomes in Chronic Pain: A Prospective Open-label Study," *The Clinical Journal of Pain, 32,* No. 12 (December 2016): 1036-1043, https://doi.org/10.1097/ AJP.0000000000000364.

392 Bruce, Douglas, et al. "Preferences for Medical Marijuana over Prescription Medications Among Persons Living with Chronic Conditions: Alternative, Complementary, and Tapering Uses." *Journal of Alternative and Complementary Medicine.* September 25, 2017, https://doi.org/10.1089/acm.2017.0184.

393 Bachhuber, Marcus A., et al. "Medical cannabis laws and opioid analgesic overdose mortality in the United States, 1999-2010," *JAMA Internal Medicine,* 174, 10, (2014): 1668-1673.

394 Jones, Jeffrey M. "In U.S., Medical Aid Top Reason Why Legal Marijuana Favored." Gallup.com, August 5, 2019. news.gallup.com/poll/258149/medical-aid-top-reason-why-legal-marijuana-favored.aspx.

395 Sewell, R., et al. "The Effect of Cannabis Compared with Alcohol on Driving." *The American Journal on Addictions.* Vol 18 (3): 185-193, 2009. https://www.ncbi.nlm.nih.gov/pmc/articles/PMC2722956/.

396 "Effects of Marijuana—With and Without Alcohol—on Driving Performance." National Institute on Drug Abuse, June 23, 2015. https://www.drugabuse.gov/news-events/news- releases/2015/06/effects-marijuana-without-alcohol-driving-performance.

397 Hartman, R. L., et al. "Cannabis Effects on Driving Longitudinal Control with and Without Alcohol." *Journal of Applied Toxicology,* Vol 36 (11): 1418-29, November 2016. https://www.ncbi.nlm.nih.gov/pubmed/26889769.

398 "Alaska, California, Maine, Massachusetts, Oregon, and Washington, D.C. use drug recognition experts to determine driver impairment, Drug-Impaired Driving Laws." Governors Highway Safety Association, 2017. http://www.ghsa.org/state-laws/issues/drugpercent20impairedpercent20 driving.

399 Odell, Morris, et al. "Residual Cannabis Levels in Blood, Urine, and Oral Fluid Following Heavy Cannabis Use," *Forensic Sci Int,* 249, 173 (2015): 173-80, 10.1016/j.forsciint.2015.01.026. Berning, Amy, et al. "Results of the 2013-2014 National Roadside Survey of Alcohol and Drug Use by Drivers," U.S. Department of Transportation, National Highway Traffic Safety Administration, February 2015. https://www.nhtsa.gov/sites/nhtsa.dot.gov/ les/812118-roadside_survey_2014.pdf.

400 "From Prohibition to Progress: A Status Report on Marijuana Legalization." Drug Policy Alliance. www.drugpolicy.org/legalization-status-report,2018.

401 Compton, Richard P. "Marijuana-Impaired Driving: A Report to Congress." NHTSA DOTHS 812 440. U.S. Department of Transportation, July 2017. https://www.nhtsa.gov/sites/nhtsa.dot.gov/files/documents/812440-marijuana-impaired-   driving-report-to-congress.pdf.

402 Logan, Barry, et al. "An Evaluation of Data from Drivers Arrested for Driving Under the Influence in Relation to Per se Limits for Cannabis." AAA Foundation for Traffic Safety, 2016. https://www.aaafoun- dation.org/sites/default/ les/EvaluationOfDriversInRelationToPerSeReport.pdf.

403 Couper, Fiona. DUI Toxicology Reports. https://media.npr.org/assets/news/2015/08/THC-1.pdf Abrams, Abigail. "Colorado's Marijuana DUIs Are Down 33 percent." Time, April 21, 2017. http://time.com/4749802/colorado-marijuana-dui-drop-33-percent-2017/.

404 Ibid.

405 Harm Reduction Journal, 6, 35. https://doi.org/10.1186/1477-7517-6-35.

406 Johnson, J. K., et al. "Heterogeneity of state medical marijuana laws and adolescent recent use of alcohol and marijuana: Analysis of 45 states, 1991-2011." Substance Abuse, 1-8, https://doi.org/10.1080/08897077.2017.1389801.

407 Anderson, D. Mark. "Association of Marijuana Laws With Teen Marijuana Use." JAMA Pediatrics, July 8, 2019. https://jamanetwork.com/journals/jamapediatrics/article-abstract/2737637.

408 "National Survey on Drug Use and Health." Substance Abuse and Mental Health Services Administration, August 20, 2019. https://www.samhsa.gov/data/data-we-collect/nsduh-national-survey-drug-use-and-health.

409 "Reports and Detailed Tables From the 2018 National Survey on Drug Use and Health (NSDUH)." Substance Abuse and Mental Health Services Administration, 2018. https://www.samhsa.gov/data/nsduh/reports-detailed-tables-2018-NSDUH.

410 According to the DEA, Schedule I drugs, substances, or chemicals are defined as drugs with no currently accepted medical use and a high potential for abuse. Some examples of Schedule I drugs are heroin, lysergic acid diethylamide (LSD), marijuana (cannabis), 3,4-methylenedioxymethamphetamine (ecstasy), methaqualone, and peyote. "Drug Scheduling." DEA. www.dea.gov/drug-scheduling.

411 The Strengthening of the Tenth Amendment Through Entrusting States (STATES) Act (S.1028 & H.R. 2093).

412 Hageseth, Christian. "Your Cannabis Company Can Get a Bank Account but Not Easily." GreenEntrepreneur, January 29, 2019. www.greenentrepreneur.com/article/326668.

413 USAspending.gov. www.usaspending.gov/#/award/67951261.

414 "26 U.S. Code § 280E—Expenditures in Connection with the Illegal Sale of Drugs." Legal Information Institute. www.law.cornell.edu/uscode/text/26/280E.

415 "H.R.1595—116th Congress (2019-2020): SAFE Banking Act of 2019." Congress.gov, June 5, 2019. www.congress.gov/bill/116th-congress/house-bill/1595/text.

416 "United Nations Convention against Illicit Traffic in Narcotic Drugs and Psychotropic Substances of 1988." United Nations Office on Drugs and Crime. https://www.unodc. org/pdf/convention_1988_en.pdf, Article 3, Paragraph 2.

417 "What Is the USA Patriot Act?" The United States Department of Justice. www.justice. gov/archive/ll/highlights.htm.

418 González, Enric. "Uruguay Loses Momentum in the Marijuana Legalization Stakes." El *País*, October 17, 2018. elpais.com/elpais/2018/10/16/inenglish/1539687522_144922.html.

419 "Consolidated Federal Laws of Canada, Cannabis Act." Cannabis Act, July 26, 2019. laws-lois.justice.gc.ca/eng/acts/C-24.5/.

420 "Legal Status of Cannabis in Belgium – an Overview." Sensi Seeds Blog, January 26, 2018. https://sensiseeds.com/en/blog/legal-status-of-cannabis-in-belgium/.

421 Sabin, Lamiat. "Cannabis Possession of up to Two Ounces Decriminalised on Bob Marley's Birthday in Jamaica." The Independent, February 9, 2015. www.independent.co.uk/news/world/americas/marijuana-in-jamaica-possession-of-up-to-two-ounces-decriminalised-on-bob-marleys-birthday-10034299.html.

422 Szalavitz, Maia. "How America Overdosed on Drug Courts." Pacific Standard, May 18, 2015. https://psmag.com/news/how-america-overdosed-on-drug-courts.

423 Abrahamson, Daniel N., and *Los Angeles Daily News*. "Drug Courts Are Not the Answer—Justice Policy Institute." Justice Policy Institute. www.justicepolicy.org/news/9204.

424 "Thurs: Briefing on Capitol Hill Responds to Finding That 'Drug Courts Are Not the Answer.'" Drug Policy Alliance. www.drugpolicy.org/news/2011/03/thurs-briefing-capitol-hill-responds-finding-drug-courts-are-not-answer.

425 Ibid.

426 Binswanger, Ingrid A., et al. "Release from Prison—A High Risk of Death for Former Inmates," *New England Journal of Medicine* 356 (2) (2007): 157.

427 Krayewski, Ed. "Drug Courts Keeping People in Jail Longer Than Their 'Sanctions,'" Lawsuit Alleges Due Process, Other Rights Violations." Reason.com. Reason, February 12, 2014. https://reason.com/2014/02/12/drug-courts-keeping-people-in-jail-longe/.

428 Ibid.

429 "Is Mandated 12-Step Attendance A Violation Of Your Constitutional Rights?" SMART Recovery, July 1, 2019. https://www.smartrecovery.org/is-mandated-12-step-attendance-a-violation-of-your-constitutional-rights/.

430 Cherkis, Jason, and Ryan Grim. "Obama Tells Outdated Opioid Treatment Industry It's Time To Change." Huffington Post, October 21, 2015. www.huffpost.com/entry/obama-opioid-addiction-treatment_n_5627b3d6e4b0bce347034174.

431 Wakeman, Sarah E. "Why It's Inappropriate Not to Treat Incarcerated Patients with Opioid Agonist Therapy." Journal of Ethics | American Medical Association. American Medical Association, September 1, 2017. https://journalofethics.ama-assn.org/article/why-its-inappropriate-not-treat-incarcerated-patients-opioid-agonist-therapy/2017-09.

432 "Harm Reduction Decade." Harm Reduction International, www.hri.global/harm-reduction-decade.

433 Vallas, Rebecca, et al. "In the US, Debtors' Prisons Are Alive and Well." Truthout, October 19, 2017. truthout.org/articles/a-poverty-expert-explains-how-we-make-it-a-crime-to-be-poor/.

434 Bearden v. Georgia 461 U.S. 660 (1983).

435 Vallas, Rebecca, et al. "In the US, Debtors' Prisons Are Alive and Well." Truthout, October 19, 2017. truthout.org/articles/a-poverty-expert-explains-how-we-make-it-a-crime-to-be-poor/.

436 Eisen, Lauren-Brooke. "Charging Inmates Perpetuates Mass Incarceration." Brennan Center for Justice at New York University School of Law, 2015, 3-5. Krauth, Barbara, and Karin Stayton, "Fees Paid by Jail Inmates: Fee Categories, Revenues, and Management Perspectives in a Sample of U.S. Jails. US Department of Justice, National Institute of Corrections, December 18, 2005.

437 Gann, Carrie. "Study: Significant number of young Americans get arrested." ABC News, December 19, 2011. http://abcnews.go.com/Health/arrests-increasing-us-youth/story?id=15180222.

438 Villines, Zawn. "The Effects of Incarceration on Mental Health." GoodTherapy.org, July 17, 2018. www.goodtherapy.org/blog/prison-incarceration-effects-mental-health-0315137.

439 Ibid.

440 Aizer, Anna, and Joseph Doyle. "What Is the Long-Term Impact of Incarcerating Juveniles?" VOX, July 16, 2013. https://voxeu.org/article/what-long-term-impact-incarcerating-juveniles.

441 "Jailing People with Mental Illness." NAMI. www.nami.org/learn-more/public-policy/jailing-people-with-mental-illness.

442 "Online Only: Report Finds Most U.S. Inmates Suffer from Substance Abuse or Addiction." The Nation's Health, American Public Health Association, April 1, 2010. thenationshealth.aphapublications.org/content/40/3/E11.

443 Bursiek, Alexandria. "Suicides Are Most Common Cause of Jail Deaths, and Many Are Preventable." The Virginian-Pilot, August 1, 2019. pilotonline.com/news/local/projects/jail-crisis/article_8a6b86a6-9756-11e8-8bbc-bb11cb63b053.html.

444 Chammah, Maurice, and Tom Meagher. "Why Jails Have More Suicides than Prisons." The Marshall Project, August 4, 2015. www.themarshallproject.org/2015/08/04/why-jails-have-more-suicides-than-prisons.

445 "National Study of Jail Suicide: 20 Years Later." National Institute of Corrections, October 17, 2018. nicic.gov/national-study-jail-suicide-20-years-later.

446 Chammah, Maurice, and Tom Meagher. "Why Jails Have More Suicides than Prisons." The Marshall Project, August 4, 2015. www.themarshallproject.org/2015/08/04/why-jails-have-more-suicides-than-prisons.

447 U.S. Department of Justice. "Mortality in Local Jails, 2000 – 2007." https://www.bjs.gov/content/pub/pdf/mlj07.pdf.

448 "Use of Electronic Offender-Tracking Devices Expands Sharply." The Pew Charitable Trusts, September 7, 2016. https://www.pewtrusts.org/en/research-and-analysis/issue-briefs/2016/09/use-of-electronic-offender-tracking-devices-expands-sharply.

449 Kilgore, James, and Emmett Sanders. "Ankle Monitors Sound Like a Great Alternative to Prison. They're Not. Here's What You Don't Know.", August 4, 2018. https://www.wired.com/story/opinion-ankle-monitors-are-another-kind-of-jail.

450 Ibid.

451 Vetterkind, Riley. "Wisconsin Doubles GPS Monitoring despite Five Years of Malfunctions, Unnecessary Jailings." WisconsinWatch.org, March 4, 2018. https://www.wisconsinwatch.org/2018/03/wisconsin-doubles-gps-monitoring-despite-five-years-of-malfunctions-unnecessary-jailings.

452 Ibid.

453 "Research Published on Electronic Monitoring." Electronic monitoring | What Works Centre for Crime Reduction, July 25, 2017. https://whatworks.college.police.uk/About/News/Pages/Electronic-monitoring.aspx.

454 Vetterkind, Riley, and Wisconsin Center for Investigative Journalism. "Opponents Claim GPS Monitoring Violates Civil Rights; Judges Not so Sure." WisconsinWatch.org, October 8, 2018. https://www.wisconsinwatch.org/2018/03/opponents-claim-gps-monitoring-violates-civil-rights-judges-not-so-sure.

455 "An Overdose Death Is Not Murder: Why Drug-Induced Homicide Laws Are Counterproductive and Inhumane." Drug Policy Alliance. www.drugpolicy.org/resource/DIH.

456 "More Imprisonment Does Not Reduce State Drug Problems." The Pew Charitable Trusts, March 8, 2018. https://www.pewtrusts.org/en/research-and-analysis/issue-briefs/2018/03/more-imprisonment-does-not-reduce-state-drug-problems.

457 Casteneda, Ruben. "Is Forcing People with Substance Use Disorder into Drug Treatment a Good Idea?" U.S. News & World Report. U.S. News & World Report, July 19, 2018. https://health.usnews.com/health-care/patient-advice/articles/2018-07-19/is-forcing-people-with-substance-use-disorder-into-drug-treatment-a-good-idea.

458   "A Federal Judge Says Mandatory Minimum Sentences Often Don't Fit the Crime." NPR, June 1, 2017. www.npr.org/2017/06/01/531004316/a-federal-judge-says-man-datory-minimum-sentences-often-dont-fit-the-crime.

459   "H.R.5682—115th Congress (2017-2018): FIRST STEP Act." Congress.gov, May 23, 2018, www.congress.gov/bill/115th-congress/house-bill/5682/text.

460   FAMM. www.FAMM.org.

461   Rondó, Jannette, and Jose Feliz. "Office of Alcoholism AndSubstance Abuse Services." Survey: Ten Percent of American Adults Report Being in Recovery from Substance Abuse or Addiction, March 6, 2012. https://www.oasas.ny.gov/pio/press/20120306Recovery.cfm.

462 "ACMT and AACT Position Statement: Preventing Occupational Fentanyl and Fentanyl Analog Exposure to Emergency Responders." American College of Medical Toxicology.   https://www.acmt.net/_Library/Positions/Fentanyl_PPE_Emergen-cy_Responders_.pdf.

463   "Opioid Overdose Prevention Programs Providing Naloxone to Laypersons—United States, 2014." Centers for Disease Control and Prevention, June 19, 2015. www.cdc.gov/mmwr/preview/mmwrhtml/mm6423a2.htm?s_cid=mm6423a2_e.

464   "No Evidence of Compensatory Drug Use Risk Behavior among Heroin Users after Receiving Take-Home Naloxone." Addictive Behaviors, Pergamon, March 9, 2017. www.sciencedirect.com/science/article/abs/pii/S0306460317301119.

465   Singer, Jeffrey A. "To Save Lives, Make Naloxone an Over-the-Counter Drug." Reason, April 27, 2018. https://reason.com/2018/04/27/to-combat-opioid-abuse-the-sur-geon-gener/.

466   "Italy's 20-Year Head Start on Stopping Overdose." Open Society Foundations, March 30, 2017. www.opensocietyfoundations.org/voices/learning-italy-s-lead-naloxone; Timms, Penny. "Heroin Overdose Cure Naloxone to Be Available over the Counter." ABC News, December 15, 2015. www.abc.net.au/news/2015-12-15/naloxone-to-be-available-over-the-counter/7031214.

467   Brauser, Deborah. "Ten-Fold Rise in Deaths from Fentanyl, Other Synthetic Opioids." Medscape, September 5, 2019. https://www.medscape.com/viewarticle/917794.

468   Pardo, Bryce, et al. "Synthetic Opioids: An Unprecedented Crisis." RAND Corporation, August 29, 2019. https://www.rand.org/pubs/research_reports/RR3117.html.

469   This infographic summarizes mortality data from 2010-2016. Please note, 15 to 25 percent of death certificates analyzed did not indicate the type of drug involved in the overdose. This was becasue drug tests were not conducted or there was a failure to record test results on death certificates. "Fentanyl and Other Synthetic Opioids Drug Overdose Deaths." National Institute on Drug Abuse (NIDA), May 29, 2018. https://www.drugabuse.gov/related-topics/trends-statistics/infographics/fentanyl-other-synthet-ic-opioids-drug-overdose-deaths.

470   Kral, Alex, and Peter Davidson, "Addressing the Nation's Opioid Epidemic: Lessons from an Unsanctioned Supervised Injection Site in the U.S.", American Journal of

Preventive Medicine, December, 2017, https://www.ajpmonline.org/article/S0749-3797(17)30316-1/fulltext.

471 "Supervised Injection Sites Are Coming to the United States. Here's What You Should Know." Blog, May 2, 2019. https://nursing.usc.edu/blog/supervised-injection-sites/.

472 Ibid.

473 "Reduction in overdose mortality after the opening of North America's first medically supervised safer injecting facility: a retrospective population-based study." The Science—Insite for Community Safety. www.communityinsite.ca/science.html.

474 Zezima, Katie. "California Assembly Approves Supervised Opioid Injection Facility, Faces Federal Opposition." The Washington Post, May 25, 2019. https://www.washingtonpost.com/national/california-assembly-approves-supervised-opioid-injection-facility-faces-federal-opposition/2019/05/25/ca9910c6-7e4c-11e9-a5b3-34f3edf1351e_story.html.

475 "AMA Wants New Approaches to Combat Synthetic and Injectable Drugs." American Medical Association, June 12, 2017. https://www.ama-assn.org/press-center/press-releases/ama-wants-new-approaches-combat-synthetic-and-injectable-drugs.

476 Kilmer, Beau, Taylor, Jirka, Caulkins, Jonathan P., Mueller, et al. "Considering Heroin-Assisted Treatment and Supervised Drug Consumption Sites in America." RAND Corporation, December 6, 2018. https://www.rand.org/pubs/research_reports/RR2693.html.

477 Weinmeyer, Richard. "Needle Exchange Programs' Status in US Politics." Journal of Ethics | American Medical Association, March 1, 2016. journalofethics.ama-assn.org/article/needle-exchange-programs-status-us-politics/2016-03.

478 "Needle Exchange Programs Promote Public Safety." American Civil Liberties Union. https://www.aclu.org/fact-sheet/needle-exchange-programs-promote-public-safety.

479 "The National Institutes of Health Consensus Development Program: Interventions to Prevent HIV Risk Behaviors." National Institutes of Health, U.S. Department of Health and Human Services. consensus.nih.gov/1997/1997PreventHIVRisk104html.htm.

480 "Most Hospital ERs Won't Treat Your Addiction. These Will." The Pew Charitable Trusts. www.pewtrusts.org/en/research-and-analysis/blogs/stateline/2018/09/21/most-hospital-ers-wont-treat-your-addiction-these-will.

481 Ibid.

482 To prescribe buprenorphine, physicians must take an eight-hour class and then apply for a special DEA number. After approval, they are restricted to treating only 30 patients in the first year, and 100 patients thereafter. There are no such restrictions on prescriptions for other drugs, including those that can be addicting. "The National Alliance of Advocates for Buprenorphine Treatment." DATA-2000 Law 30/100 Patient Limit on Prescribing Suboxone (Buprenorphine / Naloxone) for the Treatment of Opioid Addiction. www.naabt.org/30_patient_limit.cfm.

483 "Doctors of Courage." Doctors of Courage. doctorsofcourage.org/.

484 Dr. Altman is the Chair of the National Advisory Commission on Addiction Treatment at the National Center on Addiction and Substance Abuse at Columbia University.

485 "Addiction Medicine: Closing the Gap between Science and Practice." Center on Addiction, April 14, 2017. www.centeronaddiction.org/addiction-research/reports/addiction-medicine-closing-gap-between-science-and-practice.

486 Reprinted with permission form the Center on Addiction,

487 National Center on Addiction and Substance Abuse at Columbia University and the Substance Abuse and Mental Health Services Administration

488 "Shoveling Up II: The Impact of Substance Abuse on Federal, State and Local Budgets." Center on Addiction, April 14, 2017. https://www.centeronaddiction.org/addiction-research/reports/shoveling-ii-impact-substance-abuse-federal-state-and-local-budgets.

489 "Addiction Medicine: Closing the Gap between Science and Practice." Center on Addiction, April 14, 2017. https://www.centeronaddiction.org/addiction-research/reports/addiction-medicine-closing-gap-between-science-and-practice.

490 "Dual Diagnosis." National Alliance on Mental Illness. https://www.nami.org/learn-more/mental-health-conditions/related-conditions/dual-diagnosis.

491 Approval is through the Accreditation Council for Graduate Medical Education.

492 "Substance Abuse Practitioner Certification." American Institute of Health Care Professionals (AIHCP). https://aihcp.net/substance-abuse-practitioner-certification.

493 "Seattle University." Program: Master of Science in Nursing/(PCNP) Psychiatric Mental Health Nurse Practitioner with Addictions Focus Specialization—Seattle University—Acalog ACMS™, 2019. http://catalog.seattleu.edu/preview_program.php?catoid=5&poid=622.

494 "Life Beyond Bars: Children with an Incarcerated Parent", Institute for Research on Poverty, University of Wisconsin, https://www.irp.wisc.edu/publications/factsheets/pdfs/Factsheet7-Incarceration.pdf.

495 "2017 NSDUH Annual National Report." 2017 NSDUH Annual National Report | CBHSQ, 2017. https://www.samhsa.gov/data/report/2017-nsduh-annual-national-report.

496 "Key Substance Use and Mental Health Indicators in the United States: Results from the 2017 National Survey on Drug Use and Health", Substance Abuse and Mental Health Services Administration. (2018).

497 "Survey: Ten Percent of American Adults Report Being in Recovery from Substance Abuse or Addiction", New York State Office of Alcoholism and Substance Abuse Services. (2012).

498 "New FBI Report: Every 20 Seconds, Someone Is Arrested for a Drug Law Violation in the U.S." Drug Policy Alliance. www.drugpolicy.org/blog/new-fbi-report-every-20-seconds-someone-arrested-drug-law-violation-us.

499 "Drug War Statistics." Drug Policy Alliance. www.drugpolicy.org/issues/drug-war-statistics.

500 "Wisconsin Laws & Penalties." The National Organization for the Reform of Marijuana Laws. norml.org/laws/item/wisconsin-penalties-2.

501 Davis, Jeanie Lerche. "Survey: Addiction Touches Many Lives." WebMD. WebMD, May 14, 2004. https://www.webmd.com/mental-health/addiction/news/20040514/survey-addiction-touches-many-lives.

502 Szalavitz, Maia. "Why the Codependency Myth of Drug Addiction Needs to Die." Vice, October 25, 2016. https://www.vice.com/en_us/article/xdmgmj/why-the-codependency-myth-of-drug-addiction-needs-to-die-heroin-opioids-abuse.

503 "Younger Americans Much More Likely to Have Been Arrested Than Previous Generations; Increase Is Largest Among Whites and Women." RAND Corporation, February 25, 2019. www.rand.org/news/press/2019/02/25.html.

504 "Enforcement." Bureau of Justice Statistics (BJS). www.bjs.gov/content/dcf/enforce.cfm.

505 "Younger Americans Much More Likely to Have Been Arrested Than Previous Generations; Increase Is Largest Among Whites and Women." RAND Corporation, February 25, 2019. www.rand.org/news/press/2019/02/25.html.

506 "Just Facts: As Many Americans Have Criminal Records As College Diplomas: Brennan Center for Justice." Brennan Center for Justice, November 17, 2015. www.brennancenter.org/blog/just-facts-many-americans-have-criminal-records-college-diplomas.

507 Smith, James P. "The Long-Term Economic Impact of Criminalization in American Childhoods." RAND Corporation, August 17, 2018. www.rand.org/pubs/external_publications/EP67678.html.
"Younger Americans Much More Likely to Have Been Arrested Than Previous Generations; Increase Is Largest Among Whites and Women." RAND Corporation, February 25, 2019. www.rand.org/news/press/2019/02/25.html.

508 Laqueur, Hannah. "Uses and Abuses of Drug Decriminalization in Portugal." Law & Social Inquiry, 2014. https://www.law.berkeley.edu/ les/Laqueur_percent282014percent29_-_ Uses_and_Abuses_of_Drug_Decriminalization_in_Portugal_-_LSI.pdf. Domoslawski, Artur. "Drug Policy in Portugal: The Benefits of Decriminalizing Drug Use." Open Society Foundations, 2011. https://www.opensocietyfoundations. org/sites/default/ les/drug-policy-in-portugal-english-20120814.pdf. Hughes,
Caitlin Elizabeth and Alex Stevens. "What Can We Learn from the Portuguese Decriminalization of Illicit Drugs?" The British Journal of Criminology, 50, 6 (2010): 999-1022. Andrade, Paula Vale de and Ludmila Carapinha. "Drug Decriminalization in Portugal," The BMJ (2010).

509 Johnson, Julie K. et al. "Heterogeneity of State Medical Marijuana Laws and Adolescent Recent Use of Alcohol and Marijuana: Analysis of 45 States, 1991-2011." U.S. National Library of Medicine, 2018. https://www.ncbi.nlm.nih.gov/pubmed/28991522.

510 Miron, Jeffrey. "The Budgetary Effects of Ending Drug Prohibition." Cato Institute, July 23, 2018, www.cato.org/publications/tax-budget-bulletin/budgetary-effects-ending-drug-prohibition.

511　"Skinner v. Railway Labor Executives' Association." Legal Information Institute. www. law.cornell.edu/supremecourt/text/489/602

512　Amendment XXI. (Ratified December 5, 1933.)
Section 1. The eighteenth article of amendment to the Constitution of the United States is hereby repealed.

Section 2. The transportation or importation into any State, Territory, or possession of the United States for delivery or use therein of intoxicating liquors, in violation of the laws thereof, is hereby prohibited.

Section 3. This article shall be inoperative unless it shall have been ratified as an amendment to the Constitution by conventions in the several States, as provided in the Constitution, within seven years from the date of the submission hereof to the States by the Congress.

513　DEA Drug Schedules are as follows:
Schedule I—Defined as drugs with no currently accepted medical use and a high potential for abuse including severe psychological or physical dependence. Surprisingly, marijuana is listed as a Schedule I drug. Other Schedule I drugs include heroin, LSD, ecstasy, methaqualone, and peyote.

Schedule II—Defined as drugs with high potential for abuse but less than Schedule I drugs. Schedule II drugs include Vicodin, methamphetamine, methadone, Dilaudid, Demerol, OxyContin, fentanyl, Dexedrine, Adderall, and Ritalin.

Schedule III—Defined as drugs having moderate to low potential for physical and psychological dependence. Schedule III drugs include Tylenol with codeine, ketamine, anabolic steroids, and testosterone.

Schedule IV—Defined as drugs with low potential for abuse and low risk of dependence. Schedule IV drugs include Xanax, Soma, Darvon, Darvocet, Valium, Ativan, Talwin, Ambien, and Tramadol.

Schedule V—Defined as having lower potential for abuse than Schedule IV drugs, and are typically preparations containing limited quantities of narcotics. Schedule V drugs including Robitussin AC, Lomotil, Motofen, Lyrica, and Parapectolin.

514　http://www.citizensopposingprohibition.org/.

515　Lopez, German. "The Deadlier Drug Crises That We Don't Consider Public Health Emergencies." Vox, October 27, 2017. www.vox.com/policy-and-politics/2017/10/27/16557550/alcohol-tobacco-opioids-epidemic-emergency.

516　Marsh, D., et al. "Comparison of Heroin and Hydromorphone in Opioid Users—Brands—2004—Clinical Pharmacology & Therapeutics—Wiley Online Library." Clinical Pharmacology & Therapeutics. February 26, 2004. ascpt.onlinelibrary.wiley.com/doi/abs/10.1016/j.clpt.2003.11.008.

517　Hall, Wayne, and Megan Weier. "Lee Robins' Studies of Heroin Use among US Vietnam Veterans." Wiley Online Library. John Wiley & Sons, Ltd (10.1111), September 20, 2016. https://onlinelibrary.wiley.com/doi/abs/10.1111/add.13584.

518　A study published by the UC Davis Law Review reports that 40 percent of drug arrests are for a quarter of a gram or less of a substance. That's .0088 of an ounce—less than the size of a penny in your hand. Twenty percent of arrests are based on between one quarter of a gram and one gram, which is still only .035 of an ounce, moving up to the size of a U.S. quarter. Less than one percent of arrests are for a kilogram or more. Kennedy, Joseph, et al. "Sharks and Minnows in the War on Drugs: A Study of Quantity, Race and Drug Type in Arrests," *UC Davis Law Review*, 2018. More than 80 percent of arrests for drug law violations are for drug possession alone. "The Drug War Mass Incarceration and Race. New York: Drug Policy Alliance, 2016.

519   "46% In U.S. Have Friend or Family Member Who's Been Addicted to Drugs." Pew Research Center. www.pewresearch.org/fact-tank/2017/10/26/nearly-half-of-americans-have-a-family-member-or-close-friend-whos-been-addicted-to-drugs/.

520   Itzoe, Maria Lisa, and Michael Guarnieri. "New Developments in Managing Opioid Addiction: Impact of a Subdermal Buprenorphine Implant." National Center for Biotechnology Information, May 10, 2017. www.ncbi.nlm.nih.gov/pmc/articles/PMC5436774/.

521   "One Little Pill Home." One Little Pill. www.onelittlepillmovie.com/.

522   MacGillis, Alec. "The Last Shot." ProPublica, March 9, 2019. www.propublica.org/article/vivitrol-opiate-crisis-and-criminal-justice.

523   "Vivitrol: When Corporate Lobbying Supplants Evidence-Based Policy." Drug Policy Alliance, July 2017. www.drugpolicy.org/blog/vivitrol-when-corporate-lobbying-supplants-evidence-based-policy.

524   Lofwall, Michelle R., and Jennifer R Havens. "Inability to Access Buprenorphine Treatment as a Risk Factor for Using Diverted Buprenorphine." Drug and Alcohol Dependence, U.S. National Library of Medicine, December 1, 2012. www.ncbi.nlm.nih.gov/pubmed/22704124.

525   Karila, Laurent, Aviv Weinstein, Henri-Jean Aubin, Amine Benyamina, Michel Reynaud, and Steven L Batki. "Pharmacological Approaches to Methamphetamine Dependence: a Focused Review." British journal of clinical pharmacology. Blackwell Science Inc, June 2010. https://www.ncbi.nlm.nih.gov/pmc/articles/PMC2883750/.

526   "Kratom Legality." Kratom Science, July 23, 2018. www.kratomscience.com/kratom-legalit.

527   Grisham, Julie. "Kratom: What Research Tells Us about This Controversial Supplement for Pain Relief." Memorial Sloan Kettering Cancer Center, August 8, 2018. https://www.mskcc.org/blog/kratom-what-research-tells-us-about-controversial-supplement.

528   Jerome, Lisa, et al. "Can MDMA Play a Role in the Treatment of Substance Abuse?" U.S. National Library of Medicine, March 2013. www.ncbi.nlm.nih.gov/pubmed/23627786.

529   Johnson, Matthew W., and Roland R. Griffiths. "Potential Therapeutic Effects of Psilocybin." SpringerLink, Springer US, June 5, 2017. link.springer.com/article/10.1007/s13311-017-0542-y; "A Radical New Approach to Beating Addiction." *Psychology Today*, May 2017. www.psychologytoday.com/us/articles/201705/radical-new-approach-beating-addiction; Nutt, David J., et al. "Effects of Schedule I Drug Laws on Neuroscience Research and Treatment Innovation." Nature News, June 12, 2013. www.nature.com/articles/nrn3530.

Index

About the Author

Colleen Cowles is an attorney, author, speaker, teacher, advocate and, most importantly, a mother who personally experienced addiction and chronic pain in her family. Her passion and expertise are focused on minimizing the pain that families experience, improving outcomes for those suffering from substance use disorder and/or chronic pain, and advocating for reform of the criminal justice system and overall drug policy.

She offers proven solutions in her book War On Us: How the War on Drugs and Myths About Addiction are a War on All of Us, and in her online course, A Parent's Guide to Addiction: Moving Past Punishment.

Colleen speaks at corporate, public, association, and university events, and is a frequent radio and TV guest expert on topics related to criminal justice reform, drug policy, and substance use disorder. Her 15 years of research, interviews with experts, work with clients and personal experience give Colleen proficiency and practical insight into this urgently important topic.

Colleen has decades of experience in advising clients on tax, business and estate planning, as well as planning strategies to protect assets when addiction or other medical issues impact a family. She loves spending time with family, and, as an avid traveler, enjoys writing and photography as a way of sharing her experiences with others.

Notes

Notes

Notes

Notes